ANTHONY HAM

MADRID
CITY GUIDE

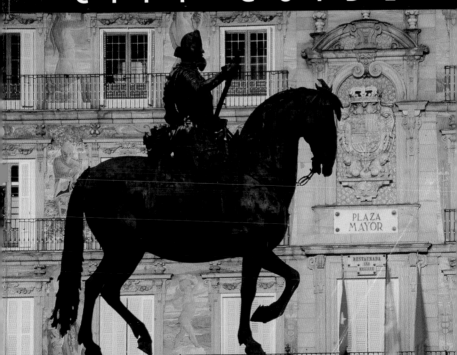

INTRODUCING MADRID

Historic buildings tower over Plaza de España (p70)

KRZYSZTOF DYDYNSKI

No city on earth is more alive than Madrid, a beguiling place whose sheer energy carries a simple message: this is one city which really knows how to live.

If Madrid was a woman, she'd be a cross between Penélope Cruz and Madonna. If it was a man, it would have to be Javier Bardem. And if you could distil the city to its essence, it would be this: Madrid is a rebellious ex-convent schoolgirl who grew up, got sophisticated but never forgot how to have a good time.

This is a city with few world-renowned landmarks and one that creeps up on you rather than necessarily overwhelming you at first. But in no time at all it is singing irresistibly in your ear. Its secret lies in its unique barrios where you'll discover that Madrid is an idea, a diverse place whose contradictory impulses are legion. Spain's capital is a wonderful year-round destination, but you'll especially appreciate being here when the weather's warm and the kaleidoscopic variety of life Madrid-style courses through the streets or takes up residence in the city's parks and plazas.

Madrid's calling cards are many: astonishing art galleries, relentless nightlife, its transformation into Spain's premier style city, an exceptional live-music scene, a feast of fine restaurants and tapas bars, and a population that's mastered the art of living the good life. It's not that other cities don't have some of these things. It's just that Madrid has all of them in bucketloads.

MADRID LIFE

It's often said that Madrid is the most Spanish of Spain's cities. It's also one of the country's most open and tolerant. If this can be summed up in a single phrase, it's the oft-heard, 'If you're in Madrid, you're from Madrid'. It's not that madrileños will knock you over with the warmth of their welcome. Rather, you'll find yourself in a bar or lost somewhere and in need of directions, and you'll suddenly be made to feel like one of their own. Just as suddenly, without knowing exactly when it happened, you'll realise that you never want to leave.

'Madrid has always been a window on the soul of the Spanish heartland'

This is a city on the upswing and there's a real feeling on the streets that Madrid's time is now. All things Spanish may be taking the world by storm, but it's here in Madrid that you'll find the laboratory of Spanish innovation, whether it be fashion, food or architecture. Dare we say it, Madrid long ago became the new Barcelona.

There are challenges though. A massive demographic shift in the past decade has seen immigrants from around the world arrive in unprecedented numbers. The global economic crisis has also shaken Spanish society to its core and the question of how to pay the bills is one of few issues guaranteed to keep madrileños awake at night for reasons other than revelry. They also worry that the country's politicians are trying to turn Spaniards into 'good Europeans', whether it's strict antismoking laws or the slow death of the siesta. 'Leave us alone to be who we are' is a typical response.

How Madrid – which has always been a window on the soul of the Spanish heartland – reacts to these challenges will most likely determine the direction of Spain's future. In the meantime, there is one simple mantra that unites madrileños wherever they come from: they remain convinced that they live in the greatest city on earth.

Cocido at Malacatín (p154)

HIGHLIGHTS

GUY MOBERLY

KRZYSZTOF DYDYNSKI

LOS AUSTRIAS, SOL & CENTRO

From the grand monuments of old Madrid to the clamour of a city converging on its busiest crossroads, Los Austrias, Sol and Centro are at once Madrid in microcosm and the city writ large.

CHRISTOPHER GROENHOUT

❶ Chocolatería San Ginés
Partake of *chocolate con churros* (Spanish donuts with chocolate) at dawn (p179)

❷ Plaza Mayor
Watch the passing parade amid stunning architecture (p61)

❸ Plaza de Oriente
Relax in one of the city's most beautiful plazas (p67)

❹ Palacio Real
Marvel at the excess in the royal palace (p67)

❺ Restaurante Sobrino de Botín
Eat suckling pig in the world's oldest restaurant (p149)

❻ Plaza de la Puerta del Sol
Take Madrid's pulse at its beating heart (p69)

LA LATINA & LAVAPIÉS

La Latina sits on the cusp of downtown Madrid, awash with restaurants and bars, where the art of taking tapas has never been more fun amid the medieval architecture of Madrid's origins. Just down the hill, Lavapiés is gritty and multicultural.

WITOLD SKRYPCZAK

KRZYSZTOF DYDYNSKI

KRZYSZTOF DYDYNSKI

❶ Tapas on Calle de la Cava Baja
Eat Madrid's best tapas along this emblematic street (p153)

❷ El Rastro
Treasure-hunt on Sunday morning in Europe's largest flea market (p74)

❸ Basílica de San Francisco El Grande
Search for Goya and St Francis of Assisi in this grand basilica (p74)

HUERTAS & ATOCHA

Huertas is best known for its nightlife, for streets that come to life after dark and capture the essence of a city that never seems to rest. The narrow lanes of the Barrio de las Letras yield to the sublime Centro de Arte Reina Sofía in Atocha.

RICHARD NEBESKY © PABLO PICASSO/SUCCESSION PICASSO. LICENSED BY VISCOPY, 2010

❶ Centro de Arte Reina Sofía
Admire Picasso's *Guernica,* as well as works by Dalí and Miró (p82)

❷ Live Jazz in Café Central or Populart
Listen to the greatest names in jazz (p186 and p187)

❸ Plaza de Santa Ana
Take up residence in this life-filled square (p86)

KRZYSZTOF DYDYNSKI

GUY MOBERLY

PASEO DEL PRADO & EL RETIRO

One of Europe's grandest boulevards, the Paseo del Prado is home to more museums and galleries than almost anywhere else on earth. Away to the east, the botanical gardens and Retiro park are glorious oases of greenery in the city centre.

KRZYSZTOF DYDYNSKI

❶ Museo Thyssen-Bornemisza
Explore centuries of the finest art in one extraordinary collection (p94)

❷ Iglesia de San Jerónimo El Real
Sigh amid the extravagance of this former royal chapel (p93)

❸ Plaza de la Cibeles
Marvel at how a roundabout can be so beautiful in this iconic plaza (p96)

❹ Parque del Buen Retiro
Take a break from city life in these glorious gardens (p97)

❺ Museo del Prado
Survey the work of Goya, Velázquez and other fine artists in this superior art gallery (p91)

❻ Caixa Forum
Enjoy the hanging garden and an innovative approach to architecture (p95)

❼ Real Jardín Botánico
Shelter from the noise of Madrid in the botanical gardens (p95)

GUY MOBERLY

BRUCE B

RICHARD NEBESKY

RICHARD NEBESKY

① Museo de la Escultura Abstracta

Stumble upon the open-air work of the country's big-name sculptors (p103)

② Salamanca Shopping

Get glamorous discovering the wonderful world of Spanish fashion (p136)

③ Museo Arqueológico Nacional

Step back into Spain's past at the archaeological museum (p101)

RICHARD NEBESKY

SALAMANCA

Madrid's most exclusive barrio for more than a century, Salamanca is all about designer shopping, restaurants and refinement. That is, at least, until you arrive at the bullring where Madrid holds fast to that most controversial Spanish pastime.

JTB PHOTO/PHOTOLIBRARY

MALASAÑA & CHUECA

Two barrios that overflow with life, Malasaña and Chueca have two vastly different personalities – the former is grungy, eclectic and always fun, while the latter is gay, extravagant and sophisticated. Together they're two of the most diverse to explore.

KRZYSZTOF DYDYNSKI

KRZYSZTOF DYDYNSKI

KRZYSZTOF DYDYNSKI

1 Malasaña Nightlife
Indulge in the hard-living fun that's a Malasaña trademark (p189)

2 Sociedad General de Autores y Editores
Ask whether Gaudí has made a sudden appearance in Madrid (p106)

3 Museo de Historia
Immerse yourself in the story of Madrid at Madrid's museum of history (p107)

CHAMBERÍ & ARGÜELLES

Chamberí is the new Salamanca, a barrio where madrileños have perfected the art of living, while Argüelles extends on the theme. Out to the west, most of the neighbourhood's sights line up along the ridge looking out towards the setting sun.

1 Templo de Debod
Relive ancient Egypt in the heart of Madrid (p114)

2 Teleférico
Ride out across the city fringe on this slow-moving cable car (p115)

DIEGO LEZAMA

MARTIN THOMAS PHOTOGRAPHY/ALAMY

NORTHERN MADRID

The north of the capital is where Madrid works hard, celebrates the fact that it has the greatest football club of all time and generally goes out to eat when money is no object.

RICHARD NEBESKY

❶ Estadio Santiago Bernabéu
Tour the temple of football or absorb the passion of Real Madrid match day (p121)

❷ Santceloni
Dine alongside royalty in this gastronomic laboratory (p170)

ADRIANA GONZÁLEZ URIBE

BEYOND THE CENTRE

Beyond the confines of inner Madrid lie many of the mega-sites that need space to accommodate the crowds, from the massive stand of trees that is Casa de Campo to a range of sights for families.

❶ Zoo Aquarium de Madrid
Talk to the animals at this fine city zoo (p126)

❷ Ermita de San Antonio de la Florida
Catch your breath under the glorious frescoes of Goya (p122)

MONDELO/EFE/CORBIS

BILDARCHIV MONHEIN GMBH/ALAMY

CONTENTS

THE AUTHOR

Anthony Ham

After years of wandering the world, Anthony has finally found his spiritual home. In 2001, Anthony fell irretrievably in love with Madrid on his first visit to the city. Less than a year later, he arrived on a one-way ticket, with not a word of Spanish and not knowing a single person in the city. Now, Anthony speaks Spanish with a Madrid accent, is married to Marina, a madrileña, and, together with their daughter Carlota, they live overlooking their favourite plaza in the city. He adores just about everything about his adopted home (with the possible exception of *cocido,* but he's working on it) and sometimes has to pinch himself to believe just how wonderfully life has turned out. When he's not writing for Lonely Planet, Anthony writes about and photographs Spain, Africa and the Middle East for newspapers and magazines around the world.

ANTHONY'S TOP MADRID DAY

Madrid is not a city that gets up early and I'm no exception. I'd start the day with breakfast on Plaza de Olavide (p118) in Chamberí while I plan my day. One of the things I love most about Madrid is that there's a different barrio to explore depending on my mood. If I've shopping in mind, it has to be Malasaña (p138) or Salamanca (p136). If I need a dose of high culture, the Paseo del Prado (p135) or the centre has enough to occupy weeks of my time. If I fancy a tapas crawl, La Latina (p152) is my destination, while for restaurants, Malasaña (p161), Chueca (p165) or Huertas (p155) are brilliant, with even more places to stay out all night afterwards. Loving live music as I do, I could also take my pick of any barrio west of the Paseo de los Recoletos and Paseo del Prado.

My best possible day begins by wandering through the lanes of Malasaña, down through the centre and to La Latina for tapas, especially along Calle de la Cava Baja and the *tortilla de patatas* at Juana La Loca (p154). After resting in Plaza Mayor (p61) or Plaza de Santa Ana (p86), I'd head down to the Museo del Prado (p90). Nearby, I can never resist the Parque del Buen Retiro (p97), or the tapas at Estado Puro (p159). I should be thinking about a siesta, but instead I'd dive into the bars of Huertas (especially the live jazz or flamenco), before cradling a *mojito* in Café Belén (p192) in Chueca or at Delic (p182) on Plaza de la Paja in La Latina for some down time. A metro ride takes me to a late dinner along Calle de Manuela Malasaña. I'm always happy to find myself nursing a *caipirinha* in Conde Duque at Kabokla (p195), before the all-night nightclubs of downtown erase all thoughts of tomorrow.

A trip to Madrid doesn't require much advance planning – it's the type of city where you can just dive in and make it up as you go along. Apart from booking your flight (p250) and accommodation (p220), just about everything else can be sorted out upon your arrival. Then again, the planning stage of your trip to Madrid can be part of the pleasure, and any preparation you do beforehand will only enhance your experience of the city.

You want to see Real Madrid play live in front of 80,000 screaming fans or you really want to see a bullfight to see what all of the fuss is about? No problem. Turn to p211 for information on how to book ahead. You've heard that Madrid's live music and jazz scenes are the best in southern Europe? Easy, simply turn to p175 and p176 respectively. Not quite sure which barrio (neighbourhood) in Madrid best suits your personality and where you'd like to be based? We've reduced the barrios to their essence in the boxed text on p65. In short, everything you could possibly want in Madrid is covered in this book. For a quick overview of some of the advance planning you may want to do, see the boxed text on p21.

When it comes to planning your budget Madrid is a destination that's well suited to all pockets with hotels and hostels spanning the full spectrum of traveller means (from terrific backpackers' hang-outs to luxurious palaces) and restaurants ranging from quick meals on the run to all that's innovative (and expensive) about nouvelle Spanish cuisine.

WHEN TO GO

There's no bad time to visit Madrid. Given that there's always something going on, the weather can be an important factor when planning your visit. In winter Madrid most often enjoys cool but crystal-clear days, although cold winds blow in off the Sierra del Guadarrama and cold snaps can be bitterly cold (snowfalls are rare but do happen). In July and August expect unrelenting heat with occasional, apocalyptic storms. In August Madrid's frenetic energy takes a break and the city is uncharacteristically quiet. City streets empty, some restaurants close and offices grind almost to a halt as locals head for the coast in search of a sea breeze or the hills in pursuit of high-altitude respite.

For more advice on Madrid's climate, turn to p257, while a list of all the official public holidays in Madrid is covered on p259.

If you have some flexibility about when you travel to Madrid, or you've a specialised interest, planning your trip around one of Madrid's many festivals (right) may well be an important consideration.

If you're only here for a short stay, consider making it a weekend (Thursday to Sunday) when Madrid's nightclubs (p177) will have you dancing until dawn. If you're here for the major art galleries and museums, avoid Mondays when many are closed; the Centro de Arte Reina Sofía (p82) is a notable exception, closing on Tuesdays. If El Rastro (p74),

Europe's largest flea market, is your thing, you'll need to be in Madrid on a Sunday morning.

FESTIVALS

Madrileños love to party. Most often that means an impromptu night out. However, there are times when there's method in the madness, whether it's Carnaval in the depths of February or the local fiestas in central Madrid's barrios in the stifling heat of August. What follows is a comprehensive guide to the major festivals, fairs and other important events in Madrid's calendar for which you may want to try to be in town. For a list of local fiestas in various Madrid barrios and surrounding towns, pick up a copy of the annual *Guía de Fiestas en la Comunidad de Madrid* (in Spanish) from the Comunidad de Madrid tourist office (p265).

January
AÑO NUEVO 1 Jan
Noche Vieja (New Year's Eve) is often celebrated at home with family before people head out after midnight to carouse and to start the new year as they mean to continue. Many madrileños gather in Plaza de la Puerta del Sol to wait for the 12 *campanadas* (bell chimes) that signal Año Nuevo (New Year's Day), whereupon they try to stuff 12 grapes (one for each chime)

into their mouths and make a wish for the new year.

REYES
6 Jan

Epifanía (the Epiphany) is also known as the Día de los Reyes Magos (Three Kings' Day), or simply Reyes, perhaps the most important day on a madrileño kid's calendar. Although the December visit from Santa Claus has caught on, traditionally young Spaniards waited until Reyes. Three local politicians dress up as the three kings (three wise men) and lead a sweet-distributing frenzy of Cabalgata de Reyes, as horse-drawn carriages and floats make their way from the Parque del Buen Retiro to Plaza Mayor at 6pm on 5 January.

MADRID FUSION
www.madridfusion.net

All the Spanish chefs who have made it big on the national and international stage come to Madrid for this gastronomy summit. It's a cooking extravaganza where the masters of the Spanish kitchen show off their latest creations. Tickets can be difficult to come by, but your tastebuds will love you for it.

February

CARNAVAL

Carnaval spells several days of fancy-dress parades and merrymaking in many barrios across the Comunidad de Madrid, usually ending on the Tuesday, 47 days before Easter Sunday. Competitions for the best costume take place in the Círculo de Bellas Artes (p87). Carnaval in Madrid is not quite as big as in other parts of Spain, such as Cádiz in Andalucía, but it can still be a wild time. Depending on when Easter falls, Carnaval can spill over into March.

FESTIVAL FLAMENCO CAJA MADRID

A combination of big names and rising talents come together for five days of fine flamenco music in one of the city's theatres, usually the Teatro Circo Price (p204). The dates are movable, but big names are guaranteed (in recent years including Enrique Morente, Carmen Linares and Diego El Cigala). The main festival often spills over into discussions and occasional performances at La Casa Encendida (p80).

top picks

UNUSUAL EVENTS

- Fiesta de San Antón The blessing of the pets takes place at the Iglesia de San Antón, home church of the patron saint of animals, on 17 January.
- Jesús de Medinaceli Up to 100,000 people crowd the Iglesia de Jesús de Medinaceli on the first Friday of Lent to kiss the right foot of a wooden sculpture of Christ (*besapié*, kissing of the foot). Pilgrims make three wishes to Jesus, of which he is said to grant one.
- Fiestas de San Isidro Labrador (p18) This is Madrid's biggest party, when *chulapos* (born-and-bred madrileños) dress in short jackets and berets, and *manolas* (the female version of a once-common Lavapiés first name) don their finest *mantón de Manila* (embroidered silk shawl). If you're lucky, they'll even dance the *choti* (a traditional working-class dance not unlike the polka).
- Fiesta de San Antonio Young women (traditionally seamstresses) flock to the Ermita de San Antonio de la Florida on 13 June to petition for a partner. Whether spiritually inclined or not, the attitude seems to be 'why chance it?' The tradition holds that a seamstress drops 13 pins into the baptismal font and dips her hand in – the number of pins that stick to her hand corresponds to the number of suitors she will have in the year ahead.
- Batalla Naval de Vallecas The mischievous Brotherhood of Sailors in the working-class barrio of Vallecas stages a 'naval battle', in other words a massive water fight, on the second or third Sunday in July to demand that the government provide Madrid with a seaport.

PASARELA CIBELES
www.cibeles.ifema.es, in Spanish

The Pasarela Cibeles, staged in the Parque Ferial Juan Carlos I, between the airport and the city centre, is becoming an increasingly important stop on the European fashion circuit, especially for spring and autumn collections; the latter take to the catwalk in September.

ARCO
www.arco.ifema.es, in Spanish

One of Europe's biggest celebrations of contemporary art, the Feria Internacional de Arte Contemporánea draws gallery reps and exhibitors from all over the world. It's staged around mid-February in the Parque

Ferial Juan Carlos I exhibition centre and lasts for five days.

March & April

JUEVES SANTO

Jueves Santo (Holy Thursday) kicks off the official holiday period known in Spain as Semana Santa (Holy Week). Local *cofradías* (lay fraternities) organise colourful and often solemn religious processions where hooded men and barefoot women dragging chains around their ankles and bearing crosses are among the parading figures. The main procession concludes by crossing Plaza Mayor to the Basílica de Nuestra Señora del Buen Consejo. For many madrileños it also marks the start of a much-needed *puente* (bridge, or long weekend) and they take the chance to escape the city.

VIERNES SANTO

Viernes Santo (Good Friday) and Easter in general are celebrated with greater enthusiasm in some of the surrounding towns. Chinchón, Ávila and Toledo in particular, are known for their lavish Easter processions.

ARTEMANÍA

The Feria de Arte y Antigüedades sees antique dealers from all over Spain converge on the Palacio de Congresos y Exposiciones on Paseo de la Castellana. You can admire anything from Picasso lithographs to ancient pottery. The fair usually lasts for a week and takes place towards the end of March, but could spill into April.

LA NOCHE DE LOS TEATROS

On 'The Night of the Theatres', Madrid's streets become the stage for all manner of performances, with a focus on comedy and children's plays. It usually takes place on the last Saturday of March, and lasts from 5pm to midnight. Check www.esmadrid .com for details.

JAZZ ES PRIMAVERA

www.sanjuanevangelista.org
Three weeks of jazz in the leading jazz venues across the city. Tickets can be bought online through www.elcorteingles.es.

May & June

FIESTA DE LA COMUNIDAD DE MADRID
2 May

On El Dos de Mayo (2 May) in 1808 Napoleon's troops put down an uprising in Madrid, and commemorating this day has become an opportunity for much festivity. The day is celebrated with particular energy in the bars of Malasaña, so much so that in recent years this fiesta has seen pitched battles between police and rowdy revellers in Malasaña, so keep your wits about you.

FIESTAS DE SAN ISIDRO LABRADOR
15 May

The merry month of May is nowhere merrier than in Madrid. In the wake of the Dos de Mayo festivities comes the city's big holiday on 15 May, when it celebrates the feast day of its patron saint, San Isidro (the 'peasant'). On this day the townsfolk gather in central Madrid to watch the colourful procession, which kicks off a week of cultural events across the city. Locals also traipse across the Puente de San Isidro to the saint's chapel and spend the day there picnicking; many are in traditional dress, and sip holy water and munch on *barquillos* (sweet pastries). Goya depicted this feast day by the river at the tail end of the 18th century. In those days you looked across green fields back to Madrid – that view is now largely obstructed by high-rises. The country's most prestigious *feria* (bullfighting season) also commences and continues for a month at the bullring Plaza de Toros Monumental de Las Ventas.

MADRID OPEN

www.madrid-open.com
Formerly known as the Madrid Masters, this is Spain's most important tennis tournament and draws most of the world's big names. It usually takes place in the first half of the month.

FESTIMAD

www.festimad.es, in Spanish
This is the biggest of Spain's year-round circuit of major music festivals. Bands from all over the country and beyond converge on Móstoles or Leganés (on the MetroSur train network), just outside Madrid, for two days of indie music indulgence. Although usually held in April or May, Festimad

sometimes spills over into (and may even begin in) June.

FIESTA DE OTOÑO EN PRIMAVERA

This busy calendar of musical and theatrical activity was held in autumn (*otoño*, hence the name) since the 1980s, but in 2010 moved to spring, beginning in May and continuing into June. The name is likely to change to the Festival de Primavera (Spring Festival) in the future. Check www.esmadrid.com for details.

FERIA DEL LIBRO

www.ferialibromadrid.com
The northeastern corner of the Parque del Buen Retiro (p97) is taken over by the Madrid Book Fair, with hundreds of stalls set up by bookshops and publishing houses from Madrid and elsewhere in Spain. It draws massive crowds with book signings and discounts of around 10%. For more information, see the boxed text, p36.

SUMA FLAMENCA

www.madrid.org/sumaflamenca,
www.teatrosdelcanal.org
Another soul-filled flamenco festival that draws some of the biggest names in the genre. The Teatros del Canal provides the main stage, but the big names may also appear in some of the better-known *tablaos* (restaurants where flamenco is performed; p175), such as Casa Patas, Las Tablas and other venues across the city. After taking place in May for much of its history, in 2010 it ran over two weeks in June.

DÍA DE SAN JUAN   24 Jun

Celebrated in other parts of Spain with fireworks and considerable gusto, the eve of this holiday is a minor affair in Madrid. The action, such as it is, takes place in the Parque del Buen Retiro.

DÍA DEL ORGULLO DE GAYS, LESBIANAS Y TRANSEXUALES

www.orgullogay.org, in Spanish, or
www.madridgaypride.com
The city's Gay and Lesbian Pride Festival and Parade take place on the last Saturday of the month. It's an international gig, with simultaneous parades occurring in cities across Europe, from Berlin to Paris. The extravagant floats begin their journey in

Plaza de la Independencia, pass through Plaza de la Cibeles, head along Gran Vía before finishing in Plaza de España. At all other times, Chueca is the place to be.

ROCK IN RIO MADRID

www.rockinriomadrid.es
The Madrid version of one of the world's foremost rock and electronica music festivals doesn't happen every year, but it did so in 2008 and 2010 to great success and certainly will again.

July
VERANOS DE LA VILLA

www.esmadrid.com/veranosdelavilla
As if the traditional local fiestas weren't enough to amuse those madrileños forced to stay behind in the broiling city summer heat, the town authorities stage a series of cultural events, shows and exhibitions known as 'Summers in the City'. Concerts, opera, dance and theatre are performed in Plaza de España, the Antiguo Cuartel del Conde Duque, the Jardines de Sabatini and outside the Templo de Debod, as well as other venues around town. The program starts in July and runs to the end of August.

August
FIESTAS DE SAN LORENZO, SAN CAYETANO & LA VIRGEN DE LA PALOMA

These three local patron saints' festivities (which revolve around La Latina and Plaza de Lavapiés) keep the otherwise quiet central districts of Madrid busy during the first fortnight of August. An almighty din fills the hot night air as locals eat, drink, dance and generally let their hair down. Why not? It's too hot to sleep anyway.

LA ASUNCIÓN   15 Aug

Also known as the Fiesta de la Virgen de la Paloma, this is a solemn date in the city's religious calendar, celebrating the Assumption of the Virgin Mary.

September
LOCAL FIESTAS

Several local councils organise fiestas in the first and second weeks of September. They include Fuencarral-El Pardo, Vallecas,

Arganzuela, Barajas, Moncloa-Aravaca and Usera. In the last week of the month you can check out the Fiesta de Otoño (Autumn Festival) in Chamartín. These are very local affairs and provide a rare insight into the barrio life of the average madrileño.

LA NOCHE EN BLANCO
http://lanocheenblanco.esmadrid.com/lanocheen blanco
'The White Night', first held in 2006 when it was a roaring success, is when Madrid (and many of its monuments, bars etc) stay open all night with a city-wide extravaganza of concerts and general revelry in 120 venues across the city. It's a participatory arts and culture festival and it rocks.

FIESTA DEL PCE
www.pce.es, in Spanish
In mid-September the Partido Comunista de España (PCE; Spanish Communist Party) holds its annual fundraiser in the Casa de Campo on the edge of the city. This mixed bag of regional-food pavilions, rock concerts and political soap-boxing lasts all weekend.

November
DÍA DE LA VIRGEN DE LA ALMUDENA
9 Nov
Castizos (traditional madrileños) gather together in Plaza Mayor to hear Mass on the feast day of the city's female patron saint.

FESTIVAL JAZZ MADRID
www.esmadrid.com/festivaljazzmadrid
Madrid loves its jazz too much to be confined to just one festival (Jazz es Primavera in spring is the other one). This one is arguably the more prestigious and groups from far and wide converge on the capital for a series of concerts in venues across town. Most of the headline acts take to the stage of Teatro Fernán Gómez (p205).

December
FESTIVAL DE GOSPEL & NEGRO SPIRITUALS
www.obrasocialcajamadrid.es
In the week running up to Christmas Madrid is treated to a feast of jazz, blues

and gospel, usually in the Teatro Fernán Gómez (p205) and La Casa Encendida (p80).

NAVIDAD
25 Dec
Navidad (Christmas) is a fairly quiet family time, with the main meal being served on Nochebuena (Christmas Eve). Elaborate nativity scenes are set up in churches around the city and an exhibition of them is held in Plaza Mayor, which is otherwise taken over by a somewhat tacky, but wildly popular, Christmas market.

COSTS & MONEY
Despite significant price rises in recent years (Madrid is the second-most-expensive city in Spain, after Barcelona, and the 26th-most-expensive city in the world in which to live) Madrid remains generally cheaper for travellers than many major world capitals. Unlike elsewhere in cities of Madrid's stature, it's also still possible to find semiluxurious boutique hotels for around €100 a double in the city centre. At the budget end of the market, dormitory beds shouldn't cost more than €20 and nice *hostales* (hostels) with private bathroom and TV rarely cost more than €60, sometimes even less. Eating out in a nice, mid-range restaurant shouldn't cost much more than about €35 per person, although you can do it for a lot less, especially if you partake in the weekday lunchtime *menú del día* (see the boxed text, p150), a fixed-price, three-course set lunch that costs around €10. The *menú del día* is a great way to experience a more-expensive restaurant without getting stung for à la carte prices. Transport (metro, city

ADVANCE PLANNING

To find out what's going to be happening in Madrid while you're there, start perusing the local Spanish-language websites that give a rundown of upcoming concerts, exhibitions and other events. The better ones include Guía del Ocio (www.guiadelocio.com), La Netro (http://madrid.lanetro.com) and Metropoli (www.elmundo.es/metropolis). If Spanish is a road too far, try the Madrid page of www.whatsonwhen.com, In Madrid (www.in-madrid.com) or the Madrid town hall's excellent multilingual website (www.esmadrid.com), which has a comprehensive calendar of events. If you find something you like, turn to the boxed text on p202 of this guide to see if you can book your concert or theatre performance online.

Although it's unlikely you'll be able to book for the smaller venues, La Noche En Vivo (www.lanocheenvivo.com, in Spanish) gives a good rundown of where and when to turn up in time for live music.

For theatre performances, Real Madrid football games and bullfighting tickets, one recommended agency is Locali-dades Galicia (www.eol.es/lgalicia). Tickets for football matches go on sale a week before the game and we would recommend trying to line up your tickets before arriving in town, especially if there's a big match on.

Most restaurants don't require bookings more than a day or two in advance during the week, but you should always book as early as possible for weekends – contact details for restaurants we recommend are found in the Eating chapter, which begins on p145. You should always book for the more expensive temples of gastronomy as soon as you know your travel dates. This is especially the case for La Terraza del Casino (p149), Santceloni (p170), Sergi Arola Gastro (p168), Jockey (p168) and Zalacaín (p170).

buses and even taxis) is still absurdly cheap and, if you time your visit well, it's possible to visit some museums at no cost (see the boxed text, p123, for more information), including the must-see Museo del Prado and the Centro de Arte Reina Sofía.

INTERNET RESOURCES

A Tapear (www.atapear.com, in Spanish) Customer reviews and rankings of tapas bars in Madrid (407 at the last count) and other Spanish cities under its 'Guía de Bares de Tapas'.

De Tapas por Madrid (www.tapaspormadrid.com, in Spanish) Occasional tapas routes (where you collect stamps in a booklet) offering discounted prices and signature tapas dishes from a range of bars.

EsMadrid.com (www.esmadrid.com) The Ayuntamiento's revamped website is super-sexy, although it can be a little tough to navigate (scroll down and try the 'Site Map' if you're having trouble). Lots of info on upcoming events. It also has a section 'Donde comer en Madrid', which gives an overview of emblematic restaurants and tapas bars.

La Cuchara (www.lacuchara.es, in Spanish) Guide to restaurants and tapas bars.

In Madrid (www.in-madrid.com) A direct line to Madrid's expat community with upcoming events, nightlife reviews, articles, a forum, classifieds and some useful practical information.

La Netro (http://madrid.lanetro.com, in Spanish) Allows you to search for bars, restaurants, nightclubs and just about any kind of Madrid business, and most have customer reviews. Its 'tops' section lists top 10s across a range of categories as voted by users.

Le Cool (www.lecool.com) Weekly updates on upcoming events in Madrid with an emphasis on the alternative, offbeat and avant-garde. The name is pretty accurate.

Lonely Planet (www.lonelyplanet.com) An overview of Madrid with hundreds of useful links, including to the Thorn Tree, Lonely Planet's online bulletin board.

Restaurantes Madrid (www.restaurantesmadrid.net, in Spanish) Rankings and reviews by the public.

Turismo Madrid (www.turismomadrid.es) Portal of the regional Comunidad de Madrid tourist office that's especially good for areas outside the city but still within the Comunidad de Madrid.

Vive Madrid (www.guiavivemadrid.com) A privately run site that has some moderately useful info on bars, restaurants, hotels and transport, as well as a booking service.

BACKGROUND

HISTORY

Founded as a Muslim garrison town in the 9th century and a squalid settlement for centuries thereafter, Madrid suddenly took centre stage in 1561 when it was unexpectedly chosen as Spain's capital. As the centre of a global empire on which the sun never set and as the seat of the Spanish royal court, Madrid was, at a stroke of the royal pen, transformed from a cultural backwater into the most important city in Spain. In the centuries that followed, the city grew into its role as capital, accumulating prestige, people from all across Spain and beyond, and the trappings of power and wealth. The end result is the most Spanish of all Spain's major cities.

ROMAN MADRID?

Amid the bustle of modern Madrid it can be difficult to imagine the scene that must have greeted the nomads who gathered along the banks of the Río Manzanares in Mesolithic and Neolithic times. If they came from the desolate plains that lie to the south or east, even Madrid's less-than-mighty river must have seemed like paradise, and the rocky bluff where Madrid would later be founded – and where the Palacio Real (p67) now stands – must have offered welcome shelter amid a landscape of unrelenting monotony. If they came from the mountains to the north or west, this combination of river and rocky perch must have felt like the last place of safety before crossing the vast plateau, the *meseta* of central Iberia.

Thousands of years later the hagiographers of imperial Spain would, in an attempt to give Madrid an historical prestige it never truly had, argued that Madrid was the site of a Roman city called Mantua Carpetana. Yes, the remains of Roman villas and inns have been found in the Madrid region, which fell under Roman control as they subdued the Celtiberian tribes between the 1st and 5th centuries AD. But the small Roman outpost known as Miacum, close to modern Madrid, was merely an obscure waystation on the important Roman road that criss-crossed the Iberian Peninsula.

MUSLIM MAYRIT

When the Muslim army of Tariq ibn Ziyad crossed the Straits of Gibraltar in the 8th century, it sparked an upheaval that would convulse the Iberian Peninsula for more than 700 years. In 756 the emirate of Córdoba was established in the south in what the Muslims called Al-Andalus. Córdoba became a beacon of religious tolerance and enlightened civilisation, and its soldiers and administrators would occupy much of the peninsula until the beginning of the 9th century.

As Iberia's Christians began the Reconquista (Reconquest) – the centuries-long campaign by Christian forces to reclaim the peninsula – the Muslims of Al-Andalus constructed a chain of fortified positions through the heart of Iberia. One of these forts was built by Muhammad I, emir of Córdoba, in 854, on the site of what would become Madrid. They called the new settlement Mayrit (or Magerit), which comes from the Arabic word *majira,* meaning water channel. At first, Mayrit was merely one of a string of such forts across the so-called Middle

TIMELINE

1st–5th centuries AD	854	End 9th century
The Roman Empire subdues the Celtiberian tribes. The Roman road that connects Mérida with the Toledo (Toletum), Segovia, Alcalá de Henares and Zaragoza (Cesaraugusta) runs close to Madrid.	Muhammad I, emir of Córdoba, establishes the fortress of Mayrit (Magerit), one of many across the so-called Middle March, a frontier land connecting Al-Andalus with the small Christian kingdoms of the north.	Muhammad I orders the construction of a wall that ran along the ridgeline, enclosed the current Catedral de Nuestra Señora de la Almudena and what is now the Plaza de Oriente.

top picks

MADRID HISTORY BOOKS

- **Madrid: A Cultural and Literary History** (Elizabeth Nash; 2001) An informative, entertaining and joyfully written account of various aspects of the city's past and present.
- **A Traveller's Companion to Madrid** (Hugh Thomas; 2005) A fascinating compendium of extracts about Madrid from the great and good.
- **The New Spaniards** (John Hooper; 2nd edition 2006) A highly readable account of the Franco years and the country's transition to democracy with Madrid taking centre stage.
- **Hidden Madrid: A Walking Guide** (Mark and Peter Besas; 2007) A quirky collection of anecdotes and curiosities about historical Madrid.
- **Historia de la Villa de Madrid** (José Antonio Vizcaíno; 2000) You'll need decent Spanish to enjoy this one, but there's no more comprehensive history of Spain's capital.
- **Illustrated Atlas of the History of Madrid** (Pedro López Carcelén; 2004) Charts Madrid's growth into a modern metropolis using historical maps and clear, Spanish text. It's more widely available in Spanish as the *Atlas Ilustrado de la Historia de Madrid*, but the English-language version is available at La Librería (p130).

March, a frontier land between Al-Andalus in the south and small Christian kingdoms of the north. As the Reconquista gathered strength, forts such as Mayrit grew in significance as part of a defensive line against Christian incursion.

With Christian forces massing to the north, Mayrit was small and vulnerable. Its hilltop location made it virtually impregnable from the north, west and south, but Mayrit lacked natural fortifications to the east. Recognising this, Muhammad I constructed a defensive wall within whose boundaries only Muslims could live; Mayrit's small Christian community lived outside, near what is now the Iglesia de San Andrés (p77). Wander down to the last remaining fragment of the Muralla Árabe (Arab Wall; p68), below the modern Catedral de Nuestra Señora de la Almudena (p68), and you can still get a sense of this isolated settlement surrounded by sweeping plains.

Above the more than 190 turrets, the imposing towers of the fort or *alcázar* (from the Arabic *al-qasr*) were visible where the Palacio Real now stands. Crouching beneath the walls was a tangle of lanes known as the *al-mudayna* (hence Almudena) in which soldiers lived with their families. It was a pattern that would be repeated over the centuries, with Madrid dominated by two mutually dependent communities who lived alongside but worlds apart – the rulers in their castle and the ordinary people in small, squalid houses nearby.

Mayrit's strategic location in the centre of the peninsula drew an increasing number of soldiers and traders. To accommodate the many newcomers, Mayrit grew into a town. The main mosque was built on what is now the corner of Calle Mayor and Calle de Bailén, although only the smallest fragment remains (see p68). Muslim Mayrit survived through agriculture (irrigated by water) and produced its own pottery and ceramics.

For all its growth and attempts at fortifications, Mayrit was dispensable to its far-off Muslim rulers. When the emirate of Córdoba broke up into a series of smaller Muslim kingdoms called *taifas* in 1008, Mayrit was attached to Toledo. As the armies of Muslim and Christian Spain battled for supremacy elsewhere, Mayrit was not considered one of the great prizes and ultimately passed into Christian hands without a fight. In 1083 Toledo's ruler gave Mayrit to King Alfonso VI of Castile during a period of rare Muslim–Christian entente.

Around 1070	1083	1110
Madrid's patron saint, San Isidro Labrador, is born among the small community of Christians clustered around the Iglesia de San Andrés (where he was buried after his death in 1130) in Muslim Mayrit.	Mayrit passes into the hands of King Alfonso VI of Castile without a fight, ending Muslim rule over Mayrit, in return for the king's assistance in capturing Valencia.	Almoravid Muslims attack Madrid in an attempt to wrest the city back from Christian rule. They succeed in destroying Madrid's walls but are unable to seize the *alcázar* before being driven back.

BEAR NECESSITIES

Madrid's emblem – a bear nuzzling a *madroño*, or strawberry tree (so named because its fruit looks like strawberries), framed by seven five-point stars and topped by a crown – may be one of the most photographed corners of the Plaza de la Puerta del Sol (p69). But its origins remain something of a mystery, even to most madrileños.

When Alfonso VI accepted Mayrit from the Muslims in 1083, it was seen as an example of things to come for Christian forces hoping to sweep across Spain from the north. Taking the theme further, a group of seven stars that lies close to the North Star in the northern hemisphere forms a shape known as the Ursa Minor, or small she-bear. Thus the bear (once a common sight in the El Pardo area north of the city) and seven stars came to symbolise Madrid. The five points of the stars later came to represent the five provinces that surround Madrid (Segovia, Ávila, Toledo, Cuenca and Guadalajara).

The crown above the frame dates from the 16th century when Carlos I allowed Madrid to use the symbol of the imperial crown in its coat of arms after he cured a fever using *madroño* leaves (a popular medicinal herb).

This coat of arms appears on a deep-violet background to form the city's flag and adorns such important Madrid icons as the shirts of Atlético de Madrid football club (but not Real Madrid's).

A MEDIEVAL CHRISTIAN OUTPOST

Madrid never again passed into Muslim hands, although the city was often besieged by Muslim forces. As the frontline gradually pushed south, Christian veterans from the Reconquista and clerics and their orders flooded into Madrid and forever changed the city's character. A small Muslim community remained and south of what is now Calle de Segovia (then a stream), in the Vistillas area, emerged the busiest of the *arrabales* (suburbs beyond the city walls). To this day the warren of streets around Vistillas (p75) is known as the *morería* – the Moorish quarter. Nearby, the Plaza de la Paja was the site of the city's main market. By the end of the 13th century, a new city wall, bordered by what are now Calle Arenal, Cava de San Miguel, Calle de la Cava Baja, Plaza de la Puerta de Moros and Calle de Bailén, was built. To give you some idea of the scale of Madrid at this time, remember that where the Plaza Mayor (p61), Plaza de España (p70) and the Plaza de la Puerta del Sol (p69) all stand then lay beyond the walls.

Madrid may have been growing, but its power was negligible. Ruled by less-than-interested and usually distant rulers, the city existed in the shadow of the more established cities of Segovia and Toledo. Whereas other Castilian cities received generous *fueros* (self-rule ordinances), Madrid had to content itself with occasional, offhand royal decrees. Left largely to their own devices, a small number of local families set about governing themselves, forming Madrid's first town council, the Consejo de Madrid. The travelling Cortes (royal court and parliament) sat in Madrid for the first time in 1309. This first sign of royal favour was followed by others – Madrid (or rather the *alcázar*) was an increasingly popular residence with the Castilian monarchs, particularly Enrique IV (r 1454–74). They found it a relaxing base from which to set off on hunting expeditions, especially for bears in the El Pardo district.

Whereas Madrid had once been susceptible to military conquest, it now succumbed to an altogether different threat, this time from poverty, isolation from power and terrible living conditions. In 1348 the horrors of the Black Death struck, devastating the population. In the same year the Castilian king began to tire of Madrid's growing independence and appointed *regidores* (governors) of Madrid and other cities in an attempt to tighten central control. Allying themselves with the royal family, a handful of families began to monopolise local power, ruling

1222	1309	1348
Madrid's emblem of seven stars and a bear nuzzling a *madroño* (strawberry tree) appears for the first time in historical records. A statue representing the image now stands in the Plaza de la Puerta del Sol.	The Cortes (royal court and parliament) sits for the first time in Madrid. During the sitting, the royals declare war on Granada; the Reconquista's demands ensure that the royal court often travel throughout Spain.	The Black Death sweeps across Spain, killing King Alfonso XI and countless numbers of his compatriots. Estimates suggest that the plague kills anywhere between 20% and 50% of Madrid's population.

as petty oligarchs through a feudal system of government, the Comunidad de Villa y Tierra, in which the *villa* (town) lorded it over the peasants who worked the surrounding *tierra* (land).

Despite growing evidence of royal attention, medieval Madrid remained dirt-poor and small-scale. As one 15th-century writer observed, 'in Madrid there is nothing except what you bring with you'. It simply bore no comparison with other major Spanish, let alone European, cities.

Beyond the small-world confines of Madrid, however, Spain was being convulsed by great events that would ultimately transform Madrid's fortunes. The marriage of Isabel and Fernando united Christian Spain for the first time. Together they expelled the last of the Muslim rulers from Granada, financed Christopher Columbus' voyages of American discovery and ordered the expulsion of Jews who would not convert to Christianity from Spain – all in 1492.

Carlos I, the grandson of Isabel and Fernando, became the King of Spain in 1516. Three years later he succeeded to the Habsburg throne and so became Carlos V, Holy Roman Emperor. His territories stretched from Austria to the Netherlands and from Spain to the American colonies, but with such a vast territory to administer, he spent only 16 years of his 40-year reign in Spain. The Spanish nobility were not amused and rose up in what came to be known as the rising of the Comuneros. In March 1520 Toledo rebelled and Madrid quickly followed suit. Carlos and his forces prevailed, after which he concentrated ever-more power in his own hands.

A TALE OF TWO CITIES

By the time that Carlos' son and successor, Felipe II, ascended the Spanish throne in 1556, Madrid was surrounded by walls that boasted 130 towers and six stone gates. Although it sounds impressive, these fortifications were largely built of mud and were designed more to impress than provide any meaningful defence of the city.

A CAPITAL CHOICE

When Felipe II decided to make Madrid Spain's capital in 1561, you could almost hear the collective gasp of disbelief from Spain's great and good, few of whom lived in Madrid. Madrid was home to just 30,000 people, whereas Toledo and Seville each boasted more than 80,000. Even Valladolid, the capital of choice for Isabel and Fernando, had 50,000 inhabitants. What's more, in the 250 years since 1309, Madrid had hosted Spain's travelling road show of royalty just 10 times, far fewer than Spain's other large cities.

Madrid's apparent obscurity may, however, explain precisely why Felipe II chose it as the permanent seat of his court. Valladolid was considered to be of questionable loyalty. Toledo, which like Madrid stands close to the geographical heart of Spain, was known for its opinionated nobles and powerful clergy who had shown an annoying tendency to oppose the king's whims and wishes. In contrast, more than one king had described Madrid as 'very noble and very loyal'. By choosing Madrid Felipe II was choosing the path of least resistance. Felipe II also wanted the capital to be 'a city fulfilling the function of a heart located in the middle of the body'.

The decision saved Madrid from a life of provincial obscurity. This was most evident in 1601 when Felipe III, tired of Madrid, moved the court to Valladolid. Within five years, the population of Madrid halved. The move was so unpopular that the king, realising the error of his ways, returned to Madrid. *'Sólo Madrid es corte'* (roughly, 'Only Madrid can be home to the court') became the catchcry and thus it has been ever since.

1426	1479–81	1492
In the midst of a devastating drought, devout madrileños take the body of San Isidro, Madrid's patron saint, out onto the streets, whereupon it begins to rain.	Isabel, Queen of Castile, marries Fernando, King of Aragón. An edict by Madrid's authorities turns Muslims into second-class citizens, forcing them to wear signs identifying their religion alongside other indignities.	The last Muslim rulers of Al-Andalus are defeated by Christian armies in Granada, uniting the peninsula for the first time in seven centuries. Jews are expelled from the peninsula and Cristóbal Colón 'discovers' the Americas.

MADRID BEYOND THE ROYAL COURT

Travellers to Madrid in the 16th and 17th centuries found occasional beauty in the brick buildings with balconies of wrought iron, but the lasting impression was of streets 'which would be beautiful if it were not for the mud and filth'. The houses, such chroniclers wrote, were 'bad and ugly and almost all made of mud'. In the absence of a functioning government that took the needs of its citizens seriously, rubbish and human excrement were thrown from the balconies, 'a thing which afterwards creates an insupportable odour'. Undaunted by the squalor of the streets, madrileños had already begun a tradition that endures to this day, as one British traveller observed: 'In the evening, the people of Madrid go out to stroll and promenade and you see nothing more than a series of carriages.' Largely abandoned to their fate by their rulers, madrileños learned how to circumvent the often onerous decrees emanating from the royal court. When, in the 17th century, all home owners were ordered to reserve the second-storey of their homes for government bureaucrats and clergy newly arrived in the city, madrileños instead built homes with just a single-storey facade at street level, building additional storeys out the back, away from prying government eyes.

Such modest claims to significance notwithstanding, Madrid was chosen by Felipe II as the capital of Spain in 1561.

Suddenly thrust into the spotlight, Madrid took considerable time to grow into its new role. Felipe II was more concerned with the business of empire and building his monastic retreat at San Lorenzo de El Escorial (p244) than in developing Madrid. Despite a handful of elegant churches, the imposing *alcázar* and a smattering of noble residences, Madrid consisted, for the most part, of precarious, whitewashed houses that were little more than mud huts. They lined chaotic, ill-defined and largely unpaved lanes and alleys. The monumental Paseo del Prado, which now provides Madrid with so much of its grandeur, was nothing more than a small creek. Even so, Madrid went from having just 2000 homes in 1563 to more than 7000 just 40 years later as opportunists, impoverished rural migrants, would-be princes and fortune-seekers flocked to the city hoping for a share of the glamour and wealth that came from being close to royalty.

With more ostentatiousness than class, Madrid's indolent royal court retreated from reality and embarked on an era of decadence. Amid the squalor in which the bulk of Madrid's people toiled, royalty and the aristocracy gave themselves over to sickening displays of wealth and cavorted happily in their make-believe world of royal splendour. The sumptuous Palacio del Buen Retiro was completed in 1630 and replaced the *alcázar* as the prime royal residence (the former Museo del Ejército building and Casón del Buen Retiro, p98), are all that remain). Countless grand churches, convents and mansions were also built and, thanks to royal patronage, this was the golden age of art in Spain (see p38): Velázquez, El Greco, José de Ribera, Zurbarán, Murillo and Coello were all active in Madrid in the 17th century. For the first time, Madrid began to take on the aspect of a city.

But for all its newfound wealth and status, Madrid suffered several handicaps compared with more illustrious capitals elsewhere in Europe: it was bereft of a navigable river, port, decent road links or the slightest hint of entrepreneurial spirit; agricultural land around the town was poor; and the immense wealth from the Americas was squandered on wars and on indulging the court. Madrid was, in fact, little more than a large grubby leech, bleeding the surrounding provinces and colonies dry.

By the middle of the 17th century Madrid had completely outgrown its capacity to cope: it was home to 175,000 people, making it the fifth-largest city in Europe. But if you took away

1520	1561	1601
Madrid joins Toledo in the rebellion of the Comuneros against Carlos I, a disastrous decision that prompts the victorious king to rein in Madrid's growing independence.	Against all the odds, Felipe II establishes his permanent court at Madrid, which was, in Felipe II's words, 'a city fulfilling the function of a heart located in the middle of the body'.	In the last serious challenge to Madrid's position as capital, Felipe III moves Spain's capital to Valladolid, but popular discontent convinces him of the error of his ways and the royal court returns to Madrid.

the court, the city amounted to nothing and when Pedro Texeiro drew the first map of the city in 1656, the place was still largely a cesspit of narrow, squalid lanes.

THE BOURBONS LEAVE THEIR MARK

Such was the extent of Spain's colonial reach that events in Madrid could still alter the course of European history. After King Carlos II died in 1700 without leaving an heir, the 12-year War of the Spanish Succession convulsed Europe. While Europe squabbled over the Spanish colonial carcass, Felipe V (grandson of Louis XIV of France and Maria Teresa, a daughter of Felipe IV) ascended the throne. He may have founded the Bourbon dynasty, which remains at the head of the Spanish state today, but he also presided over the loss of most of Spain's European territories and was left with just Spain and a handful of colonial territories over which to rule.

Felipe proved more adept at nation building than military strategy, however. His centralisation of state control and attempts at land reform are viewed by some historians as the first steps in making Spain a modern European nation, and the former clearly cemented Madrid's claims to being Spain's pre-eminent city. He preferred to live outside the noisy and filthy capital, but when in 1734 the *alcázar* was destroyed in a fire, the king laid down plans for a magnificent new Palacio Real (Royal Palace) to take its place.

His immediate successors, especially Carlos III (r 1759–88), also gave Madrid and Spain a period of comparatively commonsense governance. Carlos (with the big nose – his equestrian statue dominates the Puerta del Sol) came to be known as the best 'mayor' Madrid had ever had. By introducing Madrid's first program of sanitation and public hygiene, he cleaned up a city that was, by all accounts, the filthiest in Europe. He was so successful that, near the end of Carlos III's reign, France's ambassador in Madrid described the city as one of the cleanest capitals in Europe. Mindful of his legacy, Carlos III also completed the Palacio Real (p67), inaugurated the Real Jardín Botánico (Royal Botanical Gardens; p95) and carried out numerous other public works. His stamp on Madrid's essential character was also evident in his sponsorship of local and foreign artists, among them Goya and Tiepolo. Carlos III also embarked on a major road-building program.

By the time Carlos III died in 1788, Madrid was in better shape than ever, even if Spain remained, despite all the improvements, an essentially poor country with a big-spending royal court.

NAPOLEON & EL DOS DE MAYO

Within a year of Carlos III's death Europe was again in uproar, this time as the French Revolution threatened to sweep away the old order of privileged royals and inherited nobility. Through the machinations of Carlos IV, the successor to Carlos III, and his self-serving minister, Manuel Godoy, Spain incurred the wrath of both the French and the British. The consequences were devastating. First, Nelson crushed the Spanish fleet in the Battle of Trafalgar in 1805. Next, Napoleon convinced a gullible Godoy to let French troops enter Spain on the pretext of a joint attack on Portugal, whereby General Murat's French detachment took control of Madrid, easily defeating General Tomás de Morla's bands of hearty but unruly armed citizenry. By 1808 the French presence had become an occupation and Napoleon's brother, Joseph Bonaparte, was crowned king of Spain.

Madrid did not take kindly to foreign rule and, on the morning of 2 May 1808 madrileños, showing more courage than their leaders, attacked French troops around the Palacio Real and

1622	Mid-17th century	1702
Seville-born Diego Rodríguez de Silva Velázquez moves to Madrid, takes up a position as a painter in the royal court and becomes synonymous with the golden age of Spanish art.	Madrid's population swells to 175,000 people, up from just 30,000 a century before. Only London, Paris, Constantinople and Naples can boast larger populations in Europe.	Felipe V is crowned king, beginning the Bourbon dynasty that still rules Spain and, save for four decades of the 20th century, has done so from Madrid.

what is now Plaza del Dos de Mayo in Malasaña (Map pp108-9). Murat moved quickly and by the end of the day the rebels were defeated. Goya's masterpieces, *El Dos de Mayo* and *El Tres de Mayo,* on display in the Museo del Prado (p90), poignantly evoke the hope and anguish of the ill-fated rebellion.

Although reviled by much of Madrid's population, Joseph Bonaparte's contribution to Madrid in five short years should not be underestimated. Working hard to win popular support, Bonaparte staged numerous free *espectáculos* – bullfights, festivals of food and drink, and religious processions. He also transformed Madrid with a host of measures necessary in a city that had grown up without any discernible sense of town planning. These measures included the destruction of various churches and convents to create public squares (such as the Plaza de Oriente (p67), Plaza de Santa Ana (p86), Plaza de San Miguel, Plaza de Santa Bárbara, Plaza de Tirso de Molina and Plaza de Callao) and widening streets. He also conceived the viaduct that still spans Calle de Segovia (p75). Under Bonaparte sanitation was also improved and cemeteries were moved to the outskirts of the city.

But madrileños never forgave Bonaparte his foreign origins and the brutality with which he suppressed uprisings against his rule, mocking his yearning for legitimacy by calling him names that included the Cucumber King, Pepe Botella and King of the Small Squares. Perhaps their scepticism of foreign rule lay in the undeniable fact that life for madrileños was as difficult as ever.

The French were finally evicted from Spanish territory in 1813 as a result of the Guerra de la Independencia (War of Independence, or Peninsular War). But when the autocratic King Fernando VII returned in 1814, Spain was in disarray and, at one point, French troops even marched back into Spain to prop him up. Though Fernando was not given to frequent bouts of enlightenment, two of his projects would stand the test of time – he opened to the public the renewed Parque del Buen Retiro (p97), which had been largely destroyed during the war, and founded an art gallery in the Prado (p90). When he died in 1833 Fernando left Spain with little more than a three-year-old daughter to rule over them, a recipe for civil war and an economy in tatters.

CAPITAL OF A COUNTRY DIVIDED

Isabel II, a toddler, was obviously not up to running the country, and power passed into the hands of her mother, María Cristina, who ruled as regent. Fernando's brother, Don Carlos, and his conservative supporters disputed Isabel's right to the throne, so María Cristina turned to the liberals for help, prompting the Carlist Wars. Throughout this period political upheaval remained part of Madrid's daily diet, characterised by alternating coups by conservative and liberal wings of the army. Madrileños must have rued the day their city became capital of this deeply fragmented country.

Apart from anything else, Madrid was incredibly backward. A discernible middle class only began to make a timid appearance from the 1830s. It was aided when the government ordered the *desamortización* (disentailment) of Church property in 1837. A speculative building boom ensued – if you've lived in Madrid since the late 1990s, you'll see that history has a habit of repeating itself – and its beneficiaries constituted the emerging entrepreneurial class. Indeed most historians agree that it was in the second half of the 19th century that Madrid's ordinary inhabitants finally began to emerge from the shadow of royalty and powerful clergy and play a defining role in the future of their city.

1734	1759–88	1808
Medieval Madrid's most enduring symbol, the *alcázar*, which had stood since the early days of the Muslim occupation, is destroyed by fire. Plans begin almost immediately for a lavish royal palace to take its place.	Carlos III, King of Spain and patron of Madrid, cleans up the city, lays out the Parque del Buen Retiro and sponsors Goya, transforming Madrid from a squalid provincial city into a sophisticated European capital.	Napoleon's troops under General Murat march into Madrid and Joseph Bonaparte, Napoleon's brother, is crowned King of Spain, but only after Madrid's citizen-defenders bravely rise up in vain to protest against foreign rule.

Nonetheless, for 25 years after Isabel began to rule in her own right in 1843, Madrid was awash with coups, riots and general discontent. It is therefore remarkable that amid the chaos the city's rulers laid the foundations for modern Madrid's infrastructure. In 1851 the city's first railway line, operating between Madrid and Aranjuez, opened. Seven years later the Canal de Isabel II, which still supplies the city with water from the Sierra de Guadarrama, was inaugurated. Street paving, the sewage system and rubbish collection were improved and gas lighting was introduced. More importantly, foreign (mostly French) capital was beginning to fill the investment vacuum.

Signs that Madrid was finally becoming a national capital worthy of the name also began to appear. In the years that followed, a national road network radiating from the capital was built and public works, ranging from the reorganisation of the Puerta del Sol to the building of the Teatro Real (p68), Biblioteca Nacional (p103) and Congreso de los Diputados (lower house of parliament), were carried out.

In the 1860s the first timid moves to create an Ensanche, or extension of the city, were undertaken. The initial spurt of building took place around Calle de Serrano, where the enterprising Marqués de Salamanca bought up land and built high-class housing. Poor old Salamanca – it was only after he died in 1883 that Salamanca became one of Madrid's most exclusive *barrios* (neighbourhoods); for more information see the boxed text on p101.

In 1873 Spain was declared a republic, but the army soon intervened to restore the Bourbon monarchy. Alfonso XII, Isabel's son, assumed power. In the period of relative tranquillity that ensued, the expansion of the Ensanche gathered momentum, the city's big train stations were constructed and the foundation stones of a cathedral were laid. Another kind of 'cathedral', the Banco de España, was completed and opened its doors in 1891. By 1898 the first city tramlines were electrified and in 1910 work began on the Gran Vía. Nine years later the first metro line started operation.

The 1920s were a period of frenzied activity, not just in urban construction but in intellectual life. As many as 20 newspapers circulated on the streets of Madrid, and writers and artists (including Lorca, Dalí and Buñuel) converged on the capital, which hopped to the sounds of American jazz and whose grand cafes resounded with the clamour of lively *tertulias* (literary discussions). The '20s roared as much in Madrid as elsewhere in Europe.

However, dark clouds were gathering against this backdrop of a culturally burgeoning city.

IN THE EYE OF THE STORM

In 1923 the captain-general of Catalonia and soon-to-be dictator, General Miguel Primo de Rivera, seized power and held it until Alfonso XIII had him removed in 1930. Madrid erupted in joyful celebration, but it would prove to be a false dawn. By now, the Spanish capital, home to more than one million people, had become the seething centre of Spain's increasingly radical politics, and the rise of the socialists in Madrid, as well as anarchists in Barcelona and Andalucía, sharpened tensions throughout the country.

Municipal elections in Madrid in April 1931 brought a coalition of republicans and socialists to power. Three days later a second republic was proclaimed and Alfonso XIII fled. The republican government opened up the Casa de Campo – until then serving as a private royal playground – to the public and passed numerous reformist laws, but divisions within the government enabled a right-wing coalition to assume power in 1933. Again the pendulum

1812	1819	1833
Thirty thousand madrileños die from hunger caused by fighting against the French in the lead-up to the Guerra de la Independencia (War of Independence). The French were expelled from Spanish soil a year later.	Fernando VII opens the Museo del Prado with 311 Spanish paintings. Originally conceived as a storehouse for royal art accumulated down through the centuries, it later becomes one of the most important art galleries in Europe.	King Fernando VII dies, leaving three-year-old Isabel II as heir-apparent. Her mother, María Cristina rules as regent and Spain descends into the Carlist civil wars, devastating Madrid in the process.

swung and in February 1936 the left-wing Frente Popular (Popular Front) barely defeated the right's Frente Nacional (National Front) to power. General Francisco Franco was exiled, supposedly out of harm's way, to the Canary Islands, but with the army supporting the right-wing parties and the extreme left clamouring for revolution, the stage was set for a showdown. In July 1936 garrisons in North Africa revolted, quickly followed by others on the mainland. The Spanish Civil War had begun.

Having stopped Franco's nationalist troops advancing from the north, Madrid found itself in the sights of Franco's forces moving up from the south. Take Madrid, Franco reasoned, and Spain would be his. By early November 1936 Franco was in the Casa de Campo. The republican government escaped to Valencia, but the resolve of the city's defenders, a mix of hastily assembled and poorly trained recruits, sympathisers from the ranks of the army and air force, the International Brigades and Soviet advisers, held firm. Madrid became an international cause célèbre, drawing luminaries as diverse as Ernest Hemingway and Willy Brandt in defence of the city. For all the fame of the brigades, the fact remains, however, that of the 40,000 soldiers and irregulars defending Madrid, more than 90% were Spaniards.

Madrid's defenders held off a fierce nationalist assault in November 1936, with the fighting heaviest in the northwest of the city, around Argüelles and the Ciudad Universitaria. The Francoist general Emilio Mola assured a British journalist that he would soon take Madrid with his four columns of soldiers (20,000 in all) massed on the city's outskirts and with the help of his 'fifth column', a phrase that has since remained in the popular lexicon that referred to Franco's right-wing sympathisers in Madrid. But Mola's predictions came to nothing. Soldiers loyal to Franco inside Madrid were overpowered by local militias and 20,000 Franco supporters sought protection inside the walls of foreign embassies. Faced with republican intransigence – symbolised by the catchphrase 'No pasarán!' ('They shall not pass!') coined by the Communist leader Dolores Ibarruri – Franco besieged Madrid, bombarded the city from the air and waited for the capital to surrender. It didn't.

German bombers strafed Madrid, one of the first such campaigns of its kind in the history of warfare, although the Salamanca district was spared, allegedly because it was home to a high proportion of Franco supporters. The Museo del Prado was not so fortunate and most of its paintings were evacuated to Valencia. As many as 10,000 people died in the Battle of Madrid; Franco's approach was summed up by his promise that 'I will destroy Madrid rather than leave it to the Marxists'.

Encircled on all sides, and with much of Spain falling to Franco's forces, madrileños lived a bizarre reality. People went about their daily business, caught the metro to work and got on with things as best they could. Like Londoners during the Blitz, madrileños who lived through the siege talk of the parallel realities of life in Madrid: the fear and the camaraderie of the bomb shelters, the mundane normalcy of daily life even as the bombs rained down. All the while, skirmishes continued around Argüelles and nationalist artillery intermittently shelled the city, particularly Gran Vía (nicknamed 'Howitzer Alley'), from the Casa de Campo. To maintain a minimum of functioning infrastructure, some of the city's vital industries were moved into disused metro tunnels.

By 1938 Madrid was in a state of near famine, with food, clothes and ammunition in short supply. As republican strongholds fell elsewhere across Spain, Madrid's republican defenders were divided over whether to continue the resistance. After a brief internal power struggle, those favouring negotiations won. On 28 March 1939 an exhausted Madrid finally surrendered.

1873	1881	1898
Spain's first, short-lived republic is declared in February, although the Bourbon monarchy returns to power in Madrid's Palacio Real with help from the army in December of the following year.	The Partido Socialista Obrero Español (PSOE; Spanish Socialist Workers' Party) is founded in a back room of Casa Labra, still one of Madrid's most prestigious tapas bars.	Spain loses its remaining colonies of Cuba, Puerto Rico and the Philippines to the USA, setting off a period of national angst. In the same year, Madrid's tramlines are electrified.

FRANCO'S MADRID

A deathly silence fell over the city as the new dictator made himself at home. Mindful that he was occupying a city that had hardly welcomed him with open arms, Franco considered shifting the capital south to the more amenable Seville. As if to punish Madrid for its resistance, he opted instead to remake Madrid in his own image and transform the city into a capital worthy of its new master. Franco and his right-wing Falangist Party maintained a heavy-handed repression, and Madrid in the early 1940s was impoverished and battle scarred, a 'city of a million cadavers', according to one observer.

In the Francoist propaganda of the day, the 1940s and 1950s were the years of *autarquía* (economic self-reliance), a policy that owed more to Spain's international isolation post-WWII due to its perceived support for Hitler than any principled philosophy. For most Spaniards, however, these were the *años de hambre* (the years of hunger). Only in 1955 did the average wage again reach the levels of 1934. Throughout the 1940s, tens of thousands of suspected republican sympathisers were harassed, imprisoned, tortured and shot. Thousands of political prisoners were shipped off to Nazi concentration camps. Many who remained were put to work in deplorable conditions, most notably to construct the grandiose folly of Franco's Valle de los Caídos (p245) monument northwest of Madrid.

The dire state of the Spanish economy forced hundreds of thousands of starving *campesinos* (peasants) to flock to Madrid, increasing the already enormous pressure for housing. Most contented themselves with erecting *chabolas* (shanty towns) in the increasingly ugly satellite suburbs that began to ring the city.

By the early 1960s, the so-called *años de desarollo* (years of development), industry was taking off in and around Madrid. Foreign investment poured in and the services and banking sector blossomed. Factories of the American Chrysler motor company were Madrid's single biggest employers in the 1960s. In 1960 fewer than 70,000 cars were on the road in Madrid; ten years later more than half a million clogged the capital's streets.

For all the signs of development in Madrid, Franco was never popular in his own capital and an increased standard of living did little to diminish madrileños' disdain for a man who held the capital in an iron grip. From 1965 opposition to Franco's regime became steadily more vocal. The universities were repeatedly the scene of confrontation and clandestine trade unions, such as Comisiones Obreras (CCOO; Workers' Commissions) and the outlawed Union General de Trabajadores (UGT; General Workers' Union), also began to make themselves heard again.

The waves of protest were not restricted to Madrid. In the Basque Country the terrorist group Euskadi Ta Askatasuna (ETA; Basque Homeland and Freedom) began to fight for Basque independence. Their first important action outside the Basque Country was the assassination in Madrid in 1973 of Admiral Carrero Blanco, Franco's prime minister and designated successor.

Franco fell ill in 1974 and died on 20 November 1975.

THE TRANSITION TO DEMOCRACY

After the initial shock caused by the death of Franco, who had cast a shadow over Spain for almost four decades, Spaniards began to reclaim their country and Madrid took centre stage.

The Partido Socialista Obrero Español (PSOE; Spanish Socialist Workers' Party), Partido Comunista de España (PCE; Spanish Communist Party), trade unions and a wide range of

1919	1920s	1931
Madrid's first metro line starts running, crossing the city from north to south, with eight stations and a total length of 3.5km from Puerta del Sol to Cuatro Caminos.	Madrid enjoys a cultural revival with Salvador Dalí, Federico García Lorca and Luis Buñuel bringing both high culture and mayhem to a city in love with jazz and *tertulias* (literary discussions).	After a period of right-wing dictatorship, Spain's Second Republic is proclaimed and King Alfonso XIII flees, leaving Spain in political turmoil and planting the seeds for civil war.

opposition figures emerged from hiding and exile. Franco's trusted advisors remained in control of both parliament and the armed forces but had neither the authority nor charisma necessary to hold back the tide of liberal optimism sweeping the country.

King Juan Carlos I, of the Bourbon family that had left the Spanish political stage with the flight of Alfonso XIII in 1931, had been groomed as head of state by Franco. But the king confounded the sceptics by entrusting Adolfo Suárez, a former moderate Francoist with whom he had long been in secret contact, with government in July 1976. With the king's approval Suárez quickly rammed a raft of changes through parliament while Franco loyalists and generals, suddenly rudderless without their leader, struggled to regroup.

Suárez and his centre-right coalition won elections in 1977 and set about writing a new constitution in collaboration with the now-legal opposition. It provided for a parliamentary monarchy with no state religion and guaranteed a large degree of devolution to the 17 regions (including the Comunidad de Madrid) into which the country was now divided.

Spaniards got the fright of their lives in February 1981 when a pistol-brandishing, low-ranking Guardia Civil (Civil Guard) officer, Antonio Tejero Molina, marched into the Cortes in Madrid with an armed detachment and held parliament captive for 24 hours. Throughout a day of high drama the country held its breath as Spaniards waited to see whether Spain would be thrust back into the dark days of dictatorship or whether the fledgling democracy would prevail. With the nation glued to their TV sets, King Juan Carlos I made a live broadcast denouncing Tejero and calling on the soldiers to return to their barracks. The coup fizzled out.

A year later Felipe González' PSOE won national elections. Spain's economic problems were legion – incomes were on a par with those of Iraq, ETA terrorism was claiming dozens of lives every year and unemployment was above 20%. But one thing that Spaniards had in abundance was optimism and when, in 1986, Spain joined the European Community (EC), as it was then called, the country had well and truly returned to the fold of modern European nations.

LA MOVIDA MADRILEÑA

Madrid's spirits could not be dampened and, with grand events taking place on the national stage, the city had become one of the most exciting places on earth. What London was to the swinging '60s and Paris to 1968, Madrid was to the 1980s. After the long, dark years of dictatorship and conservative Catholicism, Spaniards, especially madrileños, emerged onto the streets with all the zeal of ex-convent schoolgirls. Nothing was taboo in a phenomenon known as '*la movida madrileña*' (the Madrid scene) as young madrileños discovered the '60s, '70s and early '80s all at once. Drinking, drugs and sex suddenly were OK. All-night partying was the norm, drug taking in public was not a criminal offence (that changed in 1992) and the city howled. All across the city, summer terraces roared to the chattering, drinking, carousing crowds and young people from all over Europe flocked here to take part in the revelry.

What was remarkable about *la movida* is that it was presided over by Enrique Tierno Galván, an ageing former university professor who had been a leading opposition figure under Franco and was affectionately known throughout Spain as 'the old teacher'. A Socialist, he became mayor in 1979 and, for many, launched *la movida* by telling a public gathering '*a colocarse y ponerse al loro*', which loosely translates as 'get stoned and do what's cool'. Unsurprisingly he was Madrid's most popular mayor ever and when he died in 1986 a million madrileños turned out for his funeral.

1936–39	1960s	1973
The Spanish Civil War breaks out. Nationalist forces bombard Madrid from the air and with artillery, besieging it for three years, before the exhausted city surrenders on 28 March 1939.	After two decades of extreme economic hardship, the decade becomes known as the *años de desarollo* (years of development) with investment and rural immigrants flooding into Madrid. Opposition to Franco's rule begins to grow.	Admiral Carrero Blanco, Franco's prime minister and designated successor, is assassinated by ETA in a car-bomb attack in Madrid's Salamanca district after the admiral left Mass at the Iglesia de San Francisco de Borga.

EYEWITNESS TO LA MOVIDA MADRILEÑA
Agatha Ruiz de la Prada, fashion designer

Madrid during *la movida* was, for me, something marvellous because it coincided with my 20s and it was then that I started my first job. And so I arrived at work and thought, 'How much fun it is to work!' Imagine that you get to your first job and you are in the heart of *la movida*. At the time, I thought that was normal.

And the people who were very clever during *la movida* are still very clever, like Pedro Almodóvar and Alaska. Alaska was only 12 years old, but she was a spectacularly clever young woman. She was 12 years old but seemed like she was 40.

And then there was a time that was quite sad, at the end of *la movida*, when lots of people died from drugs. In the middle of the 1980s HIV was running wild and we were all very afraid. They were very black years, very sad, but I remember *la movida* as a wonderful thing, both for me and for Madrid. It was a moment during which there was so much freedom.

As told to Anthony Ham

But *la movida* was not just about rediscovering the Spanish art of *salir de copas* (going out for a drink). It was also accompanied by an explosion of creativity among the country's musicians, designers and film-makers keen to shake off the shackles of the repressive Franco years. The most famous of these was film director Pedro Almodóvar (see the boxed text, p43). Still one of Europe's most creative directors, his riotously colourful films captured the spirit of *la movida*, featuring larger-than-life characters who pushed the limits of sex and drugs. Although his later films became internationally renowned, his first films, *Pepi, Luci, Bom y Otras Chicas del Montón* (Pepi, Luci, Bom and the Other Girls; 1980) and *Laberinto de Pasiones* (Labyrinth of Passion; 1982) are where the spirit of the movement really comes alive. When he wasn't making films, Almodóvar immersed himself in the spirit of *la movida*, doing drag acts in smoky bars that people-in-the-know would frequent.

Among the other names from *la movida* that still resonate, the designer Agatha Ruiz de la Prada (see the boxed text, above) stands out. Also, start playing anything by Alaska, Los Rebeldes, Radio Futura or Nacha Pop and watch madrileños' eyes glaze over with nostalgia. By one estimate, Madrid was home to 300 rock bands and 1500 fashion designers at the time.

At the height of *la movida* in 1981, Andy Warhol, like Hemingway before him, regretted that he could not spend the rest of his days here. In 1985, the *New York Times* anointed the Spanish capital 'the new cultural capital of the world and the place to be'.

So what happened to *la movida*? Many say that it died in 1991 with the election of the conservative Popular Party's José María Álvarez del Manzano as mayor. In the following years rolling spliffs in public became increasingly dangerous and creeping clamps (ie closing hours) were imposed on the almost-lawless bars. Pedro Almodóvar was even heard to say that Madrid had become 'as boring as Oslo'. Things have indeed quietened down a little, but you'll only notice if you were here during the 1980s. If only all cities were this 'boring'.

MADRID SOBERS UP

Madrid is not a city that shifts its loyalties easily. After 12 years of Socialist rule, Madrid's political landscape fundamentally changed in 1991 with the election of its first democratically elected conservative mayor, José María Álvarez del Manzano of the Popular Party (PP), who earned

1975–78	1980s	1986
Following a year-long illness Franco dies in his bed in Madrid on 20 November 1975, after 39 years in power. Without an obvious successor to Franco, Spain returns to democratic rule three years later.	*La movida madrileña* takes over the city, and becomes a byword for hedonism. The era produces such zany creative talents as Pedro Almodóvar, Agatha Ruiz de la Prada and Alaska.	Spain joins the European Community (EC), which would later become the European Union (EU). EU subsidies and other assistance will later be credited with building the prosperous foundations of the modern Spanish economy.

A CITY OF IMMIGRANTS

In a country where regional nationalisms abound – even Barcelona, that most European of cities, is fiercely and parochially Catalan – Madrid is notable for its absence of regional sentiment. If you quiz madrileños as to why this is so, they most often look mystified and reply, 'but we're all from somewhere else'.

It has always been thus in Madrid. In the century after the city became the national capital in 1561, the population swelled by more than 500%, from 30,000 to 175,000. Most were Spaniards (peasants and would-be nobles) who left behind the impoverished countryside and were drawn by the opportunities that existed on the periphery of the royal court.

During the first three decades of the 20th century Madrid's population doubled from half a million to almost one million; in 1930 a study found that less than 40% of the capital's population was from Madrid. The process continued in the aftermath of the civil war, and in the 1950s alone more than 600,000 arrived from elsewhere in Spain.

In the late 20th century the process of immigration took on a new form, as Spain became the EU's largest annual recipient of immigrants. By 2009, more than 16% of Madrid's population were foreigners, more than double the national average.

Unsurprisingly, true madrileños are something of a rare breed. Those who can claim four grandparents born in the city are dignified with the name gatos (cats). Although you could be forgiven for thinking that it reflects their tendency to crawl around the city until all hours, the term actually dates from when one of Alfonso VI's soldiers artfully scaled Muslim Mayrit's formidable walls in 1083. 'Look,' cried his comrades, 'he moves like a cat!'

the dubious distinction of bringing an end to the hedonistic Madrid of the 1980s. Álvarez del Manzano, who remained in power until 2003, became known as 'The Tunnelator' for beginning the ongoing mania of Madrid governments for semipermanent roadworks and large-scale infrastructure projects. His party remains in power to this day.

González and the PSOE remained in power at a national level until 1996 when the rightwing PP, which had been created by former Franco loyalists, picked up the baton under José María Aznar.

From 1996 until 2004, the three levels of government in Madrid (local, regional and national) remained the preserve of the PP, a dominance that prompted observers from other regions to claim that the PP overtly favoured development of the capital at the expense of Spain's other regions. Whatever the truth of such accusations, the city has moved ahead in leaps and bounds, and as the national economy took off in the late 1990s, Madrid reaped the benefits. Extraordinary expansion programs for the metro, highways, airport, outer suburbs and for innercity renewal are unmistakable signs of confidence. By one reckoning, up to 75% of inward foreign investment into Spain is directed at the capital.

11-M

On 11 March 2004, just three days before the country was due to vote in national elections, Madrid was rocked by 10 bombs on four rush-hour commuter trains heading into the capital's Atocha station. When the dust cleared, 191 people had died and 1755 were wounded, many of them seriously. It was the biggest such terror attack in the nation's history. Madrid was in shock and, for 24 hours at least, this most clamorous of cities fell silent. Then, some 36 hours after the attacks, more than three million madrileños streamed onto the streets to protest against

1991	1992	11 March 2004
Madrid elects a conservative mayor, José María Álvarez del Manzano of the Partido Popular (PP; Popular Party), for the first time, bringing an end to la movida.	In the same year that Barcelona hosts the Summer Olympics, Madrid is designated a European Capital of Culture. Drug taking in public is finally outlawed in the capital.	Terrorist bombings on four Madrid commuter trains kill 191 people and injure 1755. The next day three million madrileños take to the streets in protest, and the PSOE wins national elections on 14 March.

the bombings, making it the largest demonstration in Madrid's history. A further eight million marched in solidarity in cities across Spain. Although deeply traumatised, the mass act of defiance and pride began the process of healing.

Visit Madrid today and you'll find a city that has resolutely returned to normal. Bars and restaurants overflow with happy crowds and people throng the streets as they always have. Yes, security is a little tighter than before, but it's no more than in most other European cities. The only reminders of the bombings are the poignant Bosque del Recuerdo (Memorial Forest) in the Parque del Buen Retiro, which was planted as a memorial to the victims, and the 11 March 2004 Memorial (p83) at Atocha station.

Given the history of ETA violence, it came as no surprise that the ruling right-wing PP government insisted that ETA was responsible. But as evidence mounted that the attack might have come from a radical Islamic group in reprisal for the government's unswerving support for the deeply unpopular invasion of Iraq, angry Spaniards turned against the government. In a stunning reversal of prepoll predictions, the PP was defeated by the PSOE, whose leader, José Luis Rodríguez Zapatero, led the Socialists back to power after eight years in the wilderness.

In addition to withdrawing Spanish troops from Iraq, the new government introduced a raft of liberalising social reforms. Gay marriage was legalised, Spain's arcane divorce laws overhauled and, in 2005, almost a million illegal immigrants were granted residence. Although Spain's powerful Catholic Church has cried foul over many of the reforms, the changes played well with most Spaniards. As always, however, Madrid would become a battleground for the great issues of the day. It was here that the reforms were embraced with the greatest fervour, even as the streets filled with demonstrators (often bussed in from other Spanish regions).

MADRID TODAY

It comes as a surprise to many visitors that free-swinging Madrid is ruled by a conservative right-wing government. The PP's Alberto Ruiz-Gallardón, who was first elected mayor in 2003, increased the PP's stranglehold over the Ayuntamiento (town hall) with a landslide victory in 2007, winning 55% of the vote. His colleague, Esperanza Aguirre, became the country's first ever woman regional president in close-run elections for the Comunidad de Madrid in October 2003, and easily extended her majority in 2007. Madrid will, it seems, be ruled by conservatives for some time to come.

Despite belonging to the same party, the political marriage between Aguirre and Ruiz-Gallardón has not always been a happy one. The personable Aguirre is a tough right-wing PP member who served as a senator and as national education and culture minister in José María Aznar's first PP government. Ruiz-Gallardón, on the other hand, comes unmistakeably from the liberal wing of the party. Aguirre makes little attempt to mask her dislike of Ruiz-Gallardón. Their simmering rivalry spilled over into open conflict on the national stage in early 2008, when the PP's leader of the national opposition, Mariano Rajoy, bowed to Aguirre's demand that Ruiz-Gallardón not be chosen as Rajoy's running mate in the national elections in March 2008, elections that the Socialists narrowly won. In the wake of Aguirre's victory, a tearful Ruiz-Gallardón announced that he would retire from politics, although he since seems to have had a change of heart.

Ruiz-Gallardón has been largely credited with feeding Madrid's burgeoning confidence, in part thanks to his aim of making Madrid 'the city of reference in Southern Europe' by encouraging

2007	2007	2010
The PP's Alberto Ruiz-Gallardón, who first won election in 2003, wins an absolute majority in municipal elections, cementing the conservatives hold over Madrid's Ayuntamiento (town hall).	Twenty-one people are convicted of involvement in the 11 March 2004 terrorist attacks, although the trial uncovers no evidence of al-Qaeda involvement in the planning or execution of the bombings.	According to the IMF, Spain becomes the last advanced economy to emerge from recession after the global economic crisis, growing by 0.1% in the second quarter even as unemployment hits 20%.

international organisations (such as the World Tourism Organization) to set up their headquarters here. It seems to be working: a 2009 survey by the lifestyle magazine *Monocle* ranked Madrid the world's 12th most liveable city and the most liveable city in southern Europe.

The failure to win the 2012 and 2016 Olympic Games (in which Madrid came third and second, respectively) was something of a blip, but the city has largely taken such setbacks in its stride. A far more serious challenge to the city's self-image has been the global economic crisis, which has hit Spain particularly hard. With national unemployment having returned to pre-boom levels of almost 20% (or 40% among young Spaniards), Madrid certainly hasn't escaped unscathed: almost half a million madrileños were registered as unemployed in March 2010, almost double the figure from three years earlier. Madrid's unemployment rate (an estimated 13% to 15%) may be well below the national average, but there's no denying that the city's inherently optimistic streak has taken a hit, a situation that's unlikely to change in the short term.

ARTS

Madrid is the cultural capital of the Spanish-speaking world and easily Spain's premier cultural stage. Yes, many quintessentially Spanish art forms may have had their origins elsewhere – flamenco, for example, has its roots in Andalucía. But it is to Madrid that Spain's major artists have always flocked in order to make their name, from the grand masters of Spanish painting down through the centuries – Velázquez and Goya are two shining examples – to Spain's famous film stars, acclaimed directors such as Pedro Almodóvar and flamenco greats like El Camarón de la Isla.

This phenomenon spills over into Spain's flourishing contemporary arts scene: just about everything that is innovative in Spanish culture has a stage in the capital at some point. In short, if it's happening in Spain, it will be happening here.

LITERATURE

From the Siglo de Oro to Pérez Galdós

Spanish literature began to come of age in the late 16th century as writers gravitated to the new capital, drawn by promises of royal patronage and endless material for stories as Madrid attracted a fascinating cast of characters eager for the glamour and opportunities that surrounded the royal court. The *Siglo de Oro* (Golden Age) of Spanish writing was very much Madrid's century and luminaries, such as Cervantes, Francisco de Quevedo and Lope de Vega (p44), were all Madrid celebrities.

With the exception perhaps of the greatest of all Spanish poets, Seville-born Luis de Góngora (1561–1627), the greatest Spanish writers of the age were either born or spent much of their time in the young capital. Francisco de Quevedo (1580–1645), whose parents served in the royal court, went in search of grittier vignettes of local life and spent much of his time in Madrid taverns scribbling some of the most biting, nasty and entertaining prose to come out of 17th-century Spain. His *La Historia de la Vida del Buscón Llamado Don Pablos* (The Swindler; 1626), tracing the none-too-uplifting life of antihero El Buscón, is laced with venom and is his most enduring work.

Miguel de Cervantes Saavedra (1547–1616), regarded as the father of the novel, was born in Alcalá de Henares, lived in the Barrio de las Letras district in Huertas and ended his tur-

---

FERIA DEL LIBRO

Bibliophiles will love being in Madrid around the last week of May and first two weeks of June for Madrid's Book Fair, the Feria del Libro de Madrid (www.ferialibromadrid.com). The Feria del Libro has been running since 1933 and draws hundreds of booksellers from all over Spain, who set up stalls in the Parque del Buen Retiro. The Feria brings together some of the biggest names in Spanish literature for book signings and public events, although strolling amid the stalls in Madrid's most beautiful park on an early summer's day is reason enough to come. The books you'll come across are mostly in Spanish, but English-language titles are fairly widespread. For the duration of the Feria stalls open from 11am to 2pm and from 6pm to 9.30pm Monday to Friday, and from 10.30am to 2.30pm and from 5pm to 9.30pm Saturday and Sunday. Unless you like massive crowds, avoid Saturday and Sunday and come on a weekday.

top picks

GREAT MADRID READS

- Fortunata y Jacinta, Benito Pérez Galdós (1887)
- La Colmena (The Beehive), Camilo José Cela (1957)
- Capital de la Gloria, Juan Eduardo Zúñiga (2003)
- Un Corazon tan Blanco (A Heart So White), Javier Marías (2002)
- Historias del Kronen, José Ángel Mañas (1994)
- Winter in Madrid, CJ Sansom (2006)
- A Load of Bull: An Englishman's Adventures in Madrid, Tim Parfitt (2006)
- The Bad Girl, Mario Vargas Llosa (2007)

bulent days in Madrid. He started writing *El Ingenioso Hidalgo Don Quijote de la Mancha* (Don Quijote) as a short story to earn a quick peseta. It turned instead into an epic tale in 1605 and is now widely considered the first and greatest novel of all time, charting the journey of the errant knight and his equally quixotic companion, Sancho Panza, through the foibles of his era. For a selection of Cervantes-centric landmarks in Madrid, see the boxed text on p87.

Benito Pérez Galdós (1843–1920), alternately referred to as Spain's Balzac or the Iberian Tolstoy, spent virtually all his adult life in Madrid. His *Fortunata y Jacinta* recounts much more than a tormented love triangle, throwing light on the social intrigues and mores of late-19th-century Madrid.

Contemporary Literature

The censors of Francoist Spain ensured that literary growth in the country was somewhat stunted; some outstanding writers emerged, but freedom of expression was limited and much of what was good in Spanish writing was penned by writers in exile. Since Spain's return to democracy in 1978 there has been a flowering of Spanish letters, and Madrid is at the heart of it.

Although not a madrileño by birth, Camilo José Cela (1916–2002) wrote one of the most talked about novels on the city in the 1950s, *La Colmena* (The Beehive). This classic takes the reader into the heart of Madrid, the beehive of the title, in what is like a photo album filled with portraits of every kind of Madrid punter in those grey days. For some readers Cela's reputation has been tarnished by rumours of his closeness to Franco's regime. Cela was nonetheless a writer of the highest quality and took the Nobel Prize in Literature in 1989 and the most important Spanish literature prize, the Premio Cervantes, six years later.

Francisco Umbral (b 1935), a prestigious journalist and winner in 2000 of the Premio Cervantes, is yet another chronicler of the city. *Trilogía de Madrid* (Madrid Trilogy; 1984), which explores a whole range of different circles of Madrid life in the Franco years, is just one of several Madrid-centric novels to his credit. Some have praised Umbral as the greatest prose writer in Spanish of the 20th century; Cela would no doubt snort in disagreement, as was his wont.

Spain and Madrid's experience of the civil war is better known through the works of foreigners such as Orwell and Hemingway, but Madrid's own Juan Eduardo Zúñiga (b 1929) has written one of the most moving portrayals of Madrid life during the resistance. *Capital de la Gloria* consists of 10 stories set during the last, desperate months before Madrid finally capitulated.

Murcia's Arturo Pérez-Reverte (b 1951), long-time war correspondent and general man's man, has latterly become one of the most internationally read Spanish novelists. In *El Capitán Alatriste* (Captain Alatriste) we are taken into the decadent hurly-burly of 18th-century Madrid. The captain in question has become the protagonist of several novels and a blockbuster movie starring Viggo Mortensen.

The author of *the* cult urban tribal novel in Madrid is without doubt José Ángel Mañas (b 1971). In *Historias del Kronen* (Stories from the Kronen; 1994) a band of young disaffected madrileños hangs out in the city's Kronen bar and throws itself into a whirlwind of sex, drugs, violence and rock 'n' roll.

Madrileño Javier Marías (b 1951; www.javiermarias.es) is a prolific and critically acclaimed novelist and essayist whose exceptional breadth and quality of work has led many to tip him as Spain's next Nobel Prize winner. His *Un Corazon tan Blanco* (A Heart So White; 2002), set in Madrid and centring on a tale of subtle family intrigue, shows a miniaturist's eye for detail throughout this outstanding work of digressive and intimate storytelling.

Another emerging talent is José Machado (b 1974), whose *Grillo* (2003) is a heavily autobiographical look at a young madrileño lad of good family determined to be a writer. It's a little like looking into a mirror that looks into a mirror. Other writers either born in Madrid or with strong connections to the city include: Lucía Etxebarría (b 1966); Almudena Grandes (b 1960), whose two novels *The Ages of Lulu* (2005) and *The Wind from the East* (2007) are both available in English; and Elvira Lindo (b 1962), who is a witty newspaper columnist for *El País* on matters of Madrid and national life as well as having written numerous books for children and adults.

PAINTING

The pantheon of master painters who called Madrid home for critical periods during their working lives runs from the old masters Velázquez, El Greco and Goya to doyens of contemporary art such as Picasso and Juan Gris. In centuries past Madrid's undeniable attraction was the patronage of Spanish kings who lavished money on the great painters of the day. Spain's kings, who began the tradition in the 16th century, were a pretty vain and decadent lot and liked nothing better than to pose for portraits and to compete with other European royals for the fleeting prestige that came from association with the great artists of the day. Perhaps they also appreciated fine art. Whatever their motives, royal money and personal patronage transformed Madrid into one of the richest producers and storehouses of paintings anywhere in the world. From the early 20th century onwards, Madrid's role as the seat of Spain's finest artistic academies has also drawn Spain's most creative talents.

The Early Days

The first Spaniard to find royal favour was Logroño-born Juan Navarrete (1526–79), also known as El Mudo (the Mute), one of Spain's first practitioners of tenebrism, a style that largely aped Caravaggio's chiaroscuro style. But Navarrete was an exception and Felipe II – the monarch who made Madrid the permanent seat of the royal court – preferred the work of Italian artists such as Titian ahead of home-grown talent. Even some foreign artists who would later become masters were given short shrift, suggesting that the king's eye for quality was far from perfect. One of these was the Cretan-born Domenikos Theotokopoulos (1541–1614), known as El Greco (the Greek; see the boxed text, p237), who was perhaps the most extraordinary and temperamental 'Spanish' artist of the 16th century, but whom Felipe II rejected as a court artist.

Velázquez & the Golden Age

As Spain's monarchs sought refuge from the creeping national malaise of the 17th century by promoting the arts, they fostered an artist who would rise above all others: Diego Rodríguez de Silva Velázquez (1599–1660). Born in Seville, Velázquez later moved to Madrid as court painter and stayed to make the city his own. He composed scenes (landscapes, royal portraits, religious subjects, snapshots of everyday life) that owe their vitality not only to his photographic eye for light and contrast but also to a compulsive interest in the humanity of his subjects, so that they seem to breathe on the canvas. His masterpieces include *Las Meninas* (The Maids of Honour) and *La Rendición de Breda* (The Surrender of Breda), both on view in the Museo del Prado (p90).

Francisco de Zurbarán (1598–1664), a friend and contemporary of Velázquez, ended his life in poverty in Madrid; it was only after his death that he received the acclaim that his masterpieces deserved. He is best remembered for the startling clarity and light in his portraits of monks, a series of which hangs in the Real Academia de Bellas Artes de San Fernando (p71).

Other masters of the era whose works hang in the Prado, though their connection to Madrid was limited, include José (Jusepe) de Ribera (1591–1652), who was influenced by Caravaggio and produced fine chiaroscuro works, and Bartolomé Esteban Murillo (1618–82).

The Madrid School, Goya & Beyond

While the stars were at work, a second tier of busy baroque artists beavered away in the capital and collectively they came to be known as the Madrid School.

Fray Juan Rizi (1600–81) did most of his work for Benedictine monasteries across Castile; some hang in the Real Academia de Bellas Artes de San Fernando. Claudio Coello (1642–93)

GOYA – A CLASS OF HIS OWN

There was nothing in the provincial upbringing of Francisco José de Goya y Lucientes (1746–1828), who was born in the village of Fuendetodos in Aragón, to suggest that he would become one of the towering figures of European art.

Goya started his career as a cartoonist in the Real Fábrica de Tapices (Royal Tapestry Workshop) in Madrid. In 1776 Goya began designing for the tapestry factory, but illness in 1792 left him deaf; many critics speculate that his condition was largely responsible for his wild, often merciless style that would become increasingly unshackled from convention. By 1799 Goya was appointed Carlos IV's court painter.

Several distinct series and individual paintings mark his progress. In the last years of the 18th century he painted enigmatic masterpieces, such as *La Maja Vestida* (The Young Lady Dressed) and *La Maja Desnuda* (The Young Lady Undressed), identical portraits but for the lack of clothes in the latter. The rumour mill suggests the subject was none other than the Duchess of Alba, with whom he allegedly had an affair. Whatever the truth of Goya's sex life, the Inquisition was not amused by the artworks, which it covered up. Nowadays all is bared in the Prado.

At about the same time as his enigmatic *Majas*, the prolific Goya executed the playful frescoes in Madrid's Ermita de San Antonio de la Florida (p122), which have recently been restored to stunning effect. He also produced *Los Caprichos* (The Caprices), a biting series of 80 etchings lambasting the follies of court life and ignorant clergy.

The arrival of the French and war in 1808 had a profound impact on Goya. Unforgiving portrayals of the brutality of war are *El Dos de Mayo* (The Second of May) and, more dramatically, *El Tres de Mayo* (The Third of May). The latter depicts the execution of Madrid rebels by French troops.

After he retired to the Quinta del Sordo (Deaf Man's House) west of the Río Manzanares in Madrid, he created his nightmarish *Pinturas Negras* (Black Paintings). Executed on the walls of the house, they were later removed and now hang in the Prado. A scandal erupted recently when it was claimed that these chilling works were painted by the artist's son, Javier, and sold as genuine Goyas by his grandson. The Prado strenuously denies the claims.

Goya spent the last years of his life in voluntary exile in France, where he continued to paint until his death.

specialised in the big picture and some of his huge canvases adorn the complex at San Lorenzo de El Escorial (p244), including his magnum opus, *La Sagrada Forma* (The Holy Form).

But these were mere window dressing compared to Goya (see the boxed text, above), who cast such a long shadow that all other artists of the period have been largely obscured.

Although no-one of the stature of Goya followed in his wake, new trends were noticeable by the latter decades of the 19th century. Valencian native Joaquín Sorolla (1863–1923) flew in the face of the French Impressionist style, preferring the blinding sunlight of the Mediterranean coast to the muted tones favoured in Paris. He lived and worked in Madrid and his work can be studied in Madrid's Museo Sorolla (p118), where he once lived.

Leading the way into the 20th century was Madrid-born José Gutiérrez Solana (1886–1945), whose disturbing, avant-garde approach to painting revels in low lighting, sombre colours and deathly pale figures. His work is emblematic of what historians now refer to as *España negra* (black Spain). A selection of his canvases is on display in the Centro de Arte Reina Sofía (p82).

Picasso, Dalí & Juan Gris

The 17th century may have been Spain's golden age, but the 20th century was easily its rival.

Málaga-born Pablo Ruiz Picasso (1881–1973) is one of the greatest and most original Spanish painters of all time. Although he spent much of his working life in Paris, he arrived in Madrid from Barcelona in 1897 at the behest of his father for a year's study at the Escuela de Bellas Artes de San Fernando. Never one to allow himself to be confined within formal structures, the precocious Picasso instead took himself to the Prado to learn from the masters, and to the streets to depict life as he saw it. Picasso went on to become the master of cubism, which was inspired by his fascination with primitivism, primarily African masks and early Iberian sculpture. This highly complex form reached its high point in *Guernica* (see the boxed text, p86), which hangs in the Centro de Arte Reina Sofía.

Picasso was not the only artist who found the Escuela de Bellas Artes de San Fernando too traditional for his liking. In 1922 Salvador Dalí (1904–89) arrived in Madrid from Catalonia, but decided that the eminent professors of the renowned fine-arts school were not fit to judge him. He spent four years living in the 'Resi', the renowned students' residence (which still functions today) where he met poet Federico García Lorca and future film director Luis Buñuel. The three self-styled anarchists and bohemians romped through the cafes and music halls of 1920s Madrid, frequenting brothels, engaging in pranks, immersing themselves in jazz and taking part in endless *tertulias* (literary discussions). Dalí, a true original and master of the surrealist form, was finally expelled from art school and left Madrid, never to return. The only remaining link with Madrid is a handful of his hallucinatory works in the Centro de Arte Reina Sofía (p82).

In the same gallery is a fine selection of the cubist creations of Madrid's Juan Gris (1887–1927), who was turning out his best work in Paris while Dalí and his cohorts were up to no good in Madrid. Along with Picasso and Georges Braque, he was a principal exponent of the cubist style and his paintings can be seen in the Museo Thyssen-Bornemisza (p94) and Real Academia de Bellas Artes de San Fernando (p71).

During the Franco years in Madrid, Antonio Saura (1930–98) was a shining light of surrealism and the dramatic brushstrokes of his portraits are sometimes seen as a reaction to the conventionality of public life under the dictator. In 1956 he publicly burned books of his paintings as a protest against Franco and the following year set up the El Paso group of artists whose aim was to provide a forum for contemporary art. Check out www.antoniosaura.org for more info.

Contemporary Art

The death of Franco in 1975 unleashed a frenzy of activity and artistic creativity was central to *la movida madrileña* (p32). The Galería Moriarty (p109) became a focal point of exuberantly artistic reference and is still going strong. A parade of artists marched through the gallery, including leading *movida* lights such as Ceesepe (b 1958; real name Carlos Sánchez Pérez), who captures the spirit of 1980s Madrid with his eight short films and busy paintings full of people and activity (but recently veering towards surrealism). Another Moriarty protégé was Ouka Lele (b 1957, whose real name is Bárbara Allende), a self-taught photographer whose sometimes weird works stand out for her tangy treatment of colour. Her photos can be seen at the Centro de Arte Reina Sofía, Museo de Historia (p107) and the Museo Municipal de Arte Contemporáneo (p107). Another *movida* photographer who still exhibits around town is Alberto García-Alix (b 1956).

The rebellious, effervescent activity in the 1980s tends to cloud the fact that the visual arts in the Franco years were far from dead, although many artists spent years in exile. The art of Eduardo Arroyo (b 1937) in particular is steeped in the radical spirit that kept him in exile for 15 years from 1962. His paintings tend in part towards pop art, brimming with ironic sociopolitical comment. Of the other exiles, one of Spain's greatest 20th-century sculptors, Toledo-born Alberto Sánchez (1895–1962), who can be seen at the open-air Museo de la Escultura Abstracta (p103), lived his last years in Moscow. He and Benjamín Palencia (1894–1980), an artist whose paintings occasionally show striking similarities with some of Sánchez' sculptures, were part of the so-called Escuela de Vallecas (Vallecas is now a working-class barrio in southern Madrid). The inheritors of their legacy, which is now more often called the *Escuela de Madrid,* include Francisco Arias, Gregorio del Olmo, Álvaro Delgado, Andrés Conejo and Agustín Redondela. Carlos Franco (b 1951) painted the frescoes on the Real Casa de la Panadería on Plaza Mayor (p64). Apart from Sánchez, all of these artists are on display at the Museo de Arte Contemporáneo.

Antonio López García (b 1936) takes a photographer's eye to his hyper-realistic paintings. Settings as simple as *Lavabo y Espejo* (Wash Basin and Mirror, 1967) convert the most banal everyday objects into scenes of extraordinary depth and the same applies to his Madrid street scenes, which are equally loaded with detail, light play and subtle colour, especially *La Granvía* (1981) and *Vallecas* (1980). He won the coveted Premio Príncipe de Asturias for art in 1985 and a couple of his works are in the Centro de Arte Reina Sofía. His contemporary, Alfredo Alcain (b 1936), whose textured paintings could at times be mistaken for aerial shots of patchwork fields, won the Premio Príncipe de Asturias in 2004.

For paintings whose subject matter is Madrid (although she also paints other cities), Málaga-born Paula Varona (www.paulavarona.com) has few peers. The Madrid section of her website (which also lists upcoming exhibitions) has a stunning overview of her work.

Many of the most prominent new abstract painters have a relatively small body of work, but Alejandro Corujeira, Alberto Reguera, Xavier Grau and Amaya Bozal are all names to watch. In the figurative tradition, the same could be said of Juan Carlos Savater, Sigfrido Martín Begué, Abraham La Calle and Fernando Bellver. All can be seen at the Museo de Arte Contemporáneo.

The big event for contemporary art in Madrid is the annual midwinter Arco contemporary art fair (p17; www.arco.ifema.es), which goes from strength to strength as a showcase for both emerging and established Spanish talent, although as it gains in prestige, it's taking on a more international flavour.

MUSIC
Classical & Opera

Madrid has never been at the forefront of great classical music and opera, and the Spanish composers of note (Isaac Albéniz, Enrique Granados, Joaquín Rodrigo and Manuel de Falla) all came from elsewhere in Spain.

The single obvious exception to the general rule is Plácido Domingo (b 1934), the country's leading opera tenor and born *gato* (slang for madrileño, literally 'cat'). Early childhood was where the charming singer's relationship with Madrid more or less ended, as his parents, *zarzuela* (satirical dance and music) performers, moved to Mexico, where he made his singing debut years later. Along with the Catalan José Carreras, Spain contributed two of the Three Tenors.

Although not much of what you'll hear in Madrid originates here, you can still find a year-round program of fine performances to choose from (see p202).

top picks

MUSIC CDS

- Lo Mejor de Miguel Bosé (Miguel Bosé) Greatest hits of this veteran of the Madrid music scene.
- La Movida de los 80 All the biggies of *la movida*, including Alaska y Los Pegamoides, Radio Futura and Nacha Pop.
- Mecanografia (Mecano) All the hit singles from one of *la movida's* iconic bands.
- Canciones Hondas (Ketama) One of Ketama's best-ever CDs of rocky flamenco fusion; it's miles better than the Gypsy Kings!
- Pafuera Telearañas (Bebe) You can hear the smoky Madrid bar scene in every chord.
- Chicote Red Lounge – Cocktail (Sandro Bianchi) Downtempo rhythms mixed by DJs at Madrid's legendary Museo Chicote.
- Grandes Exitos: Todos Hablan de Ti (Joaquín Sabina) One of the poets of modern Spanish music; this includes the much-loved 'Pongamos Que Hablo de Madrid' about the city.
- Follow the City Lights (Dover) Catchy indie rock from Madrid's English-language sensations.
- El Mundo Se Equivoca (La Quinta Estación) Latin Grammy award-winning album in 2007.
- Con Otro Aire (Chambao) The latest flamenco fusion from Spain's hottest group of the moment.

Contemporary Music

At the height of *la movida madrileña* in the 1980s, Madrid's nights rocked to the sounds of more than 300 local rock bands. Most such groups fell by the wayside, but some have survived. Seguridad Social is a good old-fashioned hard-rock group that has remained a surprisingly constant force since it first started in 1982. Another legend is rock poet Rosendo Mercado, who started off with the group Leño in the late 1970s, later went solo and hasn't stopped since. Others that defined 1980s Madrid – Radio Futura, El Último de la Fila, Gabinete Caligari and Nacha Pop (and punkier ensembles such as Alaska and Kaka de Luxe) – came and went, but their music still holds a special place in the hearts of madrileños of a certain age.

One enduring group from *la movida*, Mecano, was the subject of a blockbuster musical *Hoy No Me Puedo Levantar* (I Can't Get Out of Bed Today), named after its debut single; the musical ran in Madrid for three years from 2005 to sell-out crowds. The musical was written by Madrid-born Nacho Cano, former band member and now one of Madrid's most creative musical producers. At its peak Mecano sang many of the theme songs for the grittier side of *la movida*, dealing with teenage boredom, drugs and experimental love. Although the group went its separate ways in 1998, Mecano still provides the soundtrack for many a Madrid night.

Although born in Panama, Miguel Bosé was another *la movida* identity to make Madrid his own. Since the craziness of his early years, Bosé has mellowed into one of Spanish music's elder statesmen and most respected musicians with a base in pop but with inflections from myriad music genres.

Other echoes of *la movida* can be heard elsewhere. Three years after his band Nacha Pop split, Madrid-born Antonio Vega put out his first solo disc in 1991 and became one of the sensations of the mid-1990s with his soft pop-rock.

Madrid's rock scene is not what it once was but nonetheless continues to churn out class acts. Dover is one such group, a Madrid quartet that belts out energetic indie rock in English. Another pop-rock group to watch is La Quinta Estación ('The Fifth Season'), three Madrid-born musicians who left Spain to find success in Mexico before returning home following a string of big hits.

Recently emerged from the rock bar scene in Malasaña is the pop quartet Balboa. Led by guitarist Carlos del Amo and his singer girlfriend, Lua Ríos, they've combined the energy of rock with a strong guitar lead and a soft-pop touch in Lua's voice and lyrics.

PEDRO ALMODÓVAR'S MADRID

Plaza Mayor (p61) *La Flor de mi Secreto* (The Flower of My Secret; 1995)

El Rastro (p74) *Laberinto de Pasiones* (Labyrinth of Passion; 1982)

Villa Rosa (p188) *Tacones Lejanos* (High Heels; 1991)

Café del Círculo de Bellas Artes (p184) *Kika* (1993)

Viaducto de Segovia (p75) *Matador* (1986)

Museo del Jamón (p151) *Carne Trémula* (Live Flesh; 1997)

Another big star to recently come out of the Madrid bar scene is Valencia-born Nieves Rebolledo, who goes by the stage name of Bebe. Her 2004 *Pafuera Telarañas* became one of the biggest albums of recent years and the signature track 'Malo' (Bad) managed that rare combination of becoming a dance-floor anthem while making serious social commentary (the song is an impassioned denunciation of domestic violence). She followed up her debut with the acclaimed *Y* in 2009.

Other names enjoying huge popularity on the Spanish music scene include Estopa, La Oreja de Van Gogh, Amaral and the enduring Alejandro Sanz.

CINEMA & TELEVISION
Cinema

The Spanish film industry, with Madrid as its uncontested capital, exists on two radically different levels. First there are the exceptional individual talents, such as Pedro Almodóvar (see the boxed text, opposite), Penélope Cruz, Antonio Banderas and Javier Bardem, who have become international (and Hollywood) stars. At the same time the local film-making industry turns out work of real quality but struggles for both funding and international success, too often drowned out by the glamour and big budgets of that same Hollywood. Public funding for local film-making has consistently fallen over the past decade or so and, although audience numbers remain quite steady, less than 20% of Spanish box office takings are for Spanish films. These two strands come together for the annual Goya awards (Spain's Oscars), which are held in Madrid in February – it's the perfect stage for taking the pulse of the industry.

Pedro Almodóvar is not the only Spanish director to have earned critical international acclaim. The still-young Alejandro Amenábar (b 1973) is already one of Spain's most respected directors. He was born in Chile but his family moved to Madrid when he was a child. He announced his arrival with *Tesis* (1996), but it was with *Abre Los Ojos* (Open Your Eyes; 1997), which was later adapted for Hollywood as *Vanilla Sky*, that his name became known internationally. His first English-language film was *The Others* (2001), which received plaudits from critics, but nothing like the clamour that surrounded *Mar Adentro* (The Sea Inside; 2004), his stunning portrayal of a Galician fisherman's desire to die with dignity, which starred Javier Bardem. His 2009 *Ágora* was a stunning follow-up and, with a budget of US$50 million, is the most expensive Spanish film ever made. Not content with directing, Amenábar also writes his own films.

Madrid-born Fernando Trueba (b 1955) has created some fine Spanish films, the best of which was his 1992 release *Belle Epoque*. It portrays gentle romps and bed-hopping on a country estate in Spain in 1931 as four sisters pursue a slightly ingenuous young chap against a background of growing political turbulence. Behind the scenes on this and many Spanish movies is the publicity-shy, Madrid-based Rafael Azcona, surely one of cinema's most prolific screenplay writers. *Belle Epoque* took an Oscar for Best Foreign Language Film in 1993. Truly versatile, Trueba is equally well known for his documentary *Calle 54* (2000), which did for Latin jazz what the *Buena Vista Social Club* (1999) did for ageing Cuban musicians. Trueba was a leading personality in the craziness that was *la movida madrileña* (see p32) in the 1980s.

Going back further, Luis Buñuel (1900–83) was another film identity obliquely associated with Madrid. He spent part of his formative professional years in Madrid, raising hell with his fellow surrealist Salvador Dalí, although he later spent much of his life in Paris and Mexico. Buñuel became something of a surrealist icon with his 1929 classic *Un Chien Andalou*, on which he collaborated with Dalí. His often-shocking films included *Los Olvidados* (The Forgotten Ones; 1950) and *Viridiana* (1961) – both won prizes at the Cannes Film Festival, although the latter was banned in Francoist Spain on the grounds of blasphemy.

Of Spain's best-loved actors, few are enjoying international popularity quite like the Oscar-winning heart-throb Javier Bardem, one of the best-known faces in Spanish cinema. Having made his name alongside Penélope Cruz in *Jamón Jamón* (1992), his best-loved roles include those in *Before Night Falls* (2000), *Mar Adentro* (The Sea Inside; 2004), *Love in the Time of Cholera* (2007) and *No Country for Old Men* (2007); remarkably his Oscar for Best Supporting Actor in 2008 was a first for Spanish actors. Like so many of Spain's best actors, Bardem has passed through the finishing school that are Pedro Almodóvar's movies, appearing in *Carne Trémula* (Live Flesh; 1997). Javier Bardem also comes from one of Spain's most distinguished film-making families: his uncle, Juan Antonio Bardem (1922–2002), is often considered Madrid's senior cinematic bard; Bardem Snr wrote the script for Luis García Berlanga's 1952 classic, *Bienvenido Mr Marshall* (Welcome Mr Marshall), followed in 1955 with *Muerte de un Ciclista* (Death of a Cyclist). Although from Spain's Canary Islands, the Bardems are Madrid identities and run a trendy tapas bar, La Bardemcilla (see p192), in the inner-city barrio of Chueca.

Penélope Cruz is another Hollywood actress with strong roots in Madrid (where she was born in 1974). In the late 1990s Penélope Cruz took a leap of faith and headed for Hollywood where she has had success in such films as *Captain Corelli's Mandolin* (2001) and *Vanilla Sky* (2001), but recognition of her acting abilities has come most powerfully for her roles in the Almodóvar classics, *Carne Trémula* (Live Flesh; 1997), *Todo Sobre Mi Madre* (All About My Mother; 1999) and *Volver* (2006); the latter was described by one critic as 'a raging love letter' to Cruz and earned her a Best Actress Oscar nomination, a remarkable achievement for a foreign-language film. She finally won an Oscar for Best Supporting Actress in 2009 for her role in Woody Allen's *Vicky Cristina Barcelona*. Her conversion into one of Almodóvar's muses seems confirmed by news that she has agreed to appear in Almodóvar's next two movies.

PEDRO ALMODÓVAR

When Pedro Almodóvar (b 1951) won an Oscar in 2000 for his 1999 hit, *Todo Sobre Mi Madre* (All About My Mother), the world suddenly discovered what Spaniards had known for decades – that Almodóvar was one of world cinema's most creative directors.

Born in a small, impoverished village in Castilla La Mancha, Almodóvar once remarked that in such conservative rural surrounds, 'I felt as if I'd fallen from another planet'. After he moved to Madrid in 1969 he found his spiritual home and began his career making underground Super-8 movies and making a living by selling second-hand goods at El Rastro flea market. He soon became a symbol of Madrid's counter-culture, but it was after Franco's death in 1975 that Almodóvar became a nationally renowned cult figure. His early films *Pepi, Luci, Bom y Otras Chicas del Montón* (Pepi, Luci, Bom and the Other Girls; 1980) and *Laberinto de Pasiones* (Labyrinth of Passion; 1982) – the film that brought a young Antonio Banderas to attention – announced him as the icon of *la movida madrileña* (p32), the explosion of hedonism and creativity in the early years of post-Franco Spain. Almodóvar had both in bucketloads; he peppered his films with candy-bright colours and characters leading lives where sex and drugs were the norm. By night Almodóvar performed in Madrid's most famous *movida* bars as part of a drag act called 'Almodóvar & McNamara'. He even appears in this latter role in *Laberinto de Pasiones*.

By the mid-1980s madrileños had adopted him as one of the city's most famous sons and he went on to broaden his fan base with such quirkily comic looks at modern Spain, generally set in the capital, as *Mujeres al Borde de un Ataque de Nervios* (Women on the Verge of a Nervous Breakdown; 1988) and *Átame* (Tie Me Up, Tie Me Down; 1990). *Todo Sobre Mi Madre* (All About My Mother; 1999) is also notable for the coming of age of the Madrid-born actress Penélope Cruz, who had starred in a number of Almodóvar films and was considered part of a select group of the director's leading ladies long before she became a Hollywood star. Other outstanding movies in a formidable portfolio include *Hable Con Ella* (Talk to Her; 2002), for which he won a Best Original Screenplay Oscar; *La Mala Educación* (Bad Education; 2004), a twisted story of a drag queen, his brother, an abusive priest and a school-friend-turned-filmmaker; and *Volver* (2006), which reunited Almodóvar with Penélope Cruz to popular and critical acclaim.

43

top picks

FILMS SET IN MADRID

Many famous movies have been filmed at least partly in Madrid, among them *Doctor Zhivago*, *El Cid* and *The Fall of the Roman Empire*. But the following are where Madrid really plays a starring role:

- Pepi, Luci, Bom y Otras Chicas del Montón (Pepi, Luci, Bom and the Other Girls; 1980) If you always wondered what Madrid was like during *la movida madrileña*, this early Almodóvar feature film takes you there in all its madness.
- La Colmena (The Beehive; 1982) Based on the classic novel by Camilo José Cela, this is a faithful rendition of Cela's portrait of Madrid during the grim 1950s.
- Historias del Kronen (Stories from the Kronen; 1994) In Montxo Armendariz' film, a slightly depressing story of alienated urban youth emerges from the heart of Madrid.
- Carne Trémula (Live Flesh; 1997) This typically kaleidoscopic love thriller by Pedro Almodóvar contains the usual tortured themes of sex, violence and love, and stars Javier Bardem.
- La Comunidad (The Community; 2000) Directed by the generally wacky Álex de la Iglesia, this cheerfully off-the-wall tale of greed in a Madrid apartment block stars Carmen Maura.
- Los Fantasmas de Goya (Goya's Ghosts; 2006) Set in 1792, this recent offering from Milos Forman tells the story of Goya, the Spanish Inquisition and the painter's many scandals; Javier Bardem and Natalie Portman play the lead roles.
- Volver (2006) This heart-warming Almodóvar film starring Penélope Cruz is set partly in the outer suburbs of Madrid.
- El Próximo Oriente (The Near East; 2006) Fernando Colomo's witty film takes an engaging journey through multicultural Lavapiés.

Although not born in Madrid, Málaga-born Antonio Banderas moved to Madrid in 1981 at the age of 19 to launch his career and soon became caught up in the maelstrom of *la movida madrileña*, where he made the acquaintance of Almodóvar. After an early role in *Laberinto de Pasiones* (Labyrinth of Passion; 1982), Banderas would return to the Almodóvar stable with *Mujeres al Borde de un Ataque de Nervios* (Women on the Verge of a Nervous Breakdown; 1988) as his glittering Hollywood career was taking off.

An eminent line-up of some of Spain's best actresses also come from Madrid, among them Victoria Abril (b 1959), Ana Belén (b 1950), Carmen Maura (b 1945), Belén Rueda (1965) and Maribel Verdú (b 1970).

Although existing in the shadow of Hollywood and its Spanish stars, *Alatriste* (2006) and *El Orfanato* (The Orphange; 2007) are among the Spanish movies to have made an international splash in recent years.

Television

At first glance, Spanish TV may seem to be dominated by clones of international reality TV – especially *Gran Hermano* (Big Brother) and *Operación Triunfo* (which propels singing unknowns to stardom) – or endless gossip programs (known by critics as *telebasura*, or TV rubbish) dissecting the lives of current celebrities.

That's true to a certain extent, but there are some excellent TV series to look out for. An outstanding series is *Cuéntame Cómo Pasó* (www.rtve.es/television/cuentame, in Spanish), which is set in 1970s' Madrid. Telecinco's *Los Serrano* (www.losserrano.telecinco.es) is a mostly-comic, sometimes-serious family drama set in a Madrid chalet and featuring well-known movie actors.

Most TVs receive six or seven channels – two from Spain's state-run Televisión Española (TVE1 and La 2), four independent (Antena 3, El Cuatro, Tele 5 and La Sexta) and the regional Telemadrid station.

News programs are generally decent (especially on TVE1 at 3pm and 9pm) and you can often catch an interesting documentary (especially on La 2) or film. Some TVs allow you to switch from the dubbed version to the original on some channels. Otherwise the main fare is a rather nauseating diet of soaps (many from Latin America) and endless talk shows.

Many private homes and better hotels have satellite TV. Foreign channels include BBC World, CNN, Eurosport, Sky News and the German SAT 1, while places with digital decoders offer endless choices.

THEATRE

The literary *Siglo de Oro* (Golden Age) that characterised 17th-century Madrid was not restricted to novelists and some of the country's all-time greatest playwrights were at work in much the same period. One of Madrid's towering literary figures, Lope de Vega (1562–1635), also an exceptional lyric poet, was perhaps the most prolific: more than 300 of the 800 plays and poems attributed to him remain. He explored the falseness of court life and canvassed political subjects with his imaginary historical plays. You can still visit his house (p86) in the Barrio de las Letras.

Other important playwrights include Calderón de la Barca (1600–81), whose statue adorns the Plaza de Santa Ana (p86), and Tirso de Molina (1581–1648); the latter's *El Burlador de Sevilla* (The Seducer of Seville) is where we first encounter the immortal Don Juan, a likable seducer who meets an unhappy end.

For advice on where to see the best in Spanish theatre, from modern plays to the work of these greats, turn to p204.

A particularly Spanish genre that originated in Madrid is the *zarzuela*, light-hearted musical comedy depicting various elements of Spanish life in which the actors occasionally burst into song. Although it spread throughout the country in the 19th century it remains very much a Madrid-centric phenomenon. The Teatro de la Zarzuela, founded in 1856, keeps busy with a year-round program of these melodic social dramas. For more information on this uniquely Spanish drama form, see the boxed text on p205.

FLAMENCO

The musical and dance form most readily identified with Spain is rooted in the *cante jondo* (deep song) of the *gitanos* (Roma people) of Andalucía, and probably influenced by North African rhythms. The melancholy *cante jondo* is performed by a singer, who may be *cantaor* (male) or *cantaora* (female), to the accompaniment of a blood-rush of guitar from the *tocaor* (guitar player). The accompanying dance (not always present) is performed by one or more *bailaores* (flamenco dancers).

The genre flourished in the 1920s, but with the civil war things went downhill. Not until the 1950s did flamenco come to life again. In those dark years of austere dictatorship, even fun was considered suspect and so the hidden world of smoky cabarets and *tablaos* (small restaurants where flamenco is performed) was born.

Flamenco in Madrid

Madrid likes to claim that the city is Spain's capital of flamenco, which is true, but only to an extent. Flamenco's roots lie in Andalucía – particularly in the Cádiz-Jerez-Seville axis – and it's there that the tradition of flamenco *peñas* (small flamenco clubs) attended by knowledge-able aficionados still finds its spiritual home. But like most genres of the Spanish arts scene, Madrid is flamenco's biggest stage, the place where the best performers of flamenco have always turned up at one time or another. And therein lies the essence of Madrid's contribution to the development of flamenco: it has always been a stage, often a prestigious one, that has brought flamenco to a wider audience, but the roots of flamenco have always grown first elsewhere and the greatest proponents of the art have learned their craft in the south. As such, most Madrid venues lack the intimate atmosphere and gritty authenticity that is an essential element of the flamenco experience, but the quality is unimpeachable.

At first the *gitanos* and Andalucians were concentrated in the area around Calle de Toledo. The novelist Benito Pérez Galdós found no fewer than 88 Andalucian taverns along that street towards the end of the 19th century. The scene shifted in the early 20th century to the streets around Plaza de Santa Ana.

As flamenco's appeal widened and became a tourist attraction, more *tablaos* sprang up throughout Madrid. For advice on Madrid's best flamenco venues, turn to p175 and see the listings throughout the Nightlife chapter (p173). A good website for all things flamenco is www.deflamenco.com. To learn more you could also pass by El Flamenco Vive (p132), which has a wide range of flamenco books and CDs. For flamenco courses see p258, while Madrid's excellent flamenco festivals are covered on p16.

Flamenco Stars

Two names loom large over the world of flamenco – Paco de Lucía and El Camarón de la Isla – who were responsible for flamenco's revival in the second half of the 20th century. Such is (or, in the case of El Camarón de la Isla, was) their dominance that theirs is the standard by which all other flamenco artists are measured.

Paco de Lucía (b 1947) is the doyen of flamenco guitarists with a virtuosity few can match. For many in the flamenco world, he is the personification of *duende*, that indefinable capacity to transmit the power and passion of flamenco. Although existing somewhat in Paco de Lucía's shadow, other guitar maestros include members of the Montoya family (some of whom are better known by the sobriquet of Los Habichuela), especially Juan (b 1933) and Pepe (b 1944).

From 1964 Paco de Lucía teamed up with madrileño guitarist Ricardo Modrego, but began, in 1968, flamenco's most exciting partnership with his friend El Camarón de la Isla (1950–92); together they recorded nine classic albums. Until his premature death, El Camarón was the leading light of contemporary *cante jondo* and it's impossible to overstate his influence on the art; his introduction of electric bass into his songs, for example, paved the way for a generation of artists to take flamenco in hitherto unimagined directions. Although born in San Fernando in Andalucía's far south, El Camarón was the artist in residence at Madrid's Tablao Torres Bermejas for 12 years, and it was during this period that his collaboration with Paco de Lucía was at its best. In his later years El Camarón teamed up with Tomatito, one of Paco de Lucía's protégés, and the results were similarly ground-breaking. The story of El Camarón's life (his real name was the far less evocative José Monje Cruz) has been made into an excellent movie (*Camarón*, 2005), directed by Jaime Chávarri. When El Camarón died in 1992 an estimated 100,000 people attended his funeral.

Another artist who has reached the level of cult figure is Enrique Morente (b 1942), referred to by one Madrid paper as 'the last bohemian'. While careful not to alienate flamenco purists, Morente, through his numerous collaborations across genres, helped lay the foundations for Nuevo Flamenco and Fusion. One of the most venerable *cantaoras* is Carmen Linares (b 1951), who has spent much of her working life in Madrid. Leading contemporary figures include the flighty, adventurous Joaquín Cortés (b 1969), and Antonio Canales (b 1962), who is more of a flamenco purist.

Nuevo Flamenco & Fusion

Possibly the most exciting recent developments in flamenco have occurred in its fusion with other musical forms. The purists loathe these changes – in the proud *gitano* world, innovation has often met with abrasive scorn – but a wider Spanish audience has enthusiastically embraced this innovative musical experimentation.

Two of the earliest groups to fuse flamenco with rock back in the 1980s were Ketama and Pata Negra, whose music is labelled by some as Gypsy rock. Ketama, in particular, have been wide-ranging in their search for complementary sounds and rhythms, and their collaborations with Malian kora (harp) player Toumani Diabaté (*Songhai I* and *Songhai II*) are underrated works of rare beauty. In the early 1990s, Radio Tarifa emerged with a mesmerising mix of flamenco, North African and medieval sounds. A more traditional flamenco performer, Juan Peña Lebrijano, better known as El Lebrijano, has created some equally appealing combinations with classical Moroccan music. Diego El Cigala, one of modern flamenco's finest voices, relaunched his career with an exceptional collaboration with Cuban virtuoso Bebo Valdés (*Lágrimas Negras*; 2004) and has released three critically acclaimed albums in the years since.

Chambao is the most popular of the Nuevo Flamenco bands doing the rounds at the moment. They first captured attention with their *Endorfinas a la Menta* (2003) and the excellent *Pokito a Poko* (2005). Also popular is Diego Amador (b 1973), a self-taught pianist. The piano is not a classic instrument of flamenco but Amador makes it work.

ARCHITECTURE

Where Barcelona is defined by the *Modernista* uniformity of many of its major buildings, Madrid's architecture spans the centuries and tells the broad sweep of Spain's historical story. The grandeur of Spain's imperial past, as exemplified in the stately Palacio Real, sits alongside *barroco madrileño* (Madrid baroque), the Spanish capital's muted contribution to world architectural textbooks. Later flights of fancy date to the *belle époque* period at the beginning of the 20th century, while Spain's love affair with innovative and eye-catching contemporary

top picks

NOTABLE OLD BUILDINGS

- Palacio Real (p67)
- Plaza de la Villa (p65)
- Real Casa de la Panadería (p64)
- Palacio de Comunicaciones (p96)
- Sociedad General de Autores y Editores (p106)
- Plaza de Toros Monumental de Las Ventas (p100)
- Edificio Metrópolis (p71)

architecture finds expression in the Caixa Forum, along the Paseo del Prado and Terminal 4 at Barajas Airport. It all comes together in the grand historical buildings – among them the Museo del Prado, Centro de Arte Reina Sofía and the Antigua Estación de Atocha – which have been transformed by stunning modern projects of regeneration.

MADRID TO THE 16TH CENTURY

Madrid's origins as a Muslim garrison town yielded few architectural treasures, or at least few that remain. The only reminder of the Muslim presence is a modest stretch of the town wall, known as the Muralla Árabe (Arab Wall; p68) below the Catedral de Nuestra Señora de la Almudena. Few examples also remain of the rich *mudéjar* style (developed by the Moors who remained behind in reconquered Christian territory) that once adorned Madrid; the bell towers of the Iglesia de San Pedro El Viejo (p79) and Iglesia de San Nicolás de los Servitas (p66) are the only modest representatives of the era.

When Felipe II decided in 1561 to establish Madrid as the capital of Imperial Spain, the city's architecture was unworthy of such grand aspirations, with little more to distinguish it than the odd grand church or palace; the elaborate edifices of Gothic architecture that prompted the erection of great soaring churches across medieval Europe largely passed Madrid by. After making Madrid his capital Felipe II became preoccupied with building his monumental mausoleum/palace/summer getaway at El Escorial (p244) and Madrid's architecture continued much as it had before. Unless you're content with the much interfered with, late-Gothic Casa de los Lujanes (p66) or the beautiful Capilla del Obispo (p77), you'll need to head for Toledo (p234), Segovia (p238) or Ávila (p241) for a greater appreciation of the genre.

MADRID BAROQUE & BEYOND

Juan de Herrera (1530–97) was perhaps the greatest figure of the Spanish Renaissance and his style, which was unlike anything else seen during the period, influenced a generation of Madrid architects and bequeathed to the city an architectural style all of its own. Herrera's austere masterpiece was the palace-monastery complex of San Lorenzo de El Escorial (p244), but the nine-arched Puente de Segovia (p76) is among the few structures he left behind in Madrid.

Herrera's trademark was to fuse the sternness of the Renaissance style with a timid approach to its successor, the more voluptuous, ornamental baroque. The result was an architectural style known as *barroco madrileño* (Madrid baroque). The most successful proponent of this

CONTEMPORARY ARCHITECTURE – FIND OUT MORE

Those keen to see beyond the major architectural landmarks of Madrid should pick up a copy of the *Plano de Arquitectura* (Architecture Map; free), which has photos of 258 distinguished Madrid buildings and a map of where to find them. It's produced annually by the Fundación Arquitectura COAM (Map p110; ☎ 91 319 16 83; www.fucoam.es, in Spanish; Calle de Piamonte 23; Ⓜ Chueca or Colón) for the Semana de la Arquitectura in October, but it's worth stopping by at any time during the year to see whether they've any to hand.

Architecture buffs will want to be in Madrid in late September or early October for the Semana de la Arquitectura (Architecture Week), with exhibitions, conferences and guided visits to signature architectural projects in Madrid. International Architecture Day, which usually falls in early October, also offers a chance to visit otherwise-closed architectural landmarks, including the Sociedad General de Autores y Editores (p106). These events are organised by the Fundación Arquitectura COAM.

To find out more about Madrid's architectural direction, the June–July 2005 issue (No 478), of *Techniques & Architecture* is entitled 'Madrid: A Challenge' and devoted solely to the Spanish capital. For this and other architectural publications, try Naos Libros (Map pp116–17; ☎ 91 547 39 16; www.naoslibros.es, in Spanish; Calle de Quintana 12).

style was Juan Gómez de Mora (1586–1648), who was responsible for laying out the Plaza Mayor (p61), as well as the Convento de la Encarnación (p70) and the Palacio de Santa Cruz (p65). Gómez de Mora's uncle, Francisco de Mora (1560–1610), added to an impressive family portfolio with the Palacio del Duque de Uceda (p66). Other exceptional examples of the style are the Real Casa de la Panadería (p64) and the main entrance of what is now the Museo de Historia (p107).

Ventura Rodríguez (1717–85) dominated the architectural scene in 18th-century Madrid much as Goya lorded it over the world of art. He redesigned the interior of the Convento de la Encarnación and conceived the Palacio de Liria (p109). He also sidelined in spectacular fountains, and it is Rodríguez whom we have to thank for the goddess Cybele in the Plaza de la Cibeles (p96) and the Fuente de las Conchas (p123) in the Campo del Moro.

Where Ventura Rodríguz leaned towards a neo-Classical style, Juan de Villanueva (1739–1811) embraced it wholeheartedly, most notably in the Palacio de Villanueva that would eventually house the Museo del Prado (p90). Villanueva also oversaw the rebuilding of the Plaza Mayor after it was destroyed by fire in 1790 and designed numerous outbuildings of the royal residences, such as San Lorenzo de El Escorial.

BELLE ÉPOQUE

As Madrid emerged from the chaos of the first half of the 19th century, a building boom began. The use of iron and glass, a revolution in building aesthetics that symbolised the embracing of modernity, became all the rage. The gorgeous Palacio de Cristal in the Parque del Buen Retiro (p97) was built at this time.

By the dawn of the 20th century, known to many as the *belle époque*, Madrid was abuzz with construction. Headed by the prolific Antonio Palacios (1874–1945), architects from all over Spain began to transform Madrid into the airy city you see today. Many looked to the past for their inspiration. Neo-*mudéjar* was especially favoured for bullrings. The ring at Las Ventas (p100), finished in 1934, is a classic example. A more bombastic (and perhaps the most spectacular) interpretation of the *belle-époque* style is Palacios' Palacio de Comunicaciones (p96) with its plethora of pinnacles and prancing ornaments, which was finished in 1917.

By the early 20th century architecture in Madrid had come to be known as the 'eclectic' style, a hybrid form of competing influences as architects mixed and matched. Among the joyous and eye-catching examples – Gran Vía (p71) is jammed with them – are the 1916 Edificio Grassy and the 1905 Edificio Metrópolis.

By the 1930s public architecture had taken on a more austere style with pretensions to grandeur. The signature building of this period was Nuevos Ministerios (1934–40; Map p121), whose architect, Segundino Zuazo, was said to have taken inspiration from San Lorenzo de El Escorial (p244), although the resemblance is more about scale than charm. Buildings such as this served as a precursor to the charmless style that would dominate the Franco years.

THE ARCHITECTURE OF DICTATORSHIP

After pounding Madrid into submission and asserting his control over the country in 1939, General Francisco Franco was eager to leave behind an architectural legacy that would consist of enduring monuments to his rule. The results were either self-glorifying or grand structures of little discernible beauty.

Belonging to the former category were the Valle de los Caídos (p245) and the triumphal Arco de Victoria (Arch of Victory; Map pp116-17), which stands immediately northwest of the Plaza de la Moncloa. Now known more prosaically as the Puerta de Moncloa (Moncloa Gate), the arch was built in 1956 to commemorate his victorious troops' entry into Madrid and was adorned with references to his triumphs. After Spain's return to democracy all references to Franco were removed from the gate and only the *quadriga* (a chariot drawn by four horses) on the summit remains.

Skyscrapers were a Franco trademark. Given Franco's paranoia when it came to communism, the echoes in the Edificio de España (1953) of a Soviet Monumentalist style are somewhat ironic. More in keeping with Franco's self-image was the Torre de Madrid (1957), which was for a time the tallest building in Europe. Both buildings overlook Plaza de España (p70). Far more striking and in keeping with the architecture of old Madrid was the Ministerio del Aire (Air Force Ministry; 1951) on the Plaza de la Moncloa (Map pp116-17).

Franco's impact on Madrid can also be seen along the grand, tree-lined Paseo de la Castellana, which took on much of its present aspect during Franco's rule. Sadly many fine old palaces that once lined the roadside were demolished in the process. These were replaced by such buildings as the none-too-elegant Torres de Colón, which was finished in 1976 after Franco's death.

CONTEMPORARY ARCHITECTURE

International architectural circles have long been buzzing with the energy and creativity surrounding Spanish architecture. At one level Spanish architects such as Santiago Calatrava (who transformed Valencia and built the Olympic stadium in Athens among other signature projects) are taking the world by storm. At the same time architects from all over the world are clamouring for Spanish contracts; the projects for urban renewal currently underway in Spain are some of the most innovative in Europe, and municipal governments are funding this extraordinary explosion of architectural ambition.

Madrid has been slow in coming to the party, but things are changing, a fact that will become immediately obvious if you're arriving in town at Terminal Four (T4) of Madrid's Barajas International Airport. Designed by Richard Rogers, it's a stunning, curvaceous work of art, which deservedly won Rogers the prestigious Stirling Prize in October 2006; Spanish architect Carlos Lamela also worked with Rogers on the project.

Another significant transformation on a grand scale is to Madrid's once-low-rise skyline, with four skyscrapers rising up above the Paseo de la Castellana in northern Madrid. Of these, the Torre Caja Madrid (250m, designed by Sir Norman Foster) is Spain's tallest building, just surpassing its neighbour, the Torre de Cristal (249.5m, designed by César Pelli). The Torre de Espacio (236m, designed by Henry Cobb) has also won plaudits for its abundant use of glass.

Among the architectural innovations that travellers to Madrid are more likely to experience up close and at greater depth, the most exciting is perhaps the extension of the Museo del Prado (p90), which opened in October 2007. The work of one of Spain's premier architects, the Madrid-based, Pritzker-prize-winning Rafael Moneo, the extension links the main gallery with what remains of the cloisters of the Iglesia de San Jerónimo el Real.

Tinkering with the 18th-century Palacio de Villanueva that houses the Prado was always going to be controversial and the appropriation of the cloisters to form part of the Prado's ever-growing empire was widely condemned when the plans were announced. The verdict, however, seems to be that Moneo has pulled it off with considerable aplomb. Much of the praise has centred around the use of traditional building materials such as granite, red brick and oak, while the director of the Museo del Prado, Miguel Zugzaga, lauded the final effect as being 'like placing a still life by Juan Gris next to one by Zurbarán…discreet, elegant and profoundly modern'. Moneo is no stranger to urban challenges. One of his first major tasks was the construction of the Bankinter building in Madrid in 1976. After the mania of the 1960s for destroying 19th-century mansions and replacing them with bland blocks, Moneo demonstrated an alternative approach and thus may have saved old Madrid from disappearing under the crushing weight of a lack of imagination. Moneo met two other major Madrid challenges with his acclaimed remodelling of the Antigua Estación de Atocha (p83) and his conversion of the Palacio de Villahermosa into the Museo Thyssen-Bornemisza (p94), both in the early 1990s.

Another landmark project in recent years has been the extension of the Centro de Arte Reina Sofía (p82) by the French architect Jean Nouvel. It's a stunning red glass-and-steel complement to the old-world Antigua Estación de Atocha across the Plaza del Emperador Carlos V and the austerity of the remainder of the museum's 18th-century structure.

top picks

NOTABLE NEW OR FUSION BUILDINGS

Centro de Arte Reina Sofía (p82)
Caixa Forum (p95)
Museo del Prado (p90)
Antigua Estación de Atocha (p83)
Teatro Valle-Inclán (p79)
Terminal 4, Barajas International Airport (p251)

Between the Reina Sofía and the Prado and opposite the Real Jardín Botánico, the Caixa Forum (p95), completed in 2008, is one of Madrid's most striking buildings. Designed by Swiss architects Jacques Herzog and Pierre de Meuron, its aesthetic seems to owe more to the world of sculpture than of architecture with its unusual iron-and-brick form. It's a worthy, surprising addition to the Paseo del Prado's grandeur.

One truly madrileño architectural team is the couple Ignacio García Pedrosa and Ángela García de Paredes, whose modern redesign of the Teatro Valle-Inclán (formerly the Teatro Olímpico; p79) on the Plaza de Lavapiés has won much admiration. Emilio Tuñon and Luis Mansilla have joined forces to undertake the delicate work-in-progress of building the Museo de Colecciones Reales (p68), close to the Palacio Real.

Other urban renewal projects are regenerating some of Madrid's satellite suburbs, such as Carabanchel to the south and Sanchinarro to the north, with innovative approaches to the city's urban sprawl.

And one final thing for those who love architecture: while in Madrid you really must stay at the Hotel Puerta América (p230), where each floor has been custom designed by a world-renowned architect.

ENVIRONMENT & PLANNING

Madrid is already feeling the effects of climate change, and although Spain and Madrid are not entirely to blame, the country's lamentable environmental record is nonetheless a major factor. At a city level some positive steps are being taken, but these pale in comparison to the problems the city itself seems to be creating, particularly when it come to pollution. On a planning front Madrid is, depending on your perspective, a massive building site or an exciting work-in-progress.

THE LAND

At 650m above sea level on a high continental plateau, Madrid is the highest capital city in Europe. The Comunidad de Madrid – in the centre of which lies Madrid in a rough triangle – covers 7995 sq km, less than 2% of Spain's territory.

Madrid's northwest boundary consists of a series of mountain ranges that run from the northeast to the southwest for 140km as part of the longer chain known as the Cordillera Central. Known by madrileños simply as the Sierra, they encompass the Somosierra, Sierra de Guadarrama and Sierra de Gredos.

GREEN MADRID

Madrid has an abundance of parks and gardens. The most central and attractive is the Parque del Buen Retiro (p97), but the Real Jardín Botánico (p95), Campo del Moro (p123), Parque del Oeste (p115) and Casa de Campo (p123) are all either central or easily accessible from downtown.

However, it must be acknowledged that this region's environmental problems are legion – until the drought broke in 2009–10 it had the worst dry period since records began; greenhouse gas emissions are more than three times the level agreed to under the Kyoto Protocol – and the consequences for Madrid are potentially devastating. In the last 30 years Madrid has seen a rise of 2.2°C in its average temperature, a greater increase than for any other European capital. The Madrid authorities have begun campaigns to encourage sensible water use among the city's residents, but the government's strategy seems to rely more on hoping for rain than on serious water conservation. (In late 2005 the 5200 inhabitants of Miraflores de la Sierra, a village 50km north of the capital in the Sierra, woke up to find that the village had simply run out of water.) The rains may have stayed away, but there is a human-made dimension to the problem – Madrid's 29 golf courses use as much water in a day as a city with a populace of 100,000 and half remain under investigation for not using recycled water.

If Madrid never seems to have enough water, it has the reverse problem with pollution. Some four million car journeys are made in the capital every day, with one million vehicles entering and leaving the city. The resulting cloud of pollution – known locally as 'the grey beret' – that settles over Madrid on windless days means that breathing Madrid's air is equivalent to smoking

11 cigarettes a day. Spain's obsession with diesel-fuelled cars (which produce seven times more pollution than cars running on unleaded petrol) only exacerbates the problem.

Madrid's city authorities have considered introducing a London-style congestion charge in order to reduce pollution, but the plan remains nothing more than that. That's not to say that some concrete steps haven't been taken. One obvious measure has been the pedestrianisation of many inner-city streets, among them Calle de Arenal and 40 hectares of streets in the barrio of Huertas, which have been closed to all but local traffic, while Calle de Serrano is in the process of being reduced to scarcely any traffic at all. The unsuccessful Socialist candidate for mayor in 2007 even proposed closing off Gran Vía to traffic.

The constant investment in Madrid's already impressive underground metro system – one of the 10 longest in the world and the third longest in Europe – ensures that Madrid's high pollution levels can in no way be blamed on inadequate public transport. Since 2000 more than 100km have been added to the network, drawing an ever-growing number of satellite towns into the system.

While rubbish is collected every night, recycling is optional and widely ignored. Noise pollution is another massive problem throughout the city. Residents in some Madrid barrios regularly suffer noise levels above 71 decibels; the World Health Organization warns that anything above 65 decibels poses a health risk, and a recent investigation found that a dozen sites consistently exceed such levels. Madrid's first noise survey found that the streets around Calle de O'Donnell, the Paseo de los Recoletos and Calle de Santa Engracia are among Madrid's noisiest. But at many points across the city, rowdy revellers, heavy traffic, late-night rubbish collection, all-night roadworks, the incessant sirens of emergency vehicles and horn-happy drivers all help to keep madrileños' nerves well jangled. Long live double glazing.

Beyond the city, the upgrading of the M-501 through the west of the Comunidad de Madrid has been hugely controversial. Environmentalists argue that the road expansion threatens 13 nesting pairs of the endangered Iberian Imperial Eagle, as well as destroying woodlands that shelter 10% of Spain's endangered species and possibly the world's most-endangered cat species, the Iberian lynx. When environmentalists announced in 2007 that they had found droppings from a lynx, a species that was long thought to have died out in the Madrid region, the regional premier Esperanza Aguirre refused to conduct an investigation and accused them of faking the findings in order to halt the road's construction.

Madrid may also be endlessly expanding to swallow up previously nonurban areas, but some small steps are being taken in compensation. Among these are ambitious plans to reforest 150 sq km of land around the Comunidad de Madrid. Within metropolitan Madrid, 6km of the M-30 beltway has recently been driven underground, to be replaced by the Parque de Manzanares, 500,000 sq metres of landscaped greenery in southwestern Madrid that the mayor calls 'a giant green carpet'; local residents are still waiting to see whether the dust stirred up by three years of massive road works will prove to be worth it.

URBAN PLANNING & DEVELOPMENT

Madrid's mayors are nothing if not ambitious. Madrid's mayor from 1991 to 2003, José María Alvarez del Manzano, became known as 'The Tunnelator' because of his passion for building tunnels and rerouting the course of the city's traffic. But he was nothing compared to his successor, Alberto Ruiz-Gallardón, who has become known as 'The Pharaoh' (see the boxed text, p52) for the sheer scale of his infrastructure projects. Scarcely surprising, therefore, that Danny DeVito, when asked for his opinion of Madrid during a visit some years back, replied 'Tell the mayor to tell me when he's dug up the treasure'.

Madrid can seem to be perennially awash with *obras* (road or infrastructure works). At one level such major works are necessary in a city for whom urban planning was, for centuries, somewhat chaotic and rarely part of an overall plan to make the city more liveable. As such, some major infrastructure projects have been long overdue, from the extraordinary upgrading of the city's metro system (see above) to the proposed Parque de Manzanares (see above). The shift towards massive skyscrapers in northern Madrid (see p49) has also been sold as a solution to Madrid's critical shortage of office and residential space. Although often heard complaining about the significant disruptions caused by the works, and often annoyed that the pedestrianisation of downtown Madrid hasn't included more places to sit (see the boxed text, p69), madrileños are generally quite proud that they live in a city that is constantly being improved.

But not all 'improvements' to the city have been welcomed. In 2006 the Baroness Carmen Thyssen-Bornemisza, who was responsible for convincing her husband to bequeath his unrivalled art collection to the Spanish capital (see p94), locked horns with Madrid's mayor Alberto Ruiz-Gallardón. The reason? The mayor planned to divert traffic away from the Museo del Prado and create a pedestrian precinct outside the Prado. Although the idea sounds good in principle, the problem is that much of the traffic would move across the boulevard to run past the Museo Thyssen-Bornemisza. The proposed works would also have seen more than 700 trees removed, among them 95 trees that date back to the 18th century, when Carlos III ruled Spain; Ruiz-Gallardón claimed that all would be replanted, the baroness threatened to chain herself to a tree. At the time of writing, the spat between two of Madrid's most powerful personalities was yet to be resolved, and it remains unclear whether Ruiz-Gallardón plans to push ahead with the project.

For all the attempts to address the problems caused by a lack of historical planning, Madrid may already have reached the point of no return. Surrounded by ever-growing concentric ring roads, Madrid just can't stop growing. Whole new suburbs are under construction and will swallow up pretty much all that remains of the available land in the Madrid municipal area by around 2020. Opposition parties and environmentalists alike have slammed the program. Whoever's to blame, it's already too late to stop Madrid's transformation from a compact, manageable and high-density city into one that sprawls endlessly to the horizon.

GOVERNMENT & POLITICS

Madrileños, like many Spaniards, have always had a fairly wary approach to the authorities who would try to rule over them. This is perhaps best summed up by the tale oft-told by straight-faced locals that every one of their compatriots carries a letter from the king that reads 'This Spaniard is entitled to do whatever he feels like doing'. Madrileños are nonetheless presided over by three layers of government.

At the national level, the PSOE (Spanish Socialist Workers' Party) of José Luis Rodríguez Zapatero has held power since March 2004, winning re-election in 2008. The national Cortes (parliament) is divided into two houses, the Congreso de los Diputados (lower house; p87) on Carrera de San Jerónimo, and the Senado (senate), south of Plaza de España.

At a provincial level, the Comunidad de Madrid, which includes Madrid and surrounding towns and is one of 17 Spanish autonomous regions, is led by Esperanza Aguirre of the conservative PP (Popular Party). Aguirre is the country's first female president of a Spanish region. After a close-run election in 2003, in 2007 she won an absolute majority of seats with 53.3% of the vote to PSOE's 33.4% (the left-wing Izquierda Unida won 8.8%).

THE PHARAOH OF MADRID

Madrid's mayor, Alberto Ruiz-Gallardón, must be one of few mayors around the world to have been re-elected (in 2007) on a promise that he begin no new major infrastructure projects during his next term in office. It was a shrewd political move by a man dubbed by his subjects as 'The Pharaoh'.

Behind the nickname was a city thoroughly exhausted by the endless road works and infrastructure projects that had made Madrid Europe's largest building site. At the height of Ruiz-Gallardón's mania for tearing down, digging up and generally recasting the city in his own image, there were, in 2005, more than 900 holes officially open across Madrid, not to mention 75 large infrastructure projects underway. Within this context of perennial noise and stirred-up dust, it was more than a little galling for madrileños to find that they could be charged with a local law prohibiting 'the abusive use of the public street', when most such abuse was the work of lawmakers themselves.

Of equal concern to madrileños is the financial cost involved. The Parque de Manzanares project alone will end up costing local taxpayers almost €4 billion, while the city's annual budget has a gaping €5 billion hole in its centre.

In any event, Ruiz-Gallardón's 2007 promise seems to have fallen by the wayside, although city officials would argue that recent infrastructure projects – including the pedestrianisation of many central Madrid streets and the major overhaul of Calle de Serrano – were planned long before the promise was made.

Thus it is that when the dust settles and the city finally falls quiet, Madrid will be vastly improved, but very much in the red.

At a city level the government has been the preserve of the PP since 1991 and is led by the *alcalde* (mayor), currently Alberto Ruiz-Gallardón. Ruiz-Gallardón easily won the May 2007 election, winning 34 out of the 57 seats, and is one of Madrid's most popular politicians of recent times. Among his councillors (and a right-wing politician to watch) is Ana Botella, wife of José María Aznar, the former PP Spanish president. After centuries of operating out of the Ayuntamiento on Plaza de la Villa in the heart of the old city, in 2007 the mayor and his town hall moved to the Palacio de Comunicaciones on Plaza de la Cibeles.

City and regional elections are set for 2011, with national elections a year later. For more information on the machinations of Madrid-style political life, see p35.

FASHION

In the 18th century madrileños rioted when told by the king that they could no longer wear the sweeping capes that so distinguished them. The days of Spanish capes may be long gone, but they still take their fashion seriously in Madrid.

The current buzz surrounding Spanish fashion began in the 1980s when Spain in general, and Madrid in particular, embraced all that was new and experimental after the fascist austerity of the Franco years; during *la movida madrileña* (p32) Madrid was said to be home to 1500 fashion designers. What has changed recently is that Madrid has arguably come to surpass Barcelona as Spain's fashion capital; Madrid's Pasarela Cibeles (p17) runway fashion shows have become increasingly important, especially for spring and autumn collections. As a result Madrid is considered by many in-the-know to rank just below the world's fashion capitals of Paris, Milan, New York and London.

One of the success stories of Spanish cultural life, the Spanish fashion industry now employs more than 500,000 people (more than three times the number employed by bullfighting and up from 180,000 in 1995). This is an industry that is aiming high and industry insiders admit that Spain's *fashionistas* won't be satisfied until Madrid has been elevated to the top tier of European fashion capitals. On current trends, they may not have long to wait.

Colour is the key to Spanish fashion's individuality. The psychedelic colours of *la movida madrileña* in the 1980s have never really gone away and the candy-bright colours of Agatha Ruiz de la Prada (p136; Andy Warhol was a fan) have now acquired something of a middle-class respectability; her work, widely available, encompasses everything from children's clothes to outrageous evening wear for adults. This stylish-but-anything-goes approach has morphed into a fashion scene dominated by bold colours equally well suited to the casual as to a more tailored look.

Classic and more conservative lines are the preserve of Loewe (p140) and Elisa Bracci (p139). A more formal/casual mix is favoured by designers like Amaya Arzuaga (p136), Purificación García (see the boxed text, p136) and Roberto Verino (see the boxed text, p136). Apart from the names already mentioned, others to watch out for on the catwalk include the madrileño Javier Larraínzar (one of the city's top haute couture icons), Pedro del Hierro, Kina Fernández, Nacho Ruiz and Montesinos Alama. More clean lined and casual is Armand Basi (p136), while the clothes of Davidelfín (p139) span the divide between edgy and exclusive.

Spain is also famous for the quality of its shoes and the designers once known only to Spaniards and madrileñas are fast becoming fixtures on the international scene. Manolo Blahnik (see the boxed text, p136) is perhaps the best known and beloved by red-carpet Hollywood stars, but the range goes all the way down to the casual cool of Camper (p137).

It's not only upmarket designer wear that is dominating the madrileño wardrobe and capturing international headlines. A host of more affordable high-street fashions is also leading the way. Just about every Madrid barrio has at least one outlet for names like Zara (with, at last count, 4607 shops in 73 countries), Adolfo Domínguez and Mango, which have in turn become some of Spain's leading exports. And where would you be without the cool and casual shoes of Camper (p137)? If these names have been your introduction to the world of Spanish fashion, you'll very much enjoy Madrid, but don't forget that these are merely an introduction to a far more varied Spanish look.

Madrid has numerous places to shop. For Spanish designers, Salamanca in general is Madrid's and Spain's fashion capital, with exclusive Chueca boutiques along Calle del Almirante, Calle del Conde de Xiquena and Calle de Argensola (Map pp108-9) and the streets that surround them.

Malasaña is the place for an altogether different fashion aesthetic with quirky, imaginative shops where the line between designer fashions and urban streetwear is decidedly blurred. Calle de Fuencarral (see the boxed text, p139) is Madrid's home of edgy urban fashion. For classy shoes and accessories at discounted prices, Chueca's Calle de Augusto Figueroa (Map p110) is the stuff of shopping legend. For more details on shopping in Madrid, turn to p129.

top picks

NEIGHBOURHOODS

Madrid may stake a strong claim to being Europe's most dynamic city, but it doesn't have the immediate cachet of Rome, Paris or even that other city up the road, Barcelona. Its architecture is beautiful, but there's no Colosseum, no Eiffel Tower, no Gaudí-inspired zaniness to photograph and then tell your friends back home, 'this is Madrid'. As such, many first-time visitors wonder what there is to see in the Spanish capital. The answer is wonderful sights in abundance, so many in fact that few travellers leave disappointed with their menu of high culture and high-volume excitement.

'The combination of stunning architecture and feel-good living has never been easier to access than in the beautiful plazas'

For a start, Madrid has three of the finest art galleries in the world and if ever there was a golden mile of fine art, it has to be the combined charms of the Museo del Prado, Centro de Arte Reina Sofía and the Museo Thyssen-Bornemisza. Masterpieces overflow from these three museums into dozens of other museums and galleries across the city.

Exploring deeper into the city, the combination of stunning architecture and feel-good living has never been easier to access than in the beautiful plazas where *terrazas* (cafes with outdoor tables) provide a front-row seat for Madrid's fine cityscape and endlessly energetic street life. This is a city, in the words of Benito Pérez Galdós, one of Spain's most-loved literary figures of the early 20th century, 'where going for a stroll counts as an occupation', and we challenge you to find a more spectacular and agreeable setting for your coffee than the Plaza Mayor, Plaza de Santa Ana or Plaza de Oriente. Throw in some outstanding city parks (the Parque del Buen Retiro in particular) and areas such as Chueca, Malasaña, Lavapiés and Salamanca, which each have their own alluring personalities, and you'll quickly end up wishing, like Ernest Hemingway, that you never had to leave.

Madrid is divided up into *distritos* (districts) and these are subdivided into barrios (neighbourhoods), the official names of which are largely ignored by madrileños. Indeed the word barrio has a very strong feel of local identity about it. Madrileños have their own city map in their heads and, since they know best, we follow them.

Los Austrias, Sol and Centro make up the bustling, compact and medieval heart of Madrid, where the former village of Mayrit came to life. This area now yields an impossibly rich heritage of palaces, churches and grand squares. La Latina and Lavapiés, two of Madrid's oldest inner-city barrios, are immediately south and southeast of the centre, and have plenty to see and even more to experience. East of here takes in Huertas and Atocha, with the former the home to a labyrinth of more vibrant nightlife than seems possible, but also with its fair share of cultural sights that are well worth tracking down. Down the hill, Atocha is a gateway to the grand boulevard of the Paseo del Prado, a haven of culture boasting the city's finest museums. Part of the same barrio, the glorious Parque del Buen Retiro is a refuge of green parkland and gardens, and serves as an entry point to the exclusive barrio of Salamanca. West of Salamanca, across the Paseo de los Recoletos, are two of modern Madrid's coolest barrios, Malasaña and Chueca, which have been transformed from gritty, working-class dives into cultural focal points. Neighbouring Chamberí and Argüelles, away to the north, have few sights to talk about but offer an ambience that is rapidly making them the barrios of choice for discerning madrileños. The outer *distritos* of Madrid offer some parks and children's attractions.

See the Transport chapter, p250, for details of how to get around Madrid.

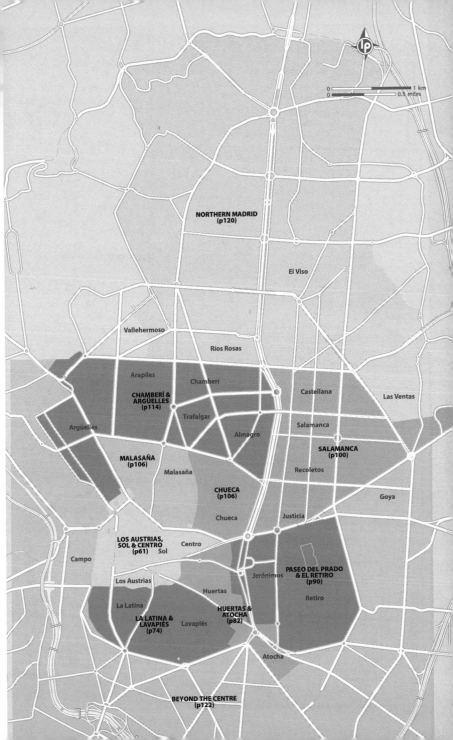

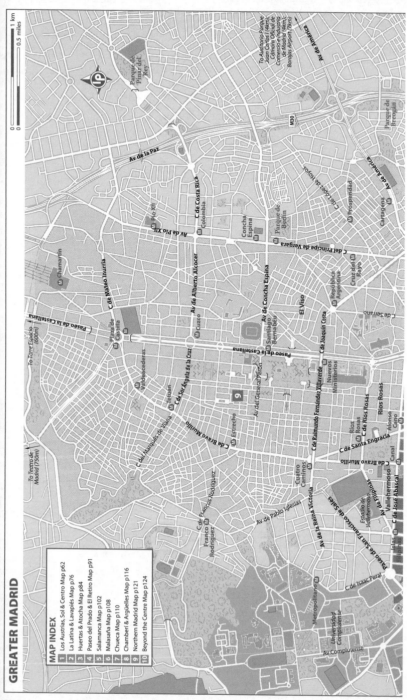

GREATER MADRID

MAP INDEX

0   1 km
0   0.5 miles

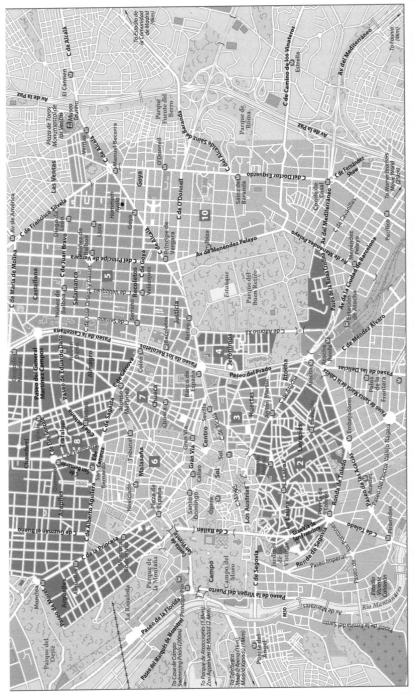

ITINERARY BUILDER

The table below allows you to plan a day's worth of activities in any area of the city. Simply select which area you wish to explore, and then mix and match from the corresponding listings to build your day. The first item in each cell represents a well-known highlight of the area, while the other items are more off-the-beaten-track gems.

ACTIVITIES	Sights	Eating	Shopping
Los Austrias, Sol & Centro	Plaza Mayor (p61) Palacio Real (p67) Real Academia de Bellas Artes de San Fernando (p71)	Restaurante Sobrino de Botín (p149) Amaya (p150) Mercado de San Miguel (p151)	Antigua Casa Talavera (p131) El Arco Artesanía (p132) El Flamenco Vive (p132)
La Latina & Lavapiés	Basílica de San Francisco El Grande (p74) Iglesia de San Andrés (p77) Museo de los Orígenes (p78)	Casa Lucio (p152) Taberna Matritum (p154) Naïa Restaurante (p153)	El Rastro (p134) Del Hierro (p133) Helena Rohner (p133)
Huertas & Atocha	Centro de Arte Reina Sofía (p82) Plaza de Santa Ana (p86) Barrio de las Letras (see the boxed text, p87)	Lhardy (p156) Casa Alberto (p156) Maceiras (p156)	México (p134) Gil (p134) Lomography (p135)
Paseo del Prado & Salamanca	Museo del Prado (p90) Museo Thyssen-Bornemisza (p94) Parque del Buen Retiro (p97)	Sula Madrid (p159) Estado Puro (p159) Biotza (p161)	Agatha Ruiz de la Prada (p136) Gallery (p137) Oriol Balaguer (p138)
Malasaña & Chueca	Sociedad General de Autores y Editores (p106) Museo del Romanticismo (p106) Museo Municipal de Arte Contemporáneo (p107)	Nina (p162) Le Cabrera (p165) Bazaar (p166)	Mercado de Fuencarral (p140) Isolée (p141) Loewe (p140)
Chamberí & Argüelles	Templo de Debod (p114) Museo de América (p115) Museo Sorolla (p118)	Sergi Arola Gastro (p168) Las Tortillas de Gabino (p169) Casa Jacinto (p169)	Antigüedades Hom (p142) Diedro (p143) Flamenco (p143)

AREA

Drinking & Nightlife p177; Eating p149; Shopping p130; Sleeping p221

Los Austrias, Sol and Centro is where the story of Madrid began and became the seat of royal power. It's also where the splendour of imperial Spain was at its most ostentatious and Spain's overarching Catholicism was at its most devout – think expansive palaces, elaborate private mansions, ancient churches and imposing convents amid the raucous clamour of modern Madrid.

From the tangle of streets tumbling down the hillside of Los Austrias and the busy shopping streets around the Plaza de la Puerta del Sol (the Gate of the Sun; more commonly known as Puerta del Sol) to the monumental Gran Vía, which marks the northern border of central Madrid, this is Madrid's most diverse corner. If other barrios all have their own distinctive character traits, then Los Austrias, Sol and Centro is the sum total of all Madrid's personalities. It's also where the madrileño world most often intersects with that of tourists and expats drawn to that feel-good Madrid vibe.

The area that slopes down the hill southwest of Plaza Mayor is Madrid's most medieval quarter and has come to be known as Madrid de los Austrias, in reference to the Habsburg dynasty, which ruled Spain from 1517 to 1700. The busy and bustling streets between the Puerta del Sol and Gran Vía form the heart and centre of Madrid, a designation that extends west to the Palacio Real, the royal jewel in Madrid's considerable crown. At the hub is the glorious Plaza Mayor.

top picks

SIGHTS IN LOS AUSTRIAS, SOL & CENTRO

- Plaza Mayor (left)
- Palacio Real (p67)
- Plaza de la Villa (p65)
- Plaza de Oriente (p67)
- Convento de las Descalzas Reales (p69)
- Real Academia de Bellas Artes de San Fernando (p71)

PLAZA MAYOR Map pp62–3

Ⓜ Sol

For centuries the centrepiece of Madrid life, the stately Plaza Mayor combines supremely elegant architecture with a history dominated by peculiarly Spanish dramas. Pull up a chair at the outdoor tables around the perimeter or laze upon the rough-hewn cobblestones as young madrileños have a habit of doing. All around you, the theatre that is Spanish street life buzzing through the plaza provides a crash course in why people fall in love with Madrid.

Ah, the history the plaza has seen! Designed in 1619 by Juan Gómez de Mora and built in typical Herrerian style, of which the slate spires are the most obvious expression, its first public ceremony was suitably auspicious – the beatification of San Isidro Labrador (St Isidro the Farm Labourer), Madrid's patron saint. Thereafter it was as if all that was controversial about Spain took place in this square. Bullfights, often in celebration of royal weddings or births, with royalty watching on from the balconies and up to 50,000 people crammed into the plaza, were a recurring theme until 1878. Far more notorious were the *autos-da-fé* (the ritual condemnations of heretics during the Spanish Inquisition) followed by executions – burnings at the stake and deaths by garrotte on the north side of the square, hangings to the south. These continued until 1790 when a fire largely destroyed the square, which was subsequently reproduced under the supervision of Juan de Villanueva who lent his name to the building that now houses the Museo del Prado (p90).

Not all the plaza's activities were grand events and, just as it is now surrounded by shops, it was once filled with food vendors. In 1673, King Carlos II issued an edict allowing the vendors to raise tarpaulins above their stalls to protect their wares and themselves from the refuse and raw sewage that people habitually tossed out of the windows above! Well into the 20th century, trams ran through Plaza Mayor.

The grandeur of the plaza is due in large part to the warm colours of the uniformly ochre apartments with 237 wrought-iron balconies offset by the exquisite frescoes

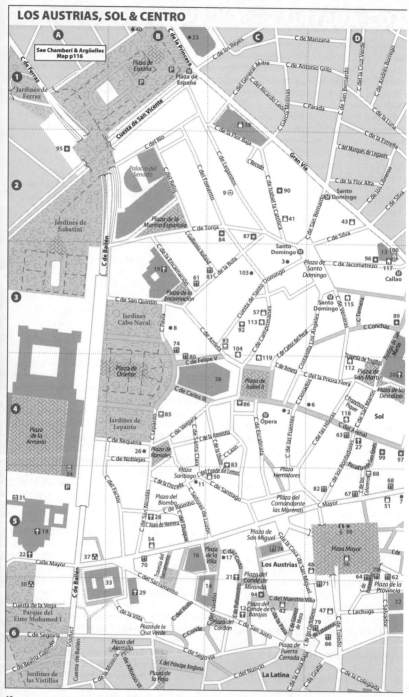

See Chamberí & Argüelles Map p116

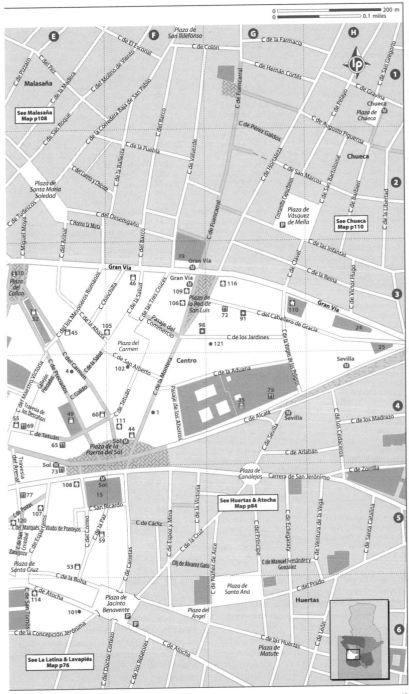

of the 17th-century Real Casa de la Panadería (Royal Bakery). The present frescoes date to just 1992 and are the work of artist Carlos Franco, who chose images from the signs of the zodiac and gods (eg Cybele) to provide a stunning backdrop for the plaza. The frescoes were inaugurated to coincide with Madrid's 1992 spell as European Capital of Culture.

In the middle of the square stands an equestrian statue of the man who ordered its construction, Felipe III. Originally placed in the Casa de Campo (p123), it was moved to Plaza Mayor in 1848, whereafter it became a favoured meeting place for irreverent madrileños who arranged to catch up 'under the balls of the horse'.

To see the plaza's epic history told in pictures, check out the carvings on the circular seats beneath the lamp posts. On Sunday mornings the plaza's arcaded perimeter is taken over by traders in old coins, banknotes and stamps, while December and early January see the plaza occupied by a Christmas market selling fairground kitsch and nativity scenes of real quality.

PALACIO DE SANTA CRUZ Map pp62-3
Plaza de la Provincia; Ⓜ Sol
Just off the southeastern corner of Plaza Mayor and dominating Plaza de Santa Cruz is this baroque edifice, which houses the Ministerio de Asuntos Exteriores (Ministry of Foreign Affairs) and hence can only be admired from the outside. A landmark with its grey slate spires, it was built in 1643 and initially served as the court prison.

BASÍLICA DE SAN MIGUEL Map pp62-3
☎ 91 548 40 11; Calle de San Justo 4; ☉ 9.45am-2pm & 5.30-9pm Mon-Fri mid-Sep-Jun, 9.45am-1pm & 5.30-9pm Mon-Fri Jul-mid-Sep; Ⓜ La Latina or Sol
Hidden away off Calle de Segovia, this basilica is something of a surprise. Its convex, late-baroque facade sits in harmony with the surrounding buildings of old Madrid. Among its fine features are statues representing the four virtues, and the reliefs of Justo and Pastor, the saints to whom the church was originally dedicated. The rococo and Italianate interior, completed by Italian architects in 1745, is another world altogether with gilded flourishes and dark, sombre domes.

CONVENTO DEL CORPUS CRISTI
Map pp62-3
Las Carboneras; ☎ 91 548 37 01; Plaza del Conde de Miranda; admission free; ☉ 9.30am-1pm & 4-6.30pm; Ⓜ Ópera
Architecturally nondescript but culturally curious, this church hides behind sober brickwork on the western end of a quiet square. A closed order of nuns occupies the convent building and, when Mass is held, the nuns gather in a separate area at the rear of the church. They maintain a centuries-old tradition of making sweet biscuits that can be purchased from the entrance just off the square on Calle del Codo (see p132).

PLAZA DE LA VILLA & AROUND
Map pp62-3
Ⓜ Ópera
There are grander plazas, but this intimate little square is one of Madrid's prettiest. Enclosed on three sides by wonderfully preserved examples of 17th-century Madrid-style baroque architecture (barroco madrileño; see p47), it was the permanent seat of Madrid's city government from the Middle Ages until recent years when Madrid's city council relocated to the grand Palacio de Comunicaciones on Plaza de la Cibeles.

The 17th-century Casa de la Villa (old town hall), on the western side of the square, is a typical Habsburg edifice with Herrerian slate-tiled spires. First planned as a prison in 1644 by Juan Gómez de Mora, who also designed the Convento de la Encarnación (p70), its granite and brick facade is a study in sobriety. The final touches to the Casa de

MADRID'S BARRIOS IN A NUTSHELL

Los Austrias, Sol & Centro Madrid's oldest quarter, home to some of Madrid's grandest monuments, as well as bars, restaurants and hotels.

La Latina & Lavapiés Narrow medieval streets, great bars for tapas, drinking venues and restaurants.

Huertas & Atocha One of Madrid's nightlife capitals and home to the Centro de Arte Reina Sofía.

Paseo del Prado & El Retiro Grand boulevard with the great art galleries along its shores and the Parque del Buen Retiro.

Salamanca Up-scale and upmarket, Madrid's home of designer shopping.

Malasaña & Chueca Inner-city barrios with eclectic nightlife, shopping and outstanding eating options.

Chamberí & Argüelles Residential barrios with a glimpse of Madrid away from the tourist crowds.

Northern Madrid High-class restaurants and the home of Real Madrid.

With the Plaza de la Puerta del Sol (Spain's Kilometre Zero) at its heart, Los Austrias, Sol and Centro is bordered by Gran Vía to the north, Plaza de España and Calle de Bailén to the west, Calle de Segovia and Calle de la Concepción Jerónima to the south and Calle de Carretas and Calle de Alcalá to the east. Aside from Calle de Segovia, which cuts a swathe through Los Austrias, other atmospheric thoroughfares include Calle Mayor, the major shopping street of Calle de Preciados and the pedestrianised Calle del Arenal, which spills into Plaza de Isabel II, home of the Teatro Real, beyond which lies the Palacio Real. Landmark plazas include cosy Plaza de la Villa and regal Plaza de Oriente.

Central Madrid is well-served by metro, although less so on its western perimeter and the southwestern corner. Along the northern rim, handy metro stops include Gran Vía (lines 1 and 5), Callao (lines 3 and 5), Santo Domingo (line 2) and Plaza de España (lines 3 and 10). In the heart of the barrio, getting out at either Sol (lines 1, 2 and 3) or Ópera (lines 2 and 5) puts you within walking distance of anywhere covered in this section.

la Villa were made in 1693, and Juan de Villanueva, of Museo del Prado fame, made some alterations a century later. The tourist office runs free tours (5pm Mon) in Spanish through various reception halls and into the Salón del Pleno (council chambers); the tours must be booked in advance through the Centro de Turismo de Madrid (p265) on Plaza Mayor. The council chambers were restored in the 1890s and again in 1986; the decoration is sumptuous neoclassical with late-17th-century ceiling frescoes. Look for the ceramic copy of Pedro Teixeira's landmark 1656 map of Madrid just outside the chambers.

On the opposite side of the square, the 15th-century Casa de los Lujanes is more Gothic in conception with a clear *mudéjar* influence (a decorative style of Islamic architecture as used on Christian buildings). The brickwork tower is said to have been 'home' to the imprisoned French monarch François I and his sons after their capture during the Battle of Pavia (1525). As the star prisoner was paraded down Calle Mayor, locals are said to have been more impressed by the splendidly attired Frenchman than they were by his more drab captor, the Spanish Habsburg emperor Carlos I.

Currently closed to the public, the Casa de Cisneros, built in 1537 by the nephew of Cardinal Cisneros, a key adviser to Queen Isabel, is plateresque in inspiration, although it was much restored and altered at the beginning of the 20th century. The main door and window above it are what remains of the Renaissance-era building. It's now home to the Salón de Tapices (Tapestries Hall), adorned with exquisite 15th-century Flemish tapestries.

Other landmarks nearby include the 18th-century baroque remake of the Iglesia del Sacramento, the central church of the Spanish army; and the Palacio del Duque de Uceda, which is now used as a military headquarters (the Capitanía General), but is a classic of the Madrid baroque architectural style and was designed by Juan Gómez de Mora in 1608.

The section of Calle Mayor that runs past the plaza witnessed one of the most dramatic moments in the history of early 20th-century Madrid. On 31 May 1906, on the wedding day of King Alfonso XIII and Britain's Victoria Eugenia, a Catalan anarchist Mateu Morral threw a bomb concealed in a bouquet of flowers at the royal couple. Several bystanders died, but the monarch and his new wife survived intact, save for her blood-spattered dress. During the Spanish Civil War, Madrid's republican government briefly renamed the street Calle Mateu Morral.

IGLESIA DE SAN NICOLÁS DE LOS SERVITAS Map pp62-3

☎ 91 548 83 14; Plaza de San Nicolás 6; admission free; 8am-1.30pm & 5.30-8.30pm Mon, 8-9.30am & 6.30-8.30pm Tue-Sat, 9.30am-2pm & 6.30-9pm Sun & holidays; Ópera

Tucked away up the hill from Calle Mayor, this intimate little church is Madrid's oldest surviving building of worship. It is believed to have been built on the site of Muslim Mayrit's second mosque. The most striking feature is the restored 12th-century *mudéjar* bell tower, although much of the remainder dates in part from the 15th century. The vaulting is late Gothic while the fine timber ceiling, which survived a fire in 1936, dates from about the same period. Despite plateresque and baroque touches, much of the interior is a study in simplicity. The architect Juan de Herrera (see p47), one of the great architects of Renaissance Spain, was buried in the crypt in 1597.

PLAZA DE RAMALES Map pp62-3 Ⓜ Ópera

This pleasant little triangle of open space is not without historical intrigue. Joseph Bonaparte ordered the destruction of the Iglesia de San Juanito to open up a pocket of fresh air in the then-crowded streets. It is believed Velázquez was buried in the church; excavations in 2000 revealed the crypt of the former church and the remains of various people buried in it centuries ago, but Velázquez was nowhere to be found. On the west side of the plaza is the Escuela Superior de Música Reina Sofía (www .escuelasuperiordemusicareinasofia.es), a prestigious musical conservatory which sometimes hosts concerts.

PLAZA DE ORIENTE Map pp62-3
Ⓜ Ópera

A royal palace that once had aspirations to be the Spanish Versailles. Sophisticated cafes watched over by apartments that cost the equivalent of a royal salary. The Teatro Real, Madrid's opera house and one of Spain's temples to high culture. Some of the finest sunset views in Madrid. Welcome to Plaza de Oriente, a living, breathing monument to imperial Madrid.

At the centre of the plaza, which the palace overlooks, is an equestrian statue of Felipe IV. Designed by Velázquez, it is the perfect place to take it all in with marvellous views wherever you look. If you're wondering how a heavy bronze statue of a rider and his horse rearing up can actually maintain that stance, the answer is simple: the hind legs are solid, while the front ones are hollow. That idea was Galileo Galilei's.

Nearby are some 20 marble statues of mostly ancient monarchs. Local legend has it that these ageing royals get down off their pedestals at night to stretch their legs.

The adjacent Jardines Cabo Naval, a great place to watch the sun set, adds to the sense of a sophisticated oasis of green in the heart of Madrid.

PALACIO REAL Map pp62-3

☎ 91 454 88 00; www.patrimonionacional.es, in Spanish; Calle de Bailén; adult/student & EU senior €10/3.50, adult without guided tour €8, free EU citizens Wed; ☾ 9am-6pm Mon-Sat, 9am-3pm Sun & holidays Apr-Sep, 9.30am-5pm Mon-Sat, 9am-2pm Sun & holidays Oct-Mar; Ⓜ Ópera

In their modern manifestation, the Bourbons who rule Spain are one of Europe's more modest royal families, but their predecessors lived far more sumptuous lifestyles.

You can almost imagine how the eyes of Felipe V, the first of the Bourbon kings, lit up when the *alcázar* (Muslim-era fortress) burned down in 1734 on Madrid's most exclusive perch of real estate. His plan? Build a palace that would dwarf all its European counterparts. The Italian architect Filippo Juvara (1678–1736), who had made his name building the Basilica di Superga and the Palazzo di Stupinigi in Turin, was called in but, like Felipe, he died without bringing the project to fruition. Upon Juvara's death, another Italian, Giovanni Battista Sacchetti, took over, finishing the job in 1764.

The result was an Italianate baroque colossus with some 2800 rooms, of which around 50 are open to the public. It's occasionally closed for state ceremonies and official receptions, but the present king is rarely in residence, preferring to live somewhere more modest.

The Farmacia Real (Royal Pharmacy), the first set of rooms to the right at the southern end of the Plaza de la Armería (Plaza de Armas; Plaza of the Armoury) courtyard, contains a formidable collection of medicine jars and stills for mixing royal concoctions, suggesting that the royals were either paranoid or decidedly sickly. West across the plaza is the Armería Real, a hoard of weapons and striking suits of armour, mostly dating from the 16th and 17th centuries.

From the northern end of the Plaza de la Armería, the main stairway, a grand statement of imperial power, leads to the royal apartments and eventually to the Salón del Trono (Throne Room). The latter is nauseatingly lavish with its crimson-velvet wall coverings complemented by a ceiling painted by the dramatic Venetian baroque master, Tiepolo, who was a favourite of Carlos III. Nearby, the Salón de Gasparini (Gasparini Room) has an exquisite stucco ceiling and walls resplendent with embroidered silks. The aesthetic may be different in the Sala de Porcelana (Porcelain Room), but the aura of extravagance continues with myriad pieces from the one-time Retiro porcelain factory screwed into the walls. In the midst of it all comes the spacious Comedor de Gala (Gala Dining Room). Only students with passes may enter the Biblioteca Real (Royal Library).

If you're lucky, you might just catch the colourful changing of the guard in full parade dress. This takes place at noon on the first Wednesday of every month (except August and September) between the palace and the Catedral de Nuestra Señora de la Almudena. There's also a less extravagant changing of the guard inside the palace compound at the Puerta del Príncipe every Wednesday from 11am to 2pm.

The French-inspired Jardines de Sabatini (9am-9pm May-Sep, 9am-8pm Oct-Apr) lie along the northern flank of the Palacio Real. They were laid out in the 1930s to replace the royal stables that once stood on the site.

Behind the Catedral de Nuestra Señora de la Almudena and adjacent to the Palacio Real, work is underway on the Museo de Colecciones Reales (Museum of Royal Collections; Map pp124-5), which is being built to house much of the palace's collection.

CATEDRAL DE NUESTRA SEÑORA DE LA ALMUDENA Map pp62-3

☎ 91 542 22 00; Calle de Bailén; admission by donation; 🕑 9am-8.30pm Mon-Sat, for Mass Sun; Ⓜ Ópera

Paris has Notre Dame and Rome has St Peter's Basilica. In fact, almost every European city of stature has its signature cathedral, a stand-out monument to a glorious Christian past. Not Madrid. Although the exterior of the Catedral de Nuestra Señora de la Almudena sits in harmony with the adjacent Palacio Real, Madrid's cathedral is cavernous and largely charmless within; its colourful, modern ceilings do little to make up for the lack of old-world gravitas that so distinguishes great cathedrals.

Carlos I first proposed building a cathedral here back in 1518, but building didn't actually begin until 1879. It was finally finished in 1992. Unsurprisingly, the pristine, bright-white neo-Gothic interior holds no pride of place in the affections of madrileños.

It's possible to climb to the cathedral's summit, with fine views. En route you climb up through the cathedral's museum; follow the signs to the Museo de la Catedral y Cúpula

(adult/child €6/4; 🕑 10am-2.30pm Mon-Sat) on the northern facade, opposite the Palacio Real.

Just around the corner in Calle Mayor, the low-lying ruins of Santa María de la Almudena are all that remain of Madrid's first church, which was built on the site of Mayrit's Great Mosque when the Christians arrived in the 11th century.

And just down the hill beneath the cathedral's southern wall on Calle Mayor is the Cripta de la Catedral de Madrid with more than 400 columns, 20 chapels and fine stained-glass windows.

MURALLA ÁRABE Map pp62-3

Cuesta de la Vega; Ⓜ Ópera

Behind the cathedral apse and down Cuesta de la Vega is a disappointingly short stretch of the original 'Arab Wall', the city wall built by Madrid's early-medieval Muslim rulers. Some of it dates as far back as the 9th century, when the initial Muslim fort was raised. Other sections date from the 12th and 13th centuries, by which time the city had been taken by the Christians. The earliest sections were ingeniously conceived – the outside of the wall was made to look dauntingly sturdy, while the inside was put together with cheap materials to save money. It must have worked, as the town was rarely ever taken by force. In summer the city council organises open-air theatre and music performances here. Just above the wall on Cuesta de la Vega, information panels show the original extent of the city walls super-imposed on a modern map; for more information, see p22.

TEATRO REAL Map pp62-3

☎ 91 516 06 96; www.teatro-real.com; Plaza de Oriente; guided tour adult/student up to 26yr & senior €5/3; 🕑 10.30am-1pm Mon & Wed-Fri, 11am-1.30pm Sat, Sun & holidays; Ⓜ Ópera

Backing onto the Plaza de Oriente, Madrid's signature opera house does not have the most distinguished of histories. The first theatre was built in 1708 on the site of public wash houses. Torn down in 1816, its successor was built in 1850 under the reign of Isabel II, whereafter it burned down and was later blown up in the civil war (when it was used as a powder store, resulting in the inevitable fireworks). It finally took its present neoclassical form in 1997 and, viewed from Plaza de Isabel II, it's a fine

ROOM TO WALK, NOWHERE TO SIT

In recent years, Madrid has closed large numbers of its downtown thoroughfares and plazas to traffic and converted them into pedestrian-only spaces. The most important have been Plaza de la Puerta del Sol, Calle del Arenal, Plaza de Isabel II, Calle de la Montera, Plaza del Callao (all Map pp62-3), Calle de Fuencarral (Map pp108-9)and Plaza de Santa Bárbara (Map p110). These welcome changes have made central Madrid an even better place to go for a stroll.

There's just one problem: apart from thinly scattered individual seats, there's nowhere to sit. In Calle de Fuencarral's 500m of pedestrianised street, for example, there are just seven seats. According to the town hall, there was some method in their madness. To add more park benches would be, the town hall argues, to turn them into obstacle courses and cause pedestrian bottlenecks. More convincingly, the town hall was keen to discourage the *botellón*, the large gatherings of young drinkers at nights, particularly at weekends.

Nonetheless, critics have ranged from local community associations to the renowned Madrid architect Rafael Moneo, who described the spaces as 'too hard' and 'unfriendly'. Until now, the complaints have fallen on deaf ears at the town hall, which is why you see so many young madrileños who can find no better place to rest than to sit on the pavement.

---

addition to the central Madrid cityscape; in Plaza de Oriente, however, it's somewhat overshadowed by the splendour of its surrounds. The 1997 renovations combined the latest in theatre and acoustic technology with a remake of the most splendid of its 19th-century decor. The guided tours (in Spanish) leave every half-hour and take about 50 minutes. See also p203.

PLAZA DE LA PUERTA DEL SOL
Map pp62-3

Ⓜ Sol

The official centrepoint of Spain is a gracious hemisphere of elegant facades and often overwhelming crowds. It is, above all, a crossroads with people forever passing through on their way elsewhere.

In early times, the Puerta del Sol (the Gate of the Sun) was the eastern gate of the city and from here passed a road through the peasant hovels of the outer 'suburbs' en route to Guadalajara, to the northeast. The name of the gate appears to date from the 1520s, when Madrid joined the revolt of the Comuneros against Carlos I and erected a fortress in the east-facing arch in which the sun was depicted. The fort was demolished around 1570.

The main building on the square houses the regional government of the Comunidad de Madrid. The Casa de Correos, as it is called, was built as the city's main post office in 1768. The clock was added in 1856 and on New Year's Eve people throng the square to wait impatiently for the clock to strike midnight, and at each gong swallow a grape – not as easy as it sounds! On the footpath outside the Casa de Correos is a

plaque marking Spain's Kilometre Zero, the point from which Spain's network of roads is measured. The semicircular junction owes its present appearance in part to the Bourbon king Carlos III (r 1759–88), whose equestrian statue (complete with his unmistakable nose) stands in the middle.

Just to the east of Carlos III, the statue of a bear nuzzling a *madroño* (strawberry tree) is the city's symbol; for more information, see the boxed text, p24.

CONVENTO DE LAS DESCALZAS REALES Map pp62-3
☎ 91 454 88 00; www.patrimonionacional.es, in Spanish; Plaza de las Descalzas 3; adult/student & EU senior €5/2.50, combined ticket with Convento de la Encarnación €6/3.40, free EU citizens Wed; ⏱ 10.30am-12.30pm & 4-5.30pm Tue-Thu & Sat, 10.30am-12.30pm Fri, 11am-1.30pm Sun & holidays; Ⓜ Callao

The grim, prisonlike walls of this one-time palace keep modern Madrid at bay and offer no hint that behind the sober plateresque facade lies a sumptuous stronghold of the faith.

The compulsory guided tour (in Spanish) leads you up a gaudily frescoed Renaissance stairway to the upper level of the cloister. The vault was painted by Claudio Coello, one of the most important artists of the 17th-century Madrid School (p38) and whose works adorn San Lorenzo de El Escorial.

You then pass several of the convent's 33 chapels – a maximum of 33 Franciscan nuns is allowed to live here (perhaps because Christ is said to have been 33 when he died) as part of a closed order.

These nuns follow in the tradition of the Descalzas Reales (Barefooted Royals), a group of illustrious women who cloistered themselves when the convent was founded in the 16th century. The first of these chapels contains a remarkable carved figure of a dead, reclining Christ, which is paraded in a moving Good Friday procession each year. At the end of the passage is the antechoir, then the choir stalls themselves, where Doña Juana – the daughter of Carlos I and who, in a typical piece of 16th-century collusion between royalty and the Catholic Church, commandeered the palace and had it converted into a convent – is buried. A *Virgen la Dolorosa* by Pedro de la Mena is seated in one of the 33 oak stalls.

In the former sleeping quarters of the nuns are some of the most extraordinary tapestries you're ever likely to see. Woven in the 17th century in Brussels, they include four based on drawings by Rubens. To produce works of this quality, four or five artisans could take up to a year to weave just 1 sq metre of tapestry.

IGLESIA DE SAN GINÉS Map pp62-3
☎ 91 366 48 75; Calle del Arenal 13; admission free; Ⓜ Sol or Ópera

Due north of Plaza Mayor, San Ginés is one of Madrid's oldest churches: it has been here in one form or another since at least the 14th century. It is speculated that, prior to the arrival of the Christians in 1085, a Mozarabic community (Christians in Muslim territory) lived around the stream that later became Calle del Arenal and that their parish church stood on this site. What you see today was built in 1645 but largely reconstructed after a fire in 1824. The church houses some fine paintings, including El Greco's *Expulsion of the Moneychangers from the Temple* (1614), which is beautifully displayed; the glass is just 6mm from the canvas to avoid reflections. The church has stood at the centre of Madrid life for centuries; Spain's premier playwright Lope de Vega was married here and novelist Francisco de Quevedo was baptised in its font. Sadly, the church is only open for Mass.

CONVENTO DE LA ENCARNACIÓN
Map pp62-3

☎ 91 454 88 00; www.patrimonionacional.es, in Spanish; Plaza de la Encarnación 1; adult/student & EU senior €3.60/2, combined ticket with Convento de las Descalzas Reales €6/3.40, free EU citizens Wed; Ⓨ 10.30am-12.45pm & 4-5.45pm Tue-Thu & Sat, 10.30am-12.45pm Fri, 11am-1.45pm Sun & holidays; Ⓜ Ópera

Founded by Empress Margarita de Austria, this 17th-century mansion built in the Madrid baroque style (a pleasing amalgam of brick, exposed stone and wrought iron) is still inhabited by nuns of the Augustine order. The large art collection dates mostly from the 17th century and among the many gold and silver reliquaries is one that contains the blood of San Pantaleón, which purportedly liquefies each year on 27 July. The convent also sits on a pretty plaza with lovely views down towards the Palacio Real.

PLAZA DE ESPAÑA Map pp62-3
Ⓜ Plaza de España

It's hard to know what to make of this curiously unprepossessing square. The 1953 Edificio de España (Spain Building; Map pp108-9) on the northeast side clearly sprang from the totalitarian recesses of Franco's imagination such is its resemblance to austere Soviet monumentalism, but there's also something strangely grand and pleasing about it. To the north stands the rather ugly and considerably taller 35-storey Torre de Madrid (Madrid Tower; Map pp116-17). Taking centre stage in the square is a statue of Cervantes. At the writer's feet is a bronze of his immortal characters Don Quijote and Sancho Panza. The monument was erected in 1927. But Plaza de España is at its best down in its lower (southwestern) reaches, where abundant trees are remarkably successful in keeping Madrid's noise at bay. It's probably best avoided after dark.

GRAN VÍA Map pp62-3

Ⓜ Gran Vía or Callao

It's difficult to imagine Madrid without Gran Vía, the grand boulevard lined with towering belle-époque facades that climbs up through the centre of Madrid from Plaza de España then down to Calle de Alcalá. But it has only existed since 1910, when it was bulldozed through what was then a labyrinth of old streets, sweeping away a lively inner-city community in the process. Plans for the boulevard were first announced in 1862 and so interminable were the delays that a famous *zarzuela* (satirical musical comedy), *La Gran Vía,* first performed in 1886, was penned to mock the city authorities and remains popular to this day. When finally completed, 14 streets disappeared off the map, as did 311 houses, including one where Goya had once lived.

It may have destroyed whole barrios, but Gran Vía is still considered one of the most successful examples of urban planning in central Madrid since the late 19th century. Throughout 2010, the street's centenary was celebrated with much fanfare.

One eye-catching building, the Carrión (Map pp62-3), on the corner of Gran Vía and Calle de Jacometrezo, was Madrid's first tower-block apartment hotel and caused quite a stir when it was put up during the pre-WWI years; it's once again a hotel. Also dominating the skyline about one-third of the way along Gran Vía is the 1920s-era Telefónica building (Map pp62-3), which was for years the highest building in the city. During the civil war, when Madrid was besieged by Franco's forces and the boulevard became known as 'Howitzer Alley' due to the artillery shells that rained down upon it, the Telefónica building was a favoured target.

Among the more interesting buildings is the stunning, French-designed Edificio Metrópolis (Map pp62-3; 1905), which marks the southern end of Gran Vía. The winged victory statue atop its dome was added in 1975 and is best seen from Calle de Alcalá or Plaza de la Cibeles. A little up the boulevard is the Edificio Grassy (with the Rolex sign; Map pp62-3), built in 1916. With its circular 'temple' as a crown, and profusion of arcs and slender columns, it's one of the most elegant buildings on the Gran Vía. Another important Gran Vía landmark is Museo Chicote (p196), one of Europe's most celebrated cocktail bars down through the decades.

Otherwise on Gran Vía, luxury hotels and cheap *hostales* (hostels), pinball parlours and dark old cinemas proliferate, as well as everything from jewellery shops, banks and high fashion to fast food and sex shops. It's home to twice as many businesses (1051 at last count) as homes (592); over 13,000 people work along the street; and up to 55,000 vehicles pass through every day (including almost 185 buses an hour during peak periods). There are 41 hotels on Gran Vía, but sadly just three of the 15 cinemas for which Gran Vía was famous remain.

REAL ACADEMIA DE BELLAS ARTES DE SAN FERNANDO Map pp62-3

☎ 91 524 08 64; http://rabasf.insde.es, in Spanish; Calle de Alcalá 13; adult/student/child under 18yr & senior €5/2.50/free, free Wed; ☷ 9am-5pm Tue-Sat, 9am-2.30pm Sun Sep-Jun, hours vary Jul & Aug; Ⓜ Sol or Sevilla

In any other city, this gallery would be a stand-out attraction, but in Madrid it often gets forgotten in the rush to the Prado, Thyssen or Reina Sofía. Nonetheless a visit here is a fascinating journey into another age of art; when we tell you that Picasso and Dalí studied at this academy (long the academic centre of learning for up-and-coming artists), but found it far too stuffy for their liking, you'll get an idea of what to expect. A centre of excellence since Fernando VI founded the academy in the 18th century, it remains a stunning repository of works by some of the best-loved old Spanish masters.

The 1st floor, mainly devoted to 16th- to 19th-century paintings, is the most noteworthy of those in the academic gallery. Among relative unknowns, you come across a hall of works by Zurbarán (especially arresting is the series of full-length portraits of white-cloaked friars) and a *San Jerónimo* by El Greco.

At a 'fork' in the exhibition, a sign points right to rooms 11 to 16, the main one showcasing Alonso Cano (1601–67) and José de Ribera (1591–1652). In the others a couple of minor portraits by Velázquez hang alongside the occasional Rubens,

Tintoretto and Bellini, which have some-how been smuggled in. Rooms 17 to 22 offer a space full of Bravo Murillo and last, but most captivating, 13 pieces by Goya, including self-portraits, portraits of King Fernando VII and the infamous minister Manuel Godoy, along with one on bullfighting.

The 19th and 20th centuries are the themes upstairs. It's not the most extensive or engaging modern collection, but you'll find drawings by Picasso as well as works by Joaquín Sorolla, Juan Gris, Eduardo Chillida and Ignacio Zuloaga, in most cases with only one or two items each.

OLD MADRID
Walking Tour
1 Plaza de Oriente
Begin in this splendid arc of greenery and graceful architecture, which could be Madrid's most agreeable plaza (p67). You'll find yourself surrounded by gardens, the Palacio Real and the Teatro Real, in a square peopled by an ever-changing cast of madrileños at play.

2 Palacio Real
Spain's seat of royal power for centuries, the Royal Palace (p67) imposes itself upon the Plaza de Oriente and stands as one of the capital's most emblematic sights. Its interior is lavish, crammed with the accumulated extravagance of royal excess.

3 Catedral de Nuestra Señora de la Almudena
Madrid's modern cathedral (p68) may lack the old-world gravitas of other Spanish cathedrals, but it's a beautiful part of the skyline when combined with the adjacent Palacio Real. Climb to the summit, then take a quick look within.

4 Plaza de la Villa
From the cathedral, climb gently up Calle Mayor, pausing to admire the last remaining ruins of Madrid's first cathedral, Santa María de la Almudena (p68), then on to Plaza de la Villa (p65), a cosy square surrounded on three sides by some of the best examples of Madrid baroque architecture.

5 Mercado de San Miguel
One of Madrid's oldest markets (dating from 1616) has become one of the coolest places to eat and mingle with locals in downtown Madrid. The recently refurbished Mercado de San Miguel (p151) is just off Calle Mayor, between Plaza de la Villa and Plaza Mayor.

6 Plaza Mayor
Head down the hill along Calle de la Cava de San Miguel, then climb up through the Arco de Cuchilleros to Plaza Mayor (p61), one of Spain's grandest and most beautiful plazas. The frescoes on the north side perfectly complement the slate spires and ochre tones that surround a square that has witnessed many of the grand events – as well as some distasteful ones – of the city's history.

7 Plaza de la Puerta del Sol
Leave Plaza Mayor via the northeast corner, down Calle de Postas to Puerta del Sol (p69). This is Madrid's heartbeat, a clamorous wedge of activity and pretty architecture dead in the centre of Madrid.

8 Iglesia de San Ginés
The pedestrianised Calle del Arenal, which leads northwest from the plaza, takes you past the pleasing brick-and-stone Iglesia de San Ginés (p70), one of the longest-standing relics of Christian Madrid. If you're able to peek inside, make straight for the El Greco masterpiece in the Santísimo Cristo Chapel.

9 Chocolatería de San Ginés
Tucked away in the lane behind the church, this bar-cafe (p179) is justifiably famous for its *churros y chocolate* (Spanish donuts fresh from the oven with a large cup of hot chocolate), the ideal Madrid hangover cure or a delicious indulgence at any hour of the day.

10 Convento de las Descalzas Reales
Across the other side of Calle del Arenal, in Plaza de San Martín, this austere convent (p69) has an extraordinarily rich interior behind the high brick walls, loaded with tapestries, master paintings and a jaw-dropping Renaissance stairway.

WALK FACTS
Start Plaza de Oriente
End Plaza de España
Distance 3km
Time Two to three hours

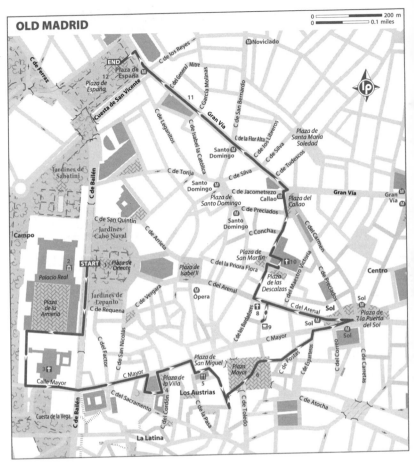

11 Gran Vía

Up the hill to the northeast lies Gran Vía (p71), the grand boulevard that consists of an endless tide of human and vehicular traffic. Along its shores are formidable examples of early 20th-century architecture, including the Telefónica and Metropolis buildings. Along its footpaths passes Madrid in all its madness.

12 Plaza de España

Down the bottom of Gran Vía to the northwest, Plaza de España (p70) is a rare stand of greenery in downtown Madrid. Watched over by architectural monuments to a dictator's folly, the plaza has a far more cultured statue of Cervantes and his two most famous literary creations in its centre.

Drinking & Nightlife p180; Eating p152; Shopping p133; Sleeping p223

La Latina combines Madrid's best selection of tapas bars and a medieval streetscape studded with elegant churches. Calle de la Cava Baja, whose path traces the long-disappeared city walls of the Middle Ages, could just be our favourite street for tapas in town. The tangle of lanes bordered by Plaza de la Paja, Calle de Segovia and Calle de Bailén once constituted the *morería*, the ancient Moorish quarter of Mayrit. It's always lively here, save for weekday mornings; while the rest of the city sleeps off its hangover from the night before, La Latina throngs with Sunday crowds on their way home from El Rastro flea market.

Lavapiés, on the other hand, is a world away from the sophistication of modern Madrid. It's at once one of the city's oldest and most traditional barrios – when madrileños dress up for the Fiestas de San Isidro Labrador (p18), they don the outfits of *chulapas* and *chulapos*, the names historically used for working-class madrileños who frequented Lavapiés in centuries past – and home to more immigrants than any other central Madrid barrio. Black Africans, Moroccans, Indians, South Americans and Chinese live cheek by jowl with fifth-generation locals; according to one count, over 50 nationalities are represented in an area made up of a couple of dozen streets. It's quirky, alternative and a melting pot all in one, a long-standing community and one constantly in the making. It's not without its problems and the barrio has a reputation for either antiglamour cool or as a no-go zone, depending on your perspective. We very much subscribe to the former.

top picks

SIGHTS IN LA LATINA & LAVAPIÉS

- El Rastro (left)
- Basílica de San Francisco El Grande (below)
- Plaza de la Paja (p77)
- La Morería (p76)
- Museo de los Orígenes (p78)

EL RASTRO Map pp76-7

Ribera de Curtidores; 8am-3pm Sun & holidays; M La Latina

The crowded Sunday flea market was, back in the 17th and 18th centuries, largely dedicated to a meat market (*rastro* means 'stain', in reference to the trail of blood left behind by animals dragged down the hill). The road leading through the market, Ribera de Curtidores, translates as Tanners' Alley and further evokes this sense of a slaughterhouse past. On Sunday mornings this is *the* place to be, with all of Madrid in all its diversity here in search of a bargain (see p134).

BASÍLICA DE SAN FRANCISCO EL GRANDE Map pp76-7

91 365 38 00; Plaza de San Francisco; adult/senior & child €3/2; Mass 8am-10.30am Mon-Sat, museum 10.30am-12.30pm & 4-6pm Mon-Sat; M La Latina or Puerta de Toledo

Lording it over the southwestern corner of La Latina, this imposing and recently restored baroque basilica is one of Madrid's grandest old churches. Its extravagantly frescoed dome is, by some estimates, the largest in Spain and the fourth largest in the world, with a height of 56m and diameter of 33m.

Legend has it that St Francis of Assisi built a chapel on this site in 1217. The

ORIENTATION & TRANSPORT: LA LATINA & LAVAPIÉS

La Latina forms a rough triangle bordered by Calle de Segovia, Calle de Bailén (which becomes the Gran Vía de San Francisco) and the Calle de Toledo, which separates it from Lavapiés. There aren't many metro stops within La Latina, although La Latina station (line 5) is the most convenient. The Puerta de Toledo stop is handy only if your business is a long way down the hill.

From Plaza de Tirso de Molina and Calle de Atocha, a series of long narrow lanes drops downhill into Lavapiés. The barrio's most obvious nerve centre is the small triangular Plaza de Lavapiés. Lavapiés is cordoned off to the south by Ronda de Toledo and Ronda de Atocha, noisy avenues that head east to Atocha station. Lavapiés metro stop (line 3) drops you in the heart of the barrio, although if you prefer a downhill walk, Tirso de Molina (line 1) and Antón Martín (line 1) are better. For El Rastro, the best stops are La Latina or Tirso de Molina.

current version was designed by Francesco Sabatini, who also designed the Puerta de Alcalá and finished off the Palacio Real. He designed the church with an unusual floor plan: the nave is circular and surrounded by chapels guarded by imposing marble statues of the 12 apostles; 12 prophets, rendered in wood, sit above them at the base of the dome. Each of the chapels is adorned with frescoes and decorated according to a different historical style, but most people rush to the neo-plateresque Capilla de San Bernardino, where the central fresco was painted by Goya in the early stages of his career – unusually, Goya has painted himself into the scene (he's the one in the yellow shirt on the right).

A series of corridors behind the high altar (accessible only as part of the guided visit) is lined with works of art from the 17th to 19th centuries; highlights include a painting by Francisco Zurbarán, and another by Francisco Pacheco, the father-in-law and teacher of Velázquez. In the sacristy, watch out for the fine Renaissance *sillería* (the sculpted walnut seats where the church's superiors would meet).

A word about the opening hours: although entry is free during morning Mass times, there is no access to the museum and the lights in the Capilla de San Bernardino won't be on to illuminate the Goya. At all other times, visit is by Spanish-language guided tour (included in the admission price). Just to confuse matters, you may face a similar problem if you're

here on a Friday afternoon or any time Saturday if there's a wedding taking place. And in summer, afternoon opening hours run from 5pm to 7pm.

LAS VISTILLAS, VIADUCT & CALLE DE SEGOVIA Map pp76-7
M Ópera

The leafy area around and beneath the southern end of the viaduct that crosses Calle de Segovia, is an ideal spot to pause and ponder the curious history of one of Madrid's oldest barrios.

Probably the best place to do this is just across Calle de Bailén where the *terrazas* (open-air cafes) of Jardines de las Vistillas (Las Vistillas) offer one of the best vantage points in Madrid for a drink, with views towards the Sierra de Guadarrama. During the civil war, Las Vistillas was heavily bombarded by Nationalist troops from the Casa de Campo, and they in turn were shelled from a republican bunker here.

The adjacent viaduct was built in the 19th century and replaced by a newer version in 1942; the plastic barriers were erected in the late 1990s to prevent suicide jumps.

Before the viaduct was built, anyone wanting to cross from one side of the road or river to the other was obliged to make their way down to Calle de Segovia and back up the other side. If you feel like re-enacting the journey, head down to Calle de Segovia and cross to the southern side. Just east of the viaduct, on a characterless apartment block wall (No 21), is a coat of arms, one of the city's oldest. The site once belonged to Madrid's Ayuntamiento. A punt would ferry people across what was then a trickling tributary of the Río Manzanares.

Climbing back up the southern side from Calle de Segovia you reach Calle de la Morería. The area south to the Basílica

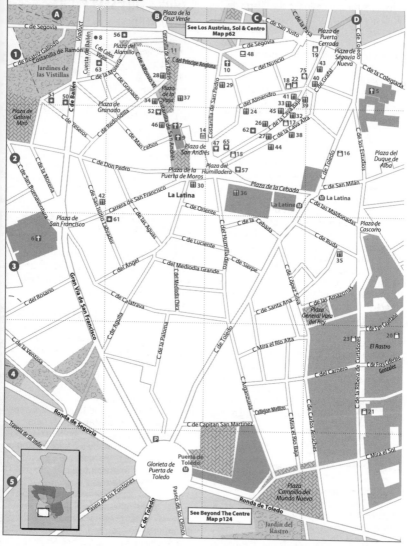

de San Francisco El Grande and southeast to the Iglesia de San Andrés was the heart of La Morería (Moorish quarter). The Muslim population of Mayrit was concentrated here following the 11th-century Christian take-over. Strain the imagination a little and the maze of winding and hilly lanes even now retains a whiff of a North African medina; for more information on the history of the period, turn to p24.

Another option is to follow Calle de Segovia west, down to the banks of the Manzanares and a nine-arched bridge, the Puente de Segovia (Map pp124-5), which Juan de Herrera built in 1584. The walk is more pleasant than the river, a view shared by the writer Lope de Vega who thought the bridge a little too grand for the 'apprentice river'. He suggested the city buy a bigger river or sell the bridge…

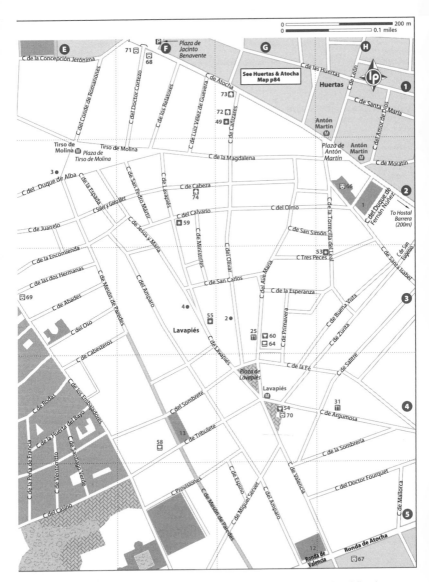

IGLESIA DE SAN ANDRÉS Map above

☎ 91 365 48 71; Plaza de San Andrés; ☻ 8am-
1pm & 6-8pm Mon-Sat, 8am-1pm Sun; Ⓜ La Latina
This proud church is more imposing than
beautiful and what you see today is the
result of restoration work completed after
the church was gutted during the civil war.

Stern, dark columns with gold-leaf
capitals against the rear wall lead your
eyes up into the dome, all rose, yellow and
green, and rich with sculpted floral
fantasies and cherubs poking out of every
nook and cranny.

Around the back, on the delightful Plaza de
la Paja (Straw Square), is the Capilla del Obispo, a
hugely important site on the historical map
of Madrid. It was here that San Isidro
Labrador, patron saint of Madrid, was first
buried. When the saint's body was discovered there in the late 13th century, two

centuries after his death, decomposition had not yet set in. Thus it was that King Alfonso XI ordered the construction in San Andrés of an ark to hold his remains and a chapel in which to venerate his memory. In 1669 (47 years after the saint was canonised) the last of many chapels was built on the site and that's what you see today.

Restoration of the chapel has been going on for years and it should – we say this with some scepticism – be open by the time you read this. If it is open, note the Gothic vaulting in the ceilings and the fine Renaissance reredos (screens), a combination that's quite rare in Madrid. But don't go looking for the saint's remains because San Isidro made his last move to the Basílica de Nuestra Señora del Buen Consejo in the 18th century.

Down the bottom (north side) of Plaza de la Paja, the walled 18th-century Jardín del Príncipe Anglona is a peaceful garden.

MADRID'S OLDEST STREET?

There are numerous candidates for the title of Madrid's oldest street. Calle del Arenal (Map pp62-3) stakes a strong claim, although the date when it ceased to be a small river and became a street remains unresolved by historical records. According to the historian Rafael Fraguas, the oldest street in Madrid is Calle de Grafal (Map pp76-7), which dates back to 1190 when it was called Calle del Santo Grial. But not that you'd notice: in the midst of La Latina's medieval streets, Calle de Grafal is not the barrio's prettiest thoroughfare, with largely modern brick apartment blocks. It runs southwest off Plaza de Segovia Nueva between Calle de Toledo and Calle de la Cava Baja.

MUSEO DE LOS ORÍGENES Map pp76-7

Casa de San Isidro; ☎ 91 366 74 15; www .munimadrid.es/museosanisidro, in Spanish; Plaza de San Andrés 2; admission free; ⏰ 9.30am-8pm Tue-Fri, 10am-2pm Sat & Sun Sep-Jul, 9.30am-2.30pm Tue-Sat Aug; Ⓜ La Latina

Next door to the Iglesia de San Andrés, this engaging museum sits on the spot where San Isidro Labrador is said to have ended his days around 1172. For an overview of Madrid's history, this place is hard to beat, with archaeological finds from the Roman period (including a 4th-century mosaic found on the site of a Roman villa in the barrio of Carabanchel), maps, scale models, paintings and photos of Madrid down through the ages. A particular highlight is the large model based on Pedro Teixera's famous 1656 map of Madrid. Of great historical interest (though not much to look at) is the 'miraculous well', where the saint called forth water to slake his master's thirst. In another miracle, the son of the saint's master fell into a well, whereupon Isidro prayed and prayed until the water rose and lifted his son to safety. The museum is housed in a largely new building with a 16th-century Renaissance courtyard and a 17th-century chapel. There were plans for major renovations so, until they finish, not all of the exhibits may be on show when you arrive.

IGLESIA DE SAN PEDRO EL VIEJO
Map pp76-7

☎ 91 365 12 84; Costanilla de San Pedro; Ⓜ La Latina
This fine old church is one of the few remaining windows on post-Muslim Madrid, most notably its clearly *mudéjar* brick bell tower, which dates from the 14th century. The church is generally closed to the public, but it's arguably more impressive from the outside (you'll probably have to take our word for it); the Renaissance doorway has stood since 1525. If you can peek inside, the nave dates from the 15th century, although the interior largely owes its appearance to 17th-century renovations. Along with the Iglesia de San Nicolás de los Servitas (p66), the Iglesia de San Pedro El Viejo is one of very few sites where traces of *mudéjar* Madrid remain *in situ*. Otherwise, you need to visit Toledo (p234), 70km south of Madrid, to visualise what Madrid once was like.

BASÍLICA DE NUESTRA SEÑORA DEL BUEN CONSEJO Map pp76-7

☎ 91 369 20 37; Calle de Toledo 37; ⊙ 8am-1pm & 6-9pm; Ⓜ Tirso de Molina or La Latina
Towering above the northern end of bustling Calle de Toledo, and visible through the arches from Plaza Mayor, this imposing church long served as the city's de facto cathedral until Catedral de Nuestra Señora de la Almudena was completed in 1992.

Still known to locals as the Catedral de San Isidro, the austere baroque basilica was founded in the 17th century as the headquarters for the Jesuits and is today home to the remains of the city's main patron saint, San Isidro (in the third chapel on your left after you walk in). His body, apparently remarkably well preserved, is only removed from here on rare occasions, such as in 1896 and 1947 when he was paraded about town in the hope he would bring rain (he did, at least in 1947). Official opening hours aren't always to be relied upon.

Next door, the Instituto de San Isidro once went by the name of Colegio Imperial and, from the 16th century on, was where many of the country's leading figures were schooled by the Jesuits. You can wander in and look at the elegant courtyard.

PLAZA DE LAVAPIÉS & AROUND
Map pp76-7

Ⓜ Lavapiés
The triangular Plaza de Lavapiés is one of the few open spaces in the barrio and it's a magnet for all that's good (a thriving cultural life) and bad (drugs and a high police presence) about the barrio. It's been cleaned up a little in recent years and the Teatro Valle-Inclán (p205), on the

southern edge of the plaza, is a stunning contemporary addition to the eclectic Lavapiés streetscape. To find out what makes this barrio tick, consider dropping in to the Asociación de Vecinos La Corrala (Map pp76-7; ☎ 91 467 05 09; www.avvlacorrala.org, in Spanish; Calle de Lavapiés 38; Ⓜ Lavapiés), the local neighbours association just up the hill from the plaza, where staff are happy to highlight all that's good about Lavapiés without dismissing its problems.

In the surrounding streets, one building that catches the community spirit of this lively barrio is La Corrala (Map pp76-7; cnr Calles de Mesón de Paredes & del Tribulete; Ⓜ Lavapiés), a partial example of an intriguing traditional (if much tidied up) tenement block, with long communal balconies built around a central courtyard; working-class Madrid was once strewn with buildings like this and very few survive. Almost opposite are the ruins (Map pp76-7; cnr Calles del Sombrete & de Mesón de Paredes; Ⓜ Lavapiés) of an old church, now converted into a library and the stunning Gaudeamus Café (p181).

LA CASA ENCENDIDA Map pp76-7

☎ 902 430 322; www.lacasaencendida.com; Ronda de Valencia 2; ⏲ 10am-10pm; Ⓜ Embajadores
This cultural centre is utterly unpredictable, if only because of the quantity and scope of its activities – everything from exhibitions, cinema sessions to workshops and more. The focus is often on international artists or environmental themes and, if it has an overarching theme, it's the alternative slant it takes on the world.

TAPAS IN MEDIEVAL MADRID
Walking Tour
1 Basílica de Nuestra Señora del Buen Consejo
If it's not Sunday and time for El Rastro (p74), begin at what once served as Madrid's interim cathedral and last resting place of the city's patron saint. At once austere and gilded in gold leaf, this imposing basilica (p79) has much greater resonance for most madrileños than the cathedral that replaced it.

2 Calle de la Cava Baja
Head across Plaza de Segovia Nueva and turn left into Calle de la Cava Baja, a winding medieval street along the site of Madrid's old city walls. This is Madrid's tapas central, with wonderful bars like Txacolina (p155), Casa Lucas (p154) and the extravagantly tiled La Chata (p154).

3 Juana La Loca
You haven't come very far, but walking La Latina means regular tapas pit stops. Purple-clad Juana La Loca (p154), just off the southwestern end of Calle de la Cava Baja, is the place for what's possibly Madrid's best *tortilla de patatas* (Spanish potato omelette) and fine wines.

4 Basílica de San Francisco El Grande
All the way down the bottom of Carrera de San Francisco, this formidable basilica (p74) looms over southwestern Madrid. Inside, note the extraordinary dome and Goya fresco and consider how far this patch of land has come since St Francis of Assisi passed through in the 13th century.

5 Las Vistillas
Calle de Bailén runs north to Las Vistillas (p75), with its sweeping views out over Madrid's sprawl, and the viaduct from where there are even better views back towards the spires and terracotta roofs of Los Austrias. You're now looking at the *morería* (Moorish quarter) from medieval times, and it's here that you're headed.

6 Plaza de la Paja
Take Calle de la Morería as far as Calle de Segovia, then climb back up to Plaza de la Paja (p77), which is unlike any other Madrid square. Feeling for all the world like you've stumbled

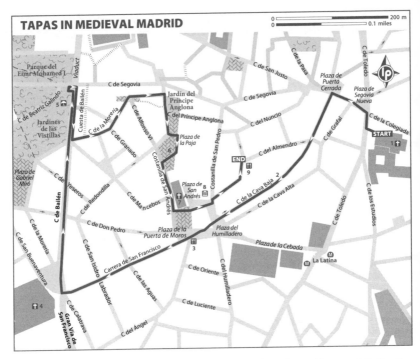

TAPAS IN MEDIEVAL MADRID

WALK FACTS

Start Basílica de Nuestra Señora del Buen Consejo
End Almendro 13
Distance 2.5km
Time Three to four hours

upon a *plaza del pueblo* (village square) in the heart of the city, Plaza de la Paja is one of our favourite corners of medieval Madrid.

7 Iglesia de San Andrés

Overlooking the plaza (although entry is from the southern side), this imposing church (p77) is glorious when floodlit at night and filled with baroque flourishes within, especially the altar and the sculpted columns.

8 Museo de los Orígenes

Time for a history lesson. Along the Plaza de San Andrés, this fine museum (p78) takes you on a journey through Madrid's history with maps, old photos and memorabilia from San Isidro.

9 Almendro 13

Rest your weary legs perched atop one of the wooden stools at Almendro 13 (p155) and cast a lingering look over the extensive menu. And hold on to your seat – this is among the most celebrated tapas bars in Madrid and tables are at a premium.

Drinking & Nightlife p184; Eating p155; Shopping p134; Sleeping p224

The noise of Huertas' nights rolls out across the city like the clamour of a not-so-distant war. If Huertas is known for anything, it's for nightlife that never seems to abate once the sun goes down. Such fame is well deserved, but there's so much more to the barrio than immediately meets the eye. At once cultural and casual, Huertas and, to a lesser extent, Atocha draw a diverse crowd that ranges from those hell-bent on having a good time to aesthetes who love the intimacy and choice that the barrio has to offer.

By day the superb Plaza de Santa Ana, with its outdoor tables, is one of Madrid's most agreeable squares. The Barrio de las Letras (Neighbourhood of Letters), a sub-barrio of Huertas that tumbles down the hill in a tight labyrinth of lanes, has landmarks dedicated to Cervantes and the esteemed 17th-century playwright Lope de Vega. At the foot of the hill, the atmosphere shifts from a culture of excess to high culture in the Centro de Arte Reina Sofía, one of the finest contemporary art galleries in Europe, home to works by Dalí and Miró, as well as Picasso's *Guernica;* while the Antigua Estación de Atocha is as much a landmark for architecture buffs as for train travellers. And littered throughout the barrio are fine restaurants, terrific bars and live music venues and offbeat shops.

top picks

SIGHTS IN HUERTAS & ATOCHA

- Centro de Arte Reina Sofía (left)
- Plaza de Santa Ana (p86)
- Antigua Estación de Atocha (opposite)
- Casa de Lope de Vega (p86)

CENTRO DE ARTE REINA SOFÍA

Map pp84–5

☎ 91 774 10 00; www.museoreinasofia.es; Calle de Santa Isabel 52; adult/student, child under 18yr & senior over 65yr €6/free, free Sun, 7-9pm Mon & Wed-Fri, 2.30-9pm Sat, headset guide adult/student €4/3; ☺ 10am-9pm Mon & Wed-Sat, 10am-2.30pm Sun; Ⓜ Atocha

Home to Picasso's *Guernica,* arguably Spain's single most famous artwork, and a host of other important Spanish artworks, the Centro de Arte Reina Sofía is Madrid's premier collection of contemporary art. In addition to plenty of paintings by Picasso, other major drawcards are works by Salvador Dalí (1904–89) and Joan Miró (1893–1983).

The collection principally spans the 20th century up to the 1980s (for more recent works, visit the Museo Municipal de Arte Contemporáneo, p107). The occasional non-Spaniard artist makes an appearance (including Francis Bacon's 1966 *Lying Figure*), but most of the collection is strictly peninsular.

The permanent collection is displayed on the 2nd and 4th floors of the main wing of the museum, the Edificio Sabatini. *Guernica's* location never changes – you'll find it in room 206 on the 2nd floor. Beyond that, the location of specific paintings can be a little confusing. After a period of grouping together works by the same artist, the museum has moved towards a more theme-based approach, which ensures that you may find works by Picasso or Miró, for example, spread across the two floors. A dynamic program of

ORIENTATION & TRANSPORT: HUERTAS & ATOCHA

The Huertas area owes its name to the mostly traffic-free Calle de las Huertas, which starts just southwest of Plaza de Santa Ana and runs through the heart of the barrio all the way down to the Paseo del Prado. The Calle del Prado also cuts a swathe through the neighbourhood. Huertas is bounded to the south by Calle de Atocha, which ends at the thundering roundabout of Plaza del Emperador Carlos V, which marks the beginning of Atocha, while Calle de Alcalá (north), Paseo del Prado (east) and Calle de Carretas (west) complete the Huertas perimeter.

The major metro stations for Huertas and Atocha all lie around the outside of the barrio, namely Sol (lines 1, 2 and 3), Sevilla (line 2) and Antón Martín (line 1). Atocha station (line 1) and, to a lesser extent, Banco de España (line 2) are useful if your business lies down the hill.

temporary exhibitions also ensures that the location of numerous paintings changes on a semi-regular basis. The only solution if you're looking for something specific is to pick up a copy of the *Planos de Museo* (Museum Floorplans) from the information desk just inside the main entrance; it lists the rooms in which each artist appears. As a companion to your visit, we also recommend the museum's *Guide to the Collection* (€22), which is available from the gift shop at the entrance and which takes a closer look at 80 of the museum's signature works.

In addition to Picasso's *Guernica* (see the boxed text, p86), which is worth the admission fee on its own, don't neglect the artist's preparatory sketches in the rooms surrounding room 206; they offer an intriguing insight into the development of this seminal work. If Picasso's cubist style has captured your imagination, the work of the Madrid-born Juan Gris (1887–1927) or Georges Braque (1882–1963) may appeal.

The work of Joan Miró (1893–1983) is defined by often delightfully bright primary colours, but watch out also for a handful of his equally odd sculptures. Since his paintings became a symbol of the Barcelona Olympics in 1992, his work has begun to receive the international acclaim it so richly deserves and the museum is a fine place to get a representative sample of his innovative work.

The Reina Sofía is also home to 20 or so canvases by Salvador Dalí, of which the most famous is perhaps the surrealist extravaganza that is *El Gran Masturbador* (1929). Among his other works is a strange bust of a certain *Joelle* done by Dalí and his friend Man Ray (1890–1976). Another well-known surrealist painter, Max Ernst (1891–1976), is also worth tracking down.

If you can tear yourself away from the big names, the Reina Sofía offers a terrific opportunity to learn more about sometimes lesser-known 20th-century Spanish artists. Among these are Miquel Barceló (b 1957); madrileño artist José Gutiérrez Solana (1886–1945); the renowned Basque painter Ignazio Zuloaga (1870–1945); Benjamin Palencia (1894–1980), whose paintings capture the turbulence of Spain in the 1930s; Barcelona painter Antoni Tàpies (b 1923); the pop art of Eduardo Arroyo (b 1937); and abstract painters such as Eusebio Sempere (1923–85) and members of the Equipo 57 group (founded in 1957 by

top picks

ARTWORKS IN THE CENTRO DE ARTE REINA SOFÍA

- Guernica (Pablo Picasso; 1937)
- Naturaleza Muerta (Pablo Picasso; 1912)
- El Gran Masturbador (Salvador Dalí; 1929)
- Muchacha en la Ventana (Salvador Dalí; 1925)
- Monumento Imperial a la Mujer Niña (Salvador Dalí; 1929)
- Pastorale (Joan Miró; 1923–24)
- Danseuse Espagnole (Joan Miró; 1928)
- L'Atelier aux Sculptures (Miquel Barceló; 1993)
- Los Cuatro Dictadores (Eduardo Arroyo; 1963)
- Retrato de Josette (Juan Gris; 1916)
- Cartes et Dés (Georges Braque; 1914)
- El Peine del Viento I (Eduardo Chillida; 1962)
- Homenaje a Mallarmé (Jorge Oteiza; 1958)
- Pintura (Antoni Tàpies; 1955)
- Otoños (Pablo Palazuelo; 1952)

a group of Spanish artists in exile in Paris), such as Pablo Palazuelo (1916–2007). Better-known as a poet and playwright, Federico García Lorca (1898–1936) is represented by a number of his sketches.

Of the sculptors, watch in particular for Pablo Gargallo (1881–1934), whose work in bronze includes a bust of Picasso, and the renowned Basque sculptors Jorge Oteiza (1908–2003) and Eduardo Chillida (1924–2002); Chillida's works are expected to move to the peaceful courtyard, there to remain in perpetuity.

Beyond its artwork, the Reina Sofía is also an important architectural landmark. Adapted from the shell of an 18th-century hospital with eye-catching external glass lifts, the Reina Sofía is a fine example of converting old-world architecture to meet the needs of a dynamic modern collection. This is especially the case in the stunning extension (the Edificio Nouvel) that spreads along the western tip of the Plaza del Emperador Carlos V and hosts temporary exhibitions, auditoriums, the bookshop, a cafe and the museum's library.

ANTIGUA ESTACIÓN DE ATOCHA
Map pp84-5

Plaza del Emperador Carlos V; Ⓜ Atocha Renfe
In 1992 the northwestern wing of the Antigua Estación de Atocha (Old Atocha

HUERTAS & ATOCHA

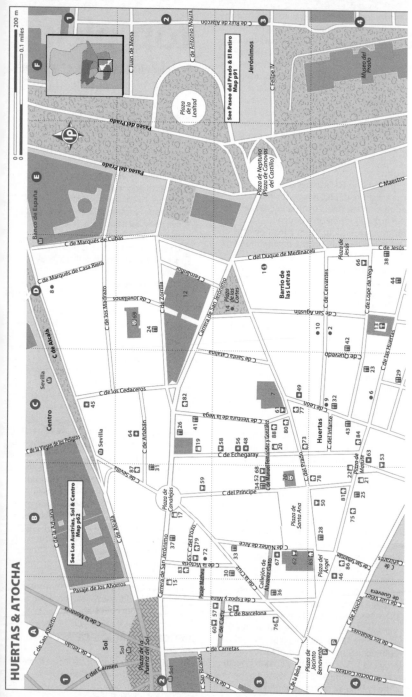

See Los Austrias, Sol & Centro Map p62

See Paseo del Prado & El Retiro Map p91

0   200 m
0   0.1 miles

Sol

Centro

Sevilla

Banco de España

Museo del Prado

Jerónimos

Barrio de las Letras

Huertas

Plaza de la Puerta del Sol

Plaza de Canalejas

Plaza de Santa Ana

Plaza del Ángel

Plaza de Jacinto Benavente

Plaza de la Lealtad

Plaza de Neptuno (Plaza de Cánovas del Castillo)

Plaza de las Cortes

Plaza de San Jerónimo

Plaza de Jesús

Plaza de Matute

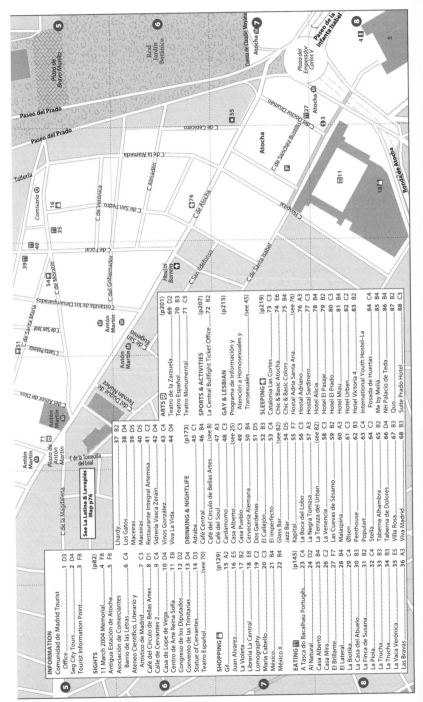

85

INFORMATION
Comunidad de Madrid Tourist
  Office 1 D3
Seg City Tours 2 D4
Tourist Information Point 3 F8

SIGHTS (p82)
11 March 2004 Memorial 4 F8
Antigua Estación de Atocha 5 F8
Asociación de Comerciantes
  Barrio de las Letras 6 C4
Ateneo Científico, Literario y
  Artístico de Madrid 7 C3
Café del Círculo de Bellas Artes .. 8 D1
Calle de Cervantes 2 .... 9 C4
Casa de Lope de Vega 10 D4
Centro de Arte Reina Sofía 11 E8
Congreso de los Diputados 12 D2
Convento de las Trinitarias 13 D4
Statue of Cervantes 14 D3
Teatro Español .... (see 70)

SHOPPING (p129)
Gil 15 A2
Juan Alvarez 16 E5
La Violeta 17 B2
Librería La Central 18 E8
Lomography 19 C2
María Cabello 20 C3
México 21 B4
México II 22 B4

EATING (p145)
A Tasca do Bacalhau Portugês .. 23 C4
Al Natural 24 D2
Casa Alberto 25 B4
Casa Mira 26 C2
El Brillante 27 F7
El Lateral 28 B4
La Biotika 29 C4
La Casa del Abuelo 30 B3
La Finca de Susana 31 B2
La Piola 32 C4
La Trucha 33 B3
La Trucha 34 B3
La Vaca Verónica 35 E5
Las Bravas 36 A3

Lhardy 37 B2
Los Gatos 38 D4
Maceiras 39 D5
Maceiras 40 D5
Restaurante Integral Artemisa .. 41 C2
Sidrería Vasca Zerain 42 D4
Vinos González 43 C4
Viva La Vida 44 D4

DRINKING & NIGHTLIFE (p173)
Adraba 45 C1
Café Central 46 B4
Café del Círculo de Bellas Artes .. (see 8)
Café del Soul 47 A3
Cardamomo 48 C3
Casa Alberto .... (see 25)
Casa Pueblo 49 C3
Cervecería Alemana 50 B4
Dos Gardenias 51 D5
El Callejón 52 B3
El Imperfecto 53 C4
Glass Bar .... (see 82)
Jazz Bar 54 D5
Kapital 55 F7
La Boca del Lobo 56 C3
La Negra Tomasa 57 A3
La Terraza del Urban .... (see 82)
La Venencia 58 C3
Las Cuevas de Sésamo 59 B2
Malaspina 60 A3
Ølsen 61 C4
Penthouse 62 B3
Populart 63 B4
Stella 64 C2
Taberna Alhambra 65 B3
Taberna de Dolores 66 D4
Villa Rosa 67 B3
Viva Madrid 68 B3

ARTS (p201)
Teatro de la Zarzuela 69 D2
Teatro Español 70 B3
Teatro Monumental 71 C5

SPORTS & ACTIVITIES (p207)
La Central Bullfight Ticket Office .. 72 B2

GAY & LESBIAN (p215)
Programa de Información y
  Atención a Homosexuales y
  Transexuales .... (see 45)

SLEEPING (p219)
Catalonia Las Cortes 73 C3
Chic & Basic Atocha 74 E6
Chic & Basic Colors 75 B4
Hostal Adria Santa Ana ..... (see 76)
Hostal Adriano 76 A3
Hostal Sardinero 77 C3
Hotel Alicia 78 B4
Hotel El Pasaje 79 B2
Hotel El Prado 80 C3
Hotel Miau 81 B4
Hotel Urban 82 C2
Hotel Victoria 4 .... 83 B2
International Youth Hostel–La
  Posada de Huertas 84 C4
Me by Meliá 85 B4
NH Palacio de Tepa 86 B4
Quo 87 B3
Suite Prado Hotel 88 C3

See La Latina & Lavapiés
Map p76

GUERNICA

Guernica is one of the most famous paintings in the world, a signature work of cubism whose disfiguration of the human form would become an eloquent symbol of a world's outrage at the horrors wrought upon the innocent by modern warfare.

After the Spanish Civil War broke out in 1936, Picasso was commissioned by the Republican government of Madrid to do the painting for the Paris Exposition Universelle in 1937. As news filtered out about the bombing of Gernika (Guernica) in the Basque Country by Hitler's Legión Condor, at the request of Franco, on 26 April 1937 (almost 2000 people died in the attack and much of the town was destroyed), Picasso committed his anger to canvas. To understand the painting's earth-shattering impact at the time, it must be remembered that the attack on Guernica represented the first use of airborne military hardware to devastating effect.

Guernica has always been a controversial work and was initially derided by many as being more propaganda than art. The 3.5m by 7.8m painting subsequently migrated to the USA and only returned to Spain in 1981, in keeping with Picasso's wish that the painting return to Spanish shores (first to Picasso's preferred choice, the Museo del Prado, then to its current home) once democracy had been restored. The Basques believe that its true home is in the Basque Country and calls to have it moved there continue unabated. Such a move is, however, unlikely to happen anytime soon with the Reina Sofía arguing that the painting is too fragile to be moved again.

train station) was given a stunning overhaul. The structure of this grand iron-and-glass relic from the 19th century was preserved, while its interior was artfully converted into a light-filled tropical garden with more than 500 plant species (and a resident turtle population), in addition to shops, cafes and the Renfe train information offices. The project was the work of architect Rafael Moneo, the man behind the Museo del Prado extension and the Thyssen–Bornemisza Museum, and his landmark achievement was to create a thoroughly modern space that resonates with the stately European train stations of another age.

In the modern northeastern corner of the station, the 11 March 2004 Memorial (Map pp84-5; admission free; 🕙 10am-2pm & 5-8pm daily Apr-Feb, 10am-8pm March; Ⓜ Atocha Renfe) is a moving monument to the victims of the 2004 terrorist attack at the station. Although partially visible from the Paseo de la Infanta Isabel, the memorial is best viewed from below. A glass panel shows the names of those killed, while the airy glass-and-perspex dome is inscribed with the messages of condolence and solidarity left by well-wishers in a number of languages in the immediate aftermath of the attack. The 12m-high dome is designed so that the sun highlights different messages at different times of the day, while the effect at night is akin to flickering candles.

PLAZA DE SANTA ANA Map pp84-5
Ⓜ Sevilla, Sol or Antón Martín

The Plaza de Santa Ana is a delightful confluence of elegant architecture and irresistible energy. Situated in the heart of Huertas, it was laid out in 1810 during the controversial reign of Joseph Bonaparte (see p27), giving breathing space to what had hitherto been one of Madrid's most claustrophobic barrios. The plaza quickly became a focal point for the intellectual life of the day, and the cafes surrounding the plaza thronged with writers, poets and artists engaging in endless *tertulias* (literary and philosophical discussions). Echoes of this literary history survive in the statues of the 17th-century writer Calderón de la Barca and Federíco García Lorca (added in 1998 on the 100th anniversary of his birth), and in the Teatro Español (formerly the Teatro del Príncipe) at the plaza's eastern end, and continue down into the Barrio de las Letras (see the boxed text, opposite). Apart from anything else, the plaza is the starting point for many a long Huertas night.

CASA DE LOPE DE VEGA Map pp84-5
☎ 91 429 92 16; Calle de Cervantes 11; admission free; 🕙 guided visits every 30 min 10am-2pm Tue-Sat; Ⓜ Antón Martín

Lope de Vega (see p44) may be little known outside the Spanish-speaking world, but he was one of the greatest playwrights ever to write in Spanish, not to mention one of Madrid's favourite and most colourful literary sons. What Real Madrid's footballers are to Madrid's celebrity rumour mill now, Lope de Vega was to Madrid society in the 17th century. Scandalously, he shared the house, where he lived and wrote for 25 years until his death in 1635, with a mistress and four children by three different women; Lope de Vega's house was a typical *casa de malicia* (house of ill repute). Today the house, which was restored in the 1950s, is filled with memorabilia related to his life and times. Out the back is a tranquil garden, a rare haven of birdsong in this somewhat claustrophobic district.

ATENEO CIENTÍFICO, LITERARIO Y ARTÍSTICO DE MADRID Map pp84–5

☎ 91 429 17 50; www.ateneodemadrid.com, in Spanish; Calle del Prado 21; Ⓜ Sevilla

Nestled away in the heart of the Barrio de las Letras, this venerable club of learned types was founded in 1821, although the building took on its present form in 1884. Its library and meetings of the great minds prompted Benito Pérez Galdós (see p37) to describe it as the most important 'intellectual temple' in Madrid and a reference point for the thriving cultural life of the Barrio de las Letras. It's not generally open to the public, although guided visits (admission €2; Ⓨ 10am–1pm Mon-Fri) for groups of 10 or more can be arranged with a prior appointment. Otherwise, no one seems to mind if you wander into the foyer, which is lined with portraits of terribly serious-looking fellows. They may even let you amble upstairs to the library, a jewel of another age, with dark timber stacks, weighty tomes and creakily quiet reading rooms dimly lit with desk lamps.

CONGRESO DE LOS DIPUTADOS

Map pp84–5

☎ 91 390 65 25; www.congreso.es, in Spanish; Plaza de las Cortes; admission free; Ⓨ guided tours 10.30am–12.30pm Sat; Ⓜ Sevilla

Spain's lower house of parliament was originally a Renaissance building, but it was completely revamped in 1850 and given a facade with a neoclassical portal. Before becoming the official seat of Spain's parliament, the building was home to a church, the Iglesia de Espíritu Santo. The imposing lions watching over the entrance were smelted from cannons used in Spain's African wars during the mid-19th century. On the day that they were mounted outside the parliament building, one irreverent Madrid newspaper wrote 'And what mouths they have! One might imagine them to be parliamentarians!' The modern extension tacked onto the building seems a rather odd afterthought. It was here, on 11 February 1981, that renegade members of Spain's Guardia Civil launched a failed coup attempt (see p31). Be sure to bring your passport if you want to visit.

CÍRCULO DE BELLAS ARTES Map pp84–5

☎ 91 360 54 00; www.circulobellasartes.com; Calle de Alcalá 42; admission €1; Ⓜ Banco de España

The 'Fine Arts Circle' has just about every kind of artistic expression on show, including exhibitions, concerts, short films and book readings. Every year in late April, the entire story of *Don Quijote* is read out

BARRIO DE LAS LETRAS

In medieval Madrid, the Barrio de las Letras – which is now bordered by Plaza de Santa Ana (west), Carrera de San Jerónimo (north), Paseo del Prado (east) and Calle de Atocha (south) – was one of Madrid's most important cultural hubs.

At Calle de Cervantes 11, Lope de Vega (1562–1635), arguably Spain's premier playwright, lived and died, and his house is now a museum (see opposite). But the street on which Lope de Vega's house sits owes its name to an even-more-famous former resident, Miguel de Cervantes Saavedra (1547–1616). Cervantes, the author of *Don Quijote*, spent much of his adult life in Madrid and lived and died at Calle de Cervantes 2; a plaque (dating from 1834) sits above the door. Sadly, the original building was torn down in the early 19th century despite a plea from King Fernando VII. When Cervantes died, his body was interred around the corner at the Convento de las Trinitarias (Calle de Lope de Vega 16), which is marked by another plaque. Still home to cloistered nuns, the convent is closed to the public, which saves the authorities embarrassment: no one really knows where in the convent the bones of Cervantes lie. A statue of Cervantes stands in the Plaza de las Cortes, or at least it should do once a major overhaul of the square been completed.

To gain a deeper insight into the Barrio de las Letras, consider taking the Wednesday 'Artes y Oficios del Barrio de las Letras' guided tour run by the tourist office as part of the Descubre Madrid program (see p262). Alternatively, stop by the office of the Asociación de Comerciantes Barrio de las Letras (Map pp84–5; ☎ 91 389 63 37; www.barrioletras .es, in Spanish; Calle de las Huertas 39; Ⓨ 9.30am–2.30pm & 4.30-6.30pm Mon-Fri; Ⓜ Antón Martín), the local small-business association, which has some useful information.

loud, often by famous Spanish figures, over two or three days in the Sala de Columnas. Overall, it's an elegant space with a program that's anything but staid, allowing it to remain at the forefront of Madrid's cultural life. There's also a fine cafe (p184).

KILLING THE NIGHT
Walking Tour
1 Plaza de Santa Ana
There are more beautiful squares in Madrid, but none more filled with life, making Plaza de Santa Ana (p86) the perfect place to begin your walking tour. To gather your energy, take up residence in a *terraza* and watch the passing parade, all the while nursing a glass of La Rioja.

2 Café Central
Across Plaza de Santa Ana and then into Plaza del Ángel takes you to the art-deco Café Central (p186), one of Europe's most celebrated venues for live jazz.

3 Casa Alberto
Just off the southeast corner of the plaza, along the iconic nightlife street of Calle de las Huertas, Casa Alberto (p156) is a classic Madrid tapas bar, laden with history and a menu even more laden with tempting choices.

4 Maceiras
Now that you're getting the hang of Huertas nights, amble all the way down Calle de las Huertas to Maceiras (p156), for the fresh tastes of Spain's northern Atlantic coast. Order what you will, but we'd be going for the *pulpo a la gallega* (octopus cooked in the Galician style, served with paprika, potatoes and rock salt).

5 Taberna de Dolores
With your stomach suitably fortified, head just around the corner to the Plaza de Jesús. There, Taberna de Dolores (p185) draws a quintessentially Madrid crowd of celebrities and casual locals drawn by the fine wines on offer.

WALK FACTS
Start Plaza de Santa Ana
End Villa Rosa
Distance 1.5km
Time All night

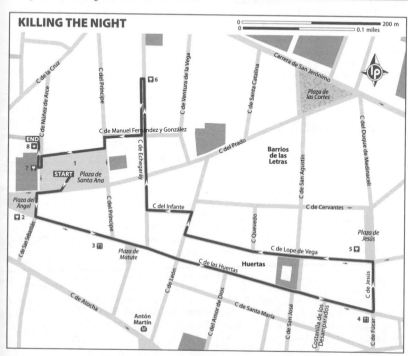

KILLING THE NIGHT

6 La Venencia

Climb up the hill along Calle de Lope de Vega, which runs through the heart of the Barrio de las Letras, then wind your way to Calle de Echegaray, home to La Venencia (p186). This is Madrid's most authentic bar for *fino* (sherry) straight from the barrel and it's a quiet place offering respite from Huertas' clamour.

7 The Penthouse

Looking down over Plaza de Santa Ana, and frequented by a groovy, upmarket crowd, The Penthouse (p185) oozes style, quite apart from letting you look out over Madrid from a whole new perspective.

8 Villa Rosa

The night is nearly at an end and, if you're like us, you just want something you can dance to without being too heavy on the ear at a place that's not too strict at the door. Villa Rosa (p188) is just such a place, with tunes you can sing along to with like-minded and similarly worse-for-wear patrons.

Eating p158; Shopping p135; Sleeping p226

From the Plaza de la Cibeles in the north, the buildings arrayed along the Paseo del Prado read like a roll-call of Madrid's most popular attractions. Temples to high culture include the Museo del Prado and Museo Thyssen-Bornemisza, which rank among the world's most prestigious art galleries, while the Caixa Forum is both architecturally stunning and home to cutting-edge contemporary exhibitions. Oases of greenery, such as the Real Jardín Botánico and, up the hill to the east, the marvellous Parque del Buen Retiro, only add to the appeal and make this one of the most attractive areas of Madrid in which to spend your time.

The Paseo del Prado – which becomes the Paseo de los Recoletos and then the Paseo de la Castellana further north – cuts through the heart of modern Madrid and is one of Europe's grandest boulevards. In Madrid's early days, the *paseo* was a stream that marked the city's eastern extremity and the surrounding *prado* (field) was the preserve of gardens and palaces that were green playgrounds for Madrid's swollen nobility. Even today, many of the trees that survive in the beautiful central pedestrian area were planted in the 18th century during the reign of King Carlos III.

top picks

SIGHTS IN PASEO DEL PRADO & EL RETIRO

- Museo del Prado (left)
- Museo Thyssen-Bornemisza (p94)
- Parque del Buen Retiro (p97)
- Plaza de la Cibeles (p96)
- Caixa Forum (p95)

MUSEO DEL PRADO Map opposite

☎ 91 330 28 00; www.museodelprado.es; Paseo del Prado; adult/student/child under 18yr & EU senior over 65yr €8/4/free, free 6-8pm Tue-Sat & 5-8pm Sun, headset guide €3.50; ☽ 9am-8pm Tue-Sun; Ⓜ Banco de España

Welcome to one of the premier art galleries anywhere in the world. The more than 7000 paintings held in the Museo del Prado's collection (although only around 1500 are currently on display) are like a window onto the historical vagaries of the Spanish soul, at once grand and imperious in the royal paintings of Velázquez, darkly tumultuous in *Las Pinturas Negras* (Black Paintings) of Goya and outward looking with sophisticated works of art from all across Europe. Spend as long as you can at the Prado or, better still, plan to make a couple of visits because it can be a little overwhelming if you try to absorb it all at once. Either way, it's an artistic feast of rare power.

Entrance to the Prado is via the eastern Puerta de los Jerónimos or northern Puerta de Goya. Either way tickets must first be purchased from the ticket office at the northern end of the building, opposite the Hotel Ritz and beneath the Puerta de Goya. One final thing before we get started on the collection: the Prado's curators are, until 2012, in the process of reorganising the collection and some room numbers are subject to change. The only sure way to find what you're looking for is to pick up the free 'Plan' from the ticket office or information desk just inside the entrance – it lists the location of 50 of the Prado's most famous works and gives current room numbers for all major artists. For more information on many of the artists covered in the Prado, turn to p38.

The masterpieces by Goya and Velázquez are the Prado's standout highlights and, although there's so much else to enjoy in

ORIENTATION & TRANSPORT: PASEO DEL PRADO & EL RETIRO

The Paseo del Prado runs north–south from Plaza de la Cibeles to Plaza del Emperador Carlos V. Huertas rises up to the west, while atop the hill to the east is the Parque del Buen Retiro, which can be reached by any of the streets running east from the *paseo*.

The only metro stations are those at either end of the Paseo del Prado – Banco de España (line 2) on Plaza de la Cibeles to the north, and Atocha (line 1) to the south. For the Parque del Buen Retiro, the best station is Retiro (line 2), but Príncipe de Vergara (lines 2 and 9) and Ibiza (line 9) also leave you on the eastern perimeter of the park.

PASEO DEL PRADO & EL RETIRO

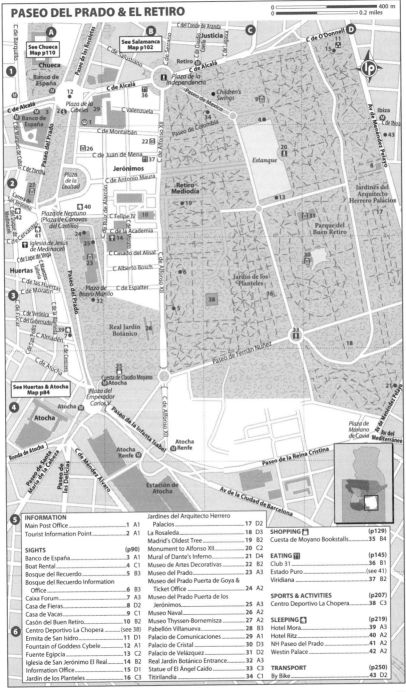

this extraordinarily rich collection, these two artists are a good place to start.

Francisco José de Goya y Lucientes (Goya; see the boxed text, p39) is found on all three floors of the Prado, but we recommend starting at the southern end of the ground or lower level. In rooms 64 and 65, Goya's *El Dos de Mayo* and *El Tres de Mayo* rank among Madrid's most emblematic paintings; they bring to life the 1808 anti-French revolt and subsequent execution of insurgents in Madrid. Alongside, in rooms 66 and 67, are some of his darkest and most disturbing works, *Las Pinturas Negras* (Black Paintings); they are so called in part because of the dark browns and black that dominate, but more for the distorted animalesque appearance of their characters. The *Saturno Devorando a Su Hijo* (Saturn Devouring His Son) captures the essence of Goya's genius. *La Romería de San Isidro* and *El Akelarre* (El Gran Cabrón) are profoundly unsettling. The former evokes a writhing mass of tortured humanity, while the latter is dominated by the compelling individual faces of the condemned souls of Goya's creation. An interesting footnote to *Las Pinturas Negras* is *El Coloso,* a Goyaesque work that was long considered part of the master's portfolio until the Prado's experts decided otherwise in 2008. The painting and its story are found adjacent to the Black Paintings.

On the 1st floor, there are more Goyas in rooms 32 and 34 to 38. Among them, in room 36, two more of Goya's best-known and most intriguing oils: *La Maja Vestida* and *La Maja Desnuda*. These portraits of an unknown woman, commonly believed to be the Duquesa de Alba (who may have been Goya's lover), are identical save for the lack of clothing in the latter. There are further Goyas, including *The Parasol* in room 85, on the top floor.

Diego Rodriguez de Silva y Velázquez (Velázquez; see p38) is another of the grand masters of Spanish art who brings so much distinction to the Prado. Of all his works, *Las Meninas* is what most people come to see. Completed in 1656, it is more properly known as *La Família de Felipe IV* (The Family of Felipe IV). It depicts Velázquez himself on the left and, in the centre, the infant Margarita. There's more to it than that: the artist in fact portrays himself painting the king and queen, whose images appear, according to some experts, in mirrors

top picks

PAINTINGS IN THE MUSEO DEL PRADO

- Las Meninas (Velázquez)
- La Rendición de Breda (Velázquez)
- La Maja Desnuda & La Maja Vestida (Goya)
- El Tres de Mayo (Goya)
- Las Pinturas Negras (Black Paintings; Goya)
- The Garden of Earthly Delights (El Jardín de las Delicias; Hieronymus Bosch)
- Adam & Eve (Adán y Eva; Dürer)
- El Lavatorio (Tintoretto)
- La Trinidad (El Greco)
- David Vencedor de Goliath (Caravaggio)
- El Sueño de Jacob (Ribera)
- The Three Graces (Las Tres Gracias; Rubens)
- Artemisa (Rembrandt)

behind Velázquez. His mastery of light and colour is never more apparent than here. An interesting detail of the painting, aside from the extraordinary cheek of painting himself in royal company, is the presence of the cross of the Order of Santiago on his vest. The artist was apparently obsessed with being given a noble title. He got it shortly before his death, but in this oil painting he has awarded himself the order years before it would in fact be his!

The rooms surrounding *Las Meninas* (most likely rooms 14, 15, 16 and 18) contain more fine works by Velázquez. Watch in particular for his paintings of various members of royalty who seem to spring off the canvas – Felipe II, Felipe IV, Margarita de Austria (a younger version of whom features in *Las Meninas*), El Príncipe Baltasar Carlos and Isabel de Francia – on horseback. But you could pick any work of Velázquez and not be disappointed.

Having experienced the essence of the Prado, you're now free to select from the astonishingly diverse works that remain. If Spanish painters have piqued your curiosity, Bartolomé Esteban Murillo, José de Ribera and the stark figures of Francisco de Zurbarán should be on your itinerary. The vivid, almost surreal works by the 16th-century master and adopted Spaniard El Greco (see the boxed text, p237), whose figures are characteristically slender and tortured, are also perfectly executed.

Another alternative is the Prado's outstanding collection of Flemish art. The fulsome figures and bulbous cherubs of Peter Paul Rubens (1577–1640) provide a playful antidote to the darkness of many of the other Flemish artists. His signature works are *Las Tres Gracias* (The Three Graces) and *Adoración de los Reyes Magos*. Other fine works in the vicinity include *The Triumph of Death* by Pieter Bruegel, Rembrandt's *Artemisa,* and those by Anton Van Dyck.

And on no account miss the weird-and-wonderful *The Garden of Earthly Delights* by Hieronymus Bosch (c 1450–1516). No one has yet been able to provide a definitive explanation for this hallucinatory work, although many have tried. While it is, without doubt, the star attraction of this fantastical painter's collection, all his work rewards inspection, especially the *Table of the Seven Deadly Sins*. The closer you look, the harder it is to escape the feeling that he must have been doing some extraordinary drugs.

And then there are the paintings by Dürer, Rafael, Tiziano (Titian), Tintoretto, Sorolla, Gainsborough, Fra Angelico, Tiepolo…

As you wander from room to room, it's worth pausing to admire the architectural masterpiece that is the building in which the Prado resides. The western wing (Edificio Villanueva) was completed in 1785, as the neoclassical Palacio de Villanueva. Originally conceived as a house of science, it later served, somewhat ignominiously, as a cavalry barracks for Napoleon's troops during their occupation of Madrid between 1808 and 1813. In 1814 King Fernando VII decided to use the palace as a museum, although his purpose was more about finding a way of storing the hundreds of royal paintings gathering dust than any high-minded civic ideals – his was an era where art was a royal preserve. Five years later the Museo del Prado opened with 311 Spanish paintings on display.

In contrast, the eastern wing (Edificio Jerónimos) is part of the Prado's stunning modern extension, which opened in 2007. Dedicated to temporary exhibitions (usually to display Prado masterpieces held in storage for decades for lack of wall space), and home to the excellent book shop and cafe, its main attraction is the 2nd-floor cloisters. Built in 1672 with local granite, the cloisters were until recently attached to the adjacent Iglesia de San Jerónimo El Real (below), but were in a parlous state. As part of their controversial incorporation into the Prado, they were painstakingly dismantled, restored and reassembled. They're a stunning way to end (or begin) your Prado visit – look in particular for the royal coats of arms on the four compass points, while the Italianate bronze and marble sculptures date back to the 16th century. For more information on the extension, see p49.

IGLESIA DE SAN JERÓNIMO EL REAL
Map p91 ☎ 91 420 35 78; Calle de Ruiz de Alarcón; admission free; ☷ 10am-1pm & 5-8.30pm Mon-Sat Oct-Jun, hours vary Jul-Sep; Ⓜ Atocha or Banco de España
Tucked away behind the Museo del Prado, this chapel was traditionally favoured by the Spanish royal family,

MUSEUM DISCOUNTS & CLOSING TIMES
For a list of museums (including the Museo del Prado and Centro de Arte Reina Sofía) offering free entry at selected times, see the boxed text p123. Remember, however, that the museums can be extremely crowded during these periods.

For other times, both the Museo del Prado and Museo Thyssen-Bornemisza drop their admission prices by one euro (to €7 in each case) if you book online through their websites.

If you plan to visit the Museo del Prado, Museo Thyssen-Bornemisza and Centro de Arte Reina Sofía while in Madrid, the Paseo del Arte ticket covers them all in a combined ticket for €17.60 and is valid for one visit to each gallery during a 12-month period; buying separate tickets would cost a total of €22. A one-year ticket for unlimited visits to the Prado, Reina Sofía and eight other museums around Spain costs €36.06.

Free admission to the three museums (and other attractions) is included in the price of the Madrid Card; see p258 for details.

Most, but not all, museums and monuments close on Monday (the Reina Sofía is an exception and closes on Tuesday). Some (including the Reina Sofía) also shut on Sunday afternoons. In July and August some close parts of their displays for want of staff, most of whom take annual leave around this time. A few minor museums close entirely throughout August.

and King Juan Carlos I was crowned here in 1975 upon the death of Franco. The sometimes-sober, sometimes-splendid mock-Isabelline interior is actually a 19th-century reconstruction that took its cues from the Iglesia de San Juan de los Reyes in Toledo (see p234); the original was largely destroyed during the Peninsular War. What remained of the former cloisters has been incorporated into the Museo del Prado (p90).

PLAZA DE NEPTUNO Map p91

Plaza de Cánovas del Castillo; M Banco de España
Officially known as Plaza de Cánovas del Castillo, the next roundabout south of Cibeles is something of a crossroads of Spanish nobility. The Ritz and the Palace, two of Madrid's most exclusive hotels, glower at each other across the plaza with self-righteous grandeur, while the Museo Thyssen-Bornemisza and the Prado do likewise in competition for the title of Madrid's best-loved repository of fine art. The centrepiece is an ornate fountain and 18th-century sculpture of Neptune, the sea god, by Juan Pascual de Mena. Madrileños, never the most reverent lot, know it better as the celebration venue of choice for fans of Atlético de Madrid, who lose all sense of decorum when their team wins a major trophy. When this happened in 1996, the hundreds of thousands of success-starved Atlético fans celebrated in anything but noble style and Neptune was relieved of a few fingers.

MUSEO THYSSEN-BORNEMISZA
Map p91

☎ 91 369 01 51; www.museothyssen.org; Paseo del Prado 8; adult/student & senior/child under 12yr €8/5.50/free, headset guide €5; ☽ 10am-7pm Tue-Sun; M Banco de España
One of the most extraordinary private collections of predominantly European art in the world, the Museo Thyssen-Bornemisza is a worthy member of Madrid's 'Golden Triangle' of art. Where the Museo del Prado or Centro de Arte Reina Sofía enable you to study the body of work of a particular artist in depth, the Thyssen is the place to immerse yourself in a breathtaking breadth of artistic styles. Most of the big names are here, sometimes with just a single painting, but the Thyssen's gift to Madrid and the art-loving public is to have them all under one roof. Its simple-to-

follow floor plan also makes it one of the most easily navigable galleries in Madrid. Not surprisingly, it often ends up being many visitors' favourite Madrid art gallery.

The collection is spread out over three floors, with the oldest works on the top floor down to the contemporary scene on the ground floor. We suggest starting on the 2nd floor and working your way down.

The 2nd floor, which is home to medieval art, includes some real gems hidden among the mostly 13th- and 14th-century and predominantly Italian, German and Flemish religious paintings and triptychs. Unless you've a specialist's eye, pause in room 5 where you'll find one work by Italy's Piero della Francesca (1410–92) and the instantly recognisable *Portrait of King Henry VIII* by Holbein the Younger (1497–1543), before continuing on to room 10 for the evocative 1586 *Massacre of the Innocents* by Lucas Van Valckenberch. Room 11 is dedicated to El Greco (with three pieces) and his Venetian contemporaries Tintoretto and Titian, while Caravaggio and the Spaniard José de Ribera dominate room 12. A single painting each by Murillo and Zurbarán add further Spanish flavour in the two rooms that follow, while the exceptionally rendered views of Venice by Canaletto (1697–1768) should on no account be missed.

Best of all on this floor is the extension (rooms A to H) built to house the collection of Carmen Thyssen-Bornemisza. Room C houses paintings by Canaletto, Constable and Van Gogh, while the stunning room H includes works by Monet, Sisley, Renoir, Pissarro and Degas.

Before heading downstairs, a detour to rooms 19 through 21 will satisfy those devoted to 17th-century Dutch and Flemish masters, such as Anton van Dyck, Jan Brueghel the Elder, Rubens and Rembrandt (one painting).

If all that sounds impressive, the 1st floor is where the Thyssen really shines. There's a Gainsborough in room 28 and a Goya in room 31 but, if you've been skimming the surface of this at times overwhelming collection, room 32 is the place to linger over each and every painting. The astonishing texture of Van Gogh's *Les Vessenots* is a masterpiece, but the same could be said for *Woman in Riding Habit* by Manet, *The Thaw at Véthueil* by Monet, Renoir's *Woman with a Parasol in a Garden* and Pissarro's quintessentially Parisian *Rue*

Saint-Honoré in the Afternoon. Room 33 is also something special with Cézanne, Gauguin, Toulouse-Lautrec and Degas, while the big names continue in room 34 (Picasso, Matisse and Modigliani), and 35 (Edvard Munch and Egon Schiele).

The baroness' eye for quality is nowhere more evident than in the 1st floor's extension (rooms I to P) where the names speak for themselves. Room K has works by Monet, Pissaro, Sorolla and Sisley, while room L is the domain of Gauguin (including his iconic *Mata Mua*), Degas and Toulouse-Lautrec. Rooms M (Munch), N (Kandinsky), O (Matisse and Georges Braque) and P (Picasso, Matisse, Edward Hopper and Juan Gris) round out an outrageously rich journey through the masters. On your way to the stairs there's Edward Hopper's *Hotel Room*.

On the ground floor, the foray into the 20th century that you began in the 1st-floor extension takes over with a fine spread of paintings from cubism through to pop art.

In room 41 you'll see a nice mix of the big three of cubism, Picasso, Georges Braque and Madrid's own Juan Gris, along with several other contemporaries. Kandinsky is the main drawcard in room 43, while there's an early Salvador Dalí alongside Max Ernst and Paul Klee in room 44. Picasso appears again in room 45, another one of the gallery's stand-out rooms; its treasures include works by Marc Chagall and Dalí's hallucinatory *Dream Caused by the Flight of a Bee Around a Pomegranate, One Second Before Waking up*.

Room 46 is similarly rich, with Joan Miró's *Catalan Peasant with a Guitar*, the splattered craziness of Jackson Pollock's *Brown and Silver I* and the deceptively simple but strangely pleasing *Green on Maroon* by Mark Rothko taking centre stage. In rooms 47 and 48 the Thyssen builds to a stirring climax, with Francis Bacon, Roy Lichtenstein, Henry Moore and Lucian Freud, Sigmund's Berlin-born grandson, all represented.

CAIXA FORUM Map p91

☎ 91 330 73 00; www.fundacio.lacaixa.es, in Spanish; Paseo del Prado 36; admission free; ☾ 10am-8pm, free guided tours 1pm Mon-Sat & 7pm Fri; Ⓜ Atocha

This extraordinary structure, which opened in early 2008 down towards the southern end of the Paseo del Prado, is one of the most exciting architectural innovations to emerge in Madrid in recent years. Seeming to hover above the ground, this brick edifice is topped by an intriguing summit of what looks like rusted iron. On an adjacent wall is the *jardín colgante* (hanging garden), a lush vertical wall of greenery almost four storeys high. Inside there are four floors of exhibition and performance space awash in stainless steel and with soaring ceilings. The exhibitions here are always worth checking out and include cover photography, painting (including, recently, Miquel Barceló) and multimedia shows. But the building itself is the star attraction.

REAL JARDÍN BOTÁNICO Map p91

☎ 91 420 30 17; www.rjb.csic.es; Plaza de Bravo Murillo 2; adult/student/child under 11yr & EU senior €2.50/1.25/free; ☾ 10am-9pm May-Aug, 10am-8pm Apr & Sep, 10am-7pm Oct & Mar, 10am-6pm Nov-Feb; Ⓜ Atocha

Although not as expansive or as popular as the Parque del Buen Retiro, Madrid's botanical gardens are another leafy oasis in the centre of town. With some 30,000 species crammed into a relatively small 8-hectare area, it's more a place to wander at leisure than laze under a tree, although there are benches dotted throughout the gardens where you can sit.

THE THYSSEN-BORNEMISZA LEGEND

The collection held in the Museo Thyssen-Bornemisza is the result of a very Spanish story that has a celebrity love affair at its heart. The paintings held in the museum are the legacy of Baron Thyssen-Bornemisza, a German-Hungarian magnate. Spain managed to acquire the prestigious collection when the baron married Carmen Tita Cervera, a former Miss España and ex-wife of Lex Barker of *Tarzan* fame. The deal was sealed when the Spanish government offered to overhaul the neoclassical Palacio de Villahermosa specifically to house the collection. Although the baron died in 2002, his glamorous wife has shown that she has learned much from the collecting nous of her late husband. In early 2000 the museum acquired two adjoining buildings, which have been joined to the museum to house approximately half of the collection of Carmen Thyssen-Bornemisza.

In the centre stands a statue of Carlos III, who in 1781 moved the gardens here from their original location at El Huerto de Migas Calientes, on the banks of the Río Manzanares. In the Pabellón Villanueva, on the eastern flank of the gardens, art exhibitions are frequently staged – the opening hours are the same as for the park and the exhibitions are usually free.

There are Spanish-language guided visits (☎ 91 420 04 38; admission free with entry ticket; ☺ noon Sat & Sun) to the gardens; advance booking by phone is essential.

MUSEO NAVAL Map p91

☎ 91 523 87 89; www.museonavalmadrid.com, in Spanish; Paseo del Prado 5; admission free; ☺ 10am-2pm Tue-Sun; Ⓜ Banco de España
A block south of Plaza de la Cibeles, this museum will appeal to those who love their ships or who have always wondered what the Spanish Armada really looked like. On display are quite extraordinary models of ships from the earliest days of Spain's maritime history to the 20th century. Lovers of antique maps will also find plenty of interest, especially Juan de la Cosa's parchment map of the known world, put together in 1500. The accuracy of Europe and Africa is astounding, and it's supposedly the first map to show the Americas (albeit with considerably greater fantasy than fact). Also of interest is the wall-sized map showing Spanish maritime journeys of discovery from the 15th to 18th centuries. Littered throughout this pleasant, though rarely cluttered, exhibition space are dozens of uniforms, weapons, flags and other naval paraphernalia. Guided Spanish-language visits operate at 11.30am on Saturday and Sunday. English speakers are better off downloading the museum's English-language brochure from the website – click on 'Información General'.

MUSEO DE ARTES DECORATIVAS
Map p91

☎ 91 532 64 99; http://mnartesdecorativas.mcu .es, in Spanish; Calle de Montalbán 12; adult/child, student & senior €3/1.50, free Sun; ☺ 9.30am-3pm Tue-Sat, 10am-3pm Sun & holidays; Ⓜ Retiro
Those who love sumptuous period furniture, ceramics, carpets, tapestries and the like will find themselves passing a worthwhile hour or two here. There's plenty to catch your eye and the ceramics from

around Spain are a definite feature, while the recreations of kitchens from several regions are curiosities. Reconstructions of regal bedrooms, women's drawing rooms and 19th-century salons also help shed light on how the privileged classes of Spain have lived through the centuries.

PLAZA DE LA CIBELES Map p91
Ⓜ Banco de España
Of all the grand roundabouts that punctuate the Paseo del Prado, Plaza de la Cibeles most evokes the splendour of imperial Madrid.

The jewel in the crown is the astonishing Palacio de Comunicaciones. Built between 1904 and 1917 by Antonio Palacios, Madrid's most prolific architect of the belle époque, it combines elements of the North American monumental style of the period with Gothic and Renaissance touches. It serves as Madrid's town hall (Ayuntamiento), with the main post office (p262) occupying the southwestern corner. Other landmark buildings around the plaza's perimeter include the Palacio de Linares and Casa de América (p101), the Palacio Buenavista (1769; p111) and the national Banco de España (1891). There are fine views east towards the Puerta de Alcalá or, even better, west towards the Edificio Metrópolis.

The spectacular fountain of the goddess Cybele at the centre of the plaza is one of Madrid's most beautiful. Ever since it was erected in

GETTING ACTIVE IN EL RETIRO

Most visitors are content to explore El Retiro on foot, but there are plenty of alternatives on offer.

Renting a row boat (per boat per 45 min €4.55; ☺ 10am-8.30pm Apr-Sep, 10am-5.45pm Oct-Mar on the lake is a very Madrid thing to do. Tickets can be bought on the lake's northern side (opposite the Casa de Vacas). The same ticket office also sells rides in the Barco Solar (Solar Boat; per person €1.20; ☺ 10am-2pm & 4pm-sunset Tue-Sun) which is somewhat less strenuous.

Cycling and rollerblading are terrific ways to range far and wide across El Retiro. By Bike (p252) rents out both forms of transport (rental fees are the same for both) and is just across the road from El Retiro's eastern edge.

And if you fancy a gym workout or a game of tennis (for which you'll need your own racquet), stop by at the Centro Deportivo La Chopera (p209).

1780 by Ventura Rodríguez, it has been a Madrid favourite. Carlos III liked it so much that he tried to have it moved to the royal gardens of the Granja de San Ildefonso, on the road to Segovia, but madrileños kicked up such a fuss that he let it be.

For all its popularity, symbolism of ancient mythology and role as exemplar of centuries-old public art, madrileños' affection for the statue is tough love. For over a century, the Cibeles fountain has been the venue for joyous and often-destructive celebrations by players and supporters of Real Madrid whenever the side has won anything of note. In recent years the frenzy of clambering all over the fountain and chipping bits off as souvenirs has seen the city council board up the statue and surround it with police on the eve of important matches.

PARQUE DEL BUEN RETIRO Map p91

admission free; 🕐 6am-midnight May-Sep, 6am-11pm Oct-Apr; Ⓜ Retiro, Príncipe de Vergara, Ibiza or Atocha

The glorious gardens of El Retiro are as beautiful as any you'll find in a European city. Littered with marble monuments, landscaped lawns, the occasional elegant building and abundant greenery, it's quiet and contemplative during the week but comes to life on weekends. Put simply, this is one of our favourite places in Madrid.

Laid out in the 17th century by Felipe IV as the preserve of kings, queens and their intimates, the park was opened to the public in 1868 and ever since, whenever the weather's fine and on weekends in particular, madrileños from all across the city gather here to stroll, read the Sunday papers in the shade, take a boat ride or nurse a cool drink at the numerous outdoor *terrazas*. Weekend buskers, Chinese masseurs and tarot readers ply their trades, while art and photo exhibitions are some-times held at the various sites around the park, but it's so big that even on weekends there are plenty of quiet corners away from the crowds (apart from the lovers under trees locked in seemingly eternal embraces).

The focal point for so much of El Retiro's life is the artificial lake *(estanque)*, which is watched over by the massive ornamental structure of the Monument to Alfonso XII on the east side, complete with marble lions. If you want to catch the essence of Madrid's

endless energy, come here as sunset approaches on a Sunday afternoon in summer – as the crowd grows, bongos sound out across the park and people start to dance.

On the southern end of the lake, the odd structure decorated with sphinxes is the Fuente Egipcia (Egyptian Fountain) and legend has it that an enormous fortune buried in the park by Felipe IV in the mid-18th century rests here. Park authorities assured us that we could put away our spade and that the legend is rot.

Hidden among the trees south of the lake is the Palacio de Cristal (☎ 91 574 66 14; 🕐 11am-8pm Mon-Sat, 11am-6pm Sun & holidays May-Sep, 10am-6pm Mon-Sat, 10am-4pm Sun & holidays Oct-Apr), a magnificent metal and glass structure that is arguably El Retiro's most beautiful architectural monument. It was built in 1887 as a winter garden for exotic flowers and is now used for temporary exhibitions organised by the Centro de Arte Reina Sofía. Just north of here, the 1883 Palacio de Velázquez is generally used for temporary exhibitions, although it was closed for renovations at the time of writing. Another building occasionally used for temporary exhibitions is the Casa de Vacas (☎ 91 409 58 19; 🕐 11am-10pm), on the north side of the lake.

At the southern end of the park, near La Rosaleda (Rose Garden) with its more than 4000 roses, is a statue of El Ángel Caído (the Fallen Angel, aka Lucifer), one of the few statues to the devil anywhere in the world. Strangely, it sits 666m above sea level… In the same vein, the Puerta de Dante, in the extreme southeastern corner of the park, is watched over by a carved mural of Dante's Inferno.

Occupying much of the southwestern corner of the park is the Jardín de los Planteles, one of the least-visited sections of El Retiro, where quiet pathways lead beneath an overarching canopy of trees. West of here is the moving Bosque del Recuerdo (Memorial Forest), an understated memorial to the 191 victims of the 11 March 2004 train bombings. For each victim stands an olive or cypress tree. About 200m north of the monument is the Bosque del Recuerdo information office (🕐 10am-2pm & 4-7pm Sat, Sun & holidays). To the north, just inside the Puerta de Felipe IV, stands what is thought to be Madrid's oldest tree, a Mexican conifer *(ahue-huete)*. Planted in 1633 and with a trunk circumference of 52m, it was used by French soldiers during the Napoleonic Wars in the early 19th century as a cannon mount.

In the northeastern corner of the park, there's another information office (◷ 10am-2pm & 4-7pm Sat, Sun & holidays) in the cute Casita del Pescador, a former royal fishing lodge. Inquire here for the free guided tours (☎ 91 588 46 20; inforetiro@munimadrid.es) of the Parque del Buen Retiro, which cover bird and plant life as well as history and architecture; reservations are essential.

A stone's throw from this information office are the pleasing ruins of the Ermita de San Isidro (cnr Calle de O'Donnell & Avenida de Menéndez Pelayo; Ⓜ Príncipe de Vergara), a small country chapel noteworthy as one of the few, albeit modest, examples of Romanesque architecture in Madrid. Parts of the wall, a side entrance and part of the apse were restored in 1999 and are all that remain of the 13th-century building. When it was built, Madrid was a small village more than 2km away.

Southeast of the hermitage, beyond the children's playgrounds and the Casa de Fieras – which served as Madrid's zoo until 1972 and was once home to camels that appeared in *Lawrence of Arabia* – are the sculpted hedgerows, wandering peacocks and lily ponds of the Jardines del Arquitecto Herrero Palacios (◷ 8am-5pm Mon-Fri).

With playgrounds dotted around the park and plenty of child-friendly activities (see the boxed text, p96), El Retiro should have more than enough space and interest to keep children happy. If they need something more, puppet shows are a summertime feature (look for signs to Titirilandia – Puppet Land – in the park's northwest). The Casa de Vacas also sometimes hosts children's theatre *(teatro infantil)* on weekends. Ask at one of the information offices to see what's on.

CASÓN DEL BUEN RETIRO Map p91
Calle de Alfonso XII 28; Ⓜ Retiro

One of the few vestiges of the 17th-century Palacio del Buen Retiro, this somewhat austere building overlooking the Parque del Buen Retiro is run as an academic library by the Museo del Prado and, as such, is mostly closed to the general public. The only exception, and it's an important one, is for the guided visits (☎ 902 107 077; ◷ 11am & 12.30pm Sun) to the stunning Hall

of the Ambassadors, which is crowned by the astonishing 1697 ceiling fresco *The Apotheosis of the Spanish Monarchy* by Luca Giordano. These visits can be arranged at the 'Educación' desk just inside the Puerta de los Jerónimos in the Museo del Prado. The remainder of the Casón del Buen Retiro has been renovated in a modern style.

PASEO DEL ARTE
Walking Tour
1 Parque del Buen Retiro
Wandering through El Retiro (p97) is one of Madrid's greatest pleasures, with its combination of expansive greenery, and marble and glass monuments littered among the trees. Start at the lake *(estanque)* and consider taking a leisurely detour via the Monument to Alfonso XII, the statue of El Ángel Caído and completing a circuit via the Ermita de San Isidro before making your way west.

2 Casón del Buen Retiro
Just outside one of the western gates of the park, the Casón del Buen Retiro (left) formed part of the royal residence in the 17th century. With El Retiro on its doorstep, you can't help but feel it must have been a lovely place to live. It was recently renovated and only opens for guided visits on Sunday.

3 Plaza de la Cibeles
Head north along Calle de Alfonso XII, admire Puerta de Alcalá, then turn left down the hill to Plaza de la Cibeles (p96), one of the world's most beautiful roundabouts. Surrounded as it is by soaring architectural triumphs, you'll nonetheless be unable to tear your eyes away from the Palacio de Comunicaciones, a glorious remnant of the belle-époque architectural period.

4 Museo Thyssen-Bornemisza
Walk south along the Paseo del Prado (in the tree-lined centre of the boulevard, not the side footpaths) until you reach the Museo Thyssen-Bornemisza (p94; closed Monday) on your right. This marvellous museum gives you a taste of the major epochs of European art before you narrow in on the more specialist collections elsewhere.

5 Museo del Prado
Diagonally across the other side of Plaza de Neptuno awaits the Prado (p90), one of the

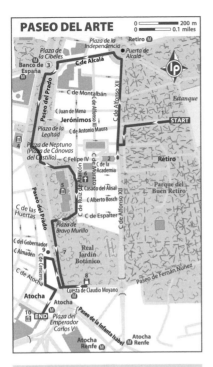

PASEO DEL ARTE

WALK FACTS

Start Parque del Buen Retiro
End Centro de Arte Reina Sofía
Distance 4km
Time Two hours, plus gallery time
Fuel stop Estado Puro (p159)

greatest galleries in the world of fine art. If time is short, restrict yourself to the works of Velázquez and Goya, the two towering masters of Spanish painting.

6 Iglesia de San Jerónimo El Real

The Museo del Prado extension has recently swallowed up the cloisters of the Iglesia de San Jerónimo El Real (p93), but the church itself has hints of the extravagance that befits the chapel of choice for the royal family and place of the coronation of Juan Carlos I.

7 Real Jardín Botánico

Skirting around to the south of the Museo del Prado, you come to Madrid's botanical gardens (p95). There's no more shady spot in central Madrid, a green oasis while the modern, mechanised world rushes past just outside. Budding botanists will love the variety of trees, but we love it more for its respite from the outside world.

8 Cuesta de Moyano Bookstalls

Outside the southern end of the Botanical Gardens, these secondhand bookstalls (p136) climb up towards the backside of El Retiro. They're something of a Madrid landmark and, while most titles are in Spanish, they are well worth casting an eye over, especially the significant collection of fine-arts books.

9 Caixa Forum

Across the other side of the Paseo del Prado, Caixa Forum (p95) is modern Madrid's most stunning architectural innovation and one of its cultural highlights. One look at its hanging garden alongside the earth-toned facade and you'll understand what we mean.

10 Centro de Arte Reina Sofía

Even if you're suffering from gallery overload, don't forsake the Reina Sofía (p82). Head straight for Picasso's *Guernica*, a breathtaking masterpiece, seek out works by Miró and Salvador Dalí, then take in the stunning new extension around the corner.

Drinking & Nightlife p189; Eating p159; Shopping p136; Sleeping p227

The barrio of Salamanca is Madrid's most exclusive quarter. Like nowhere else in the capital, this is where stately mansions set back from the street share barrio space with designer boutiques from the big local and international fashionistas, and where the unmistakeable whiff of old money mingles comfortably with the aspirations of Spain's nouveaux riches. In short, it's the sort of place to put on your finest clothes, regardless of your errand, and simply be seen, to stroll into shops with an affected air and resist asking the prices. Salamanca's sprinkling of fine restaurants, designer tapas bars and niche museums are also very much at home here. For more earthy delights, the Plaza de Toros and Museo Taurino to the east of the barrio are the spiritual home of Spanish bullfighting; it's technically part of Salamanca, although the señoras of the barrio would love to disown it, even as their husbands sneak out for an occasional *corrida* (bullfight).

top picks

SIGHTS IN SALAMANCA

- Plaza de Toros & Museo Taurino (left)
- Museo Lázaro Galdiano (p103)
- Museo de la Escultura Abstracta (p103)

PLAZA DE TOROS & MUSEO TAURINO off Map p102
Ⓜ Las Ventas

The Plaza de Toros Monumental de Las Ventas (often known simply as Las Ventas) is not the most beautiful bullring in the world – that honour probably goes to Ronda in Andalucía – but it is the most important.

A classic example of the neo-*mudéjar* style, it was opened in 1931 and hosted its first *corrida* (bullfight) three years later. Like all bullrings, the circle of sand enclosed by four storeys, which can seat up to 25,000 spectators, evokes more a sense of a theatre than a sports stadium – it also hosts concerts; see p199. To be carried high on the shoulders of aficionados out through the grand and decidedly Moorish Puerta de Madrid is the ultimate dream of any torero (bullfighter) – if you've made it at Las Ventas, you've reached the pinnacle of the bullfighting world. The gate is known more colloquially as the 'Gate of Glory'. Guided visits (conducted in English and Spanish) take you out onto the sand and into the royal box, last 40 minutes and start on the hour. For reservations, contact Tauro Tour (☎ 91 556 92 37; gregorio@trazopublicidad.es; 4th fl, Paseo de la Castellana 115; adult/child €7/5; ☼ 10am-2pm Tue-Sun Jun-Sep).

If your curiosity is piqued, wander into the Museo Taurino (☎ 91 725 18 57; www.las-ventas .com, in Spanish; Calle de Alcalá 237; admission free; ☼ 9.30am-2.15pm Mon-Fri & 10am-12.45pm Sun Jun-Sep), and check out the collection of paraphernalia, costumes, photos and other bullfighting memorabilia up on the top floor above one of the two courtyards by the ring.

The area where the Plaza de Toros is located is known as Las Ventas because, in times gone by, several wayside taverns *(ventas)*, along with houses of ill repute, were to be found here.

ORIENTATION & TRANSPORT: SALAMANCA

Paseo de los Recoletos and its continuation, Paseo de la Castellana, delineate the western end of Salamanca's neat grid of streets tacked onto the northern perimeter of the Parque del Buen Retiro. Calle de María de Molina, Calle de Francisco Silvela and Calle de Alcalá rule Salamanca off neatly to the north, east and southeast. The posher parts of Salamanca centre around Calle de Serrano, Calle del Príncipe de Vergara and Calle de Goya. The lifeblood and undoubted focal point of the barrio is, however, Calle de Serrano, a supremely elegant thoroughfare that promises to be even better once the massive roadworks designed to reduce vehicle traffic have been completed.

The most useful metro stations that encircle the barrio's perimeter include Colón (line 4), Banco de España (line 2), Retiro (line 2), Príncipe de Vergara (lines 2 and 9), Goya (lines 2 and 4), Manuel Becerra (lines 2 and 6) and Gregorio Marañón (lines 7 and 10). Those that deposit you in the heart of the barrio include Serrano (line 4), Velázquez (line 4) and Núñez de Balboa (lines 5 and 9).

SALAMANCA'S DIFFICULT BIRTH

Salamanca, with its expensive boutiques, high-class restaurants and luxury apartments, was born with a silver spoon in its mouth. When Madrid's authorities were looking to expand beyond the newly inadequate confines of the medieval capital, the Marqués de Salamanca, a 19th-century aristocrat and general with enormous political clout, heard the call. He threw everything he had into the promotion of his barrio in the 1870s, buying up land cheaply, which he hoped to sell later for a profit. He was ahead of his time: the houses he built contained Madrid's first water closets, the latest in domestic plumbing and water heating for bathrooms and kitchens, while he also inaugurated horse-drawn tramways. In the year of his death, 1883, the streets got electric lighting. Hard as it is now to imagine, there was little enthusiasm for the project and the *marqués* quickly went bankrupt. Towards the end of his life, he wrote 'I have managed to create the most comfortable barrio in Madrid and find myself the owner of 50 houses, 13 hotels and 18 million feet of land. And I owe more than 36 million *reales* on all of this. The task is completed but I am ruined.' It was only later that madrileños saw the error of their ways.

PUERTA DE ALCALÁ Map p102
Plaza de la Independencia; Ⓜ **Retiro**
This imposing triumphal gate was once the main entrance to the city (its name derives from the fact that the road that passed under it led to Alcalá de Henares) and was surrounded by the city's walls. It was here that the city authorities controlled access to the capital and levied customs duties.

The first gate to bear this name was built in 1599, but Carlos III was singularly unimpressed and had it demolished in 1764 to be replaced by another, the one you see today. It's best appreciated from the east for fine views through the arch down towards central Madrid. Our only complaint? It could do with a clean. Twice a year, in autumn and spring, cars abandon the roundabout and are replaced by flocks of sheep being transferred in an age-old ritual from their summer to winter pastures (and vice versa). And the Puerta de Alcalá was immortalised in the cultural lexicon in 1986 when Ana Belén and Victor Manuel's mediocre but strangely catchy song 'La Puerta de Alcalá' became an unlikely smash hit.

PALACIO DE LINARES & CASA DE AMÉRICA Map p102
☎ 91 595 48 00; www.casamerica.es, in Spanish; **Plaza de la Cibeles 2; adult/child/student & senior €7/free/4;** ◷ **guided tours 11am, noon & 1pm Sat & Sun;** Ⓜ **Banco de España**
So extraordinary is the Palacio de Comunicaciones on Plaza de la Cibeles that many visitors fail to notice this fine 19th-century pleasure dome that stands watch over the northeastern corner of the plaza. Built in 1873, the Palacio de Linares is a worthy member of the line-up of grand facades on the plaza, while its

interior is notable for the copious use of Carrara marble. Tours take an hour and can be reserved on ☎ 902 400 222 or booked online at www.entradas.com. Alternatively, you can purchase tickets at the ticket office (◷ 9am-8pm Mon-Fri, 11am-1pm Sat & Sun); tickets often sell out in advance, so don't leave it until the last minute. In the palace's grounds is the Casa de América, a modern exhibition centre, which also hosts all sorts of events and concerts.

MUSEO ARQUEOLÓGICO NACIONAL
Map p102
National Archaeology Museum; ☎ **91 577 79 12; http://man.mcu.es, in Spanish; Calle de Serrano 13; admission free;** ◷ **9.30am-8pm Tue-Sat, 9.30am-3pm Sun & holidays;** Ⓜ **Serrano**
On the east side of the building housing the Biblioteca Nacional, the showpiece Museo Arqueológico Nacional contains a sweeping accumulation of artefacts behind its towering facade. The large collection includes stunning mosaics taken from Roman villas across Spain, intricate Muslim-era and *mudéjar* handiwork, sculpted figures such as the *Dama de Ibiza* and *Dama de Elche,* examples of Romanesque and Gothic architectural styles and a partial

THINGS THEY SAID ABOUT... THE PLAZA DE TOROS

'The next afternoon all the world crowds to the Plaza de Toros. You need not ask the way; just launch into the tide, which in these Spanish affairs will assuredly carry you away. Nothing can exceed the gaiety and sparkle of a Spanish public going, eager and full dressed, to the fight.'
Richard Ford, *Gatherings from Spain* (1861)

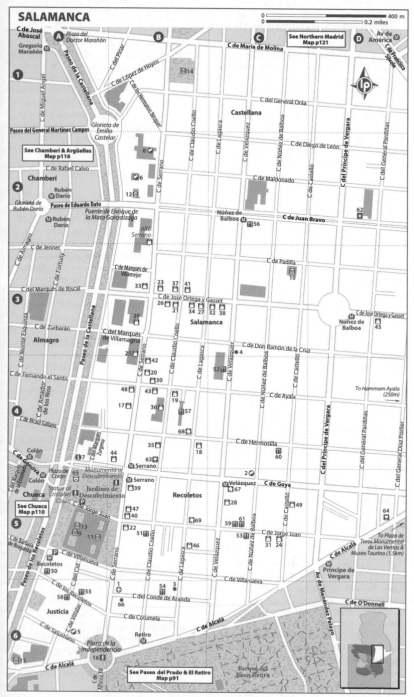

SALAMANCA

0 — 400 m
0 — 0.2 miles

See Northern Madrid Map p121

See Chamberí & Argüelles Map p116

See Chueca Map p110

See Paseo del Prado & El Retiro Map p91

copy of the prehistoric cave paintings of Altamira (Cantabria).

Sadly, until 2012 (and more likely 2013), only a small sample of the museum's riches will be on display as the building undergoes major (and long overdue) renovations. When finished, the museum will almost certainly be one of Madrid's finest, but no one really knows when that will be. An admission charge (probably around €3 for adults) will apply once the museum reopens in all its glory.

BIBLIOTECA NACIONAL & MUSEO DEL LIBRO Map opposite

☎ 91 580 78 05; www.bne.es, in Spanish; Paseo de los Recoletos 20; admission free; Ⓜ Colón

Perhaps the most impressive of the grand edifices erected along the Paseo de los Recoletos in the 19th century, the 1892 Biblioteca Nacional (National Library; ☺ 9am-9pm Mon-Fri, 9am-2pm Sat) dominates the southern end of Plaza de Colón. The reading rooms are more for use by serious students. Downstairs, and entered via a separate entrance, the fascinating and recently overhauled Museo del Libro (☺ 10am-9pm Tue-Sat, 10am-2pm Sun), otherwise known as the Museo de la Biblioteca Nacional, is a must for bibliophiles, with interactive displays on printing presses and other materials, illuminated manuscripts, the history of the library, and literary cafes, although our favourites are the 1626 map of Spain and Picasso's *Mademoiselle Léonie en un Sillón* in the Sala de las Musas. Mercifully, there's not an e-book in sight.

MUSEO DE LA ESCULTURA ABSTRACTA Map opposite

www.munimadrid.es/museoairelibre; Paseo de la Castellana; Ⓜ Rubén Darío

This fascinating open-air collection of 17 abstract sculptures includes works by the renowned Basque artist Eduardo Chillida, the Catalan master Joan Miró, as well as Eusebio Sempere and Alberto Sánchez, one of Spain's foremost sculptors of the 20th century. The sculptures are beneath the overpass where Paseo de Eduardo Dato crosses Paseo de la Castellana, but somehow the hint of traffic grime and pigeon shit only adds to the appeal. All but one are on the eastern side of Paseo de la Castellana.

MUSEO LÁZARO GALDIANO Map opposite

☎ 91 561 60 84; www.flg.es, in Spanish; Calle de Serrano 122; adult/student €4/2, free Sun; ☺ 10am-4.30pm Wed-Mon; Ⓜ Gregorio Marañón

This is just the sort of place you expect to find along Calle de Serrano, with an imposing early-20th-century Italianate stone mansion set discreetly back from the street. And Don José Lázaro Galdiano (1862–1947), a successful and cultivated businessman, was just the sort of person you'd expect to find in Salamanca. A patron of the arts, he built up an astonishing private collection that he bequeathed to the city upon his death. It was no mean inheritance, with some 13,000 works of art and *objets d'art,* a quarter of which are on show at any time.

The highlights are the works by Zurbarán, Claudio Coello, Hieronymus Bosch, Esteban Murillo, El Greco, Lucas Cranach, Constable and there's even a painting in room 11 attributed to Velázquez. But the undoubted star of the show is Goya, who dominates room 13, while the ceiling of the adjoining room 14 features a collage from some of Goya's more famous works in honour of the genius.

The ground floor is largely given over to a display setting the social context in which Galdiano lived, with hundreds of curios from all around the world on show. The lovely 1st floor is dominated by Spanish artworks arrayed around the centrepiece of the former ballroom and beneath lavishly frescoed ceilings. The 2nd floor contains numerous minor masterpieces from Italian, Flemish, English and French painters, while the top floor is jammed with all sorts of ephemera, including some exquisite textiles in room 24.

The labelling throughout the museum is excellent, appearing in both English and Spanish, and is accompanied by photos of each room as it appeared in Galdiano's prime.

FUNDACIÓN JUAN MARCH Map p102
☎ 91 435 42 40; www.march.es; Calle de Castelló 77; admission free; ⏱ 11am-8pm Mon-Sat, 10am-2pm Sun & holidays; Ⓜ Núñez de Balboa
This foundation organises some of the better temporary exhibitions in Madrid each year and it's always worth checking its website, the listings pages of local papers or *EsMadrid Magazine* (from the tourist office) to see what exhibitions are happening. The foundation also stages concerts and other events throughout the year (see p203 for more info).

DESIGNER BARRIO
Walking Tour
1 Plaza de la Independencia
From this roundabout crowned with the monumental Puerta de Alcalá (p101), you've many of Madrid's highlights on your doorstep. Southeast is the Parque del Buen Retiro, down the hill to the west is the glorious Plaza de la Cibeles and, beyond, the city centre. But you're headed north, into the distinguished Salamanca barrio.

2 Calle de Serrano
Sweeping away to the north is Calle de Serrano (see the boxed text, p136), which is to Madrid what Blvd Haussmann is to Paris. Undergoing a major overhaul to widen the footpaths

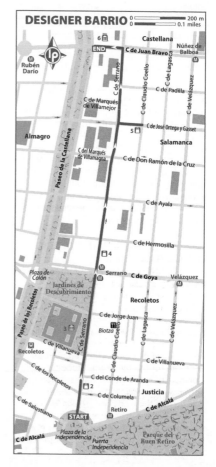

WALK FACTS

Start Plaza de la Independencia
End Museo de la Escultura Abstracta
Distance 4km
Time Two hours, plus shopping time
Fuel stop Biotza (p161)

at the time of writing, this street is glamour central, the most prestigious shopping street in Spain.

3 Museo Arqueológico Nacional

Just before you reach Plaza de Colón (it's the one with the largest Spanish flag you'll ever see) is the grand Museo Arqueológico Nacional (p101). If the renovations have finished, take the time to wander through this fascinating journey spanning Spanish prehistory through to the glories of Muslim Spain.

4 Calle de Serrano Part Two

Back on Calle de Serrano, stop in at Loewe (see the boxed text, p136). Thus initiated into

the world of classy Spanish fashion, continue north to the cheerful, bright colours of Agatha Ruiz de la Prada (p136) before toning things down a little in the boutique of Roberto Verino (see the boxed text, p136).

5 Calle de José Ortega y Gasset

Shopping in Salamanca can give you a newly acquired Spanish look, but Calle de José Ortega y Gasset (see the boxed text, p137) is all about international glamour, with just about every mainstream luxury clothes designer having a shop front here. To treat yourself, head east as far as Oriol Balaguer (p138), where chocolate becomes art.

6 Museo de la Escultura Abstracta

Retrace your steps to Calle de Serrano, turn right, then left on Calle de Juan Bravo. Beneath the bridge where the street starts to cross the Paseo de la Castellana, the open-air Museo de la Escultura Abstracta (p103) is about Spanish design of a more enduring kind, with the works of big-name Spanish sculptors on permanent display.

Drinking & Nightlife p189; Eating p161; Shopping p138; Sleeping p228

The two inner-city barrios of Malasaña and Chueca are where Madrid gets up close and personal. Yes, there are rewarding museums and examples of landmark architecture sprinkled throughout. But these two barrios are more about doing than seeing. Here, it's more an experience of life as it's lived by madrileños than the traditional traveller experience of ticking off from a list of wonderful, if more static, attractions that may have made the city famous but which only tell half the story. These are barrios with attitude and personality, barrios where Madrid's famed nightlife, shopping and eating choices live and breathe and take you under the skin of the city.

Malasaña lives to an agreeable extent in the past. The barrio, where locals rose up in rebellion against the French occupiers in 1808 (p27), has never quite lost its rebellious spirit. It was here, two centuries later in the 1980s, that *la movida madrileña* (p32) found its most authentic expression, rebelling against Spain's Franco past and pushing hedonism to new limits. Most of the city may have moved on, but Malasaña still holds fast to *la movida's* spirit. All along its narrow streets, shop fronts announce names like 'True Love Tattoo' and 'Retro City' alongside graffiti and posters of heavy-rocking bands that have become an integral part of its gritty urban charm. From the Plaza del Dos de Mayo in the heart of the barrio, the clamour of Malasaña rolls out across the city, reminding madrileños where they came from. Slightly more refined and less clamorous, the sub-barrio of Conde Duque, to the west, has the best of Malasaña without quite the same grit and noise.

If Malasaña holds fast to its roots, Chueca has become a symbol for all the extravagance, tolerance and sophistication of the new Madrid. Chueca wears its heart on its sleeve, a barrio that gays and lesbians have transformed from a down-at-heel symbol of urban decay into one of the coolest places in Spain. Sometimes it's in your face, but more often it's what locals like to call not 'gay friendly' but 'hetero friendly'. The diversity of the gay and lesbian communities who have made Chueca their own is reflected in its polyglot character: it's a place of rainbow flags and open-fronted gay bookshops, of bars for bears and boutiques for an exclusive clientele. The further east you go, the more sophisticated Chueca becomes, but above all, it's a feel-good barrio whose moment is very much now.

top picks

SIGHTS IN MALASAÑA & CHUECA

- Museo de Historia (opposite)
- Museo Municipal de Arte Contemporáneo (opposite)
- Sociedad General de Autores y Editores (left)

SOCIEDAD GENERAL DE AUTORES Y EDITORES Map p110

☎ 91 349 95 50; www.sgae.es, in Spanish; Calle de Fernando VI 4; Ⓜ Alonso Martínez

This swirling, melting wedding cake of a building is as close as Madrid comes to the work of Antoni Gaudí, which so illuminates Barcelona. It's a joyously self-indulgent ode to modernismo and is virtually one of a kind in Madrid. Casual visitors are actively discouraged, although what you see from the street is impressive enough. The only exceptions are on the first Monday of October, International Architecture Day, and during the Noche en Blanco festivities (see p20). We've had a peek inside and its interior staircase alone is reason enough to come if you're here at one of these times.

MUSEO DEL ROMANTICISMO Map p110

☎ 91 448 10 45; http://museoromanticismo.mcu .es, in Spanish; Calle de San Mateo 13; adult/child/student €3/free/1.50, free Sat after 2.30pm; ⌚ 9.30am-8.30pm Tue-Sat & 10am-3pm Sun May-Oct, 9.30am-6.30pm Tue-Sat & 10am-3pm Sun Nov-Apr; Ⓜ Tribunal

After eight years of renovations (!), this intriguing museum has finally reopened and is devoted to the Romantic period of the 19th century. The museum occupies a late-18th-century mansion which was converted into a museum by the Marqués de la Vega-Inclán (who was involved in the creation of the chain of luxury hotels known as the *paradores*) in 1924. It houses a minor treasure trove of mostly 19th-century paintings, furniture, porcelain, books, photos and other bits and bobs

Malasaña is enclosed by Gran Vía (south), Calle de la Princesa (west), Calle de Alberto Aguilera (north) and Calle de Fuencarral (east). The heart of Chueca starts not far east of Calle de Fuencarral and extends down as far as the Paseo de los Recoletos, with Gran Vía and Calle de Génova enclosing Chueca to the south and north, respectively. The major, roughly north–south thoroughfares through the area are Calle de San Bernardo, Calle de Fuencarral and Calle de Hortaleza.

Six out of the 10 main metro lines pass through one of these two barrios or deposit you conveniently around the perimeter. For Malasaña, Bilbao (lines 1 and 4) and San Bernardo (lines 2 and 4) sit on the barrio's northern rim and allow a downhill walk into the barrio, while Noviciado (lines 2 and 10) lies where Malasaña segues into Conde Duque. Alonso Martínez (lines 4, 5 and 10) allows a downward stroll into Chueca, while Colón (line 4) and Banco de España (line 2) also surround the barrio. Gran Vía (lines 1 and 5), at the southern end, and Tribunal (lines 1 and 10) are handy for both barrios. Chueca (line 5) sits in the heart of the barrio of the same name. Plaza de España (lines 3 and 10) is helpful for the lower corner of Malasaña and Conde Duque.

from a bygone age and offers an insight into what upper-class houses were like in the 19th century. There's a limit of 100 visitors inside the museum at any one time. The best-known work in the collection is Goya's *San Gregorio Magno, Papa*.

MUSEO DE HISTORIA Map pp108-9

Museo Municipal; ☎ 91 588 86 72; www.munimadrid .es/museodehistoria; Calle de Fuencarral 78; Ⓜ Tribunal

Closed for major renovations until at least 2011 and possibly beyond, this fine museum (formerly the Museo Municipal) is arguably the best of the museums that take you through Madrid's history; the others are the Museo de los Orígenes (p78) and Museo de la Ciudad (p120). Once it reopens, you'll find paintings and other exhibits relating to Madrid de los Austrias (Habsburg Madrid) and Bourbon Madrid, as well as an absorbing scale model/map of 1830s Madrid; in particular, note the long-disappeared bullring next to the Puerta de Alcalá and the absence of the Gran Vía through the centre of Madrid.

In the meantime, if it's not covered in scaffolding, you can admire the extraordinary restored baroque entrance, a flight of churrigueresque fancy raised in 1721 by Pedro de Ribera.

MUSEO MUNICIPAL DE ARTE CONTEMPORÁNEO Map pp108-9

☎ 91 588 59 28; www.munimadrid.es/museoarte contemporaneo, in Spanish; Calle del Conde Duque 9-11; admission free; Ⓥ 10am-2pm & 5.30-9pm Tue-Sat, 10.30am-2.30pm Sun & holidays; Ⓜ Noviciado or San Bernardo

Spread over two floors, this is a rich collection of modern Spanish art, mostly paintings and graphic art with a smattering of photography, sculpture and drawings. Running throughout much of the gallery are works showcasing creative interpretations of Madrid's cityscape – avant-garde splodges and almost old-fashioned visions of modern Madrid side by side – and, for many lay visitors, therein lies the museum's greatest appeal. Some examples include Juan Moreno Aquado's *Chamartín* (2000), Luis Mayo's *Cibeles* (1997) and a typically fantastical representation of the Cibeles fountain by one-time icon of *la movida madrileña*, Ouka Lele. The 1st floor is a mix of works acquired between 1999 and 2001, while the 2nd floor contains a chronological display (starting with the 1920s). The many talented artists represented here include Eduardo Arroyo and Basque sculptor Jorde Oteiza.

ANTIGUO CUARTEL DEL CONDE DUQUE Map pp108-9

☎ 91 588 57 71; Calle del Conde Duque 9-11; Ⓜ Noviciado or San Bernardo

This grand former barracks dominates Conde Duque on the western fringe of Malasaña with its imposing facade stretching 228m down the hill. Built in 1717 under the auspices of architect Pedro de Ribera, its highlight is the extravagant 18th-century doorway, which is a masterpiece of the baroque churrigueresque style. These days it's home by day to a cultural centre, which hosts government archives, libraries, the Hemeroteca Municipal (the biggest collection of newspapers and magazines in Spain), temporary exhibitions and the Museo Municipal de Arte Contemporáneo (left). By night, in summer, one of the two large patios becomes an atmospheric venue

MALASAÑA

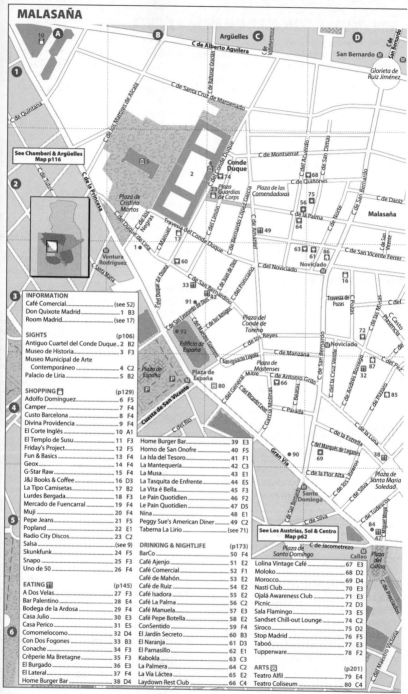

See Chamberí & Argüelles Map p116

See Los Austrias, Sol & Centro Map p62

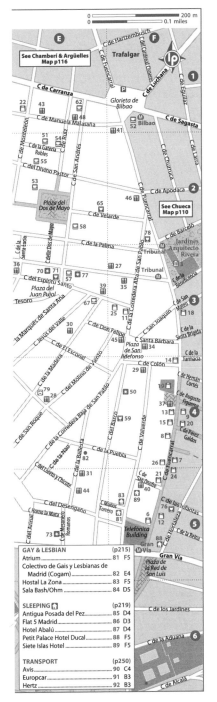

See Chamberí & Argüelles Map p116

See Chueca Map p110

TRIBALL – THE NEW MALASAÑA

Although Malasaña is unlikely to shed its carefully cultivated retro image any time soon, a new project run by local businesses is seeking to change the way people think about Malasaña. Entitled Triángulo Ballesta (www.triballmadrid.com, in Spanish), it's named after the once famously seedy Calle de Ballesta, close to Gran Vía, and includes streets such as Calle del Desengaño, Calle de Valverde, Calle de la Corredera Baja de San Pablo and surrounds. The project is one of regeneration and involves cleaning up the streets, as well as encouraging new businesses and the avant-garde arts community to make it their barrio of choice. They have promised not to stop until they have transformed Malasaña into the new Soho.

for concerts; programs for exhibitions and concerts are posted outside. The southwestern end of the complex was undergoing major renovations at the time of research, so expect some disruptions until they finish. In the gardens to the northeast of the building, most mornings you'll find old men playing *petanca* (boules) under the trees like a scene from Madrid's village past.

GALERÍA MORIARTY Map p110
☎ 91 531 43 65; www.galeriamoriarty.com; Calle de la Libertad 22; ⏱ 11am-2pm & 5-8.30pm Tue-Sat; Ⓜ Chueca

During *la movida madrileña* in the 1980s, Galería Moriarty (then in Calle del Almirante) was one of Madrid's most important meeting places of culture and counterculture, drawing the iconic Agatha Ruiz de la Prada, film-maker Pedro Almodóvar and photographer García Alix among others to attend its exhibitions and parties. It may have moved, but it remains one of the most important small galleries in Madrid, with all manner of interesting contemporary exhibitions.

PALACIO DE LIRIA Map left
☎ 91 547 53 02; Calle de la Princesa 20; ⏱ guided visit 11am & noon Fri; Ⓜ Ventura Rodríguez

This 18th-century mansion, rebuilt after a fire in 1936, nestles amid the modern architecture just north of Plaza de España as a reminder of the days when the streets were lined with mansions like these. It holds an impressive collection of art, period furniture and *objets d'art*. To join a guided

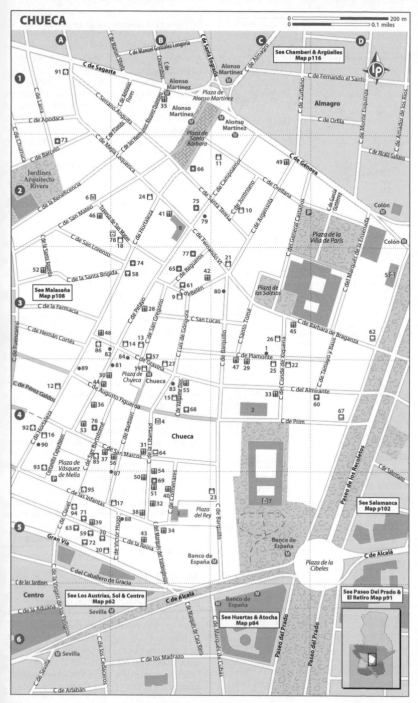

CHUECA

0 — 200 m
0 — 0.1 miles

See Chamberí & Argüelles
Map p116

See Malasaña
Map p108

See Los Austrias, Sol & Centro
Map p62

See Salamanca
Map p102

See Huertas & Atocha
Map p84

See Paseo Del Prado &
El Retiro Map p91

visit, you need to send a formal request with your personal details to the palace, which is home to the Duke and Duchess of Alba, one of the grandest names in Spanish nobility. The waiting list is long and most mere mortals content themselves with staring through the gates into the grounds.

PALACIO BUENAVISTA & CASA DE LAS SIETE CHIMENEAS Map opposite

M Banco de España

Set back amid gardens on the northwest edge of Plaza de la Cibeles stands the Palacio Buenavista, now occupied by the army. It once belonged to the Alba family, and the young Duchess of Alba, Cayetana, who was widely rumoured to have had an affair with the artist Goya in the 18th century, lived here for a time.

A block behind it to the west, on the tiny Plaza del Rey, is the Casa de las Siete Chimeneas, a 16th-century mansion that takes its name from the seven chimneys it still boasts. It's a tantalising glimpse of the sort of residences that once lined the Paseo de la Castellana. They say that the ghost of one of Felipe II's lovers still runs about here in distress on certain evenings. Nowadays, it's home to the Ministry of Education, Culture and Sport.

MUSEO DE CERA Map opposite

☎ 91 319 26 49; www.museoceramadrid.com; Paseo de los Recoletos 41; adult/child under 10yr €16/12; ☉ 10am-2.30pm & 4.30-8.30pm Mon-Fri, 10am-8.30pm Sat, Sun & holidays; M Colón

If wax museums are your thing, this one with more than 450 characters is a fairly standard version of the genre. With models ranging from the Beatles to Bart Simpson, and from Raúl to Cervantes, Dalí and Picasso, it's a typically broad-ranging collection of international and Spanish

For those with an interest in contemporary art that extends beyond what you'll find at the Centro de Arte Reina Sofía (p82) or the Museo Municipal de Arte Contemporáneo (p107), central Madrid is studded with small galleries showcasing both up-and-coming and longer-established painters, sculptors and photographers. For a near-complete list, check out Arte Madrid (www.artemadrid.com, in Spanish); its brochure of the same name, available online in PDF format, contains a map and program of upcoming exhibitions. Many of these galleries are regulars at Madrid's Arco fair (p17).

figures down through the centuries. If you're drawn to the darker side of life, there's everything from the Inquisition to Freddy Krueger, while the Tren del Terror is not for the faint hearted. Other attractions include the Simulador, which shakes you up a bit as though you were inside a washing machine, and the Multivisión journey through Spanish history. It claims to be Madrid's seventh most visited museum, although it's hard to see why, unless you've got kids.

OFF THE TOURIST TRAIL
Walking Tour
1 Plaza de Chueca

Welcome to the heart of gay Madrid, a barrio of over-the-top sexuality and devil-may-care hedonism. If you like what you see and plan to come back after dark, take note of Antigua Casa Ángel Sierra (p193), right on the plaza, and Café Acuarela (p216), to later catch the buzz.

2 Sociedad General de Autores y Editores

Take Calle Luis de Góngora heading north to Calle de Belén, mark the location of Café Belén (p192) for a *mojito* later, then make for Calle de Fernando VI, where the Sociedad General

WALK FACTS

Start Plaza de Chueca
End El Jardín Secreto
Distance 5km
Time Three hours
Fuel stop Café Pepe Botella (p191)

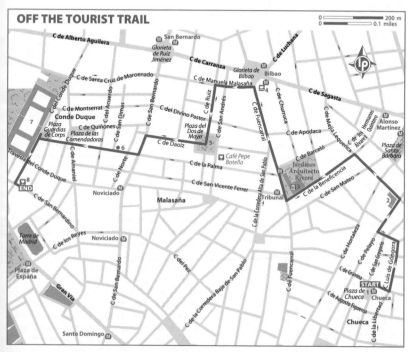

OFF THE TOURIST TRAIL

de Autores y Editores (p106) is housed in a modernista masterpiece that would have made Gaudí proud.

3 Museo de Historia
Continue northwest along Calle de Mejía Lequerica, then left on Calle de la Beneficencia. At the end of this street on the right is the Museo de Historia (p107), an intriguing repository of historical Madrid artworks. If the renovations haven't finished, you can at least admire its astonishing baroque doorway.

4 Café Comercial
Calle de Fuencarral heads north to the Glorieta de Bilbao and it's here that you'll find the old-world literary Café Comercial (p190). One of the most famous old cafes in Madrid, a coffee here is a journey back to the thriving intellectual life of Madrid in the 1950s.

5 Plaza del Dos de Mayo
Crossing into Malasaña, stroll west along Calle de Manuela Malasaña, a name you'll want to remember for its fine range of restaurants (see the boxed text, p161). We especially like La Isla del Tesoro (p162), Nina (p162) and La Musa (p162), but

they're all good. Down the hill to the south is Plaza del Dos de Mayo, the beating heart of Malasaña.

6 Conde Duque
Any of the streets heading west out of Malasaña lead down to Calle de San Bernardo, across which lies the barrio de Conde Duque. Its impossibly narrow streets shelter a number of excellent live-music venues, among them Kabokla (p195) and Café La Palma (p194).

7 Antiguo Cuartel del Conde Duque
Make your way down to the Plaza Guardias de Corps, a pleasing little square overshadowed by the Antiguo Cuartel del Conde Duque (p107). This immense cultural space is architecturally distinguished, but its treasures lie within, most notably in the Museo Municipal de Arte Contemporáneo (p107).

8 El Jardín Secreto
You've covered a lot of ground. Now your reward lies in El Jardín Secreto. There's no more romantic cafe in Madrid than this cosy, candlelit bar (p192), with its exotic decor and wide range of drinks.

CHAMBERÍ & ARGÜELLES

Drinking & Nightlife p197; Eating p168; Shopping p142; Sleeping p229

Chamberí, north of the city centre, is one of the most *castizo* (typically madrileño) barrios in Madrid. At once traditional and sophisticated, this leafy barrio has in recent years become one of the most sought-after addresses in Madrid and prices have even begun to surpass those of Salamanca. In the early 19th century, the barrio was an insignificant village beyond the then city boundaries – Napoleon himself is believed to have spent the night here in December 1808, in the early months of his occupation of Spain.

Argüelles is similar, a predominantly residential barrio whose streets are lined with elegant early-20th-century apartment buildings, although it's far from uniform. The barrio was the scene of heavy fighting during the Spanish Civil War, acting as the buffer between Franco's forces in the Ciudad Universitaria area and downtown Madrid. Argüelles, like Chamberí, is home to a smattering of small shops and restaurants that are very much a part of barrio life.

You don't come to Chamberí or Argüelles for the sights, although there are some fine museums, as well as outstanding places to eat, drink and watch live music. More than that, Chamberí and, to a lesser extent, Argüelles may be fairly well off today, but they lack the snootiness of Salamanca. As such, it's here perhaps more than anywhere else in Madrid that you get a sense of Madrid as the madrileños experience it, away from the tourist crowds.

top picks

SIGHTS IN CHAMBERÍ & ARGÜELLES

- Templo de Debod (left)
- Museo de América (opposite)
- Museo Sorolla (p118)
- Estación de Chamberí (p117)

TEMPLO DE DEBOD Map pp116-17

☎ 91 366 74 15; www.munimadrid.es/templodebod, in Spanish; Calle de Ferraz 1; admission free; ☯ 10am-2pm & 6-8pm Tue-Fri, 10am-2pm Sat & Sun Apr-Sep, 9.45am-1.45pm & 4.15-6.15pm Tue-Fri, 10am-2pm Sat & Sun Oct-Mar; Ⓜ Ventura Rodríguez

Yes, that *is* an Egyptian temple in downtown Madrid. No matter which way you look at it, there's something incongruous about finding the Templo de Debod in the Parque de la Montaña northwest of Plaza de España. How did it end up in Madrid? The temple was saved from the rising waters of Lake Nasser in southern Egypt as Egyptian president Gamal Abdel Nasser built the Aswan High Dam. After 1968 it was sent block by block to Spain as a gesture of thanks to Spanish archaeologists in the Unesco team that worked to save the monuments that would otherwise have disappeared forever.

Begun in 2200 BC and completed over many centuries, the temple was dedicated to the god Amon of Thebes, about 20km south of Philae in the Nubian desert of southern Egypt. According to some authors of myth and legend, the goddess Isis gave birth to Horus in this very temple, although obviously not in Madrid.

The views from the surrounding gardens towards the Palacio Real are some of Madrid's prettiest.

ORIENTATION & TRANSPORT: CHAMBERÍ & ARGÜELLES

For the purposes of this book, Chamberí and Argüelles stretch westward from Paseo de la Castellana across Calle de la Princesa and then dog-leg south; Chamberí occupies the east, Argüelles the west. Sloping parkland along Paseo del Pintor Rosales closes off the area to the west. Calle de Cea Bermúdez and Calle de José Abascal seal the area off to the north, while Calle de Génova, Calle de Sagasta, Calle de Carranza and Calle de Alberto Aguilera demarcate the south from Chueca and Malasaña.

Numerous metro stations circle the area. The most useful are Colón (line 4), Gregorio Marañón (lines 7 and 10), Islas Filipinas (line 7), Moncloa (lines 3 and 6), Argüelles (lines 3, 4 and 6), San Bernardo (lines 2 and 4), Bilbao (lines 1 and 4) and Alonso Martínez (lines 4, 5 and 10). In the heart of Chamberí you'll find Quevedo (line 2) and Iglesia (line 1).

MUSEO DE CERRALBO Map pp116-17

☎ 91 547 36 46; http://museocerralbo.mcu.es; Calle de Ventura Rodríguez 17; Ⓜ Ventura Rodríguez

Huddled beneath the modern apartment buildings northwest of Plaza de España, this noble old mansion is like an apparition of how wealthy madrileños once lived. The former home of the 17th Marqués de Cerralbo (1845–1922) – politician, poet and archaeologist – is a study in 19th-century opulence. The museum was closed for renovations at the time of writing.

When it reopens, the upper floor boasts a gala dining hall and a grand ballroom. The mansion is jammed with the fruits of the collector's eclectic meanderings – from Oriental pieces to religious paintings and clocks.

On the main floor are spread suits of armour from around the world, while the Oriental room is full of carpets, Moroccan kilims, tapestries, musical instruments and 18th-century Japanese suits of armour, much of it obtained at auction in Paris in the 1870s. The music room is dominated by a gondola of Murano glass and pieces of Bohemian crystal. The house is also replete with porcelain, including Sèvres, Wedgwood, Meissen and local ceramics. Clearly the *marqués* was a man of diverse tastes and it can all be a little overwhelming, especially once you factor in artworks by Zurbarán, Ribera, van Dyck and El Greco.

MUSEO DE AMÉRICA Map pp116-17

☎ 91 549 26 41; http://museodeamerica.mcu.es, in Spanish; Avenida de los Reyes Católicos 6; adult/student €3/1.50, free Sun; ⏰ 9.30am-3pm Tue, Wed, Fri & Sat, 9.30am-3pm & 4-7pm Thu, 10am-3pm Sun & holidays; Ⓜ Moncloa

Empire may have become a dirty word but it defined how Spain saw itself for centuries. Spanish vessels crossed the Atlantic to the Spanish colonies in Latin America carrying adventurers one way and gold and other looted artefacts from indigenous cultures on the return journey. These latter pieces – at once the heritage of another continent and a fascinating insight into imperial Spain – are the subject of this excellent museum.

The two levels of the museum show off a representative display of ceramics, statuary, jewellery and instruments of hunting, fishing and war, along with some

of the paraphernalia of the colonisers. The display is divided into five thematic zones: El Conocimiento de América (which traces the discovery and exploration of the Americas), La Realidad de América (a big-screen summary of how South America wound up as it has today), and others on society, religion and language, which each explore tribal issues, the clash with the Spanish newcomers and its results. The Colombian gold collection, dating as far back as the 2nd century AD, and a couple of shrunken heads are particularly eye-catching.

Temporary exhibitions with various Latin American themes are regularly held here.

FARO DE MADRID Map pp116-17

☎ 91 544 81 04; Avenida de los Reyes Católicos; lift (elevator) €1.20; Ⓜ Moncloa

If it ever reopens after the slow-moving renovations, this odd tower just in front of the Museo de América is the place to go for panoramic views of western Madrid. It was built in 1992 to commemorate the 500th anniversary of the discovery of America and to celebrate Madrid's role that year as the European Capital of Culture.

TELEFÉRICO Map pp116-17

☎ 91 541 11 18; www.teleferico.com, in Spanish; one-way/return €3.55/5.15; ⏰ hours vary; Ⓜ Argüelles

One of the world's most horizontal cable cars (it never hangs more than 40m above the ground), the Teleférico putters out from the slopes of La Rosaleda (the rose garden of Parque del Oeste). The 2.5km journey takes you into the depths of the Casa de Campo, Madrid's enormous green (in summer a more dry olive hue) open space to the west of the city centre. It's relaxing, a very local thing to do and offers some good views of Madrid's skyline. Try to time it so you can settle in for a cool lunch or evening tipple on one of the *terrazas* along Paseo del Pintor Rosales.

PARQUE DEL OESTE Map pp116-17

Avenida del Arco de la Victoria; Ⓜ Moncloa

Sloping down the hill behind the Moncloa metro station, Parque del Oeste (Park of the West) is quite beautiful, with plenty of shady corners where you can recline under a tree in the heat of the day and fine views out to the west towards Casa de Campo. It has been a madrileño favourite

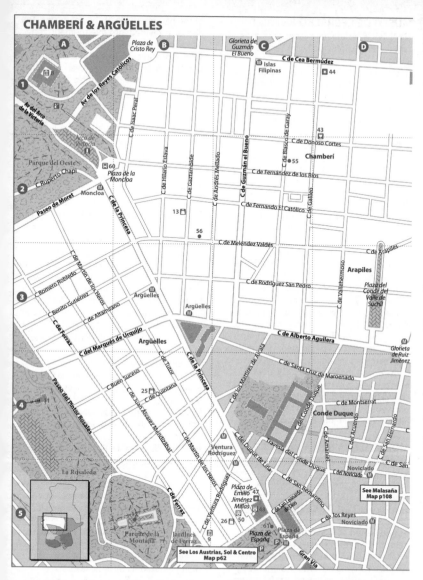

CHAMBERÍ & ARGÜELLES

ever since its creation in 1906, and one of the country's greatest-ever writers, Benito Pérez Galdós (see p36), took his last ride in Madrid here in August 1919. He soon fell ill and died in his house in Salamanca in January 1920.

In recent years the park has become the unofficial base of some new madrileños, the large Latin American community, who gather here on week-

end afternoons in large numbers to pass the time with barbecues and impromptu football games.

Until a few years ago, the Paseo de Camoens, a main thoroughfare running through the park, was lined with prostitutes by night. To deprive the prostitutes of clients, the city authorities now close the park to wheeled traffic from 11pm on Friday until 6am on Monday.

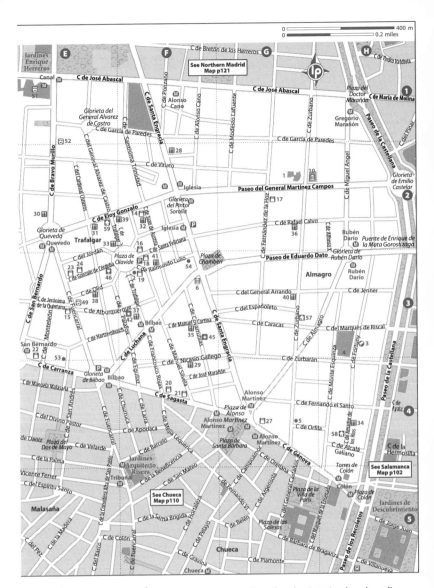

ESTACIÓN DE CHAMBERÍ Map above

Andén Cero; cnr Calles de Santa Engracia & de Luchana; admission free; ☺ 11am-7pm Tue-Fri, 11am-3pm Sat & Sun; Ⓜ Iglesia or Bilbao

For years, madrileños wondered what happened to the metro station called Chamberí – they knew it existed, yet it appeared on no maps and no trains ever stopped there. Over four decades later, the mystery has been solved. The answer was that Chamberí station lay along line 1, between the stops of Bilbao and Iglesia, until 1966 when Madrid's trains (and, where possible, platforms) were lengthened. Logistical difficulties meant that Chamberí could not be extended and the station was abandoned. In 2008 the Estación de Chamberí finally reopened to the public, if not for trains, serving as a museum piece that recreates the era of the station's inauguration in 1919 with advertisements from the time (including Madrid's then four-digit phone numbers), ticket offices and other memorabilia almost a century old. It's an engaging journey down memory lane.

MUSEO SOROLLA Map pp116-17
☎ 91 310 15 84; http://museosorolla.mcu.es, in Spanish; Paseo del General Martínez Campos 37; adult/child under 18yr & senior/student €3/free/1.50, free Sun; ☽ 9.30am-8pm Tue-Sat, 10am-3pm Sun & holidays; Ⓜ Gregorio Marañón or Rubén Darío

The Valencian artist Joaquín Sorolla immortalised the clear Mediterranean light of the Valencian coast. His Madrid house, a quiet mansion surrounded by lush gardens that he designed himself, was inspired by what he had seen in Andalucía and now contains the most complete collection of the artist's works.

On the ground floor there's a cool *patio cordobés,* an Andalucian courtyard off which is a room containing collections of Sorolla's drawings. The 1st floor, with the main salon and dining areas, was mostly decorated by the artist himself. On the same floor are three separate rooms that Sorolla used as studios. In the second one is a collection of his Valencian beach scenes. The third was where he usually worked.

Upstairs, works spanning Sorolla's career are organised across four adjoining rooms.

FROM TRADITIONAL BARRIO LIFE TO EGYPT
Walking Tour
1 Plaza de Olavide
This lovely circular plaza is a real slice of barrio life, with bars around the perimeter, children's playgrounds and a fountain as its centrepiece. It's a wonderful place to begin your walking tour, even if it will make you wish that you, too, could call it home.

2 Calle de Fuencarral
Take Calle de Gonzalo de Córdoba, which runs southwest from the plaza into Calle de Fuencarral. Another barrio favourite, this wide street has more pedestrians than cars and is lined with shops and cinemas. On Sunday mornings from 10am to 2pm, it's closed to traffic and the kids come out to play.

3 Museo de América
You've a long walk ahead of you, down through the east–west running streets of residential Argüelles. You'll eventually reach the Plaza de la Moncloa, watched over by the eye-catching Air Force Ministry. Beyond the monumental gate to the northwest, the Museo

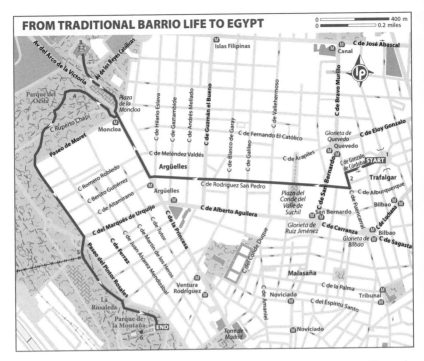

FROM TRADITIONAL BARRIO LIFE TO EGYPT

WALK FACTS

Start Plaza de Olavide
End Templo de Debod
Distance 4km
Time Three hours

de América (p115) promises a close-up look at the treasures looted from Spain's Latin American colonies. It's one of the more interesting museums in Madrid with insights into how Spain sees its own history.

4 Parque del Oeste

Across the busy road to the south, the sloping lawns and shady nooks of the Parque del Oeste (p115) are a pleasure to wander through. They may lack the grandeur of the Parque del Buen Retiro, but they're a delightful place to stroll as you make your way roughly south-southeast.

5 Teleférico

Emerging from the park along the Paseo del Pintor Rosales, you'll see the station for the Teleférico (p115) on your right. If you've the time, take a return trip out to the Casa de Campo, enjoying the views of central Madrid on the return journey.

6 Templo de Debod

With your feet back on the ground, the Paseo del Pintor Rosales leads to the Templo de Debod (p114), a 4200-year-old Egyptian temple transplanted into the heart of Madrid. It's an intriguing apparition. Don't neglect to wander in the gardens behind the temple for fine views (especially at sunset) towards the Palacio Real.

NORTHERN MADRID

Drinking & Nightlife p198; Eating p170; Shopping p144; Sleeping p230

Madrileños like to keep business and play separate and, for the most part, northern Madrid primarily concerns itself with the former. Most of the gracious old palaces and mansions that once lined the Paseo de la Castellana were long ago replaced by office buildings and apartments, many of which have appeared since the 1940s. Even so, it's home to Real Madrid's Estadio Santiago Bernabéu, a worthy but little-visited museum, upmarket restaurants and some terrific nightlife.

ESTADIO SANTIAGO BERNABÉU
Map opposite

☎ 91 398 43 00, 902 291 709; www.realmadrid .com; Avenida de Concha Espina 1; tour adult/child under 14yr €15/10; ⏱ 10am-7.30pm Mon-Sat, 10.30am-6.30pm Sun, except match days; Ⓜ Santiago Bernabéu

Football fans and budding Madridistas (Real Madrid supporters) will want to make a pilgrimage to this temple to all that's extravagant and successful in football. For a tour of the stadium, buy your ticket at ticket window 10 (next to gate 7). The self-guided tours take you up into the stands for a panoramic view of the stadium, then pass through the presidential box, press room, dressing rooms, players' tunnel and even onto the pitch itself. The tour ends in the extraordinary Exposición de Trofeos (trophy exhibit). On match days, tours cease five hours before the game is scheduled to start, although the Exposición de Trofeos is open until two hours before

game time. For details on getting tickets to a Real Madrid game, turn to p211, while the club's astonishing history is covered on p210. Details of Real Madrid's club shop are found on p144.

MUSEO DE LA CIUDAD Map opposite

☎ 91 588 65 99; Calle del Príncipe de Vergara 140; admission free; ⏱ 9.30am-8pm Tue-Fri, 10am-2pm Sat & Sun; Ⓜ Cruz del Rayo

The highlights of this museum are the scale models of various Madrid landmarks, among them the Plaza de Toros. Other models cover whole barrios or features, such as Plaza de la Villa and Paseo de la Castellana. The exhibits take you from Madrid and its beginnings to the Enlightenment, through the 19th century and to the present. The displays on the airport and how the gas, electricity and telephone systems work, however, are as dry as dust and may offer just a bit too much discovery for some tastes.

ORIENTATION & TRANSPORT: NORTHERN MADRID

Just about everything you're likely to need in northern Madrid is on, or just off, Paseo de la Castellana, which runs through the striking Torres Puerta de Europa on Plaza de Castilla close to its northern end. These remarkable leaning towers are 115m high with a 15-degree tilt, and have become a symbol of modern Madrid. Just northeast of the towers is the Chamartín train station.

The main metro stations you're likely to need are Gregorio Marañón (lines 7 and 10), Nuevos Ministerios (lines 6, 8 and 10), Santiago Bernabéu (line 10) and Chamartín (lines 1 and 10).

NORTHERN MADRID

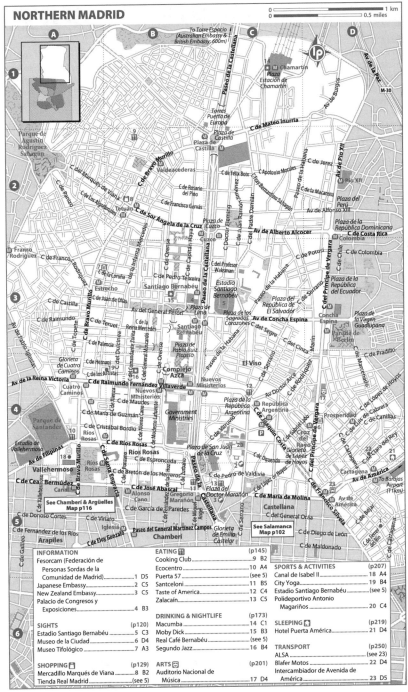

Eating p171

In general the attractions beyond Madrid's central barrios are spread pretty far and wide and, in most cases, there's little reason to do anything other than see the sight and come back. There are, however, exceptions. The Ermita de San Antonio de la Florida, which on no account should be missed, lies just beyond the Argüelles district and is easily reached by public transport. The Real Fábrica de Tapices and Casa de la Moneda are similarly close, away to the east and southeast.

ERMITA DE SAN ANTONIO DE LA FLORIDA Map pp124-5

☎ 91 542 07 22; Glorieta de San Antonio de la Florida 5; admission free; ⊙ 9.30am-8pm Tue-Fri, 10am-2pm Sat & Sun Sep-Jun, hours vary Jul & Aug; Ⓜ Príncipe Pío

Simply extraordinary: the frescoed ceilings of this humble hermitage are among Madrid's most surprising secrets. Recently restored – and also known as the Panteón de Goya – the southern of the two chapels is one of the few places to see Goya masterworks in their original setting, as painted by the master in 1798 on the request of Carlos IV.

Figures on the dome depict the miracle of St Anthony. The saint, who lived in Padua in Italy, heard word from his native Lisbon that his father had been unjustly accused of murder. The saint was whisked miraculously to his home town from northern Italy, where he tried in vain to convince the judges of his father's innocence. He then demanded that the corpse of the murder victim be placed before the judges. Goya's painting depicts the moment in which St Anthony calls on the corpse (a young man) to rise up and absolve his father. Around them swarms a typical Madrid crowd. It was customary in such works that angels and cherubs appear in the cupola, above all the terrestrial activity, but Goya, never one to let himself be confined within the mores of the day, places the human above the divine.

The painter is buried in front of the altar. His remains were transferred in 1919 from

top picks

SIGHTS BEYOND THE CENTRE

- Ermita de San Antonio de la Florida (left)
- Warner Brothers Movie World (p127)
- Casa de Campo (opposite)
- Matadero Madrid (p126)
- Faunia (p128)
- Real Fábrica de Tapices (p126)

Bordeaux (France), where he had died in self-imposed exile in 1828. Oddly, the skeleton that was exhumed in Bordeaux was missing one important item – the head.

On 13 June every year, it is a Madrid tradition for seamstresses to come here to pray for a partner, although the tradition now extends to young women from all walks of life.

CEMENTERIO DE LA FLORIDA
Map pp124-5

Calle de Francisco Jacinto y Alcantara; Ⓜ Príncipe Pío

Across the train tracks from the Ermita de San Antonio de la Florida is the cemetery where 43 rebels executed by Napoleon's troops lie buried. They were killed on the nearby Montaña del Príncipe Pío in the predawn of 3 May 1808, after the Dos de Mayo uprising. The event was immortalised by Goya in his *Dos de Mayo* and *Tres de Mayo* paintings, which hang in the Museo

ORIENTATION & TRANSPORT: BEYOND THE CENTRE

You'll find the Casa de Campo west of the city centre; it's also home to the Zoo Aquarium de Madrid and Parque de Atracciones. The Museo del Ferrocarril is about 1km south of Atocha station in the former Las Delicias train station. South of Madrid, near the town of San Martín de la Vega, is Madrid's answer to Disney World: Warner Brothers Movie World. Faunia is southeast of the city centre.

The most efficient way to get to the sights in this section (with the exception of Warner Brothers Movie World, which requires a regional train) is by metro or bus. The appropriate transport options are indicated in each entry.

del Prado (p90). A plaque was placed here in 1981. The forlorn cemetery, established in 1796, is often closed.

CAMPO DEL MORO Map pp124-5

☎ 91 454 88 00; www.patrimonial.es; Paseo de la Virgen del Puerto; ⏲ 10am-8pm Mon-Sat, 9am-8pm Sun & holidays Apr-Sep, 10am-6pm Mon-Sat, 9am-6pm Sun & holidays Oct-Mar; Ⓜ Príncipe Pío
From this attractive park you can gain an appreciation of Madrid in its earliest days – it was from here, in what would become known as Campo del Moro (Moor's Field), that an Almoravid army laid siege to the city in 1110. The troops occupied all but the fortress (where the Palacio Real now stands), but the Christian garrison held on until the Almoravid fury abated and their forces retired south. The 20 hectares of gardens that now adorn the site were first laid in the 18th century, with major overhauls in 1844 and 1890. The gardens combine quiet corners that feel like an expansive private garden with the monumental grandeur designed to mimic the gardens surrounding the palace at Versailles; nowhere is the latter more in evidence than along the east–west Pradera, a lush lawn with the Palacio Real as its backdrop. The gardens' centrepiece, which stands halfway along the Pradera, is the elegant Fuente de las Conchas (Fountain of the Shells) designed by Ventura Rodríguez, the Goya of Madrid's 18th-century architecture scene. The only entrance is from Paseo de la Virgen del Puerto.

CASA DE CAMPO off Map pp124-5

Ⓜ Batán
Sometimes called the 'lungs of Madrid', this 17 sq km stand of greenery stretches west of the Río Manzanares. There are prettier and more central parks in Madrid but such is its scope that there are plenty of reasons to visit. And visit the madrileños do, nearly half a million of them every weekend, celebrating the fact that the short-lived Republican government of the 1930s opened the park to the public (it was previously the exclusive domain of royalty).

For city-bound madrileños with neither the time nor the inclination to go further afield, it has become the closest they get to nature, despite the fact that cyclists, walkers and picnickers overwhelm the byways and trails that criss-cross the park. There are

top picks

IT'S FREE

Admission is free at the following sights all the time or at the times listed.

- Museo del Prado (p90) From 6pm to 8pm Tuesday to Saturday and from 5pm to 8pm Sunday.
- Centro de Arte Reina Sofía (p82) From 7pm to 9pm Monday and Wednesday to Friday, 2.30pm to 9pm Saturday, and 10am to 2.30pm Sunday.
- Ermita de San Antonio de la Florida (opposite)
- Caixa Forum (p95)
- Museo Sorolla (p118) Sunday.
- Plaza de Toros & Museo Taurino (p100)
- Museo Municipal de Arte Contemporáneo (p107)
- Estación de Chamberí (p117)
- Matadero Madrid (p126)
- Museo de los Orígenes (p78)
- Templo de Debod (p114)
- Museo de América (p115) Sunday.
- Museo de la Escultura Abstracta (p103)
- Museo de la Ciudad (p120)
- Casa de Lope de Vega (p86)
- Museo Naval (p96)
- Museo del Romanticismo (p106) After 2.30pm Saturday.
- Museo del Libro (p103)

tennis courts and a swimming pool, as well as a zoo (Zoo Aquarium de Madrid, p126) and an amusement park (Parque de Atracciones, p127). At Casa de Campo's southern end, restaurants specialise in wedding receptions, ensuring plenty of bridal parties roam the grounds in search of an unoccupied patch of greenery where they can take photos. Also in the park, the Andalucian-style ranch known as Batán is used to house the bulls destined to do bloody battle in the Fiestas de San Isidro Labrador.

Although it's largely for the better, something has definitely been lost from the days before 2003 when unspoken intrigues surrounded the small artificial lake (Ⓜ Lago), where several lakeside terrazas and eateries were frequented by an odd combination of day trippers, working girls and clients. By night, prostitutes jockeyed for position while punters kept their places around the lakeside chiringuitos (open-air bars or kiosks) as though nothing out of the ordinary was happening. The traffic in the middle of the night here was akin to rush hour in the city

BEYOND THE CENTRE

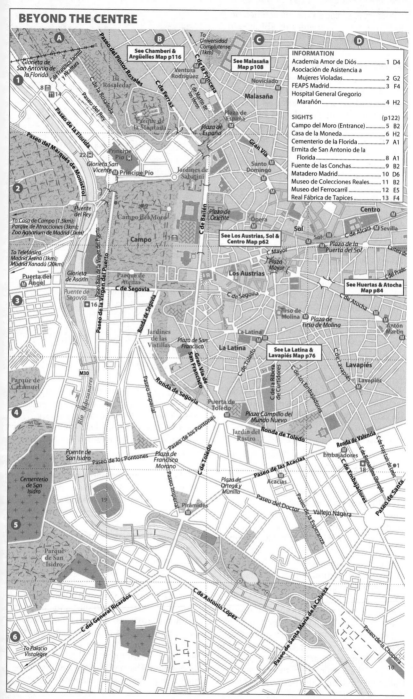

See Chamberí & Argüelles Map p116

See Malasaña Map p108

See Los Austrias, Sol & Centro Map p62

See Huertas & Atocha Map p84

See La Latina & Lavapiés Map p76

INFORMATION

Academia Amor de Diós	1	D4
Asociación de Asistencia a Mujeres Violadas	2	G2
FEAPS Madrid	3	F4
Hospital General Gregorio Marañón	4	H2

SIGHTS (p122)

Campo del Moro (Entrance)	5	B2
Casa de la Moneda	6	H2
Cementerio de la Florida	7	A1
Ermita de San Antonio de la Florida	8	A1
Fuente de las Conchas	9	B2
Matadero Madrid	10	D6
Museo de Colecciones Reales	11	B2
Museo del Ferrocarril	12	E5
Real Fábrica de Tapices	13	F4

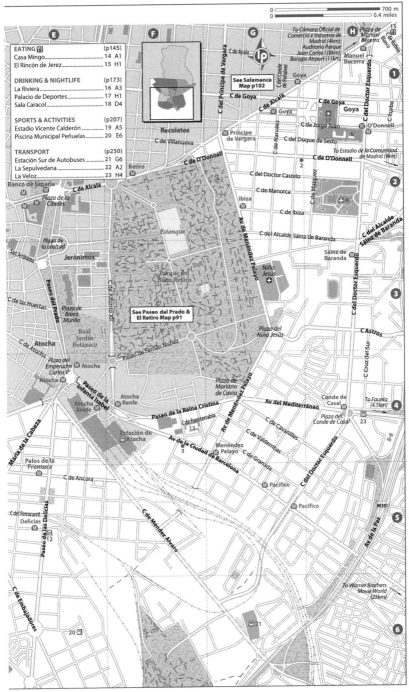

EATING 🍴 (p145)
Casa Mingo...................................... 14 A1
El Rincón de Jerez............................ 15 H1

DRINKING & NIGHTLIFE (p173)
La Riviera.. 16 A3
Palacio de Deportes......................... 17 H1
Sala Caracol.................................... 18 D4

SPORTS & ACTIVITIES (p207)
Estadio Vicente Calderón................. 19 A5
Piscina Municipal Peñuelas............. 20 E6

TRANSPORT (p250)
Estación Sur de Autobuses.............. 21 G6
La Sepulvedana............................... 22 A2
La Veloz.. 23 H4

See Salamanca
Map p102

To Cámara Oficial de
Comercio e Industria de
Madrid (4km);
Auditorio Parque
Juan Carlos I (8km);
Barajas Airport (11km)

See Paseo del Prado &
El Retiro Map p91

To Estadio de la Comunidad
de Madrid (9km)

To Faunia
(4.5km)

To Warner Brothers
Movie World
(25km)

0 — 700 m
0 — 0.4 miles

125

centre. The police shut this scene down and, thankfully, there are no more louche traffic jams, at least on weekends.

MATADERO MADRID Map pp124-5

☎ 91 252 52 53; www.mataderomadrid.com; Paseo de la Chopera 14; admission free; ⏱ 4-10pm Tue-Fri, 11am-10pm Sat & Sun; Ⓜ Legazpi

This contemporary arts centre, opened in 2007, is a stunning multipurpose space south of the centre. Occupying the converted buildings of the old Arganzuela livestock market and slaughterhouse, Matadero Madrid will, when completed, cover 148,300 sq metres and host cutting-edge drama, musical and dance performances and exhibitions on architecture, fashion, literature and cinema. It will also be the site for the Centro Nacional de la Moda (National Fashion Centre). It's already worth a visit but, as the site expands its program, it's definitely one to watch for the future.

REAL FÁBRICA DE TAPICES Map pp124-5

☎ 91 434 05 50; www.realfabricadetapices.com; Calle de Fuenterrabía 2; admission €4; ⏱ 10am-2pm Mon-Fri Sep-Jul, guided tours every half-hour; Ⓜ Atocha Renfe or Menéndez Pelayo

If a wealthy Madrid nobleman wanted to impress, he came here to the Real Fábrica de Tapices (Royal Tapestry Workshop) where royalty commissioned the pieces that adorned their palaces and private residences. The Spanish government, Spanish royalty and the Vatican were the biggest patrons of the tapestry business: Spain alone is said to have collected four million tapestries. With such an exclusive clientele, it was a lucrative business and remains so, 300 years after the factory was founded. Goya began his career here, first as a cartoonist and later as a tapestry designer. Given such an illustrious history, it is, therefore, somewhat surprising that coming here today feels like visiting a carpet shop with small showrooms strewn with fine tapestries. There is a permanent exhibition on show and a sales area. If you're lucky, you'll get to see how they're made.

CASA DE LA MONEDA Map pp124-5

☎ 91 566 65 44; www.fnmt.es; Calle del Doctor Esquerdo 36; admission free; ⏱ 10am-5.30pm Tue-Fri, 10am-2pm Sat, Sun & holidays; Ⓜ O'Donnell or Goya

top picks

FOR CHILDREN

- Warner Brothers Movie World (opposite)
- Teleférico (p115)
- Faunia (p128)
- Estadio Santiago Bernabéu (p120)
- Parque del Buen Retiro (p97)
- Museo de Cera (p111)
- Museo del Ferrocarril (p127)
- Parque de Atracciones (opposite)
- Zoo Aquarium de Madrid (below)
- Madrid Snow Zone (p210)

The national mint (literally the 'house of coin') is a collectors' treasure trove of coins from ancient Greece and Roman Spain, proceeding through the Byzantine, Visigothic and Islamic periods. The last period is particularly well represented. Coins from the days of the Catholic Monarchs abound, and the collection continues through to the establishment of the peseta as the Spanish currency, consigned to history by the introduction of the euro in 2002. Paper money ranges from a 14th-century Chinese note to revolutionary Russian cash. Also on display is an extensive collection of prints, *grabados* (etchings), lottery tickets since 1942 and stamps. You can also follow the processes involved in coining money and even strike your own medal. If you're an old-money buff, a visit to the Plaza Mayor (p61) on Sunday morning, when the porticoes are crowded with dealers selling coins, stamps and banknotes, will nicely complement your visit to the mint.

ZOO AQUARIUM DE MADRID
off Map pp124-5

☎ 902 345 014; www.zoomadrid.com; Casa de Campo; adult/child 3-7yr & senior €18.65/15.10; ⏱ hours vary; Ⓜ Casa de Campo or bus 37 from Intercambiador de Príncipe Pío

Madrid's zoo, in the Casa de Campo, is a fairly standard European city zoo and is home to about 3000 animals. Exhibits range from white Siberian tigers to mambas, Atlas lions, zebras, giraffes, rhinoceroses, flamingos, koalas and a pair of celebrity pandas. There's also a fine aquarium and you can watch dolphins and sea lions get up to their tricks. Shows are held at least a couple of times a day. The 3000 sq metre Aviario (aviary) contains some 60 species of eagle, condor and vulture. Spend long enough here, however, and the Disneyfication of the zoo and their penchant for charging for everything (€0.60 for the map!) will start to grate. Arriving by bus is the best option as it leaves you right at the door; if you take the metro to Casa de Campo, you've a 15-minute walk from the station, or you can take bus 37 from the station for one stop.

PARQUE DE ATRACCIONES
off Map pp124-5

☎ 91 463 29 00; www.parquedeatracciones .es; Casa de Campo; admission €10.60, admission & unlimited rides adult/child under 7yr €29/22; ⌚ hours vary; Ⓜ Batán or bus 37 from Intercambiador de Príncipe Pío

There's not much that's especially Spanish about this amusement park, located about 300m from the Parque de Atracciones, but it's got the usual collection of high-adrenaline rides, shows for the kids and kitsch at every turn. In the Zona de Máquinas (the rather ominous sounding Machines Zone) are most of the bigger rides, such as classic roller coasters, the Lanzadera (which takes you up 63m and then drops you in a simulated bungee jump), La Máquina (a giant wheel that spins on its axis) and the favourite of all, the Tornado, a kind of upside-down roller coaster that zips along at up to 80km/h. Strictly for those with cast-iron stomachs.

After all that gut-churning stuff, you'll be grateful for the Zona de Tranquilidad, where you can climb aboard a gentle Ferris wheel, take a theme ride through the jungle or just sit back for a snack. Of course, tranquillity is relative – El Viejo Caserón (haunted house) is not for the nervous among you (in our experience, it's the adults who get spooked). La Zona de la Naturaleza (Nature Zone) offers, among other things, Dodgems and various water rides.

Finally, in the Zona Infantil, younger kids can get their own thrills on less hair-raising rides, such as a Ford-T, the Barón Rojo (Red Baron) and Caballos del Oeste (Horses of the Wild West).

The park, in the Casa de Campo, has all sorts of timetable variations, so it is always a good idea to check before committing yourself.

WARNER BROTHERS MOVIE WORLD
off Map pp124-5

☎ 902 024 100; www.parquewarner.com; San Martín de la Vega; adult/child €38/29; ⌚ hours vary; cercanías train (line C3 for Aranjuez, change at Pinto) from Atocha, get out at Parque de Ocio station

Disney World it ain't but this movie theme park, 25km south of central Madrid, has much to catch the attention. Kids will love the chance to hang out with Tom and Jerry, while the young-at-heart film buffs among you will be similarly taken with the Wild West or remakes of the studio sets for such Hollywood 'greats' as Police Academy. Entrance to the park is via Hollywood Boulevard, not unlike LA's Sunset Boulevard, whereafter you can choose between Cartoon World, the Old West, Hollywood Boulevard, Super Heroes (featuring Superman, Batman and the finks of Gotham City) and finally Warner Brothers Movie World Studios. It's all about the stars of the silver screen coming to life as life-sized cartoon characters roam the grounds, and rides and high-speed roller coasters distract you if attention starts to wane. There are also restaurants and shops.

To get here by car, take the N-IV (the Carretera de Andalucía) south out of Madrid and turn off at Km22 for San Martín de la Vega, about 15km east of the exit. Follow the signs to the car park, where parking is available for €8.

Opening times are complex and do change; check before heading out.

MUSEO DEL FERROCARRIL Map pp124-5
☎ 902 228 822; www.museodelferrocarril.org; Paseo de las Delicias 61; adult/student, senior & child 4-12yr €4.50/3; ⌚ 10am-3pm Tue-Sun Sep-Jul; Ⓜ Delicias

You don't have to be a trainspotter to enjoy this railway museum – you'll see as many kids as anoraks – but it helps. Housed in the disused 1880s Estación de Delicias south of Lavapiés, this museum has about 30 pieces of rolling stock lined up along the platforms, ranging from the earliest steam locomotives to a sleeping car from the late 1920s and the Talgo II, which ran on the country's long-distance routes until 1971. Several rooms off the platforms are set aside for dioramas of train stations, memorabilia, station clocks and the like. There are plenty of model trains, tracks and other modelling products in the shop on the way out.

FAUNIA off Map pp124-5

☎ 91 301 62 10; www.faunia.es, in Spanish; Avenida de las Comunidades 28; 8yr & older/under 8yr & senior €25.50/19.50; ⏰ 10am-8pm Mon-Fri & 10am-9pm Sat & Sun Jun-Aug, shorter hr rest of year; Ⓜ Valdebernardo

This modern animal theme park takes you through a range of thematic areas, including an aviary, an insectarium, a parade of more than 70 penguins in the polar ecosystem, an Amazon jungle scene (complete with simulated tropical storm), an African forest and performing dolphins and sea lions. Faunia is located east of the M-40, about 7km from the city centre. Opening hours vary and they close for much of January and February, so check the website before setting out. Tickets are €1 to €2 cheaper if bought online.

SHOPPING

top picks

What's your recommendation? www.lonelyplanet.com/madrid

SHOPPING

Shopping in the Spanish capital is about so much more than Zara, bull postcards and tacky flamenco posters. If we had to identify our favourite aspect of shopping here, it would have to be the small boutiques and quirky shops that you find all across the city and which enable you to escape the over-commercialisation of mass-produced Spanish culture. Often run by the same family for generations, these engaging little outposts of traditional Spanish culture sell everything from handcrafted *abanicos* (Spanish fans) and old-style ceramics to rope-soled espadrilles, and from guitars favoured by the Beatles, Eric Clapton and numerous flamenco greats to corner shops specialising in Spanish wines and food delicacies. Madrid is also Spain's fashion capital and the streets are lined with shops that showcase all the colour and creativity of Spanish and international designers, from haute couture to earthy street wear.

The key to shopping Madrid-style is knowing where to look. Salamanca and parts of Chueca are the home of upmarket fashions. Malasaña, Salamanca's alter ego, is all about fashion that's as funky as it is offbeat and ideal for that studied underground look that will fit right in with Madrid's after-dark crowd. Huertas and Chamberí defy easy categorisation with their engaging, often old-style little boutiques, while La Latina has become a magnet for some of Spain's most imaginative jewellery designers. The downtown area close to the Puerta del Sol throws up plenty of individual surprises but, in keeping with the character of central Madrid, there's a little bit of everything on offer. That sense is multiplied a hundredfold in El Rastro market, where madrileños converge in epic numbers on Sunday to pick through the junk in search of treasure.

LOS AUSTRIAS, SOL & CENTRO

The maze of streets around the Plaza Mayor that extend up towards Gran Vía have something for everyone. Recurring themes include excellent bookshops, large-scale department stores and classy souvenir shops that help you forget the stores selling tacky tourist kitsch all across the centre.

CASA DEL LIBRO Map pp62-3   Bookshop
☎ 91 524 19 00; www.casadellibro.com; Gran Vía 29; ✆ 9.30am-9.30pm Mon-Sat, 11am-9pm Sun; Ⓜ Gran Vía
Spain's answer to Borders, this sprawling megabookshop has titles on just about any topic you can think of. There's a large English-language literature section on the mezzanine level above the information desk, as well as novels in French, Italian and German. Nonfiction books in English are mixed elsewhere alongside Spanish titles.

FNAC Map pp62-3   Bookshop & Multimedia
☎ 91 595 61 00; www.fnac.es, in Spanish; Calle de Preciados 28; ✆ 10am-9.30pm Mon-Sat, noon-9.30pm Sun; Ⓜ Callao
This four-storey megastore has a terrific range of CDs ranging from flamenco and world music to classical, as well as DVDs, video games, electronic equipment and books; English-language books are on the 3rd floor, and there's a large children's section on the 4th floor.

LA LIBRERÍA Map pp62-3   Bookshop
☎ 91 454 00 18; Calle Mayor 80; ✆ 10am-8pm Mon-Fri, 11am-2pm Sat; Ⓜ Ópera or Sol
This bookshop may be small, but it's the place to find books (mostly in Spanish) covering everything to do with Madrid, from coffee-table books to histories of every barrio in the capital.

PETRA'S INTERNATIONAL BOOKSHOP Map pp62-3   Bookshop
☎ 91 541 72 91; www.petrasbookshop.com; Calle de Campomanes 13; ✆ 11am-9pm Mon-Sat; Ⓜ Ópera or Santo Domingo
A wonderful little bookshop (with mostly secondhand stock), Petra's has a great selection in all major languages and across most major genres; it's also something of a meeting place for the lively expat community. They also have plans to sell a range of new Lonely Planet guides and the friendly owners can point you in the direction of activities in English and other languages. We also like a bookshop with a cat – Pet Ra is its name.

top picks

FOR QUALITY GIFTS

- Antigua Casa Talavera (below)
- Antigüedades Hom (p142)
- El Arco Artesanía (p132)
- Gil (p134)
- México (p134)
- Casa de Diego (p132)

ANTIGUA CASA TALAVERA

Map pp62-3   Ceramics
☎ 91 547 34 17; Calle de Isabel la Católica 2;
☒ 10am-1.30pm & 5-8pm Mon-Fri, 10am-1.30pm
Sat; Ⓜ Santo Domingo
The extraordinary tiled facade of this
wonderful old shop conceals an Aladdin's
cave of ceramics from all over Spain. This
is not the mass-produced stuff aimed at a
tourist market, but comes from the small
family potters of Andalucía and Toledo,
ranging from the decorative (tiles) to the
useful (plates, jugs and other kitchen
items). The old couple who run the place
are delightful.

ASÍ Map pp62-3   Children's Toys & Clothes
☎ 91 548 28 28; www.tiendas-asi.com, in Spanish;
Gran Vía 47; ☒ 10am-8.30pm Mon-Sat; Ⓜ Callao
or Santo Domingo
Exquisite handmade children's dolls, all
beautifully attired and overflowing from
the shop window, are proffered here. Inside
it also sells children's clothes, toys and
intricate dolls' houses that are works of art;
for the last, every single item (furniture,
saucepans etc) can be purchased
individually. None of it's cheap, but they're
once-in-a-lifetime purchases.

FLIP Map pp62-3   Clothes & Accessories
☎ 91 366 44 72; www.flipmadrid.com; Calle Mayor
19; ☒ 10.30am-9pm Mon-Sat, noon-8pm 1st & last
Sun of month; Ⓜ Sol
Too cool for its own good, Flip is funky
and edgy, with its designer T-shirts, G-Star
jeans and brand names like Franklin
Marshall, Carhartt, Guess and Diesel, as well
as a groovy and often offbeat collection of
belts, caps and bags. Staff are as hip as the
clothing and always ready with advice. The
changing rooms, however, require a con-
tortionist's flexibility.

SALVADOR BACHILLER

Map pp62-3   Clothes & Accessories
☎ 91 559 83 21; www.salvadorbachiller.com; Gran
Vía 65; ☒ 10am-9.30pm Mon-Sat; Ⓜ Plaza de
España or Santo Domingo
The stylish and high-quality leather bags,
wallets, suitcases and other accessories
of Salvador Bachiller are a staple of
Spanish shopping aficionados. This is
leather with a typically Spanish twist – the
colours are dazzling in bright pinks, yellows
and greens. Sound garish? You'll change
your mind once you step inside. It also has
an outlet (Map p110; ☎ 91 523 30 37; Calle de Gravina
11; ☒ 10.30am-9.30pm Mon-Thu, 10.30am-11pm Fri
& Sat, noon-9pm Sun; Ⓜ Chueca) in Chueca for
superseded stock.

EL CORTE INGLÉS

Map pp62-3   Department Store
☎ 91 379 80 00; www.elcorteingles.es, in Spanish;
Calle de Preciados 3; ☒ 10am-10pm Mon-Sat; Ⓜ Sol
In the great tradition of department stores
the world over, there's everything you need
here, from food and furniture to clothes,
appliances, toiletries, electronics, books and
music. Although you'll usually pay extra for
the convenience of one-stop shopping,

TAXES & REFUNDS

Value-added tax (VAT) is known in Spain as *impuesto sobre el valor añadido* (IVA, pronounced 'ee-ba'). On accommodation and restaurant prices, IVA is 7% and is usually – but not always – included in quoted prices. On retail goods IVA
is 16%.

   Visitors are entitled to a refund of the 16% IVA on purchases costing more than €90.15 from any shop if the goods
are taken out of the European Union (EU) within three months. Ask the shop for a cashback refund form showing the
price and IVA paid for each item, and identifying the vendor and purchaser; then present the form at the customs booth
for IVA refunds when you depart from Spain (or elsewhere from the EU). At this point, you'll need your passport and a
boarding card that shows you're leaving the EU. The officer will stamp the invoice and you hand it in at a bank at the
departure point for the reimbursement. There are refund offices in terminals T1, T2 and T4 at Barajas airport as you're
departing Madrid.

the after-sales service is better than most. They also open on the first Sunday of every month, and every day in December. Branches are scattered throughout the city, including one in Malasaña (Map pp108-9; ☎ 91 454 60 00; Calle de la Princesa 56; ⊗ 10am-10pm Mon-Sat; Ⓜ Argüelles) and one in Salamanca (Map p102; ☎ 91 432 54 90; Calle de Serrano 47; ⊗ 10am-10pm Mon-Sat; Ⓜ Serrano).

CONVENTO DEL CORPUS CRISTI
Map pp62-3   Food & Drink

Las Carboneras; ☎ 91 548 37 01; Plaza del Conde de Miranda; ⊗ 9.30am-1pm & 4-6.30pm; Ⓜ Ópera

The cloistered nuns at this convent also happen to be fine pastry chefs. You make your request through a door, then grille on Calle del Codo and the products are delivered through a little revolving door that allows the nuns to remain unseen by the outside world.

EL FLAMENCO VIVE Map pp62-3   Music

☎ 91 547 39 17; www.elflamencovive.es; Calle del Conde Lemos 7; ⊗ 10am-2pm & 5-9pm Mon-Sat; Ⓜ Ópera

This temple to flamenco has it all, from guitars and songbooks to well-priced CDs, polka-dotted dancing costumes, shoes, colourful plastic jewellery and literature about flamenco. It's the sort of place that will appeal as much to curious first timers as to serious students of the art. It also organises classes in flamenco guitar (see p258).

EL ARCO ARTESANÍA Map pp62-3   Souvenirs

☎ 91 365 26 80; www.elarcoartesania.com; Plaza Mayor 9; ⊗ 11am-9pm; Ⓜ Sol or La Latina

This original shop in the southwestern corner of Plaza Mayor sells an outstanding array of homemade designer souvenirs, from stone and glass work to jewellery and home fittings. The papier mâché figures are gorgeous, but there's so much else here to turn your head.

CASA DE DIEGO Map pp62-3   Specialist

☎ 91 522 66 43; www.casadediego.com; Plaza de la Puerta del Sol 12; ⊗ 9.30am-8pm Mon-Sat; Ⓜ Sol

This classic shop has been around since 1858, making, selling and repairing Spanish fans, shawls, umbrellas and canes. Service is old style and occasionally grumpy, but the fans are works of antique art. They have

another shop and workshop (Map pp62-3; ☎ 91 531 02 23; Calle del los Mesoneros Romanos 4; ⊗ 9.30am-1.30pm & 4.45-8pm Mon-Sat; Ⓜ Callao or Sol) nearby.

CASA HERNANZ Map pp62-3   Specialist

☎ 91 366 54 50; Calle de Toledo 18; ⊗ 9am-1.30pm & 4.30-8pm Mon-Fri, 10am-2pm Sat; Ⓜ La Latina or Sol

Comfy, rope-soled *alpargatas* (espadrilles), Spain's traditional summer footwear, are worn by everyone from the King of Spain down, and you can buy your own pair at this humble workshop, which has been hand-making the shoes for five generations; you can even get them made to order. Prices range from €5 to €40 and queues form whenever the weather starts to warm up.

JOSÉ RAMÍREZ Map pp62-3   Specialist

☎ 91 531 42 29; www.guitarrasramirez.com; Calle de la Paz 8; ⊗ 10am-2pm & 4.30-8pm Mon-Fri, 10.30am-2pm Sat; Ⓜ Sol

José Ramírez is one of Spain's best guitar makers and his guitars have been strummed by a host of flamenco greats and international musicians (even the Beatles). Using Honduran cedar, Cameroonian ebony and Indian or Madagascan rosewood, among other materials, and based on traditions dating back over generations, this is craftsmanship of the highest order. Out the back there's a little museum with guitars dating back to 1830.

MATY Map pp62-3   Specialist

☎ 91 531 32 91; www.maty.es, in Spanish; Calle del Maestro Victoria 2; ⊗ 10am-1.45pm & 4.30-8pm Mon-Fri, 10am-2pm & 4.30-8pm Sat; Ⓜ Sol

Wandering around central Madrid, it's easy to imagine that flamenco outfits have been reduced to imitation dresses sold as souvenirs to tourists. That's why places like Maty matter. Here you'll find dresses, shoes and all the accessories that go with the genre, with sizes for children and adults. It also does quality disguises for Carnaval. These are the real deal, with prices to match, but they make brilliant gifts.

SANTARRUFINA Map pp62-3   Specialist

☎ 91 522 23 83; www.santarrufina.com; Calle de la Paz 4; ⊗ 10am-2pm & 4.30-8pm Mon-Fri, 10am-2pm Sat; Ⓜ Sol

This outpost of Spanish Catholicism has to be seen to be believed. Churches, priests

SALES & OPENING HOURS

The peak shopping season is during *las rebajas,* the annual winter and summer sales, when prices are slashed on just about everything. The winter sales begin around 7 January, just after Three Kings' Day, and last well into February. Summer sales begin in early July and last into August.

The shopping day starts at about 10am and is often broken up by a long lunch from 2pm to 5pm, except in larger stores. Shops reopen after lunch and stay busy until 8pm or even later. Shops selling music and books, as well as some convenience stores, are the only outlets allowed to open every Sunday, although all shops may (and most usually do) open on the first Sunday of every month and throughout December. There are plans to allow more shops to open on Sunday.

and monasteries are some of the patrons of this overwhelming three-storey shop full of everything from simple rosaries to imposing statues of saints and even a litter used to carry the Virgin in processions. Head downstairs for a peek at the extravagant chapel.

LA LATINA & LAVAPIÉS

La Latina is very much an after-dark and weekend barrio. That said, this is one of the most popular barrios for a hip, well-to-do urban crowd and the small boutiques dotted around the narrow streets reflect this clientele, especially when it comes to designer jewellery. But it's also the barrio that throngs with Sunday bargain hunters drawn here by El Rastro (which tumbles down into Lavapiés) and you'll also come across curio shops so specialised that you wonder how they ever keep going.

DEL HIERRO Map pp76-7   Clothes & Accessories
☎ 91 364 58 91; Calle de la Cava Baja 6;
🕑 11.30am-2.30pm & 5-9pm Mon-Sat, noon-3pm Sun; Ⓜ La Latina or Tirso de Molina
This small boutique has an exceptional selection of handbags from designers such as Iñaki Sampedro, Quique Mestre and Carlos de Caz. The look is sophisticated but colourful.

ALMA DE IBÉRICO Map pp76-7   Food & Wine
☎ 91 366 15 24; www.julianbecerro.com, in Spanish; Calle de la Cava Baja 41; 🕑 10am-10pm; Ⓜ La Latina

This purveyor of some of the finest *embutidos* (cured meats) is perfectly at home on this, one of Madrid's culinary streets. The *jamón* comes from the renowned Salamanca region of Castilla y León, with cheeses and other products from around Spain.

CARAMELOS PACO Map pp76-7   Food & Wine
☎ 91 365 42 58; www.caramelospaco.com, in Spanish; Calle de Toledo 53-55; 🕑 9.30am-2pm & 5-8.30pm Mon-Fri, 9.30am-2pm Sat; Ⓜ La Latina
A sweet shop that needs to be seen to be believed, Caramelos Paco has been indulging children and adults alike since 1934. There's almost nothing you can't find here and even the shop window is a work of art.

CARMEN SÁNCHEZ Map pp76-7   Jewellery
☎ 91 366 74 01; Calle de la Cava Baja 25;
🕑 noon-3pm & 7-10pm Tue-Sat, noon-4pm Sun; Ⓜ La Latina
This charming little boutique serves up sophisticated, individually crafted jewellery with the occasional quirky twist. Silver, enamel and beautiful colour combinations are the hallmarks.

DE PIEDRA Map pp76-7   Jewellery
☎ 91 365 96 20; www.depiedracreaciones.com, in Spanish; Calle del Almendro 10; 🕑 11am-2pm & 5.30-9pm Mon-Fri, 11.30am-2.30pm & 5.30-9pm Sat, noon-3pm Sun; Ⓜ La Latina
Necklaces, earrings, bracelets and home decorations fill this lovely showroom. Silver and semiprecious stones are the mainstays and many of the items have been imported from India, Brazil and Morocco.

HELENA ROHNER Map pp76-7   Jewellery
☎ 91 365 79 06; www.helenarohner.com; Calle del Almendro 4; 🕑 9am-8.30pm Mon-Fri, noon-2.30pm & 3.30-8pm Sat, noon-3pm Sun; Ⓜ La Latina or Tirso de Molina
One of Europe's most creative jewellery designers, Helena Rohner has a spacious boutique in La Latina. Working with silver, stone, porcelain, wood and Murano glass, she makes inventive pieces and her work is a regular feature of Paris fashion shows. In her own words, she seeks to recreate 'the magic of Florence, the vitality of London and the luminosity of Madrid'. She has also recently branched out into home wares.

EL RASTRO & THE FLEA MARKETS OF MADRID

Flea markets, fresh markets, crafts markets…bargain hunters will have a field day in Madrid. The city's biggest and best-known market is El Rastro, by some accounts the largest flea market in Europe and a thriving mass of vendors, buyers, pickpockets and the generally curious. This classic flea market, open on Sunday morning only, has been an open-air market for half a millennium.

The madness begins at the Plaza de Cascorro, near La Latina metro stop, and worms its way downhill along the Calle de la Ribera de Curtidores and the streets off it. The shopping starts at about 8am and lasts until 2pm or 3pm but, for many madrileños, the best of El Rastro comes after the stalls have shut and everyone crowds into the nearby bars of La Latina for an *aperitivo* (appetiser) of vermouth and tapas.

Apart from El Rastro, other curious local markets include the following:

Art Market (Map pp62-3; Plaza del Conde de Barajas; ☺ 10am-2pm Sun; Ⓜ Sol) Local art and prints of the greats.

Cuesta de Moyano Bookstalls (p136)

Mercadillo Marqués de Viana (El Rastrillo; Map p121; Calle del Marqués de Viana; ☺ 9am-2pm Sun; Ⓜ Tetuán) A calmer version of El Rastro in northern Madrid.

Mercado de Monedas y Sellos (Map pp62-3; Plaza Mayor; ☺ 9am-2pm Sun; Ⓜ Sol) Old coins and stamps.

SHOPPING HUERTAS & ATOCHA

EL RASTRO Map pp76-7 — Market
Calle de la Ribera de Curtidores; ☺ 8am-3pm Sun; Ⓜ La Latina, Puerta de Toledo or Tirso de Molina

A Sunday morning at El Rastro is a Madrid institution. You could easily spend an entire morning inching your way down the Calle de la Ribera de Curtidores and through the maze of streets that hosts El Rastro flea market every Sunday morning. Cheap clothes, luggage, old flamenco records, even older photos of Madrid, faux designer purses, grungy T-shirts, household goods and electronics are the main fare. For every 10 pieces of junk, there's a real gem (a lost masterpiece, an Underwood typewriter) waiting to be found.

Antiques are also a major drawcard for traders and treasure hunters alike with a concentration of stores at Nueva Galerías (Ribera de Curtidores 12) and Galerías Piquer (Ribera de Curtidores 30); most of the shops open 10am to 2pm and 5pm to 8pm Monday to Saturday and not all open during El Rastro.

A word of warning: pickpockets love El Rastro as much as everyone else, so keep a tight hold on your belongings and don't keep valuables in easy-to-reach pockets.

For more information on El Rastro, see p74.

HUERTAS & ATOCHA

Shopping in Huertas is akin to being on a treasure hunt. Small, quirky shops – some run by the same family for generations, others devoted to the most specialised of niches – pop up in the most unlikely places, with especially rich pickings in the tangle of lanes that make up the Barrio de las Letras.

MÉXICO Map pp84-5 — Antiques
☎ 91 429 94 76; Calle de las Huertas 20; ☺ 9am-2pm & 5-8pm Mon-Fri, 9am-2pm Sat; Ⓜ Antón Martín

A treasure chest of original old maps, this is a great place to find a unique souvenir of Spain. Some 160 folders hold antique, original maps of Madrid, Spain and the rest of the world. These are all originals or antique copies, not modern reprints, so prices range from a few hundred to thousands of euros. Just down the road, México II (☎ 91 429 58 12; Calle de las Huertas 17) sells cheaper reprints.

LIBRERÍA LA CENTRAL Map pp84-5 Bookshop
☎ 91 787 87 82; www.lacentral.com, in Spanish; Ronda de Atocha 2; ☺ 10am-9pm Mon-Sat, 10am-2pm Sun; Ⓜ Atocha

Part of the stunning extension to the Centro de Arte Reina Sofía, La Central is Madrid's best gallery bookshop, with a range of posters and postcards as well as extensive sections on contemporary art, design, architecture and photography. Most, but by no means all, books are in Spanish.

GIL Map pp84-5 — Clothes & Accessories
☎ 91 521 25 49; Carrera de San Jerónimo 2; ☺ 9.30am-1.30pm & 4.30-8pm Mon-Sat; Ⓜ Sol

You don't see them much these days, but the exquisite fringed and embroidered *mantones* and *mantoncillos* (traditional

Spanish shawls worn by women on grand occasions) and delicate *mantillas* (Spanish veils) are stunning and uniquely Spanish gifts. Gil also sells *abanicos* (Spanish fans). Inside this dark shop, dating back to 1880, the sales clerks still wait behind a long counter to attend to you; the service hasn't changed in years and that's no bad thing. Our only complaint? Kitsch tourist souvenirs (T-shirts and the like) have made an appearance here.

LA VIOLETA Map pp84-5   Food & Drink
☎ 91 522 55 22; Plaza de Canalejas 6; ⏰ 10am-2pm & 4.30-8.30pm Mon-Sat Sep-Jul; Ⓜ Sevilla or Antón Martín
In the early 20th century, *violetas* (small violet-coloured sweets and frosted petals from the violet flower) took on an iconic status and remain one of the city's most typical sweets. This tiny shop evokes that era in its decor and they don't serve much else other than the elegantly wrapped sweets.

MARÍA CABELLO Map pp84-5   Food & Drink
☎ 91 429 60 88; Calle de Echegaray 19; ⏰ 9.30am-2.30pm & 5.30-9pm Mon-Fri, 10am-2.30pm & 6.30-9.30pm Sat; Ⓜ Sevilla or Antón Martín
All wine shops should be like this. This family-run corner shop really knows its wines and the decoration has scarcely changed since 1913, with wooden shelves and even a faded ceiling fresco. There are fine wines in abundance (mostly Spanish, and a few foreign bottles), with some 500 labels on show or tucked away out the back.

LOMOGRAPHY Map pp84-5   Specialist
☎ 91 369 17 99; www.lomography.com; Cuesta de Echegaray 5; ⏰ 11am-8.30pm Mon-Fri; Ⓜ Sevilla or Sol
Dedicated to the Lomo LC-A, a 1980s-era Russian Kompakt camera that has acquired cult status for its zany colours, fisheye lenses and anticool clunkiness, this eclectic shop sells the cameras (an original will set you back €295) and offbeat design items, from bags and mugs to retro memorabilia loved by adherents of 'lomography'. You can even develop your Lomo photos here. They have another shop (Map p110; ☎ 91 310 44 18; Calle de Argensola 1; ⏰ 11am-8.30pm Mon-Fri, 11.30am-2.30pm & 5.30-8.30pm Sat; Ⓜ Alonso Martínez or Chueca) in Chueca.

CLOTHING SIZES

Women's clothing

Aus/UK	8	10	12	14	16	18
Europe	36	38	40	42	44	46
Japan	5	7	9	11	13	15
USA	6	8	10	12	14	16

Women's shoes

Aus/USA	5	6	7	8	9	10
Europe	35	36	37	38	39	40
France only	35	36	38	39	40	42
Japan	22	23	24	25	26	27
UK	3½	4½	5½	6½	7½	8½

Men's clothing

Aus	92	96	100	104	108	112
Europe	46	48	50	52	54	56
Japan	S		M	M		L
UK/USA	35	36	37	38	39	40

Men's shirts (collar sizes)

Aus/Japan	38	39	40	41	42	43
Europe	38	39	40	41	42	43
UK/USA	15	15½	16	16½	17	17½

Men's shoes

Aus/UK	7	8	9	10	11	12
Europe	41	42	43	44½	46	47
Japan	26	27	27½	28	29	30
USA	7½	8½	9½	10½	11½	12½

Measurements approximate only; try before you buy

JUAN ALVAREZ Map pp84-5   Specialist
☎ 91 429 20 33; Calle de San Pedro 7; ⏰ 5-8pm Mon, 10am-1.30pm & 5-8pm Tue-Fri, 10am-1.30pm Sat; Ⓜ Antón Martín
The shop and workshop may be tiny, but Juan Alvarez is one of the most celebrated guitar makers in Spain. Like his father before him, Juan has been making classical and flamenco guitars for longer than he can remember (the family business dates back to 1945) and former clients include Eric Clapton, Compay Segundo and a host of flamenco greats. Prices start at €145 and don't stop until they reach €12,000.

PASEO DEL PRADO & EL RETIRO

The Paseo del Prado is more about grand art galleries (with shops attached) and afternoon promenades, but there is one Madrid shopping tradition that you really must seek out.

CUESTA DE MOYANO BOOKSTALLS

Map p91
Bookshop

Cuesta de Claudio Moyano; ⏰ 9am-dusk Mon-Sat, 9am-2pm Sun; Ⓜ Atocha

Madrid's answer to the booksellers that line the Seine in Paris, these secondhand bookstalls are an enduring Madrid landmark. Most titles are in Spanish, but there's a handful of offerings in other languages. Some of the stalls close at lunchtime.

SALAMANCA

Salamanca is where you discover that there's so much more to Spanish fashion than Zara and Mango. Fashions range from classically elegant to cool and cutting edge, from both leading and upcoming Spanish designers and the big names in international fashion. As such, the exclusive boutiques of the barrio are the ideal place to take the pulse of the Spanish fashion scene and you'll likely find it in rude health – for the low-down on Spain's fashion industry, turn to p53. Shopping here is a social event, where people put on their finest and service is often impeccable, if a little stuffy. Throw in a sprinkling of gourmet food shops and designer home wares and you could easily spend days doing little else but shopping.

DE VIAJE Map p102
Bookshop

☎ 91 577 98 99; www.deviaje.com, in Spanish; Calle de Serrano 41; ⏰ 10am-8.30pm Mon-Fri, 10.30am-2.30pm & 5-8pm Sat; Ⓜ Serrano

Whether you're after a guidebook, a coffee-table tome or travel literature, De Viaje, Madrid's largest travel bookshop, probably has it. Covering every region of the world, it has mostly Spanish titles, but plenty in English as well. Staff are helpful and there's also a travel agency.

IMAGINARIUM Map p102
Toys

☎ 91 781 33 37; www.imaginarium.es, in Spanish; Calle de Claudio Coello 45; ⏰ 10am-9pm Mon-Sat; Ⓜ Serrano

This wonderfully personal toy shop sells creative toys, books and games; it treats kids respectfully, with separate entrances for kids and adults. There are other branches all across town, including one in Argüelles (Map pp116-17; ☎ 91 444 56 09; Calle de Carranza 20; ⏰ 10am-8.30pm Mon-Sat; Ⓜ San Bernardo).

AGATHA RUIZ DE LA PRADA

Map p102
Clothes & Accessories

☎ 91 319 05 01; www.agatharuizdelaprada.com; Calle de Serrano 27; ⏰ 10am-8.30pm Mon-Sat; Ⓜ Serrano

This boutique has to be seen to be believed, with pinks, yellows and oranges everywhere you turn. It's fun and exuberant, but not just for kids. It also has serious and highly original fashion; Agatha Ruiz de la Prada is one of the enduring icons of Madrid's 1980s outpouring of creativity known as *la movida madrileña*.

AMAYA ARZUAGA

Map p102
Clothes & Accessories

☎ 91 426 28 15; www.amayaarzuaga.com; Calle de Lagasca 50; ⏰ 10.30am-8.30pm Mon-Wed, 10.30am-9pm Thu-Sat; Ⓜ Velázquez

Amaya Arzuaga has sexy, bold options. She loves mixing black with bright colours (one season it's 1980s fuchsia and turquoise, the next it's orange or red) and has earned a reputation as one of the most creative designers in Spain today.

ARMAND BASI Map p102
Clothes & Accessories

☎ 91 577 79 93; www.armandbasi.com; Calle de Claudio Coello 52; ⏰ 10am-8.30pm Mon-Sat; Ⓜ Serrano

---

SHOPPING STREET – CALLE DE SERRANO

Sophisticated Calle de Serrano (Map p102; Ⓜ Serrano) is lined with big-name Spanish designers – opening a boutique along this street is an announcement of arrival as a national fashion icon. The colours of Agatha Ruiz de la Prada (above) find their classy (and exclusive) counterpoint in Loewe (p140), whose clothes and accessories are regulars on the Paris catwalk. Purificación García (☎ 91 435 80 13; www.purificaciongarcia.com, in Spanish; Calle de Serrano 28; ⏰ 10am-8.30pm Mon-Sat; Ⓜ Serrano) is one of the most successful Spanish designers, offering elegant, mature designs for men and women that are as at home in the workplace as at a wedding. Roberto Verino (☎ 91 426 04 75; www.robertoverino.com; Calle de Serrano 33; ⏰ 10am-8.30pm Mon-Sat; Ⓜ Serrano) purveys simple, classy designs for men and women. Manolo Blahnik (☎ 91 575 96 48; www.manoloblahnik.com; Calle de Serrano 58; ⏰ 10am-8.30pm Mon-Sat; Ⓜ Serrano) is one of Spain's women's shoe designers *par excellence;* the shoes are displayed in the shop like works of art and have appeared more times at the Oscars than Penélope Cruz.

SHOPPING STREET – CALLE DE JOSÉ ORTEGA Y GASSET

The world's most prestigious international designers occupy what is known as *la milla del oro* (the golden mile) along Calle de José Ortega y Gasset (Map p102; M Núñez de Balboa), close to the corner with Calle de Serrano. All of the following shops are open from 10am to 8.30pm Monday to Saturday unless otherwise stated.

On the south side of the street, there's Giorgio Armani (☎ 91 577 58 07; www.armani.com; Calle de José Ortega y Gasset 16), Dolce & Gabbana (☎ 91 781 09 10; www.dolcegabbana.es; Calle de José Ortega y Gasset 14), Chanel (☎ 91 431 30 36; www.chanel.com; Calle de José Ortega y Gasset 14; ☷ 10am–8pm Mon-Sat), Hermès (☎ 91 577 76 09; www.hermes.com; Calle de José Ortega y Gasset 12; ☷ 10am–8pm Mon-Sat), Burberry (☎ 91 575 82 99; www.burberry.com; Calle de José Ortega y Gasset 8; ☷ 11am–8pm Mon-Sat) and Dior (☎ 91 781 08 10; www.dior .com; Calle de José Ortega y Gasset 6). Just across the road is Louis Vuitton (☎ 91 575 13 08; www.louisvuitton.com; Calle de José Ortega y Gasset 17), Jimmy Choo (☎ 91 781 86 08; www.jimmychoo.com; Calle de José Ortega y Gasset 15) and Cartier (☎ 91 576 22 81; www.cartier.com; cnr Calles de José Ortega y Gasset & de Serrano; ☷ 10am-8.30pm Mon-Fri, 11am-8pm Sat). Also in the vicinity is Gucci (☎ 91 431 17 17; www.gucci.com; cnr Calles de José Ortega y Gasset & de Serrano). What more could you want?

With hip, urban designs for men and women, this is the place to go when you want to look fashionable but carelessly casual; the look is perfectly suited to a night out in the city's bars, especially in Chueca.

CAMPER Map p102   Clothes & Accessories
☎ 91 578 25 60; www.camper.es; Calle de Serrano 24; ☷ 10am-8.30pm Mon-Sat; M Serrano
Spanish fashion is not all *haute couture*, and this world-famous cool and quirky shoe brand from Mallorca offers bowling-shoe chic with colourful, fun designs that are all about quality coupled with comfort. There are other outlets throughout the city, including a shop (☎ 91 531 23 47; www .camper.com; Calle de Fuencarral 42; M Gran Vía or Tribunal) in Malasaña – check out their website for locations.

EKSEPTION & EKS
Map p102   Clothes & Accessories
☎ 91 577 43 53; Calle de Velázquez 28; ☷ 10.30am-2.30pm & 5-9pm Mon-Sat; M Velázquez
This elegant showroom store consistently leads the way with the latest trends, spanning catwalk designs alongside a more informal, though always sophisti-cated, look. The unifying theme is urban chic and their list of designer brands includes Balenciaga, Prada Sport, Marc Jacobs and Dries van Noten. Next door is the preserve of younger, more casual lines, including a fantastic selection of jeans. Victoria Beckham was a regular customer here in her Madrid days; make of that what you will.

GALLERY Map p102   Clothes & Accessories
☎ 91 576 79 31; www.gallerymadrid.com; Calle de Jorge Juan 38; ☷ 10.30am-8.30pm Mon-Sat; M Príncipe de Vergara or Velázquez
This stunning showpiece of men's fashions and accessories (shoes, bags, belts and the like) is the new Madrid in a nutshell – stylish, brand conscious and all about having the right look. There are creams and fragrances to indulge the metrosexual in you, as well as quirkier items such as designer crash helmets. With an interior designed by Tomas Alia, it's one of the city's coolest shops for men.

BOMBONERÍAS SANTA
Map p102   Food & Wine
☎ 91 576 86 46; www.bombonerias-santa.com, in Spanish; Calle de Serrano 56; ☷ 10am-8.30pm Mon-Sat Sep-Jun, shorter hours in summer; M Serrano
If your style is as refined as your palate, the exquisite chocolates in this tiny shop will satisfy. The packaging is every bit as pretty as the *bombones* within, but they're not cheap – count on paying around €60 per kilo of chocolate.

LAVINIA Map p102   Food & Wine
☎ 91 426 06 04; Calle de José Ortega y Gasset 16; ☷ 10am-9pm Mon-Sat; M Núñez de Balboa
Although we love the intimacy of old-style Spanish wine shops, they can't match the selection of Spanish and international wines available at Lavinia, which has more than 4500 bottles to choose from. It also organises wine courses (see p185), wine tastings and excursions to nearby bodegas (wineries).

top picks

SPANISH FASHION ICONS

- Agatha Ruiz de la Prada (p136)
- Amaya Arzuaga (p136)
- Camper (p137)
- Custo Barcelona (see the boxed text, opposite)
- Davidelfin (opposite)
- Elisa Bracci (opposite)
- Loewe (p140)
- Manolo Blahnik (see the boxed text, p136)
- Purificación García (see the boxed text, p136)

MANTEQUERÍA BRAVO

Map p102   Food & Wine

☎ 91 576 02 93; Calle de Ayala 24; ⏰ 9.30am-
2.30pm & 5.30-8.30pm Mon-Fri, 9.30am-2.30pm
Sat; Ⓜ Serrano

Behind the attractive old facade lies a
connoisseur's paradise, filled with local
cheeses, sausages, wines and coffees.
The products here are great for a gift,
but everything's so good that you won't
want to share. Mantequería Bravo won
the prize for Madrid's best gourmet
food shop or delicatessen – it's as simple
as that.

ORIOL BALAGUER Map p102   Food & Wine

☎ 91 401 64 63; www.oriolbalaguer.com; Calle
de José Ortega y Gasset 44; ⏰ 9am-9pm Mon-Sat,
9am-2.30pm Sun; Ⓜ Núñez de Balboa

Catalan pastry chef Oriol Balaguer has a
formidable CV – he worked in the kitchens
of Ferran Adrià in Catalonia and won the
prize for the World's Best Dessert (the
'Seven Textures of Chocolate') in 2001. His
hugely anticipated chocolate boutique
opened with much fanfare in Madrid in
March 2008 and it's a combination of a
small art gallery and a fashion boutique,
except that it's dedicated to exquisite finely
crafted chocolate collections and cakes.
You'll never be able to buy ordinary
chocolate again after a visit here.

VINÇON Map p102   Home Wares

☎ 91 578 05 20; www.vincon.com, in Spanish;
Calle de Castelló 18; ⏰ 10am-8.30pm Mon-Sat;
Ⓜ Príncipe de Vergara

Conceived in Barcelona when the city was
Europe's centre of cool, Vinçon's popularity

here recognises the fact that cutting-edge
Catalan *disseny* (design) has also taken hold
in the Spanish capital. Sleek and often fun
home wares and all sorts of gadgets that
you never knew you needed – but suddenly
feel you must have – are what it's all about.

CUARTO DE JUEGOS Map p102   Toys

☎ 91 435 00 99; www.cuartodejuegos.es; Calle
de Jorge Juan 42; ⏰ 10am-2pm & 5-8pm Mon-Fri,
5-8pm Sat; Ⓜ Velázquez or Príncipe de Vergara

We're not sure if it's an official rule, but
batteries seem to be outlawed at this
traditional toy shop, where all kinds of old-
fashioned board games, puzzles and toys
are still sold. Yes, there's ludo, Chinese
checkers and backgammon, but there's so
much more here and they're not just for kids.

MALASAÑA & CHUECA

Malasaña is one of Madrid's quirkiest barrios in which to shop, home to edgy clothing
stores, shops where mainstream designers
show off their street cred, and highly original
jewellery boutiques. Shop staff here won't
look down their noses at you no matter what
you wear – they've seen it all before. Chueca,
on the other hand, can be zany or elegant
and caters as much for gay clubbers as for a
refined gay sensibility. Where Chueca eases
gently down the hill towards the Paseo de los
Recoletos and beyond to Salamanca, especially in Calle de Piamonte, Calle del Conde
de Xiquena and Calle del Almirante, niche
designers take over with exclusive boutiques
and the latest individual fashions. In short,
it's Madrid in microcosm and ideal for
those style-conscious shoppers who value an
alternative look at life.

J&J BOOKS & COFFEE

Map pp108-9   Bookshop

☎ 91 521 85 76; www.jandjbooksandcoffee.com;
Calle del Espíritu Santo 47; ⏰ 11am-midnight
Mon-Thu & Sat, 11am-2am Fri, 4-10pm Sun;
Ⓜ Noviciado

Downstairs from this bar-cafe that serves
as a meeting place for Madrid's expats
(they have international exchange nights
from 8pm on Wednesday and Thursday),
this place claims to have more than
150,000 books for sale. A fair proportion
of these are in English and the bar is the
perfect place to flick through those you're
considering buying.

SHOPPING STREET – CALLE DE FUENCARRAL

Calle de Fuencarral (Map pp108-9; M Gran Vía or Tribunal) is best known for being Madrid's home of alternative street fashion, with the Mercado de Fuencarral (p140) as its spiritual home. But in recent years, a host of Spanish and international brand names has moved in, adding breadth and depth to the experience of shopping along this iconic street. All of the following shops are open 10am to 9pm Monday to Saturday unless otherwise stated and some open their doors on some Sundays.

For landmark casual Spanish fashion, there's the colourful and consciously cool Adolfo Domínguez (☎ 91 523 39 38; www.adolfodominguez.com, in Spanish; Calle de Fuencarral 5; M Gran Vía), often-outlandish Custo Barcelona (☎ 91 360 46 36; www.custo-barcelona.com; Calle de Fuencarral 29; M Gran Vía), Spain's casual shoe king Camper (p137) and Divina Providencia (☎ 91 521 10 95; www.divinaprovidencia.com, in Spanish; Calle de Fuencarral 42; M Tribunal), whose offbeat retro and Asian influences have made the transition to mainstream stylish.

International names with an outlet along the street include Geox (☎ 91 531 64 62; Calle de Fuencarral 53; 10am-8.30pm Mon-Sat; M Tribunal), Fun & Basics (☎ 91 522 07 95; Calle de Fuencarral 43; M Tribunal), Salsa (☎ 91 523 43 50; Calle de Fuencarral 42; M Tribunal), G-Star Raw (☎ 91 523 80 48; Calle de Fuencarral 39; M Gran Vía or Tribunal), Pepe Jeans (☎ 91 701 06 42; Calle de Fuencarral 23; M Gran Vía or Tribunal), Skunkfunk (☎ 91 521 65 01; Calle de Fuencarral 20; M Gran Vía) and Friday's Project (☎ 91 522 93 00; Calle de Fuencarral 6; M Gran Vía).

BIBLIOKETA Map p110 Bookshop
☎ 91 391 00 99; www.biblioketa.com, in Spanish; Calle de Justiniano 4; 10.30am-2pm & 5-8pm Mon-Sat; M Alonso Martínez
Biblioketa is perhaps the best multilingual children's bookshop in Madrid, with a range of quality titles in English, Spanish and French. Check out the basement 'cave', where it runs a range of activities offering an 'apprenticeship' in reading with an emphasis on fun.

COORLEONE'S COMPANY
Map p110 Clothes & Accessories
☎ 91 521 47 46; www.coorleonecompany.com, in Spanish; Calle de Hortaleza 37; 11am-9pm Mon-Sat; M Gran Vía or Chueca
This stunning shop has been used to film TV series, advertisements and movies, but you come here primarily for designer clothing, belts and handbags from international designers and a few big local names thrown in, among them Davidelfín and Locking Shocking.

DAVIDELFÍN Map p110 Clothes & Accessories
☎ 91 702 07 60; www.davidelfin.com; Calle de San Gregorio 1; 12.30-8.30pm Mon-Fri, 11.30am-8.30pm Sat; M Chueca
This young Spanish designer combines catwalk fashions with a rebellious spirit. The look is young, sometimes edgy and an enthusiastic nod to the avant-garde. Having recently made the move from Salamanca, they're still settling in to their new quarters

and told us that permanent opening hours are yet to be decided.

EL TEMPLO DE SUSU
Map pp108-9 Clothes & Accessories
☎ 91 523 31 22; Calle del Espíritu Santo 1; 11am-2.30pm & 5.30-8.30pm Mon-Sat; M Tribunal
It won't appeal to everyone, but El Templo de Susu's secondhand clothes from the 1960s and 1970s have clearly found a market among Malasaña's too-cool-for-the-latest-fashions types. It's kind of like charity shop meets unreconstructed hippie, which is either truly awful or retro cool, depending on your perspective.

EL TINTERO Map p110 Clothes & Accessories
☎ 91 308 14 18; www.eltintero.es, in Spanish; Calle de Gravina 5; 10.30am-2pm & 5-9pm Mon-Sat; M Chueca
Terrific T-shirts are all that El Tintero sells. So if you're looking for a colourful *camiseta* with Spanish-language slogans that translate as 'I'm tired of being good' or 'Looking for a habitable planet', this is your place. They also take a similar approach with kids' wear, from newborns to those aged 10 years.

ELISA BRACCI Map p110 Clothes & Accessories
☎ 91 435 03 05; www.elisabracci.es, in Spanish; Calle de Bárbara de Braganza 2; 10.30am-2.30pm & 5.30-8.30pm Mon-Sat; M Alonso Martínez or Colón

One of the most enduring and respected names of Spanish catwalk fashion, Elisa Bracci is the place to find that evening dress for a special occasion. Just entering this store makes you feel like a celebrity and the mix of colours and unrestrained elegance suggests a confident designer who long ago reached the pinnacle of her profession.

H.A.N.D. Map p110   Clothes & Accessories
☎ 91 521 51 52; www.hand-haveaniceday.es, in Spanish; Calle de Hortaleza 26; ◷ 11am-2.30pm & 5-9pm Mon-Sat; Ⓜ Gran Vía or Chueca
Looking for all the world like a small slice of Paris, H.A.N.D. (as in 'Have A Nice Day') is an effortlessly chic little boutique where you find dresses, skirts and other clothing from a range of predominantly French designers such as Les Petites, Manoush and Malene Birger. The look is classy with a fresh and sometimes vaguely vintage feel.

LA TIPO CAMISETAS
Map pp108-9   Clothes & Accessories
☎ 91 547 78 39; www.latipo.es, in Spanish; Calle del Conde Duque 7; ◷ 11am-2.30pm & 5-9pm Mon-Sat; Ⓜ Plaza de España or Ventura Rodríguez
T-shirts in bright colours, T-shirts you'd have to be feeling pretty preppy to wear and T-shirts with witty (Spanish-language) slogans that rarely stray into the questionable taste that can be Malasaña's forte are what this shop is all about. It's all good, clean fun that would be out of place in the heart of hard-rocking Malasaña, but they've found a good home here in Conde Duque.

L'HABILLEUR Map p110   Clothes & Accessories
☎ 91 531 32 22; Plaza de Chueca 8; ◷ 11am-2pm & 5-9pm Mon-Sat; Ⓜ Chueca
This popular Paris boutique now has a branch on Plaza de Chueca and the deal is the same: designer names at discounted prices, especially downstairs. For women, top names include Forte-Forte, Dr Fango, Marlota and Sofie Doore, while men are served by Hartford, Ganesh and Vintage.

LOEWE Map p110   Clothes & Accessories
☎ 91 522 68 15; www.loewe.com; Gran Vía 8; ◷ 10am-8.30pm Mon-Sat; Ⓜ Gran Vía
Born in 1846 in Madrid, Loewe is arguably Spain's signature line in high-end fashion

and its landmark store on Gran Vía is one of the most famous and elegant stores in the capital. Classy handbags and accessories are the mainstays and prices can be jaw-droppingly high, but it's worth stopping by here, even if you don't plan to buy. There's another branch (Map p102; ☎ 91 426 35 88; Calle de Serrano 26 & 34; ◷ 10am-8.30pm Mon-Sat; Ⓜ Serrano) in Salamanca.

LURDES BERGADA
Map p110   Clothes & Accessories
☎ 91 531 99 58; Calle del Conde de Xiquena 8; ◷ 10.30am-8.30pm Mon-Sat; Ⓜ Chueca or Colón
Lurdes Bergada and Syngman Cucala, a mother-son designer team from Barcelona, offer classy and original men's and women's fashions using neutral colours and all-natural fibres. They've developed something of a cult following for their clothes that are stylish yet casual in a very Chueca kind of way. It's difficult to leave without finding something that you just have to have. They have another branch (Map pp108-9; ☎ 91 521 88 18; Calle de Fuencarral 70; ◷ 10.30am-8.30pm Mon-Sat; Ⓜ Tribunal) in Malasaña.

MERCADO DE FUENCARRAL
Map pp108-9   Clothes & Accessories
☎ 91 521 41 52; www.mdf.es, in Spanish; Calle de Fuencarral 45; ◷ 11am-9pm Mon-Sat; Ⓜ Tribunal
Madrid's home of alternative club cool is still going strong, revelling in its reverse snobbery. With shops like Fuck, Ugly Shop and Black Kiss, it's funky, grungy and filled to the rafters with torn T-shirts and more black leather and silver studs than you'll ever need. This is a Madrid icon and when it was threatened with closure in 2008, there was nearly an uprising.

PIAMONTE Map p110   Clothes & Accessories
☎ 91 523 07 66; www.piamonteshop.com, in Spanish; Calle de Piamonte 16; ◷ 10.30am-8.30pm Mon-Sat; Ⓜ Chueca
Carefully selected accessories of every kind – handbags, purses, belts, shoes and jewellery – have made this a point of reference for female shoppers in the capital. They have another branch (Map p102; ☎ 91 702 55 61; Calle de Lagasca 28; ◷ 10.30am-8.30pm Mon-Sat; Ⓜ Serrano) in Salamanca.

SNAPO Map pp108-9   Clothes & Accessories
☎ 91 532 12 23; Calle del Espíritu Santo 5; ◷ 11am-2pm & 5-8.30pm Mon-Sat; Ⓜ Tribunal

Snapo is rebellious Malasaña to its core, thumbing its nose at the niceties of fashion respectability – hardly surprising given that its line of clothing is called Fucking Bastardz Inc. It does jeans, caps and jackets, but its T-shirts are the Snapo trademark. Expect a mocked-up cover of 'National Pornographic' or Pope John Paul II with fist raised and 'Vatican 666' emblazoned across the front. Need we say more?

CACAO SAMPAKA Map p110   Food & Wine
☎ 91 319 58 40; www.cacaosampaka.com; Calle de Orellana 4; ☽ 10am-9.30pm; Ⓜ Alonso Martínez

If you thought chocolate was about fruit 'n' nut, think again. This gourmet chocolate shop is a chocoholic's dream come true, with more combinations to go with humble cocoa than you ever imagined possible. If you only come to one chocolate shop in Madrid, make it this one.

ISOLÉE Map p110   Food & Wine
☎ 902 876 136; www.isolee.com; Calle de las Infantas 19; ☽ 10am-10pm Mon-Thu, 10am-1am Fri & Sat, 4-10pm Sun; Ⓜ Gran Vía or Chueca

Multipurpose lifestyle stores were late in coming to Madrid, but they're now all the rage and there's none more stylish than Isolée. It sells a select range of everything from clothes (Levi's to Davidelfín) and shoes to CDs and food. It also has a trendy cafe. They have another branch (Map p102; Calle de Claudio Coello 55; ☽ 10.30am-8.30pm Mon-Sat; Ⓜ Serrano) in Salamanca.

PATRIMONIO COMUNAL OLIVARERO
Map p110   Food & Wine
☎ 91 308 05 05; www.pco.es, in Spanish; Calle de Mejía Lequerica 1; ☽ 10am-2pm & 5-8pm Mon-Fri, 10am-2pm Sat; Ⓜ Alonso Martínez

You could buy your Spanish olive oil at El Corte Inglés, but to catch the real essence of the country's olive-oil varieties (Spain is the world's largest producer), Patrimonio Comunal Olivarero is perfect. With examples of the extra-virgin variety (and nothing else) from all over Spain, you could spend ages agonising over the choices. The staff know their oil and are happy to help out if you speak a little Spanish.

RESERVA Y CATA Map p110   Food & Wine
☎ 91 319 04 01; www.reservaycata.com, in Spanish; Calle del Conde de Xiquena 13; ☽ 11am-

2.30pm & 5-9pm Mon-Fri, 11am-2.30pm Sat; Ⓜ Colón or Chueca

This old-style shop stocks an excellent range of local wines, and the knowledgeable staff can help you pick out a great one for your next dinner party or a gift for a friend back home. It specialises in quality Spanish wines that you just don't find in El Corte Inglés and there's often a bottle open so that you can try before you buy.

ALDABA Map p110   Home Wares
☎ 91 308 38 33; Calle de Belén 4; ☽ 10am-8.30pm Mon-Sat; Ⓜ Chueca

You never quite know what you'll find in this densely packed designer home wares store on a quiet street towards the northern end of Chueca. There's a specialist kitchen section but every corner of your house is catered for, as is your every mood – products range from Alessi to 'ex-lover's voodoo dolls'.

FUTURAMIC Map p110   Home Wares
☎ 91 531 63 57; www.futuramics.com, in Spanish; Calle de Válgame Dios 5; ☽ 11am-2.30pm & 5-8pm Mon-Fri, 11am-2.30pm Sat; Ⓜ Chueca

Looking for that 1960s jukebox? Or a real-life parking meter? Just about anything you can imagine in memorabilia (either original or in replica) from the 1930s to the 1980s is available here. Not everything is for sale (the life-size London phone booth, for example), as many of the items are in demand for movie sets, but much of it is. Ring before you head here as the staff are often out on location.

UNO DE 50 Map pp108-9   Jewellery
☎ 91 523 99 75; www.unode50.com; Calle de Fuencarral 25; ☽ 10am-8.30pm Mon-Sat; Ⓜ Gran Vía or Tribunal

Close to where in-your-face Malasaña intersects with could-go-either-way Chueca, Uno de 50 offers up silver jewellery that wouldn't look out of place in either barrio. It's chunky and loud and not very subtle, but there are some great pieces here and they're as original as the manner in which they're displayed.

RADIO CITY DISCOS Map pp108-9   Music
☎ 91 547 77 67; www.radiocitydiscos.com, in Spanish; Plaza Guardias de Corps 2; ☽ 11am-2pm & 5-9pm Mon-Sat; Ⓜ Plaza de España or Ventura Rodríguez

In these days of music megastores and internet downloads, it's nice to find small, specialist music shops still going strong. True to Malasaña's roots, Radio City Disco's small collection of CDs and vinyl spans the 1970s, roots, funk, rock and indie, with a small section devoted to Brazil's Tropicalismo. If they don't have it, they promise to track it down for you.

MUJI Map pp108-9   Paper Products & Home Wares
☎ 91 521 08 47; www.muji.com/es, in Spanish; Calle de Fuencarral 36; ⏰ 10.30am-8pm Mon-Sat; Ⓜ Tribunal

From clean-lined notebooks and folders to all manner of home wares small and large, this shop is almost impossible to pass. The look has all the clean lines of Japanese design wedded to functionality – not only do you need everything here, you'll want to display it prominently. They've another branch (☎ 91 576 44 24; Calle de Goya 9; ⏰ 10.30am-8pm Mon-Sat; Ⓜ Serrano) in Salamanca.

LA JUGUETERÍA Map p110   Sex Shop
☎ 91 308 72 69; Travesía del San Mateo 12; ⏰ noon-3pm & 5-10pm Mon-Sat; Ⓜ Alonso Martínez

We don't normally include sex shops in our guides but this softly lit one tickled our fancy. Home to sultry staff and carefully chosen feathers and erotic toys, there's nothing brown paper bag and men in anoraks about this place; you won't feel guilty entering. It's very Chueca.

MACCHININE Map p110   Specialist
☎ 91 701 05 18; Calle de Barquillo 7; ⏰ 10am-2pm & 4.30-8.30pm Mon-Sat; Ⓜ Banco de España

Collectors and children will love this small shop in equal measure, packed as it is with perfectly created replica model cars and wooden and metal figures. There are also games, toys without batteries and all manner of perfectly proportioned knick-knacks.

POPLAND Map pp108-9   Specialist
☎ 91 591 21 20; www.popland.es, in Spanish; Calle de Manuela Malasaña 24; ⏰ 11am-8.30pm Mon-Sat; Ⓜ San Bernardo

'Curiosity and Retro' are the buzzwords here and Popland has both by the vinyl-suitcase load. 'Go Eighties' T-shirts, Pink Panther dolls, Elvis card games, candy handcuffs, mirrored disco balls, Space

Invaders handbags… If you can't find it here, it simply didn't exist in the world of street pop art.

CHAMBERÍ & ARGÜELLES

One of Madrid's trendiest barrios, Chamberí is dotted with great shops, although we love it more for the small stores, some of which haven't changed in decades and are all the better for it. Some of it spills over into Argüelles, which is primarily residential and not generally known for its shopping.

ANTIGÜEDADES HOM
Map pp116-17   Antiques
☎ 91 594 20 17; Calle de Juan de Austria 31; ⏰ 5-8pm Mon-Wed, noon-2pm & 5-8pm Thu & Fri; Ⓜ Iglesia

Specialising in antique Spanish fans, this tiny shop is a wonderful place to browse or to find a special gift, especially delicately painted fans and those made with bone. It's open mostly afternoons only because the owner spends the mornings restoring the fans you see for sale. It's also a purveyor of other treasures and bric-a-brac.

ALTAÏR Map pp116-17   Bookshop
☎ 91 543 53 00; www.altair.es, in Spanish; Calle de Gaztambide 31; ⏰ 10am-2pm & 4.30-8.30pm Mon-Fri, 10.30am-2.30pm Sat; Ⓜ Argüelles

One of the best travel bookshops in Madrid, Altaïr has an exceptional range of books, maps and magazines covering Spain and every other major region of the world. Most are in Spanish, but there are loads of English-language titles scattered

top picks

CHILDREN'S SHOPS

- Así (p131)
- Imaginarium (p136)
- Los Bebés de Chamberí (opposite)
- Biblioketa (p139)
- Cuarto de Juegos (p138)
- Agatha Ruiz de la Prada (p136)
- Bazar Matey (p144)
- Macchinine (left)

throughout, as well as calendars and world-music CDs. Altaïr is the Spanish distributor for Moleskine notebooks, once beloved of Hemingway and Chatwin, and now enjoying a revival.

BOOKSELLERS Map pp116-17 Bookshop

☎ 91 442 79 59; Calle de Fernández de la Hoz 40; ⏱ 9.30am-2pm & 5-8pm Mon-Fri, 10am-2pm Sat; Ⓜ Iglesia

This suburban bookshop has close to the largest selection of English-language titles in town, covering novels, history, travel literature and Spanish themes. There's another Booksellers (☎ 91 702 79 44; Plaza de Olavide 10; ⏱ 9.30am-2pm & 5-8pm Mon-Fri, 10am-2pm Sat; Ⓜ Bilbao, Iglesia or Quevedo) that specialises in English-language children's books.

PASAJES LIBRERÍA INTERNACIONAL
Map pp116-17 Bookshop

☎ 91 310 12 45; www.pasajeslibros.com; Calle de Génova 3; ⏱ 10am-8pm Mon-Fri, 10am-2pm Sat; Ⓜ Alonso Martínez

Definitely one of the best English-language bookshops in Madrid, Pasajes has an extensive English section (downstairs at the back), which includes high-quality fiction (if it's a new release, it'll be the first bookshop in town to have it), history, Spanish subject matter and travel, as well as a few literary magazines. There are also French, German, Italian and Portuguese books, children's books and DVDs, and a useful noticeboard.

LOS BEBÉS DE CHAMBERÍ
Map pp116-17 Clothes & Accessories

☎ 91 444 05 96; www.losbebesdechamberi.com, in Spanish; Calle de Gonzalo de Córdoba 7; ⏱ 11am-2.30pm & 5.30-8.30pm Tue-Sat; Ⓜ Quevedo

This small shop showcases the wonderful individuality of Spanish children's clothes; you'll leave laden with bags for your own kids and for those of friends back home. Bright colours are a recurring theme, the stuffed toys are always more original than you'll find elsewhere and the wares cater to all ages from newborns to six-year-olds.

DIEDRO Map pp116-17 Clothes & Accessories

☎ 91 444 59 59; www.diedro.com; Calle de Sagasta 17; ⏱ 10am-10pm Mon-Sat, noon-10pm Sun; Ⓜ Bilbao or Alonso Martínez

One of the most innovative gift shops in Madrid, Diedro has designer jewellery,

top picks

FOR ENGLISH-LANGUAGE BOOKS

Pasajes Librería Internacional (left)
Petra's International Bookshop (p130)
Booksellers (left)
J&J Books & Coffee (p138)
Altaïr (opposite)
De Viaje (p136)
Fnac (p130)
Casa del Libro (p130)

clothes, stationery and home wares. It's a wonderful space spread over three floors that span just about every taste, as long as it's design conscious. Leading brand names include Calvin Klein, Pandora, Guess, Bodum and Alessi.

FLAMENCO Map pp116-17 Clothes & Accessories

☎ 91 591 30 79; www.flamencochic.com; Calle de Sagasta 25; ⏱ 10am-9pm Mon-Sat; Ⓜ Alonso Martínez

The name of this vibrant and relentlessly creative clothing store may be slightly misleading, but only up to a point: it has little to do with Spain's best-known musical form other than seeming to capture the spirit and passion that lies at the heart of the genre. Bright colours are the hallmark of its dresses, jackets, tops and other clothing; there's a line in equally colourful children's clothing downstairs. It has another branch (Map p102; ☎ 91 577 48 16; Calle de Ayala 13; ⏱ 10am-9pm Mon-Sat) in Salamanca.

LA QUITA PENAS
Map pp116-17 Clothes & Accessories

☎ 91 448 02 57; www.laquitapenas.com, in Spanish; Calle de Fuencarral 146; ⏱ 10am-8.30pm Mon-Sat; Ⓜ Quevedo

One of the most original little shops in the barrio, La Quita Penas offers regalos con suerte (lucky gifts) that range from clothing and jewellery to a handful of children's toys. Every item is carefully chosen and Inés, the owner who is usually there until 3pm, is a delight.

CALZADOS CANTERO Map pp116-17 Shoes

☎ 91 447 07 35; Plaza de Olavide 12; ⏱ 10am-2pm & 4.45-8.30pm Mon-Sat; Ⓜ Quevedo, Iglesia or Bilbao

A charming old-world shoe store, Calzados Cantero sells a range of shoes at rock-bottom prices. But it's most famous for its rope-soled *alpargatas* (espadrilles), which start from €5.50. This is a barrio classic, the sort of store that parents bring their children as their own parents did a generation before.

BAZAR MATEY Map pp116-17 Specialist
☎ 91 446 93 11; www.matey.com, in Spanish; Calle de Fuencarral 127; 9.30am-1.30pm & 4.30-8pm Mon-Sat; M Bilbao or Quevedo

A wonderful old store, Bazar Matey caters for collectors of model trains, aeroplanes and cars, as well as all sorts of accessories. The items here are the real deal, with near-perfect models of everything from old Renfe trains to aircrafts of obscure international airlines. Prices can be sky high, but that doesn't deter the legions of collectors who stream in from all over Madrid on Saturdays. The kids will love it, too.

CASA CARRIL Map pp116-17 Specialist
☎ 91 447 05 12; www.casacarril.com, in Spanish; Calle de Raimundo Lulio 4; 9am-8pm Mon-Fri; M Bilbao

You could go to any photography shop in Madrid for your camera needs, but why not go where the professionals in Madrid have been going for the past 60 years? This place has knowledgeable staff who are as savvy with older cameras as with digital

ones. It also develops photos and sells a range of other accessories, including camera bags.

OCHO Y MEDIO Map pp116-17 Specialist
☎ 91 559 06 28; www.ochoymedio.com; Calle de Martín de los Heros 11; 10am-2pm & 5-8.30pm Mon-Sat; M Plaza de España

Close to a number of the best foreign-language cinemas in Madrid, this is a terrific resource for film buffs, with a huge range of books, posters, magazines and other memorabilia. Much of the stock is in Spanish, but there's a smattering of English- and French-language titles and the friendly staff knows its films.

NORTHERN MADRID

TIENDA REAL MADRID Map p121 Specialist
☎ 91 398 43 00; Gate 57, Estadio Santiago Bernabéu, Avenida de Concha Espina 1; 10am-8.30pm Mon-Sat, 10.30am-8pm Sun; M Santiago Bernabéu

The club shop of Real Madrid sells replica shirts, posters, caps and just about everything under the sun to which it could attach a club logo. From the shop window, you can see down onto the stadium itself. For information on stadium tours, turn to p120. There's another shop (Map pp62-3; ☎ 91 521 79 50; Calle del Carmen 3; 10am-8.45pm Mon-Sat, 10am-6.45pm Sun; M Sol) in the centre of town.

top picks

- **Restaurante Sobrino de Botín** (p149)
- **Santceloni** (p170)
- **Sula Madrid** (p159)
- **Le Cabrera** (p165)
- **Estado Puro** (p159)
- **Bazaar** (p166)
- **La Musa** (p162)
- **Nina** (p162)

After holding fast to its rather unexciting local cuisine for centuries (aided, it must be said, by loyal locals who never saw the need for anything else), Madrid has finally become one of Europe's culinary capitals.

This is a city that grew and became great because of immigrants from all over Spain who made Madrid their home. On their journey to the capital, these immigrants carried with them recipes and ingredients from their villages, thereby bequeathing to the city an astonishing variety of regional flavours that you just don't find anywhere else. Travel from one Spanish village to the next and you'll quickly learn that each has its own speciality; travel to Madrid and you'll find them all. Throw in some outstanding restaurants serving international cuisine and the choice of where to eat well is almost endless.

There's not a barrio where you can't find a great meal. Restaurants in Malasaña, Chueca and Huertas range from glorious old *tabernas* (taverns) to boutique eateries across all price ranges. For more classically elegant surrounds, Paseo del Prado, El Retiro, Salamanca and northern Madrid are generally pricey but of the highest standard and are ideal for spotting royalty and celebrities. In the central barrios of Los Austrias, Sol and Centro, as is their wont, there's a little bit of everything. Splendid tapas bars abound everywhere, but La Latina is the undoubted king.

Aside from the myriad tastes on offer, it's the buzz that accompanies eating that defines the city as a memorable gastronomic experience. Here, eating is not a functional pastime to be squeezed in between other more important tasks; instead, it is one of life's great pleasures, a social event always taken seriously enough to allocate hours for the purpose and to be savoured like all good things in life.

Madrid celebrates a number of food festivals. In addition to Madrid Fusion (p17) in January, there's the Taller de los Sentidos Gourmets (www.gourmets.com, in Spanish) in April, where you can sample products from around the world on the sidelines of a major food trade fair, and the Feria de la Tapa (Tapas Festival) held in the Casa de Campo in mid-June.

If you read Spanish, watch out for the annual (and indispensable) *Guía Metropoli – Comer y Beber en Madrid*. It's available from news kiosks for €11.90 and has reviews of over 1800 Madrid restaurants and bars by the food critics of *ABC* newspaper. And for a range of websites, some of which cover Madrid's food scene, see p21.

ETIQUETTE

Love them or hate them, Spanish waiters are unlikely to leave you indifferent. In smarter establishments, waiters are often young, attentive and switched on to the needs of patrons. In more traditional places, waiting is a career, often a poorly paid one, which is the preserve of old men (sometimes one old man; sometimes one grumpy old man) in white jackets and bow ties, for whom service with a smile is not part of the job description. In such places, they shuffle amid the tables, the weight of the world upon their shoulders, struggling with what seems a Sisyphean task. Getting their attention can be a challenge. On the other hand, they know their food and, if you speak Spanish, they can help tailor your order in the best possible way.

If you're just eating tapas, in many bars you can either take a small plate and help yourself or point to the morsel you want. If you do this, it's customary to keep track of what you eat (by holding on to the toothpicks for example) and then tell the barman when it comes time to pay. Otherwise, most bars have a list of tapas up behind the bar which you can order as a *pincho* (*tapa*), *media ración* (half ration) or *ración* (full ration). In some bars you'll also get a small (free) *tapa* when you buy a drink.

In simpler restaurants, you may keep the same knife and fork throughout the meal. As each course is finished, you set the cutlery aside and the waiter whisks away the plates.

Don't jump out of your seats if people passing your table address you with a hearty *'buen provecho!'* They're just saying 'Enjoy your meal!'

And if you're in a bar, don't be surprised to see people throwing their serviettes and olive stones on the floor – you might as well join them because a waiter will come around from time to time to sweep them all up.

BEST FOR...

Cocido a la Madrileña
- Taberna La Bola (p150)
- Malacatín (p154)
- Lhardy (p156)
- Restaurante Los Galayos (p150)

Roast Lamb or Suckling Pig
- Restaurante Sobrino de Botín (p149)
- El Pedrusco (p169)
- Restaurante Los Galayos (p150)

Tortilla de Patatas
- Juana La Loca (p154)
- Bodega de la Ardosa (p163)
- Estado Puro (p159)
- Las Tortillas de Gabino (p169)

Croquetas
- Bar Melo's (p155)
- Casa Julio (p164)

- Casa Labra (p151)
- Casa Alberto (p156)
- Baco y Beto (p166)
- Las Tortillas de Gabino (p169)

Patatas Bravas
- Las Bravas (p158)
- Le Cabrera (p165)
- Bodega de la Ardosa (p163)

Huevos Rotos
- Almendro 13 (p155)
- Casa Lucio (p152)

Rice & Paella
- Costa Blanca Arrocería (p169)
- Casa Perico (p162)
- La Paella de la Reina (p165)

Chocolate con Churros
- Chocolatería de San Ginés (p179)
- Chocolatería Valor (p178)
- El Brillante (p158)

SPECIALITIES

On the bleak *meseta* (plateau) of inland Spain, food in medieval Madrid was a necessity, good food a luxury, and the dishes that developed were functional and well suited to a climate dominated by interminable, bitterly cold winters. The city's traditional local cuisine is still dominated by these influences and, when the weather turns chilly, that means *legumbres* (legumes), such as *garbanzos* (chickpeas), *judías* (beans) and *lentejas* (lentils). Hearty stews are the order of the day and there are none more hearty than *cocido a la madrileña*; it's a kind of hotpot or stew that starts with a noodle broth and is followed by, or combined with carrots, chickpeas, chicken, *morcilla* (blood sausage), beef, lard and possibly other sausage meats – there are as many ways of eating *cocido* as there are madrileños. *Repollo* (cabbage) sometimes makes an appearance. Madrileños love *cocido*. They dream of it while they're away from home and they wonder why it hasn't caught on elsewhere. There was even a hit song written about it in the 1950s. However, we'll put this as gently as we can: you have to be a madrileño to understand what all the fuss is about because it may be filling but it's not Spain's most exciting dish.

Other popular staples in Madrid include *cordero asado* (roast lamb), *croquetas* (croquettes), *patatas con huevos fritos* (baked potatoes with eggs, also known as *huevos rotos*), *tortilla de patatas* (a thick potato omelette) and endless variations on *bacalao* (cod).

But this is only half the story. Madrid has wholeheartedly embraced dishes – and the innovations that accompany them – from across the country. The city has a thriving tapas culture and has become one of the biggest seafood-consuming cities in the world. Every day, tonnes of fish and other seafood are trucked in from Mediterranean and Atlantic ports to satisfy the madrileño taste for the sea to the extent that, remarkably for a city so far inland, Madrid is home to the world's second-largest fish market (after Tokyo).

VEGETARIANS & VEGANS

Pure vegetarianism remains something of an alien concept in most Spanish kitchens; cooked vegetable dishes, for example, often contain ham. That said, Madrid has a growing cast of vegetarian restaurants. Even in those restaurants that serve meat or fish, salads are a Spanish staple and, in some places, can be a meal in themselves. You'll also come across the odd vegetarian paella, as well as dishes such as *verduras a la plancha* (grilled vegetables), *garbanzos con espinacas* (chickpeas and spinach) and numerous potato dishes, such as *patatas bravas* (potato chunks bathed in spicy tomato sauce) and the *tortilla*

top picks

FOR VEGETARIANS & VEGANS

- La Isla del Tesoro (p162)
- El Estragón (p155)
- La Galette (p160)
- Restaurante Integral Artemisa (p157)
- Viva La Vida (p155)
- La Biotika (p158)

de patatas (potato and onion omelette). The prevalence of legumes ensures that *lentejas* and *judías* are also easy to track down, while *pan* (bread), *quesos* (cheeses), *alcachofas* (artichokes) and *aceitunas* (olives) are always easy to find. If vegetarianism is rare among Spaniards, vegans will feel as if they've come from another planet. However, some of the established vegetarian restaurants may have certain vegan dishes; otherwise, self-catering is an option (see opposite).

COOKING COURSES

There are plenty of places to learn Spanish cooking. In most cases, you'll need at least passable Spanish, but some run special classes for English speakers.

Alambique (Map pp62-3; ☎ 91 547 42 20; www
.alambique.com; Plaza de la Encarnación 2; Ⓜ Ópera or Santo Domingo) Cooking classes start at around €50, with a handful of English- and French-speaking courses.

Apunto – Centro Cultural del Gusto (Map p110; ☎ 91
702 10 41; www.apuntolibreria.com, in Spanish; Calle de Pelayo 60; Ⓜ Chueca) At this engaging little bookstore, whose subtitle translates as 'Cultural Centre of Taste', cooking classes across a range of cuisines start at around €25.

Cooking Club (Map p121; ☎ 91 323 29 58; www
.club-cooking.com, in Spanish; Calle de Veza 33;
Ⓜ Valdeacederas) This regular, respected program of classes encompasses a range of cooking styles.

Gaudeamus Café (p181) This fine Lavapiés cafe runs classes in Spanish and international cooking.

PRACTICALITIES

Most visitors complain not about the quality of Spanish food but about its timing. *Comida/almuerzo* (lunch) rarely begins before 2pm (restaurant kitchens usually open from 1pm until 4pm). For *cena* (dinner), few madrileños would dream of turning up before 9.30pm,

although most restaurants open 8.30pm to midnight, later on weekends. On weekends some restaurants take reservations for two sittings, one starting at 9pm, the other at 11pm! Stay in Madrid long enough and you'll soon get used to it. In this chapter, 'lunch' means a venue is open 1pm to 4pm, and 'dinner' means 8.30pm to midnight; exceptions are noted in reviews.

In the intervening hours, many bars serve tapas and *raciones* throughout the day. *Bocadillos* (filled rolls, usually without butter) are another option. Cafes tend to open from 8am or 9am through to at least 9pm, and often to midnight or beyond if they double as bars. Most restaurants are shut on Christmas Eve and many on New Year's Eve (or Christmas Day and New Year's Day), while some have a night off on Sunday and many don't open at all on Monday. Some close over Easter and a good many shut for at least part of August as well.

Desayuno (breakfast) is generally a no-nonsense affair taken at a bar on the way to work. A *café con leche* (half coffee and half warm milk) with a *bollo* (pastry) is the typical breakfast. Croissants or a cream-filled pastry are also common. Some people prefer a savoury start – try a *sandwich mixto*, a toasted ham and cheese sandwich; or a Spanish *tostada*, which is simply buttered toast. Others, especially party animals heading home at dawn after a night out, go for an all-Spanish favourite, *chocolate con churros*, a deep-fried stick of plain pastry immersed in thick hot chocolate.

A full meal generally comprises an *entrante* (entrée), *plato principal* (main course) and *postre* (dessert). Bread is routinely served with meals, but you pay extra for it (usually around €1.20). If you can't face a full menu, a simpler option is the *plato combinado*, basically a meat-and-three-veg dish that will hardly excite taste buds but will have little fiscal impact.

In the following pages a 'meal' is understood to mean an entrée, main course and dessert, including a little modestly priced wine.

PRICE GUIDE

Throughout this chapter, restaurants are listed according to the barrio (area of Madrid), then by price range from most expensive to least expensive. Each place is accompanied by one of the following symbols:

€€€	more than €50 a meal
€€	€20-50 a meal
€	less than €20 a meal

At many of the midrange restaurants and simpler taverns with *comedores* (dining rooms) you can generally turn up and find a spot without booking ahead. You should reserve a table at sit-down restaurants, especially on Friday or Saturday night.

Tipping

A service charge is generally calculated into most bills in Madrid, so any further tipping is a matter of personal choice. Spaniards themselves are pretty stingy when it comes to tipping and often leave no more than €1 per person or nothing more than small change. If you're particularly happy, 5% on top would be fine.

Self-Catering

Some of the better food markets in town:

Mercado de la Cebada (Map pp76-7; Plaza de la Cebada; 9am-2pm & 5.30-8.30pm Mon-Fri, 9am-2.30pm Sat; La Latina) Slated for long-overdue major renovations.

Mercado de la Paz (Map p102; off Calle de Ayala; 9am-8pm Mon-Sat; Serrano)

Other specialist food stores include Maison Blanche (p167), Mantequería Bravo (p138) and Alma de Ibérico (p133). For Spanish and other European cheeses, Poncelet (Map p110; ☎ 91 308 02 21; www .poncelet.es; Calle de Argensola 27; 10.30am-8.30pm Mon-Sat; Alonso Martínez) should be your first stop.

For more international flavours, try the following:

Taste of America (Map p121; ☎ 91 411 46 42; Calle de Serrano 149; 9am-9pm Mon-Fri, 10am-9pm Sat, 11am-3pm Sun; República Argentina) Betty Crocker chocolate chip cookie mix, jelly beans and other US staples.

Things You Miss (Map pp116-17; ☎ 91 447 07 85; www.thethingsyoumiss.com; Calle de Juan de Austria 11; 10am-2.30pm & 5-8.30pm Mon-Fri, 10.30am-2.30pm Sat Sep-Jul; Iglesia or Bilbao) For all things British.

LOS AUSTRIAS, SOL & CENTRO

From the world's oldest restaurant to downtempo fusion places, from regional tapas to Asian flavours, and from old Spanish bars where the ambience owes everything to impromptu theatre to brightly painted vegetarian restaurants, downtown Madrid has a little bit of everything. This is the part of the capital where you're most likely to find English menus (which we welcome), as well

as loads of places with brightly photographed paellas out the front (of which we're always suspicious). Around here, you'll also find waiters roaming outside touting for business – we haven't listed such places here. A far better guide to the quality of the food on offer is if the place is filled with locals.

LA TERRAZA DEL CASINO
Map pp62-3   Spanish €€€
☎ 91 521 87 00; www.casinodemadrid.es; Calle de Alcalá 15; meals €100-140; lunch & dinner Mon-Fri, dinner Sat; Sevilla
Perched atop the landmark Casino de Madrid building, this temple of haute cuisine is overseen, albeit from afar, by Ferran Adrià (Spain's premier celebrity chef), but is mostly in the hands of his acolyte Paco Roncero. It's all about culinary experimentation and a menu that changes with each new idea that emerges from the laboratory and into the kitchen. Other celebrity chefs occasionally make an appearance. You may not eat here often, but doing so just once will leave you in raptures. The *menu degustación* (tasting menu) costs €140.

TABERNA DEL ALABARDERO
Map pp62-3   Spanish €€
☎ 91 547 25 77; www.grupolezama.es; Calle de Felipe V 6; meals €45-50; lunch & dinner daily; Ópera
This fine old Madrid *taberna* is famous for its croquettes, fine *jamón* (ham), *montaditos de jamón* (small rolls of cured ham) and *montaditos de bonito* (small rolls of cured tuna) in the bar, while out the back the more classic cuisine includes *rabo de toro estofado* (bull's tail, served with honey, cinnamon, mashed potato and pastry with herbs; €18.50). Prices aren't cheap, but Madrid's notoriously fussy diners generally accept that it's worth it. Their sister restaurant around the corner in Plaza de Oriente, La Mar del Alabardero (Map pp62-3; ☎ 91 541 33 33; www.grupolezama.es; Plaza de Oriente 6; meals €35-40; lunch & dinner daily; Ópera), is renowned for its high-quality seafood.

RESTAURANTE SOBRINO DE BOTÍN
Map pp62-3   Spanish €€
☎ 91 366 42 17; www.botin.es; Calle de los Cuchilleros 17; set menu €40.90, meals €40-45; La Latina or Sol
It's not every day that you can eat in the oldest restaurant in the world (the *Guinness*

Book of Records has recognised it as the oldest – established in 1725) that has also appeared in many novels about Madrid, most notably Hemingway's *The Sun Also Rises*. The secret of its staying power is fine *cochinillo* (roast suckling pig; €22.90) and *cordero asado* (roast lamb; €22.90) cooked in wood-fired ovens. Eating in the vaulted cellar is a treat. Yes, it's filled with tourists. And yes, staff are keen to keep things ticking over and there's little chance to linger. But the novelty value is high and the food excellent. They also run tours (The Botín Experience; ☎ 91 447 38 66; tour incl lunch €55; 🕑 12.30pm Mon-Fri) of the restaurant.

RESTAURANTE LOS GALAYOS
Map pp62-3   Spanish €€
☎ 91 366 30 28; www.losgalayos.net; Calle de Botoneros 5; meals €30-35; 🕑 1pm-12.30am; Ⓜ Sol

Most of the restaurants surrounding Plaza Mayor are tourist traps, but Los Galayos, a few steps off the plaza's southeastern corner, is an exception. Renowned for its roasted meats (roast suckling pig or spring lamb for €21.75), *cocido* (€18; lunch only), it's a good place to sample traditional local cooking from around Spain, sometimes with the merest hint of a creative twist.

TABERNA LA BOLA Map pp62-3   Madrileño €€
☎ 91 547 69 30; www.labola.es; Calle de la Bola 5; meals €30-35; 🕑 lunch & dinner Mon-Sat, lunch Sun; Ⓜ Santo Domingo

In any poll of food-loving locals seeking the best and most traditional Madrid cuisine, Taberna La Bola (going strong since 1870 and run by the sixth generation of the Verdasco family) always features near the top. We're inclined to agree and, if you're going to try *cocido a la madrileña* (€19) while in Madrid, this is a good place to do

so. It's busy and noisy and very Madrid. It also serves other Madrid specialities, such as *callos* (tripe) and *sopa castellana* (garlic soup).

AMAYA Map pp62-3   Tapas €€
☎ 91 366 82 07; www.viviramaya.com, in Spanish; Plaza de la Provincia 3; meals €25-30; 🕑 noon-5pm & 8pm-late Tue-Sat, noon-5pm Sun; Ⓜ Sol

This new place is one of our favourite tapas bars in central Madrid. Warm colours and modern decor mark a welcome change from the traditional ambience of many places close to the Plaza Mayor. The range of tapas, salads and Spanish wines is a moveable feast that mixes surprising tastes with reassuring Spanish staples.

LA GLORIA DE MONTERA
Map pp62-3   Spanish €€
☎ 91 523 44 07; Calle del Caballero de Gracia 10; meals €25-30; 🕑 lunch & dinner daily; Ⓜ Gran Vía

La Gloria de Montera combines classy decor with eminently reasonable prices. It's not that the food is especially creative, but rather the tastes are fresh and the surroundings sophisticated. You'll get a good initiation into Spanish cooking without paying over the odds. It doesn't take reservations, so turn up early or be prepared to wait.

KITCHEN STORIES Map pp62-3   Spanish €€
☎ 91 366 97 71; www.kitchenstories.es; Calle de los Cuchilleros 3; meals €20-30; 🕑 noon-1am; Ⓜ Sol or La Latina

Cafe, restaurant and food store in one, Kitchen Stories, at the foot of the Arco de Cuchilleros stairs, is a refreshing break from the often classical cooking in the area, with a bright modern space and Spanish flavours blended with international tastes.

MENÚ DEL DÍA

One great way to cap prices at lunchtime Monday to Friday is to order the *menú del día*, a full set meal (usually with several options), water, bread and wine. These meals start from around €9, although €10 and up is increasingly the norm. You'll be given a menu with five or six entrées, the same number of mains and a handful of desserts – choose one from each category. It is usually possible to choose two starters as your first two courses, but not two mains.

The philosophy behind the *menú del día* is that, during the working week, few madrileños have time to go home to have their lunch. Taking a packed lunch is just not the done thing, so the majority of people end up eating in restaurants, and all-inclusive three-course meals are as close as they can get to eating home-style food without breaking the bank. It's worth remembering that quantities are usually slightly smaller than the equivalent à la carte dishes and most places don't include their signature specialities in the *menú del día*.

YERBABUENA Map pp62-3 Vegetarian €€

☎ 91 548 08 11; www.yerbabuena.ws, in Spanish; Calle de los Bordadores 3; meals €20-25; ☺ 11am-midnight; Ⓜ Sol or Ópera

Cheerful bright colours, a full range of vegetarian staples (soya-bean burgers, biological rice and homemade yogurt) and plenty of creatively conceived salads add up to one of central Madrid's best restaurants for vegetarians and vegans.

BANGKOK THAI RESTAURANT

Map pp62-3 Thai €€

☎ 91 559 16 96; 1st fl, Calle de los Bordadores 15; meals €20; ☺ noon-4pm & 8pm-midnight; Ⓜ Sol or Ópera

Great Thai food, reasonable prices, good service and a Thai-style dining area make for a terrific meal in the heart of town. If you're lucky, you'll get one of the tables overlooking the busy pedestrian thoroughfare of Calle del Arenal. In addition to their à la carte choices, they offer a well-priced *menú del día* (€11.50) that's available for lunch seven days a week, a *menú de noche* (evening set menu; €15) and a *menú de degustación* (tasting menu; €19.50). Their opening hours are particularly friendly to non-Spanish stomachs.

MERCADO DE SAN MIGUEL

Map pp62-3 Tapas & Delicatessen €€

www.mercadodesanmiguel.es, in Spanish; Plaza de San Miguel; ☺ 10am-midnight Sun-Wed, 10am-2am Thu-Sat; Ⓜ Sol

One of Madrid's oldest and most beautiful markets, the Mercado de San Miguel has undergone a stunning major renovation and bills itself as a 'culinary cultural centre'. Within the early-20th-century glass walls, the market has become an inviting space strewn with tables (difficult to nab) where you can enjoy the freshest food or a drink. Apart from the fresh fish corner, you can order tapas at most of the counter-bars. La Casa de Bacalao (stall 17), for example, serves up a range of tempting small toasts for €1 each, while an outpost of the classic Madrid restaurant Lhardy (p156) can be found at stalls 61 and 62. But everything here (from caviar to chocolate) is as tempting as the market is alive.

CASA LABRA Map pp62-3 Tapas €

☎ 91 532 14 05; www.casalabra.es; Calle de Tetuán 11; meals €15-20; ☺ 11am-3.30pm & 6-11pm; Ⓜ Sol

Casa Labra has been going strong since 1860, an era that the decor strongly evokes. Locals love their *bacalao* (cod) and ordering it here – either as deep-fried tapas (*una tajada de bacalao* goes for €1.25) or as *una croqueta de bacalao* (€0.80 per croquette) – is a Madrid rite of initiation, as the lunchtime queues will attest; they go through more than 700kg of cod every week. This is also a bar with history – it was where the Partido Socialista Obrero Español (PSOE; Spanish Socialist Party) was formed on 2 May 1879. It was a favourite of Lorca, the poet, as well as appearing in Pío Baroja's novel *La Busca*. It's the sort of place that fathers bring their sons, just as their fathers did before them.

CASA REVUELTA Map pp62-3 Tapas €

☎ 91 366 33 32; Calle de Latoneros 3; meals €15-20; ☺ 10.30am-4pm & 7-11pm Mon & Wed-Sat, 10.30am-4pm Sun Sep-Jul; Ⓜ Sol or La Latina

Casa Revuelta puts out some of Madrid's finest tapas of *bacalao* (€2.60 per *tapa*) bar none. While aficionados of Casa Labra may disagree, the fact that the octogenarian owner, Señor Revuelta, painstakingly extracts every fish bone in the morning and serves as a waiter in the afternoon wins the argument for us. Early on a Sunday afternoon, as the Rastro crowd gathers here, it's filled to the rafters, although locals who've been coming here for decades always manage to find room. It's also famous for its *callos* (tripe), *torreznos* (bacon bits) and *albóndigas* (meatballs).

MUSEO DEL JAMÓN Map pp62-3 Spanish €

☎ 91 531 45 50; www.museodeljamon.com, in Spanish; Calle Mayor 7; meals €15-20; ☺ 8am-midnight; Ⓜ Sol

Famous for having appeared in Pedro Almodóvar's 1997 film *Carne Trémula* (Live Flesh), and equally beloved by first-time visitors to Spain for the sight of hundreds of hams hanging from the ceiling, Museo del Jamón is definitely a local landmark. Prices for a *ración/bocadillo* start at €2.50/1.50 and go much higher depending on the quality of the *jamón*.

FAST GOOD Map pp62-3 Healthy Fast Food €

☎ 91 523 04 56; www.fast-good.com, in Spanish; Calle de Tetuán 2; meals €10-15; ☺ 1-10pm Sun-Tue, 1-11pm Wed & Thu, 1pm-midnight Fri & Sat; Ⓜ Sol

When Ferran Adrià, the star Catalan chef, became concerned about Spaniards' growing obsession with fast food, he decided to do something about it. Fast Good is a wonderfully simple concept (food that's fast but healthy) and it's a terrific place to get a freshly prepared hamburger using Spanish ground beef with olive tapenade, roast chicken, sandwiches with Spanish ham, panini, or French fries cooked in fresh olive oil. The opening hours will appeal to those not yet used to Spanish eating hours, and they have set menus ranging from €9.50 to €11.

CERVECERÍA 100 MONTADITOS
Map pp62-3 Bocadillos €

☎ 91 354 02 68; www.cerveceria100montaditos.com; Calle Mayor 22; meals €5-10; 🕒 10am-11.30pm Sun-Thu, 10am-1.30am Fri & Sat; Ⓜ Sol

This bar with outlets all across the city serves up no fewer than 100 different varieties of mini-*bocadillos* (filled rolls, without butter) that span the full range of Spanish staples, such as chorizo, *jamón, tortilla,* a variety of cheeses and seafood, in more combinations than you could imagine; there are even two possibilities with chocolate. Each one costs a princely €1 to €2 and four will satisfy most stomachs. You fill out your order, take it up to the counter and your name is called in no time. Menus are available in English.

BAR LA IDEAL Map pp62-3 Bocadillos €

☎ 91 365 72 78; Calle de los Botaderos 4; bocadillos €2.30; 🕒 lunch & dinner until late; Ⓜ Sol

Spanish bars don't come any more basic than this, but it's the purveyor of an enduring and wildly popular Madrid tradition – *bocadillo de calamares*. If it's closed, which is rare, Cervecería La Campana next door is the same deal.

LA LATINA & LAVAPIÉS

La Latina is our pick for the best barrio in Madrid for tapas, complemented by a fine selection of sit-down restaurants. If you're planning only one tapas crawl while in town, do it here in Calle de la Cava Baja and surrounding streets.

Lavapiés is more eclectic and multicultural and, generally speaking, the further down the hill you go, the better it gets, especially along Calle de Argumosa.

CASA LUCIO Map pp76-7 Spanish €€

☎ 91 365 32 52; www.casalucio.es, in Spanish; Calle de la Cava Baja 35; meals €45-50; 🕒 lunch & dinner Sun-Fri, dinner Sat Sep-Jul; Ⓜ La Latina

Lucio has been wowing madrileños with his light touch, quality ingredients and

MADRID FOR THE SWEET TOOTH

Tapas may be a Spanish institution, but what madrileños really love are their pastries, especially at breakfast, although any excuse will do. These are our favourite classic Madrid pastry shops, which we were forced to visit (purely for research purposes, of course).

Chocolatería de San Ginés (p179) The best known of Madrid's *chocolate con churros* vendors. Sedate by day, by night it fills with clubbers with the munchies, pouring out of the city's nearby dance palaces.

Horno de San Onofre (Map pp108-9; ☎ 91 532 90 60; Calle de San Onofre 3; 🕒 8am-9pm; Ⓜ Gran Vía) Everything's a speciality, from cakes and pastries to bite-sized sweets and Christmas *turrón* (a nougat-like sweet).

Horno de Santiguesa (Map pp62-3; ☎ 91 559 62 14; Calle Mayor 73; 🕒 8am-9pm; Ⓜ Ópera) Owned by the same family as Horno de San Onofre.

Casa Mira (Map pp84-5; ☎ 91 429 88 95; Carrera de San Jerónimo 30; 🕒 10am-2pm & 5-9pm Mon-Sat; Ⓜ Sol) The turning, wedding-cake-like display in the window is laden with sweets, cakes, fat pastries and candied fruits. The shop is especially known for its *turrónes*.

La Duquesita (Map p110; ☎ 91 308 02 31; Calle de Fernando VI 2; 🕒 9.30am-2.30pm & 5-9pm Tue-Sun; Ⓜ Alonso Martínez) Another lavish step back in time with wonderful traditional pastries.

La Mallorquina (Map pp62-3; ☎ 91 521 12 01; Plaza de la Puerta del Sol 8; 🕒 9am-9.15pm; Ⓜ Sol) A classic pastry shop that's packed to the rafters by madrileños who just couldn't pass by without stopping. Treat yourself to a takeaway *ensaimada* (a light pastry dusted with icing sugar) from Mallorca.

Confitería El Riojano (Map pp62-3; ☎ 91 366 44 82; Calle Mayor 10; 🕒 10am-2pm & 5-9pm Mon-Fri, 10am-2.30pm & 5.30-9pm Sat & Sun; Ⓜ Sol) Founded in 1855, this place serves the usual suspects, as well as traditional Madrid offerings such as *azucarillos* (meringue-like sugar bombs) of lemon, coffee or strawberry and *bartolillos* (sweet filled pastries).

EAT STREETS – CALLE DE LA CAVA BAJA

Calle de la Cava Baja (Map pp76-7; **M** La Latina) is jam-packed with great tapas bars and sit-down restaurants. For tapas, we love Txacolina (p155), La Chata (p154) and Casa Lucas (p154). Other outstanding choices include the tapas from Extremadura in Taberna de Conspiradores (☎ 91 366 58 69; Calle de la Cava Baja 7; meals €20-25), La Camarilla (☎ 91 354 02 02; www.lacamarillarestaurante.com, in Spanish; Calle de la Cava Baja 21; meals €25-30, tapas tasting menu €19; ☽ lunch & dinner Mon, Tue, Fri & Sat, lunch only Thu & Sun) and the Galician cuisine of Orixe (☎ 91 354 04 11; www.orixerestaurante.com, in Spanish; Calle de la Cava Baja 17; meals €30-35; ☽ lunch & dinner Tue-Sat, lunch Sun, dinner Mon).

For a sit-down meal, it's difficult to beat Casa Lucio (opposite), but other bastions of tradition worth splashing out include the Madrid-through-and-through Posada de la Villa (☎ 91 366 18 60; Calle de la Cava Baja 9; meals €50-55; ☽ lunch & dinner Mon-Sat, lunch Sun Sep-Jul), in a restored 17th-century inn, and the refined Navarran cooking of Restaurante Julián de Tolosa (☎ 91 365 82 10; Calle de la Cava Baja 8; meals €50-55; ☽ lunch & dinner Mon-Sat, lunch Sun).

home-style local cooking for ages – think roasted meats and, a Lucio speciality, eggs in abundance. There's also *rabo de toro* (bull's tail) during the Fiestas de San Isidro Labrador and plenty of *rioja* (red wine) to wash away the mere thought of it. Casa Lucio draws an august, always well-dressed crowd, which has included the king of Spain, former US president Bill Clinton and Penélope Cruz.

ENE RESTAURANTE
Map pp76-7   Tapas & Fusion €€
☎ 91 366 25 91; www.enerestaurante.com; Calle del Nuncio 19; meals €35-40; **M** La Latina
Just across from Iglesia de San Pedro El Viejo, one of Madrid's oldest churches, Ene is anything but old world. The design is cutting edge and awash with reds and purples, while the young and friendly waiters circulate to the tune of lounge

top picks
TAPAS

- Estado Puro (p159)
- Le Cabrera (p165)
- Sagaretxe (p170)
- Biotza (p161)
- Txacolina (p155)
- Almendro 13 (p155)
- Taberna Matritum (p154)
- Juana La Loca (p154)
- La Colonial de Goya (p160)
- Baco y Beto (p166)
- Bocaito (p166)
- Gastromaquia (p167)

music. The food is Spanish-Asian fusion and there are also plenty of *pintxos* (Basque tapas) to choose from. The chill-out beds downstairs are great for an after-dinner cocktail or even a meal, although they're always reserved well in advance.

NUNC EST BIBENDUM
Map pp76-7   Spanish €€
☎ 91 366 52 10; Calle de la Cava Alta 13; meals €30-35; ☽ lunch & dinner Mon-Sat, lunch Sun; **M** La Latina
Calle de la Cava Alta doesn't have the sex appeal (or the crowds) of its neighbour, but it has some wonderful little bar-restaurants. Nunc Est Bibendum combines a classy but casual clean-lined look with a varied menu that defies categorisation – sometimes it's a Basque base; other flavours come from Italy or the south or from France. But it's always good, with riffs on the theme of meat, rice and fish. The 50-strong wine list is also thoughtfully chosen, with some lesser-known Spanish wines.

NAÏA RESTAURANTE
Map pp76-7   Fusion €€
☎ 91 366 27 83; www.naiarestaurante.com, in Spanish; Plaza de la Paja 3; meals €30-35; ☽ lunch & dinner Tue-Sun; **M** La Latina
On the lovely Plaza de la Paja, Naïa has a real buzz about it, with a cooking laboratory overseen by Carlos López Reyes, modern Spanish cuisine and a chill-out lounge downstairs. The emphasis throughout is on natural ingredients, healthy food and exciting tastes. The *chilli con carne con chocolate negro* (chilli with meat and dark chocolate) is typical of what to expect. The kitchen stays open until 12.30am on Friday and Saturday nights.

JUANA LA LOCA Map pp76-7 Tapas €€

☎ 91 364 05 25; Plaza de la Puerta de Moros 4; meals €25-30; ⏰ lunch & dinner Tue-Sun, dinner Mon; Ⓜ La Latina

You can't miss 'Juana the Crazy One', with its bright purple facade, and nor would you want to. Juana La Loca does a range of creative tapas with tempting options lined up along the bar and more on the menu that they prepare to order. But locals love it above all for its *tortilla de patatas* (€4 per *tapa*), which is distinguished from others of its kind by the caramelised onions – simply wonderful.

SANLÚCAR Map pp76-7 Tapas €€

☎ 91 354 00 52; Calle de San Isidro Labrador 14; meals €25-30; ⏰ lunch & dinner Tue-Sat, lunch Sun; Ⓜ La Latina

The seafood-dominated cooking of the Andalucian province of Cádiz is what this place is all about, with every imaginable sea creature (usually lightly fried) sharing the menu with gazpacho (cold soup) served in a tall drinking glass. Quiet at lunchtimes (except on Sundays), it can be hard to find a place in the evenings.

LA BUGA DEL LOBO Map pp76-7 Spanish €€

☎ 91 467 61 51; www.labocadellobo.com; Calle de Argumosa 11; meals €25-30; ⏰ 11am-2am Wed-Mon; Ⓜ Lavapiés

La Buga del Lobo has been one of the 'in' places in cool and gritty Lavapiés for years now and it's still hard to get a table. The atmosphere is Bohemian and inclusive, with funky, swirling murals, contemporary art exhibitions and jazz or lounge music. The food's good and traditional, with meat and fish dishes for mains and *croquetas,* cheeses or salads for entrées, but it's best known for its groovy vibe at any time of day or night.

LA CHATA Map pp76-7 Tapas €€

☎ 91 366 14 58; Calle de la Cava Baja 24; meals €25-30; ⏰ lunch & dinner Thu-Mon, dinner Wed; Ⓜ La Latina

Behind the lavishly tiled facade, La Chata looks for all the world like a neglected outpost of the past. The decor may be rundown and the bullfighting memorabilia not to everyone's taste, but this is an essential stop on a tapas tour of La Latina. The dishes are mainstays of the local diet (tripe and plenty of seafood), but don't come here without ordering a *cazuela* (stew cooked and served in a ceramic pot).

LA MUSA LATINA Map pp76-7 Fusion €€

☎ 91 354 02 55; www.lamusalatina.com; Costanilla de San Andrés 1; meals €25-30; ⏰ lunch & dinner daily; Ⓜ La Latina

Laid-back La Musa Latina has an ever-popular dining area and food that's designed to bring a smile to your face. It's the same deal as at its other restaurants (p162) in Malasaña. The downstairs bar in the former wine cellar is ideal for an after-dinner drink.

MALACATÍN Map pp76-7 Madrileño €€

☎ 91 365 52 41; www.malacatin.com; Calle de Ruda 5; meals €25-30; ⏰ lunch Mon-Wed & Sat, lunch & dinner Thu & Fri; Ⓜ La Latina

If you want to see madrileños enjoying their favourite local food, this is one of the best places to do so. The clamour of conversation bounces off the tiled walls of the cramped dining area adorned with bullfighting memorabilia. The speciality is as much *cocido* (stew) as you can eat (€18). The *degustación de cocido* (taste of *cocido;* €5) at the bar is a great way to try Madrid's favourite dish without going all the way, although it's a bit like smoking without inhaling.

TABERNA MATRITUM Map pp76-7 Tapas €€

☎ 91 365 82 37; Calle de la Cava Alta 17; meals €25-30; ⏰ lunch & dinner Thu-Sun, dinner Mon-Wed; Ⓜ La Latina

This little gem is reason enough to detour from the more popular Calle de la Cava Baja next door. The seasonal menu here encompasses terrific tapas, salads and generally creative cooking (there's even bull's tail with an aroma of truffles) and some of the desserts come from the master Catalan chocolatier Oriol Balaguer. The wine list runs into the hundreds and it's sophisticated without being pretentious.

CASA LUCAS Map pp76-7 Tapas €€

☎ 91 365 08 04; www.casalucas.es; Calle de la Cava Baja 30; meals €20-30; ⏰ lunch & dinner Thu-Tue, dinner Wed; Ⓜ La Latina

Receiving plaudits from food critics and ordinary punters alike, Casa Lucas takes a sideways glance at traditional Spanish tapas and heads off in new directions (the foie gras with port and caramelised fruits, for example). There are a range of hot and cold tapas (€5 to €7) and larger *raciones* (€15). The menu changes regularly as they come up with new ideas.

THE ORIGIN OF TAPAS

There are many stories concerning the origins of tapas. One holds that, in the 13th century, doctors to King Alfonso X advised him to accompany his small sips of wine between meals with small morsels of food. So enamoured was the monarch with the idea that he passed a law requiring all bars in Castile to follow suit. Another version attributes tapas to bar owners who placed a saucer with a piece of bread on top of a sherry glass either to deter flies or prevent the punter from drinking on an empty stomach and getting too tipsy. As for the name, *tapa* (which means 'lid') is said to have attained widespread usage in the early 20th century when King Alfonso XIII stopped at a beachside bar. When a strong gust of wind blew sand in the king's direction, a quick-witted waiter rushed to place a slice of *jamón* atop the king's glass of sherry. The king so much enjoyed the idea (and the *jamón*) that, wind or no wind, he ordered another and the name stuck.

EL ESTRAGÓN Map pp76-7 Vegetarian €€

☎ 91 365 89 82; Plaza de la Paja 10; meals €20-25; ⓨ lunch & dinner daily; Ⓜ La Latina

A delightful spot for crêpes, vegie burgers and other vegetarian specialities, El Estragón is undoubtedly one of Madrid's best vegetarian restaurants, although attentive vegans won't appreciate the use of butter. Apart from that, we're yet to hear a bad word about it, and the *menu del día* (from €8) is one of Madrid's best bargains.

ALMENDRO 13 Map pp76-7 Tapas €

☎ 91 365 42 52; Calle del Almendro 13; meals €15-20; ⓨ lunch & dinner daily; Ⓜ La Latina

Almendro 13 is a charming, wildly popular *taberna* where you come for traditional Spanish tapas with an emphasis on quality rather than frilly elaborations. Cured meats, cheeses, omelettes and many variations on these themes dominate the menu; it serves both *raciones* and half-sized plates – a full *ración* of the famously good *huevos rotos* (literally, 'broken eggs') served with *jamón* and thin potato slices (€8.80) is a meal in itself. The only problem is that the wait for a table (low, with wooden stools) requires the patience of a saint, so order a fine wine or manzanilla (dry sherry) and soak up the buzz. Unusually, it opens at 7.30pm (8pm on weekends), when your chances of finding a perch are better.

TXACOLINA Map pp76-7 Tapas €

☎ 91 366 48 77; Calle de la Cava Baja 26; meals €15-20; ⓨ dinner Mon & Wed-Fri, lunch & dinner Sat, lunch Sun; Ⓜ La Latina

Txacolina calls its *pintxos* 'high cuisine in miniature' – the first part is true, but these are some of the biggest *pintxos* (€2.80 to €5) you'll find and some are a meal in themselves. If ordering tapas makes you nervous because you don't speak Spanish or you're not quite sure how it works, it couldn't be easier here – they're lined up on the bar, Basque style, in all their glory and you can simply point. Whatever you order, wash it down with a *txacoli*, a sharp Basque white.

VIVA LA VIDA Map pp76-7 Tapas €

☎ 91 366 33 49; www.vivalavida.vg; Costanilla de San Andrés 16; veg buffet per 100g €2.10; ⓨ noon-midnight; Ⓜ La Latina

The enticing vegetarian buffet with hot and cold food, always filled with flavour, is one of the best deals in town. On the cusp of Plaza de la Paja, this place has a laid-back vibe and is a great place at any time of the day, especially outside normal Spanish eating hours when your stomach's rumbling. It has another branch (Map pp84-5; ☎ 91 369 72 54; Calle de las Huertas 57; Ⓜ Antón Martín) in Huertas, although it's more takeaway, with only a handful of stools.

BAR MELO'S Map pp76-7 Tapas & Bocadillos €

☎ 91 527 50 54; Calle del Ave María; meals €15-20; ⓨ 9pm-2am Tue-Sat; Ⓜ Lavapiés

One of those Spanish bars that you'd normally walk past without a second glance, Bar Melo's is famous across the city for its *zapatillas* (great, spanking *bocadillos* of *lacón* – cured shoulder of pork – and cheese). They're big, they're greasy and they're damn good; the place is packed on Friday and Saturday nights when a *zapatilla* is the perfect accompaniment to a night of drinking. The *croquetas* are also famously good, not to mention epic in scale.

HUERTAS & ATOCHA

The noise surrounding Huertas nightlife can obscure the fact that the barrio is a terrific place to eat out. Its culinary appeal lies in a hotchpotch of styles rather than any overarching personality. Bastions of traditional cooking, from those serving pheasant in refined surrounds to down-and-dirty tapas bars selling *oreja* (pig's ear), coexist here with restaurants serving Basque, Galician, Andalucian, Scandinavian and Italian cuisine. When you factor in the barrio's fine bars and pulsing nightlife (see p184), it's difficult to find a good reason to leave the barrio once the sun goes down.

LHARDY Map pp84-5 Madrileño €€€

☎ 91 521 33 85; www.lhardy.com; Carrera de San Jerónimo 8; meals €60-70; ☽ lunch & dinner Mon-Sat, lunch Sun Sep-Jul; Ⓜ Sol or Sevilla

This Madrid landmark (since 1839) is an elegant treasure trove of takeaway gourmet tapas downstairs, while the six upstairs dining areas are the upmarket preserve of traditional Madrid dishes with an occasional hint of French influence. House specialities include *cocido a la madrileña* (€35.50), pheasant in grape juice (€31.50) and lemon soufflé (€13.50). The quality and service are unimpeachable. A favourite haunt of royalty in the 19th century, Lhardy has drawn the great and good of Madrid ever since.

SIDRERÍA VASCA ZERAÍN

Map pp84-5 Basque €€

☎ 91 429 79 09; Calle de Quevedo 3; meals €35-40; ☽ lunch & dinner Mon-Sat Sep-Jul; Ⓜ Antón Martín

In the heart of the Barrio de las Letras, this sophisticated Basque restaurant is one of the best places in town to sample Basque cuisine. The essential staples include cider, *bacalao* and wonderful steaks, while there are also a few splashes of creativity thrown in (the secret's in the sauce). We highly recommend the *menú sidrería* (cider-house menu; €36.50).

A TASCA DO BACALHAU PORTUGÊS

Map pp84-5 Portuguese €€

☎ 91 429 56 75; www.atascadobacalhauportuges .com, in Spanish; Calle de Lope de Vega 14; meals €30-40; ☽ lunch & dinner Tue-Sat, lunch Sun; Ⓜ Antón Martín

One of the few authentic Portuguese restaurants in Madrid, A Tasca do Bacalhau doesn't have a particularly extensive menu, but it's dominated by excellent *bacalhau* (cod) and rice dishes. They claim to have 412 different recipes for cod, although thankfully only a handful of these appear on the menu. If you're not familiar with Portuguese cooking, this is a good place to have your first taste.

LA VACA VERÓNICA

Map pp84-5 Italian & Argentine €€

☎ 91 429 78 27; www.lavacaveronica.es, in Spanish; Calle de Moratín 38; meals €30-35; ☽ lunch & dinner Mon-Sat, lunch Sun; Ⓜ Antón Martín

Plenty of red meat, pastas and salads are the staples of this long-standing local favourite in the Paseo del Prado hinterland. There's an agreeable buzz about this place most nights and the service is excellent. If there's two of you, try the *bandeja de la vaca* (€35), a meat platter that groans under the weight of steak, chorizo, *morcilla* (blood sausage), *mollejas* (sweetbreads), potatoes…

CASA ALBERTO

Map pp84-5 Traditional Spanish €€

☎ 91 429 93 56; www.casaalberto.es, in Spanish; Calle de las Huertas 18; meals €25-30; ☽ noon-1.30am Tue-Sat, noon-4pm Sun; Ⓜ Antón Martín

One of the most atmospheric old *tabernas* of Madrid, Casa Alberto has been around since 1827 and occupies a building where Cervantes is said to have written one of his books. The secret to its staying power is vermouth on tap, excellent tapas at the bar and fine sit-down meals; Casa Alberto's *rabo de toro* is famous among aficionados. As the antique wood-panelled decoration will suggest straight away, the *raciones* have none of the frilly innovations that have come to characterise Spanish tapas. *Jamón,* Manchego cheese and *croquetas* are recurring themes.

LOS GATOS Map pp84-5 Tapas €€

☎ 91 429 30 67; Calle de Jesús 2; meals €25-30; ☽ noon-1am Sun-Thu, noon-2am Fri & Sat; Ⓜ Antón Martín

Tapas you can point to without deciphering the menu and eclectic old-world decor (from bullfighting memorabilia to a fresco of skeletons at the bar) make this a popular choice down the bottom end of Huertas. The most popular orders are the canapés (tapas on toast), which, we have to say, are rather delicious.

MACEIRAS Map pp84-5 Galician €€

☎ 91 429 15 84; Calle de las Huertas 66; meals €20-30; ☽ lunch & dinner daily; Ⓜ Antón Martín

Galician tapas (think octopus, green peppers etc) never tasted so good as in this agreeably rustic bar down the bottom of the Huertas hill, especially when washed down with a crisp white Ribeiro. The simple wooden tables, loyal customers and handy location make this a fine place to rest after (or en route to) the museums along the Paseo del Prado. Galician music plays in the background and the kitchen stays open until 12.45am on Fridays and Saturdays. There's another branch (Map pp84-5; Calle de Jesús 7; ☼ lunch & dinner Tue-Sun, dinner Mon) around the corner.

RESTAURANTE INTEGRAL ARTEMISA
Map pp84-5   Vegetarian €€
☎ 91 429 50 92; Calle de Ventura de la Vega 4; meals €20-30; ☼ lunch & dinner daily; Ⓜ Sevilla
With a couple of options for meat eaters, this mostly vegetarian restaurant does a brisk trade with its salads, moussaka and rice dishes. The decor is simple, the service is no-nonsense and there are more than 50 dishes to choose from. The salads are what marks this place out as worthy of a visit. Alternatively, try the *plato degustación* (€24.95) for a range of tastes.

LA FINCA DE SUSANA
Map pp84-5   Mediterranean €€
☎ 91 369 35 57; www.lafinca-restaurant.com; Calle de Arlabán 4; meals €20-25; ☼ lunch & dinner daily; Ⓜ Sevilla
It's difficult to find a better combination of price, quality cooking and classy atmosphere anywhere in Huertas. The softly lit dining area is bathed in greenery and the sometimes innovative, sometimes traditional food draws a hip young crowd. The duck *confit* with plums and turnips is a fine choice. It doesn't take reservations.

LA TRUCHA
Map pp84-5   Tapas €€
☎ 91 532 08 90; Calle de Núñez de Arce 6; meals €20-25; ☼ lunch & dinner daily; Ⓜ Sol
'The Trout' is an outpost of Andalucía in central Madrid and is one of Madrid's longest-standing and most popular tapas bars. Beneath Andalucian tile work, the counter is loaded with enticing choices, but the fish cookery – especially the trout and *pescaito frito* (fried fish) – is why most people come here and the bar staff will have their own idea about what's good to try. The menu lists a staggering 95 possibilities. If it's too

crowded, try the other branch (Map pp84-5; ☎ 91 429 58 33; Calle de Manuel Fernández y González 3) nearby.

LA CASA DEL ABUELO
Map pp84-5   Tapas €€
☎ 902 027 334; Calle de la Victoria 12; meals €20-25; ☼ 8.30am-midnight Sun-Thu, 8am-1am Fri & Sat; Ⓜ Sol
The 'House of the Grandfather' is an ageless, popular place, which recently passed its centenary. The traditional order here is a *chato* (small glass) of the heavy, sweet El Abuelo red wine (made in Toledo province) and the heavenly *gambas a la plancha* (grilled prawns) or *gambas al ajillo* (prawns sizzling in garlic on little ceramic plates). They cook more than 200kg of prawns here on a good day.

VINOS GONZÁLEZ
Map pp84-5   Deli-Cafe €€
☎ 91 429 56 18; Calle de León 12; meals €20-25; ☼ 9am-midnight Tue-Thu, 9am-1am Fri & Sat; Ⓜ Antón Martín
Ever dreamed of a deli where you could choose a tasty morsel and sit down and eat it right there? Well, here you can. On offer is a tempting array of cheeses, cured meats and other typically Spanish delicacies and there's an all-you-can-eat buffet (€10) from 1pm to 4pm Tuesday to Friday. The tables are informal, cafe style and it also does takeaway, but we recommend lingering.

AL NATURAL
Map pp84-5   Vegetarian €
☎ 91 369 47 09; www.alnatural.biz; Calle de Zorrilla 11; meals €15-25; ☼ lunch & dinner Mon-Sat, lunch Sun; Ⓜ Sevilla or Banco de España
Tucked behind the Spanish parliament, Al Natural has an intimate ambience and terrific organic vegetarian food. There are the usual suspects, such as salads and pastas, but some welcome creative touches, including grilled provolone cheeses, make this a good choice. Their lunch/dinner menus (€11.60/12.60) are terrific value.

LA PIOLA
Map pp84-5   Italian Cafe €
Calle de León 9; meals €15-20; ☼ 10am-1am Mon-Thu, 10.30am-2am Fri, 11am-2.30am Sat; Ⓜ Antón Martín
This charming Italian place is part cafe and part bar. The small range of pasta on offer is well priced and filled with subtle flavours. In addition to the rustic tables and bar stools, there's a sofa that has to be the

best seat in the house. You're likely to find it full most nights of the week, which has as much to do with the atmosphere as the food.

LAS BRAVAS Map pp84-5 Tapas €
☎ 91 522 85 81; Callejón de Álvarez Gato 3; meals €15; ⏰ lunch & dinner daily; Ⓜ Sol or Sevilla

Las Bravas has long been the place for a *caña* (small glass of beer) and the best *patatas bravas* (fried potatoes with a spicy tomato sauce; €3.15) in town. In fact, their version of the *bravas* sauce is so famous that they patented it. Other good orders include *calamares* (calamari) and *oreja a la plancha* (grilled pig's ear). The antics of the bar staff are enough to merit a stop, and the distorting mirrors are a minor Madrid landmark. Elbow your way to the bar and be snappy about your orders.

LA BIOTIKA Map pp84-5 Vegetarian €
☎ 91 429 07 80; www.labiotika.es, in Spanish; Calle del Amor de Dios 3; meals €10-15; ⏰ 10am-11.30pm Mon-Sat, 10am-4pm Sun; Ⓜ Antón Martín

The macrobiotic, cafe-style La Biotika, out the back of a health-food shop, takes its vegetarianism seriously, with an emphasis on simplicity and healthy eating with not too many creative twists: *seitan* (wheat meat), tofu-based dishes and generous salads. If you're a vegetarian, you'll love it. If you're not, you might want to go elsewhere as the variety is limited.

EL BRILLANTE Map pp84-5 Bocadillos €
☎ 91 528 69 66; Calle del Doctor Drumén 7; bocadillos €4.50-6.50; ⏰ 6.30am-12.30am; Ⓜ Atocha

Just by the Centro de Arte Reina Sofía, this breezy, no-frills bar-eatery is a Madrid institution for its *bocadillos* (the *bocadillo de calamares* is an old favourite) and other snacks (*raciones* cost €7.50 to €12). It's also famous for *chocolate con churros* or *porras* (deep-fried doughnut strips) in the wee hours after a hard night on the tiles. There's another branch (Map pp116-17; ☎ 91 448 19 88; Calle de Eloy Gonzalo 14; Ⓜ Quevedo) in Chamberí.

PASEO DEL PRADO & EL RETIRO

In the discreet residential enclave between the Parque del Buen Retiro and the Paseo del Prado you'll find a handful of exclusive restaurants where eating is taken seriously, classic charm is the pervasive atmosphere, and limousines wait outside to ferry the well-heeled back home. On the western shore of the *paseo* is one of Madrid's most exciting new tapas bars.

VIRIDIANA Map p91 Spanish €€€
☎ 91 523 44 78; www.restauranteviridiana.com; Calle de Juan de Mena 14; meals €80-90; ⏰ lunch & dinner Mon-Sat; Ⓜ Banco de España

The chef here, Abraham García, is a much-celebrated Madrid figure and his larger-than-life personality is reflected in

BRUNCH

Madrid's restaurants are clamouring to ride the wave of the brunch trend, which came late to town but has arrived with a vengeance. Brunch Madrid-style almost always consists of a selection of pastries, a choice of cooked main courses, as well as orange juice, coffee etc. In true Spanish style, it usually stretches long into the afternoon. These are some of our favourites:

Café Oliver (Map p110; ☎ 91 521 73 79; http://cafeoliver.com, in Spanish; Calle del Almirante 12; €25; ⏰ brunch 11.30am-4pm Sat & Sun; Ⓜ Chueca)

Nina (p162; €21.90; ⏰ brunch noon-5.30pm Sat & Sun; Ⓜ Bilbao)

Ene Restaurante (p153; €22; ⏰ brunch 12.30-4.30pm Sat & Sun; Ⓜ La Latina)

Bristol Bar (p192; €16-21; ⏰ brunch 11.30am-3pm Sat & holidays; Ⓜ Antón Martín)

La Mantequería (Map pp108-9; ☎ 91 541 75 43; Calle de San Bernardino 7; €18; ⏰ brunch noon-2.30pm Sat & Sun; Ⓜ Plaza de España or Noviciado)

La Camarilla (see the boxed text, p153; brunch €19, drunch €19; ⏰ brunch 11.30am-2pm Sat & Sun, drunch 5.30-8.30pm Sun) In addition to brunch, they also do an afternoon equivalent 'drunch', which is either a weird idea or the start of a whole new trend...

WOULD YOU LIKE SMOKE WITH THAT, SIR?

If you're from a country where smoking is banned in restaurants, you're in for a rude shock in Madrid, although not for much longer.

Since 1 January 2006, all Spanish bars, restaurants, offices and other enclosed public places have, in theory, become subject to strict antismoking legislation. Smoking is now banned in all workplaces, schools, sports and cultural centres, and on public transport. The law also extends to bars and restaurants, although these have an opt-out clause, and therein lies the key. Those establishments over 100 sq metres must have designated smoking areas, while smaller bars must make a choice – ban smoking or make the bar off limits to children. In practice, and despite polls showing that up to 70% of Spaniards support the law, many restaurants and most bars remain dominated by *zonas de fumadores* (smoking sections).

But there are changes afoot. In late 2009, the government announced that it planned to ban smoking, without exception, in all public places (including bars and restaurants) in 2010. The laws had yet to pass parliament at the time of writing and may not come into effect until 2011 or even later.

Viridiana's wide-ranging menu. Many influences are brought to bear on the cooking here, among them international innovations and ingredients and well-considered seasonal variations. This place was doing fusion cooking long before it became fashionable and has developed a fiercely loyal clientele as a result.

CLUB 31 Map p91   Spanish €€€
☎ 91 531 00 92; www.club31.net; Calle de Alcalá 58; meals €70-80; 🕙 lunch & dinner daily Sep-Jul; Ⓜ Retiro or Banco de España

An old Madrid classic, Club 31 has a vaguely contemporary design with long black seats, leaning wall mirrors and bright white designer lamps hanging from the ceiling, but the cuisine here is classic. The accent is on fish and game, with the occasional modern touch. You could set your watch by the old-style, professional service. Last time we were here, royalty were at the next table.

ESTADO PURO Map p91   Tapas €€
☎ 91 330 24 00; www.tapasenestadopuro.com, in Spanish; Plaza de Cánovas del Castillo 4; tapas €1.95-9.50; 🕙 11am-1am Tue-Sat, 11am-4pm Sun; Ⓜ Banco de España or Atocha

Most places to eat along or around the Paseo del Prado are either tourist traps or upmarket temples to fine dining, but this place bucks the trend. A slick but casual tapas bar attached to the NH Paseo del Prado hotel, Estado Puro serves up fantastic tapas, many of which have their origins in Catalonia's world-famous El Bulli restaurant, such as the *tortilla española siglo XXI* (21st-century Spanish omelette, served in a glass). The kitchen here is

overseen by Paco Roncero, the head chef at La Terraza del Casino (p149), who learned his trade with master chef Ferran Adrià. Most of the tapas involve spectacular riffs on traditional Spanish themes. There's a funky indoor area and outdoor tables (often reserved and with higher prices) and the long opening hours are a treat for those whose appetites don't conform to Spanish eating hours.

SALAMANCA

Eating out in Salamanca is, true to barrio form, almost always a suave affair. In the same way that the barrio's fashion boutiques seem intent on pushing the city in stylish new directions, Salamanca's restaurants invite you to rub shoulders with the young and the beautiful and experiment with cuisine dreamed up by celebrity chefs. Gourmet tapas bars are a Salamanca speciality, while Calle de Jorge Juan has some of the coolest places to eat in the city.

SULA MADRID Map p102   Fusion €€€
☎ 91 781 61 97; www.sula.es; Calle de Jorge Juan 33; meals €60-70, menú degustación €60; 🕙 lunch & dinner Mon-Sat; Ⓜ Velázquez

A gastronomic temple that combines stellar cooking with clean-lined sophistication, Sula Madrid – a gourmet food store, super-stylish tapas bar and top-notch restaurant all rolled into one – is one of our favourite top-end restaurants in Madrid. It's the sort of place where Madrid celebrities are on first-name terms with the waiters. The name dropping continues in the kitchen, where wunderkind Quique Dacosta (voted Spain's best chef in 2005) prepares a range

EATING SALAMANCA

of Mediterranean dishes – some traditional, some with the most creative of twists – that you won't find anywhere else. Design touches added by Amaya Arzuaga help to make this one of Madrid's coolest, black-clad spaces. Despite the clientele, there's nothing snooty about the atmosphere, especially at lunchtime when the *menú del día* (€21.15) is a great way to sample what all the fuss is about.

AL-MOUNIA Map p102 Moroccan €€

☎ 91 435 08 28; www.almounia.es, in Spanish; Calle de los Recoletos 5; meals €40-50; ⊙ lunch & dinner Mon-Sat Sep-Jul; Ⓜ Recoletos
One of the longest-standing Moroccan restaurants in town, Al-Mounia has a loyal following. The best couscous in Madrid (it bears little relation to the couscous you buy in a packet) is a menu highlight, as are the subtly spiced lamb *tagines* (stew cooked in a ceramic pot) and the *asado berebere* (Berber roast; €26). The handcrafted traditional decor is breathtaking and greatly complements the cuisine.

O'LIVE Map p102 Fusion €€

☎ 91 431 59 53; www.restauranteolive.com, in Spanish; Calle de Jorge Juan 29; meals €40-45; ⊙ lunch & dinner; Ⓜ Velázquez
Places like this have transformed Calle de Jorge Juan into one of the trendiest eating streets in Madrid. The charcoal-grey and lime-green decor sets the scene for the culinary experimentations (such as pumpkin soup with foie gras and chestnuts) of chef George Urquiz. It's an especially good place for lunch, with a *menú del día* that can cost as little as €6, depending on the season.

LA COCINA DE MARÍA LUISA

Map p102 Castilla y León €€
☎ 91 781 01 80; www.lacocinademarialuisa.es; Calle de Jorge Juan 42; meals €35-45; ⊙ lunch & dinner Mon-Sat Sep-Jul; Ⓜ Velázquez
The home kitchen of former parliamentarian María Luisa Banzo has one of Salamanca's most loyal followings. The cooking is a culinary journey through the central Spanish region of Castilla y León, accompanied by well-chosen regional wines and rustic decor that add much warmth to this welcoming place. Dishes like sirloin of wild boar with raisins and pine nuts (half/full serve €14.20/21.80) set the standard.

MUMBAI MASSALA Map p102 Indian €€

☎ 91 435 71 94; www.wineanddine.es, in Spanish; Calle de los Recoletos 14; meals €35; ⊙ lunch & dinner daily; Ⓜ Retiro
Enter through the heavy red curtain into a brightly coloured Indian world where the food and service are good and the ambience is very laid-back. Servings aren't enormous, but they're superbly done, with dishes spanning the subcontinent from southern India (think hot and spicy) to Pakistan. If you can't decide, it has a range of set menus (€14.75 to €26) to choose from, including the 'Menu Bollywood'. It also does brunch (€26) on weekends.

LA GALETTE Map p102 Vegetarian & European €€

☎ 91 576 06 41; Calle del Conde de Aranda 11; meals €30-35; ⊙ lunch & dinner Mon-Sat, lunch Sun; Ⓜ Retiro
This lovely little restaurant combines an intimate dining area with checked tablecloths and cuisine that the owner describes as 'baroque vegetarian'. The food is a revelation, blending creative flavours with a strong base in traditional home cooking. The *croquetas de manzana* (apple croquettes) are a house speciality, but the truth is that everything on the extensive menu is good. The only problem is that the tables are so close together you get the feeling that diners need to breathe in at the same time for everyone to fit.

LE CAFÉ Map p102 Spanish €€

☎ 91 781 15 86; Calle de los Recoletos 13; meals €30-35; ⊙ lunch & dinner Mon-Sat, lunch Sun; Ⓜ Retiro
It can be almost impossible to get a table here at lunchtime on weekdays, when locals stream in from surrounding offices. The atmosphere is bright and informal and the food is largely traditional Spanish fare (rice dishes are a recurring theme), which is done well, but dishes such as steak tartare of venison with onion, cashews and wasabi mayonnaise show more than a touch of flair.

LA COLONIAL DE GOYA Map p102 Tapas €€

☎ 91 575 63 06; www.restauranterincondegoya.es; Calle de Jorge Juan 34; tapas €2.20-4.20, meals €30-35; ⊙ 1pm-midnight Mon-Fri, 1pm-1am Sat; Ⓜ Velázquez
A mere 63 varieties of canapé should be sufficient for most, but they also serve a

range of carpaccios, croquettes and main dishes at this engaging little tapas bar. The atmosphere is casual, the all-white decor of wood and exposed brick walls is classy, and some of the dishes (such as the grilled cuttlefish with mint mayonnaise) are Spanish nouvelle cuisine at its best.

EL LATERAL Map p102 — Tapas €€
☎ 91 435 06 04; www.cadenalateral.es; Calle de Velázquez 57; per tapa around €3.50, tasting menu €15-19; ⏰ 1pm-midnight; Ⓜ Velázquez or Núñez de Balboa

El Lateral does terrific *pinchos* (tapas), which serve as the perfect accompaniment to the fine wines on offer. At around €3.50 per *pincho*, you could easily pass an evening savouring every bite. This being Salamanca, they draw a pretty upmarket crowd, but you'd be surprised how rapidly the ties loosen up after work. Service is restaurant standard, rather than your average tapas-bar brusqueness. They have another branch (Map pp108-9; ☎ 91 531 68 77; Calle de Fuencarral 43; ⏰ 1pm-midnight; Ⓜ Tribunal) in Malasaña, with a further bar-restaurant (Map pp84-5; ☎ 91 420 15 82; Plaza de Santa Ana 12; ⏰ noon-1am; Ⓜ Sol or Antón Martín) in Huertas.

RESTAURANTE ESTAY Map p102 — Tapas €€
☎ 91 578 04 70; www.estayrestaurante.com; Calle de Hermosilla 46; tapas €1.75-4.70, 6-tapas set menus from €13.25; ⏰ 8am-12.30am Mon-Sat; Ⓜ Velázquez

Restaurante Estay is partly a standard Spanish bar, where besuited waiters serve *café con leche* (it does breakfasts), and one of the best-loved tapas bars in town. The long list of hot and cold tapas concentrates mostly on Spanish staples, with a selection of more adventurous combinations, such as quail with onion and chocolate. Like this last dish, it all seems rather an odd mix, but it somehow works.

BIOTZA Map p102 — Basque Tapas €€
☎ 91 781 03 13; Calle de Claudio Coello 27; tapas €2.60-3.30; ⏰ 9am-midnight Mon-Thu, 9am-1am Fri & Sat; Ⓜ Serrano

This breezy Basque tapas bar is one of the best places in Madrid to sample the creativity of bite-sized *pintxos* as only the Basques can make them. It's the perfect combination of San Sebastián bars laden with food and Madrid-style pale-green and red-black decoration and unusual angular

benches. To sample the flavours on offer, we suggest one of the *degustación de pintxos* (tasting menus; €17 to €21), where you get a selection. The prices quickly add up, but it's highly recommended nonetheless.

MALASAÑA & CHUECA

Cool barrios. Cool places to eat. Chueca and Malasaña may be radically different, one newly modern, the other firmly rooted in the past, but their restaurants are remarkably similar. Blending old *tabernas* with laid-back temples to Spanish nouvelle cuisine, eating here revolves around an agreeable buzz, innovative cooking and casual but stylish surrounds. Some streets stand out, especially Calle de Manuela Malasaña (see the boxed text, below) in Malasaña and Calle de la Libertad (see the boxed text, p166) in Chueca. For cheap but decent international cuisine (eg Asian, Indian, Thai, Persian), head down to Calle de San Bernardino at the lower end of Calle del Conde Duque in Malasaña.

MALASAÑA

LA TASQUITA DE ENFRENTE
Map pp108-9 — Spanish €€€
☎ 91 532 54 49; www.latasquitadeenfrente .com, in Spanish; Calle de la Ballesta 6; meals €70; ⏰ lunch & dinner Tue-Sat; Ⓜ Gran Vía

To succeed on the international stage, Spain's celebrity chefs have to take experimentation to new levels, but to succeed at home they usually have to maintain a greater fidelity to traditional bases before heading off in new directions. And therein lies the success of Chef Juanjo López: it's difficult to overstate how popular this place

---

EAT STREETS – CALLE DE MANUELA MALASAÑA

Calle de Manuela Malasaña (Map pp108-9; Ⓜ Bilbao) has long been one of Madrid's best streets for eating out, its appeal founded on creative approaches to Mediterranean cuisine and designer decor. While the buzz has revolved around three flagship restaurants – Nina (p162), La Musa (p162) and La Isla del Tesoro (p162) – others have been drawn here to transform the street into one of Madrid's most varied eating experiences. Wander along the street and you'll soon discover what we mean.

is among people in the know in Madrid's food scene. His seasonal menu never ceases to surprise (he was preparing cream of pea soup with caviar and hamburgers with foie gras and truffles when we were there) but also combines simple Spanish staples, such as squid with broad beans, to stunning effect. His *menu degustación* (€48) and *menú de Juanjo* (€65) would be our choice if this is your first time. Reservations are essential.

LA ISLA DEL TESORO
Map pp108-9   Vegetarian €€

☎ 91 593 14 40; www.isladeltesoro.net; Calle de Manuela Malasaña 3; meals €30-40; ☽ lunch & dinner daily; Ⓜ Bilbao

Unlike some vegetarian restaurants that seem to work on the philosophy that basic decor signifies healthy food, the dining area here is like someone's fantasy of a secret garden come to life. The cooking is assured and wide ranging in its influences; the jungle burger is typical in a menu that's full of surprises. The weekday lunchtime *menú del día* (€10) is more varied than most in Madrid. Our only complaint? The otherwise friendly waiters are often too keen to free up your table for the next punters on weekends.

NINA Map pp108-9   Mediterranean Fusion €€

☎ 91 591 00 46; Calle de Manuela Malasaña 10; meals €30-40; ☽ lunch & dinner daily; Ⓜ Bilbao

Sophisticated, intimate and wildly popular, Nina has an extensive menu (available in English) of Mediterranean nouvelle cuisine that doesn't miss a trick; boned pig's trotters filled with boletus mushrooms, foie gras and truffles with fried prawns is as weird and wonderful as it sounds. We like the decor, all exposed brick and subtle lighting, and we love just about everything on the menu, but we adore the honey-and-*sobrasada*-glazed grilled ostrich steak with a salmon and raspberry crust. What we're not so keen on is the policy of two sittings (at 9.15pm and 11.30pm), which inevitably means that staff can start to hover when your time's nearly up. The weekend brunch (with two courses, plus juice and coffee €21.90; noon to 5.30pm Saturday and Sunday) is excellent.

CASA PERICO Map pp108-9 Traditional Spanish €€

☎ 91 532 81 76; Calle de la Ballesta 18; meals €25-30; ☽ lunch & dinner Mon-Fri, lunch Sat Sep-Jul; Ⓜ Gran Vía

One look at the glowing reviews from the local press plastered across the facade and you'll quickly learn what this place is about: fine traditional cooking at a reasonable price. Going strong since the 1940s, they do everything from legume-based stews to ribs, but their signature dish is *arroz a lo cutre* (literally 'coarse rice', actually a delicious creamy rice dish). When you push open the door, it is not entirely clear you're in a restaurant – the handful of check-cloth-covered tables are huddled behind a mess of wine bottles, crates and who knows what else. A great, quirky place to eat.

LA MUSA Map pp108-9   Fusion €€

☎ 91 448 75 58; www.lamusa.com.es; Calle de Manuela Malasaña 18; meals €25-30; ☽ 9am-1.30am Sun-Thu, 9am-2.30am Fri & Sat; Ⓜ Bilbao or San Bernardo

Snug yet loud, a favourite of Madrid's hip young crowd yet utterly unpretentious, La Musa is all about designer decor, lounge music on the sound system and food (breakfast, lunch and dinner) that will live long in the memory and is always fun and filled with flavour. The menu is divided into three types of tapas – hot, cold and BBQ; among the hot varieties is the fantastic *jabalí con ali-oli de miel y sobrasada* (wild boar with honey mayonnaise and *sobrasada* – a soft, mildly spicy sausage from Mallorca). It doesn't take reservations, so sidle up to the bar, add your name to the waiting list and soak up the ambient buzz of Malasaña at its best. If you don't fancy waiting, try the sister restaurant nearby, Ojalá Awareness Club (p193).

CON DOS FOGONES
Map pp108-9   Spanish & International €€

☎ 91 559 63 26; www.condosfogones.com, in Spanish; Calle de San Bernardino 9; meals €20-30, day/night set menu €10/18; ☽ lunch & dinner daily; Ⓜ Plaza de España

Con Dos Fogones is cool and classy, with bright colours softly lit by designer lamps. The food is everything from salads and quality hamburgers to great slabs of fine Argentine beef with plenty of unexpected twists, like brie tempura or cod pâté. Their evening set menus are excellent value.

A DOS VELAS Map pp108-9   Spanish €€

☎ 91 446 18 63; www.adosvelas.net, in Spanish; Calle de San Vicente Ferrer 16; meals €20-30, evening set menu €17; ☽ lunch & dinner Mon-Sat; Ⓜ Tribunal

We're fans of this place and Madrid's discerning restaurant public clearly agrees. The food is always creative with Mediterranean cooking fused with occasional Indian or even Argentine flavours, a lovely dining area with soft lighting and exposed brick, and service that's attentive without being intrusive.

COMOMELOCOMO

Map pp108-9   Spanish & International €€

☎ 91 523 13 23; www.comomelocomo.com, in Spanish; Calle de Andrés Borrego 16; meals €20-25; Ⓨ lunch & dinner daily; Ⓜ Noviciado

Run by the same group that brought you Con Dos Fogones (opposite) and A Dos Velas (opposite), Comomelocomo, down Malasaña's lower end, offers excellent-value traditional Spanish dishes given the odd international twist to suit 21st-century palates. Elsewhere, beautifully presented meals and agreeable surrounds too often mean meagre portions, but not here. The friendly service is another winner.

LE PAIN QUOTIDIEN

Map pp108-9   Bakery & Fusion €€

☎ 91 593 09 39; www.lepainquotidien.com; Calle de Fuencarral 95; meals €20-25; Ⓨ 8am-midnight Mon-Thu, 8am-1am Fri, 9am-1am Sat, 9am-midnight Sun; Ⓜ Tribunal

From Paris to New York and now in Madrid, this bakery-cum-restaurant has taken the world by storm. Based around a philosophy of homemade bread and ecologically friendly principles, it's as good for a loaf of bread and creative breakfasts as for light meals that include Middle Eastern dips and Spanish staples. There are other branches in the centre (Map pp108-9; ☎ 91 523 40 04; Gran Vía 46; Ⓨ 8am-midnight Sun-Thu, 9am-midnight Fri & Sat; Ⓜ Callao) and Salamanca (Map p102; ☎ 91 431 13 12; Calle de Velázquez 92; Ⓨ 8am-midnight Sun-Thu, 9am-midnight Fri & Sat; Ⓜ Núñez de Balboa).

TABERNA LA LIRIO

Map pp108-9   Tapas €€

☎ 91 521 39 58; Calle del Espíritu Santo 30; meals €20-25; Ⓨ 5.30pm-1am Mon-Thu, 1.30pm-1am Fri-Sun; Ⓜ Tribunal

This softly lit and thoroughly agreeable tapas bar does the simple things well and it's a winning combination. The no-frills tapas – such as large tostas (toasts) topped with anchovies with Manchego cheese – and dishes like fried green tomatoes are part of its appeal, but this is as much a

place to drink and is just the spot to settle in for the evening.

CONACHE

Map pp108-9   Spanish €

☎ 91 522 95 00; www.restauranteconache.es, in Spanish; Plaza de San Ildefonso; meals €15-25; menú del día €9; Ⓨ 9.30am-1.30am Mon-Thu, 9.30am-2.30am Fri & Sat; Ⓜ Tribunal

With Asian and African decoration, creative Mediterranean cooking and a noisy Spanish clientele, Conache is a hub of barrio life and is as good for breakfast as for dinner. The food is outstanding; the salmorejo (cold tomato soup made with bread, oil, garlic and vinegar) is among the best we've tasted this far from Córdoba.

CRÊPERIE MA BRETAGNE

Map pp108-9   Crêpes €

☎ 91 531 77 74; Calle de San Vicente Ferrer 9; meals €15-20; Ⓨ dinner daily; Ⓜ Tribunal

What a wonderful little place this is – dark, candle lit and all about delicious crêpes. After eating a main meal of crêpes from the rustic wooden tables, there are more crêpes, this time sweet, for dessert. You'll never want to see a crêpe again after overindulging here, but it's a great way to go out.

BODEGA DE LA ARDOSA

Map pp108-9   Tapas €

☎ 91 521 49 79; Calle de Colón 13; meals €15-20; Ⓨ 8.30am-1am; Ⓜ Tribunal

Going strong since 1892, the charming, wood-panelled bar of Bodega de la Ardosa could equally be recommended as a favourite Malasaña drinking hole. Then again, to come here and not try the salmorejo, croquetas, patatas bravas or tortilla de patatas would be a crime. On weekend nights there's scarcely room to move.

HOME BURGER BAR

Map pp108-9   Hamburgers €

☎ 91 522 97 28; www.homeburgerbar.com, in Spanish; Calle del Espíritu Santo 12; meals €15-20; Ⓨ lunch & dinner daily; Ⓜ Tribunal

There are times when you just need a burger. Home Burger Bar is terrific, with an interesting mix of vegetarian, gourmet and classic hamburgers served by friendly waiters in an American-diner-style setting. The meat is 'ecologically sound' and, in the Spanish style, medium-rare (the chef will cook it more if you ask). They have another, larger restaurant (Map pp108-9; ☎ 91 115 12 79; Calle de Silva 25; ✤ lunch & dinner daily; Ⓜ Callao) close to Gran Vía, and another (Map p110; ☎ 91 521 85 31; Calle de San Marcos 26; ✤ lunch & dinner daily; Ⓜ Chueca) in Chueca.

CASA JULIO Map pp108-9
Croquetas €

☎ 91 522 72 74; Calle de la Madera 37; meals €10-15; ✤ lunch & dinner Mon-Sat; Ⓜ Tribunal
A city-wide poll for the best *croquetas* in Madrid would see half of those polled voting for Casa Julio and the remainder not doing so only because they haven't been yet. They're that good that celebrities and mere mortals from all over Madrid come here to sit alongside crusty old locals and sample the traditional *jamón* variety or more creative versions such as spinach with raisins and gorgonzola. Six/12 pieces go for €5/10.

PEGGY SUE'S AMERICAN DINER
Map pp108-9
Hamburgers €

☎ 91 521 85 60; www.peggysues.es, in Spanish; Calle de Amaniel 20; meals €10-15; ✤ lunch & dinner daily; Ⓜ Noviciado
American-style burgers have developed something of a cult following in Madrid in recent years and this place has been at the forefront of the trend. The decor recreates 1950s America and the jukebox belts out Aretha Franklin and Chuck Berry at regular intervals. The burgers (from €5.35) are the genuine article and as good as you'll find in town. Among their three other restaurants in Madrid, there's a branch (Map p110; ☎ 91 308 30 93; Calle de Belén 5; Ⓜ Chueca or Alonso Martínez) in Chueca.

BAR PALENTINO Map pp108-9
Tapas €

☎ 91 532 30 58; Calle del Pez 8; meals €5-10; ✤ 7am-2pm Mon-Sat; Ⓜ Noviciado
Formica tables, not a single attention to decor detail, and yet… This ageless Malasaña bar is a reminder of an important lesson in eating Spanish style: don't be fooled by appearances. Wildly popular with young and old alike, Bar Palentino has an irresistible charm, thanks in large part to its owners María Dolores (who is there in the morning and early afternoon and claims to be 'the house speciality') and Casto (evenings, and one of few septuagenarians to have his own MySpace profile). And the food? Simple traditional tapas and bocadillos (filled rolls) that have acquired city-wide fame, not least for their price (€1.50 to €1.80).

GOOD PLACES FOR A SNACK

In the not-too-distant past, the choice for those visitors unaccustomed to eating a big meal at lunchtime (as is the local custom) was limited to grazing on tapas. Although this still represents snacking at its best, there are increasingly places where you can get a sandwich or light meal. These include the following:

Cacao Sampaka (Map p110; ☎ 91 521 56 55; www.cacaosampaka.com; Calle de Orellana 4; meals €10-15; ✤ 10am-9pm Mon-Fri, 10am-2pm & 3.30-9pm Sat & Sun; Ⓜ Alonso Martínez) A gourmet chocolate shop (see p141) with a cafe attached, where they serve sandwiches, pastries, cakes and the like.

Magasand (Map p110; ☎ 91 319 68 25; www.magasand.com, in Spanish; Travesía de San Mateo 16; meals €10; ✤ 9.30am-10pm Mon-Fri, noon-8pm Sat; Ⓜ Alonso Martínez) Comfy sofas, bar stools, free wi-fi and designer magazines elevate this above your average sandwich bar. They do creative sandwiches and bagels, as well as salads and hot soups.

El Burgado (Map pp108-9; ☎ 91 521 28 77; Calle del Espíritu Santo 40; meals €10-15; ✤ 11am-5pm & 8-11.30pm Mon-Wed, until 1am Thu, until 2am Fri & Sat; Ⓜ Noviciado) Nine varieties of gourmet bocadillos (filled rolls) are the staples in this bright corner snackery, but there are also sandwiches, salads, toasts and other snacks.

Un y 2 (Map p110; ☎ 91 522 71 92; www.unydos.es, in Spanish; Calle de la Libertad 12; meals €5-10; ✤ 9.30am-1.30pm & 3.30-8.30pm; Ⓜ Chueca) Salads, sandwiches and cakes while you enjoy the free wi-fi in a bright, modern space.

Diurno (p191) In addition to great coffee throughout the day, they also serve sandwiches (€3.80), bocadillos (from €4.90), and light pasta dishes (€3.95).

Bar Palentino (above)

Fast Good (p151)

La Vita é Bella (opposite)

LA VITA É BELLA

Map pp108-9   Italian Takeaway €

☎ 91 521 41 08; www.lavitaebella.com.es, in
Spanish; Plaza de San Ildefonso 5; meals €5-10;
☽ noon-midnight Sun-Thu, noon-1am Fri & Sat;
Ⓜ Tribunal

With tasty, authentic Italian dishes that
would put many sit-down restaurants to
shame, the Italian-run La Vita é Bella does a
roaring trade in pizza, pasta, calzone, salad
and tiramisu. Take the plate of your choice
down to Plaza del Dos de Mayo and watch
the barrio life. They've another branch (Map
p110; ☎ 91 523 17 41; Calle de Pelayo 22; ☽ noon-
midnight Sun-Thu, noon-1am Fri & Sat; Ⓜ Chueca) in
Chueca.

CHUECA

JANATOMO Map p110   Japanese €€

☎ 91 521 55 66; Calle de la Reina 27; meals €30-
35; ☽ lunch & dinner Tue-Sun; Ⓜ Gran Vía

Restaurateurs Tomoyuki and Eiko Ikenaga
arrived in Spain in the 1950s and have
watched Spaniards slowly become
accustomed to foreign cuisines. Their
patience has paid off and now their
restaurant, Janatomo, has undergone a
style overhaul, adding a Zen ambience to
its splendid Japanese cooking. The sight of
tour groups from the home country piling
in is all the confirmation we need.

LE CABRERA Map p110   Tapas €€

☎ 91 319 94 57; www.lecabrera.com, in Spanish;
Calle de Bárbara de Braganza 2; meals €30-35;
☽ lunch & dinner Tue-Sat; Ⓜ Colón or Alonso
Martínez

One of the most exciting new tapas bars to
open in Madrid in recent years, this place
is the brainchild of Catalan wonder chef
Sergi Arola and his partner in innovation
Benjamín Benoussan. They describe it as
a 'Cocktail and Gastrobar' and as much
thought has gone into the decoration (with
mirrors that resemble shattered glass) as
the cooking. Perhaps more than other
denizens of Spanish nouvelle cuisine, they
work overwhelmingly from a traditional
base – the emphasis here is on quality
rather than experimentation, although
some well-known Spanish dishes do head
off in all manner of surprising directions.
Sergi's trademark *patatas bravas* (roasted
potatoes in a spicy tomato sauce) has a cult
following, but think of sardines marinated

in passionfruit juice, or liquefied cheese-
cake and you get the idea of what this
place is all about. The downstairs cocktail bar
(p195) is one of the coolest spots in town.

TEPIC Map p110   Mexican €€

☎ 91 522 08 50; www.tepic.es, in Spanish; Calle
de Pelayo 4; meals €30-35; ☽ lunch & dinner daily;
Ⓜ Chueca

Chueca's young professional crowd loves
these sorts of places – chic dining rooms,
gay-friendly service and international
flavours that come with a label, in this
case 'Urban Mexican Food'. Tepic's
signature dish is the Acapulco Tropical, a
cheese taco with meat and pineapple, but
it's all good and leaves you with none of
that heavy after-dinner feel that spoils the
aftermath of so many Mexican meals. Their
menú degustación (€26) is outstanding and
there are lots of Mexican beers to choose
from.

EL ORIGINAL Map p110   Traditional Spanish €€

☎ 91 522 90 69; www.eloriginal.es, in Spanish;
Calle de las Infantas 44; meals €25-30; ☽ lunch &
dinner Mon-Sat Sep–mid-Aug; Ⓜ Chueca or Banco
de España

With the best products, signature dishes
from each of the regions of Spain and a
kitchen overseen by respected Madrid chef
Julio Reoyo, you might expect El Original
to be a bastion of traditionalism. It does
indeed describe its cooking as classic
Spanish. Instead of messing with some
of Spain's favourite dishes, they've gone
for creativity in the decor – trees grow
throughout the dining area and the
decoration is pleasingly contemporary.
Prices are reasonable, another reason why
this relatively new place seems to be
lasting the distance.

LA PAELLA DE LA REINA

Map p110   Paella €€

☎ 91 531 18 85; www.lapaelladelareina.com,
in Spanish; Calle de la Reina 39; meals €25-30;
☽ lunch & dinner daily; Ⓜ Banco de España

Madrid is not renowned for its paella
(Valencia is king in that regard), but
Valencianos who can't make it home are
known to frequent La Paella de la Reina.
Like any decent paella restaurant, you
need two people to make an order but,
that requirement satisfied, you've plenty
of choice. The typical Valencia paella is

EAT STREETS – CALLE DE LA LIBERTAD & AROUND

You can eat well in most corners of Chueca, but Calle de la Libertad (Map p110; **M** Chueca) and its immediate vicinity stand out for variety and value for money. Central to the street's appeal are Bazaar (below), Bocaito (below), Restaurante Momo (opposite) and Diurno (p191), one of Chueca's most popular cafes.

Restaurante Extremadura (☎ 91 531 88 22; www.restauranteextremadura.com, in Spanish; Calle de la Libertad 13; meals €35-40; 🕙 lunch Mon, lunch & dinner Tue-Sun) is a complete change of pace, with hearty, meat-dominated cooking from the Spanish interior; *jamón* is a key fixture (some of the best *jamón* comes from Extremadura). Down the hill to the south, Irureta Martini (☎ 91 521 95 19; Calle de la Libertad 3; meals €20-25; 🕙 lunch Mon, lunch & dinner Tue-Sat, dinner Sun) has dishes that range from northern Spain to Italy, but it's especially popular for its more-creative-than-most lunchtime *menú del día* (€10) from Monday to Friday. Just down the road, El Original (p165) lives up to its name.

cooked with beans, chicken and rabbit, but there are also plenty of seafood varieties on offer, including *arroz negro* (black rice, whose colour derives from squid ink).

BACO Y BETO Map p110 — Tapas €€

☎ 91 522 84 81; www.bacoybeto.com, in Spanish; Calle de Pelayo 24; meals €20-25; 🕙 dinner Mon-Thu, lunch & dinner Fri & Sat; **M** Chueca

Friends of ours in Madrid begged us not to include this place in the guide and we must admit that we were tempted to keep this secret all to ourselves. Some of the tastiest tapas in Madrid are what you find here, either ordered as a *tapa* (eg quail's eggs with *salmorejo*) or *raciones* (eg aubergine with parmesan). Their *croquetas* are wonderful and they're not averse to bringing international influences into their dishes. The clientele is predominantly gay, but they, like our friends, can't have it all to themselves.

BAZAAR Map p110 — Spanish Nouvelle Cuisine €€

☎ 91 523 39 05; www.restaurantbazaar.com; Calle de la Libertad 21; meals €20-25; 🕙 lunch & dinner daily; **M** Chueca

Bazaar's popularity among the well heeled and famous shows no sign of abating. Its pristine white interior design, with theatre-style lighting and wall-length windows, may draw a crowd that looks like it stepped out of the pages of *Hola!* magazine, but the food is extremely well priced and innovative and the atmosphere is casual. For years we've been recommending the *carpaccio de gambas con vinagreta de setas* (prawn carpaccio with mushroom vinaigrette) and see no reason to stop doing so. It doesn't take reservations, so get there early or be prepared to wait, regardless of whether you're famous or not.

BOCAITO Map p110 — Tapas €€

☎ 91 532 12 19; www.bocaito.com, in Spanish; Calle de la Libertad 4-6; meals €20-25; 🕙 lunch & dinner Mon-Fri, dinner Sat; **M** Chueca or Banco de España

Film-maker Pedro Almodóvar once described this traditional bar and restaurant as 'the best antidepressant'. Forget about the sit-down restaurant and jam into the bar shoulder to shoulder with the casual crowd, order a few Andalucian *raciones* off the menu, slosh them down with some gritty red or a *caña* (small glass of beer) and enjoy the theatre in which these busy barmen excel. Specialities include the smoked fish salad and tiger mussels.

KIMBUMBU Map p110 — African €€

☎ 91 521 26 81; Calle de Colmenares 7; meals €20-25; 🕙 lunch & dinner Mon-Sat, lunch Sun; **M** Chueca or Banco de España

Stepping inside this fine African restaurant, with stunning African decor and a tranquil air, is like entering another world. The *menú de degustación* (€21) is a good way to get acquainted with Cameroonian, Ghanaian, Kenyan and Tanzanian tastes. Then again, the *gambas con mango y batata dulce* (prawns with mango and sweet potato) are pretty self-explanatory and very tasty.

LA MORDIDA Map p110 — Mexican €€

☎ 91 308 20 89; www.lamordida.com, in Spanish; Calle de Belén 13; meals €20-25; 🕙 lunch & dinner Sun-Fri, 1.30pm-1am Sat; **M** Chueca

If your idea of Mexican food was born in Taco Bell, La Mordida, owned by singer-songwriter Joaquin Sabina, will show you a whole new world. This is home-style Mexican cooking, the sort of place where most of the names on the menu will need explanation from the waiters. With Mexican cantina-style decor and Coronitas in abundance, this could just be our favourite Mexican restaurant in a city of many.

RIBEIRA DO MIÑO Map p110   Seafood €€
☎ 91 521 98 54; Calle de la Santa Brígida 1; meals €20-25; ☽ lunch & dinner Tue-Sat; Ⓜ Tribunal
This riotously popular seafood bar and restaurant is where madrileños with a love for seafood indulge their fantasy. The *mariscada de la casa* (€32 for two) is a platter of seafood so large that even the hungriest of visitors will be satisfied. Leave your name with the waiter and be prepared to wait up to an hour for a table on weekends.

ARABIA Map p110   Middle Eastern €€
☎ 91 532 53 21; Calle de Piamonte 12; meals €20; ☽ lunch & dinner Tue-Sun; Ⓜ Chueca
Fine Middle Eastern cuisine, reasonable prices and the aesthetics of an Arab diwan with cushions strewn around some of the softly lit, low-lying tables make for a fine change from your all-Spanish diet. We especially enjoyed the *cordero con miel y piñones* (lamb with honey and pine nuts) and the *cuscus de pollo con pasas y cebolla* (couscous with raisins and onion). It's worth ringing ahead as their opening hours were in flux at the time of research.

MAISON BLANCHE Map p110   Gourmet Cafe €€
☎ 91 522 82 17; www.maisonblanche.com; Calle de Piamonte 10; meals €20; ☽ 10am-midnight Mon-Sat, noon-6pm Sun; Ⓜ Chueca
If you have a friend from Barcelona who's too cool for Madrid, bring them here and they might just change their mind. A gourmet food store and designer cafe, this has become one of the most fashionable places in town for A-list celebrities; one newspaper called it 'paradise for sybarites'. The food ranges far and wide, but quiche Lorraine and duck are among the most popular choices. It also serves up live jazz from 2.30pm to 4.30pm on Sunday. This is the new Madrid and it's very cool.

RESTAURANTE MOMO Map p110   Spanish €€
☎ 91 532 73 48; Calle de la Libertad 8; meals €20; ☽ lunch & dinner Mon-Sat; Ⓜ Chueca
Momo is a Chueca beacon of reasonably priced home cooking for a casual crowd. It has an artsy vibe and is ideal for those

who want a hearty meal without too much elaboration; the trout with soy and lemon sauce is recommended. Unusually, the well-priced three-course set menus spill over into the evening and the famous chocolate *moco* (literally 'snot', but really homemade chocolate pudding) is the tastiest of dessert dishes despite the worrying name. It's a mostly gay crowd, but everyone's welcome.

WAGABOO Map p110   Fusion €
☎ 91 531 65 67; www.wagaboo.com; Calle de Gravina 18; meals €15-25; ☽ 1pm-midnight; Ⓜ Chueca
Wagaboo offers cheap and cheerful pasta and noodle dishes in a trendy setting with a clientele to match. They have restaurants across the city and, in addition to the main eating hours, they've recently decided to stay open after lunch (from 4.30pm to 8.45pm) for snacks, salads and cakes – we hope it lasts. There's another Wagaboo (☎ 91 523 02 32; Calle de San Marcos 28; ☽ 1pm-midnight daily; Ⓜ Chueca) not far away.

GASTROMAQUIA Map p110   Tapas €
☎ 91 522 64 13; Calle de Pelayo 8; meals €15; ☽ lunch Mon, lunch & dinner Tue-Thu & Sat, dinner Fri; Ⓜ Chueca
The exciting reimagining of tapas that would have Hemingway turning in his grave swept through Madrid long ago, but few places have recognised the possibilities of bringing world cuisines (eg couscous) into the mix. The philosophy behind Gastromaquia (the brainchild of renowned chef Ivan Sánchez) is to encourage Spaniards to relearn the art of eating tapas, taking them on a journey into what he calls 'universal tapas'. To do so, Gastromaquia maintains a base in Spanish cooking (helped by its location in an old Chueca *taberna*), but the tastes are always fresh and surprising. Opening hours change as often as new ideas emerge from the kitchen.

FRESC CO Map p110   Buffet €
☎ 91 521 60 52; www.frescco.com; Calle de Sagasta 30; meals from €8.95; ☽ noon-5pm & 8-11.30pm; Ⓜ Alonso Martínez
If you just can't face deciphering another Spanish menu or are in dire need of a do-it-yourself salad, Fresc Co is a fresh, well-priced and all-you-can-eat antidote. OK, so the atmosphere is cafeteria-style and none too exciting, but the extensive choice of

LATE BITES & DAWN DINING

There's no tradition in Madrid of heading for a curry or kebab in the wee small hours and for all the Spanish love of eating late, most restaurant kitchens close by midnight, and even earlier on weekdays. Kitchens in the following places stay open, or food is otherwise available later (Friday and Saturday only, unless stated):

Until 12.45am
Con Dos Fogones (p162)
Maceiras (p156)

Until 1am
El Estragón (p155)
La Vita é Bella (p165)
Le Cabrera (p165)
La Mordida (p166)

Until 1.30am
Cervecería 100 Montaditos (p152)

Until 2am
Bar La Ideal (p152) No one quite knows when they close – could be earlier, could be later.
Bar Melo's (p155) Opens until 2am from Tuesday to Saturday.
Crêperie Ma Bretagne (p163) Opens until 1am Sunday to Thursday, and until 2am Friday and Saturday.
Malaspina (p186)

Later
Chocolatería de San Ginés (p179) Open for *chocolate con churros* (Spanish doughnuts with chocolate) until 7am every day.

self-service salads, soups, pasta and pizza more than makes up for it; the price includes a drink and queues often go out the door at lunchtime. There's another branch (Map pp62-3; ☎ 91 524 06 79; Calle del Caballero de Gracia 8; Ⓜ Gran Vía) just off Gran Vía in the centre.

CHAMBERÍ & ARGÜELLES

At first glance Chamberí and Argüelles seem more residential than great places to go out. With so many young and upwardly mobile madrileños clamouring to live here, however, there are some fine choices if you know where to look. Another advantage is that there's rarely another tourist in sight.

SERGI AROLA GASTRO
Map pp116-17   Nouvelle Cuisine €€€
☎ 91 310 21 69; www.sergiarola.es; Calle de Zurbano 31; set menus €95-235; Ⓨ lunch & dinner Mon-Fri, dinner Sat; Ⓜ Alonso Martínez
Sergi Arola, a young Catalan acolyte of the world-renowned chef Ferran Adrià, has opened his very own personalised temple to all that's innovative in Spanish gastronomy. You pay for the privilege of eating here – the showpiece *menú gastro* costs €160 without wine and taxes, although the *basico* menu covers seven signature dishes for €105. But this is culinary indulgence at its finest, the sort of place where creativity, presentation and taste are everything. And oh, what tastes…

JOCKEY Map pp116-17   Spanish €€€
☎ 91 319 24 35; www.restaurantejockey.net; Calle de Amador de los Ríos 6; meals €78-100; Ⓨ lunch & dinner Mon-Sat Sep-Jul; Ⓜ Colón
Fine Spanish cooking, with the occasional nod to international sophistication, and celebrities and royalty dotted around the dining room (Prince Felipe, heir to the Spanish throne, and Letizia Ortiz chose the Jockey chefs for their wedding banquet in May 2004) make for a top-quality dining experience. The menu is more traditionally European than most in this price range, although there are some innovative flourishes. Otherwise, it's along the lines of Persian caviar, snails and soufflés. If we could choose one dish, it would probably be lobster ragout with truffles and fresh

pasta, while the *special menú* (€78) is outstanding. Men must wear a tie and a jacket – it's that sort of place.

LA FAVORITA Map pp116-17 Navarran €€
☎ 91 448 38 10; www.restaurante-lafavorita.com; Calle de Covarrubias 25; meals €40-50; ☽ lunch & dinner Mon-Fri, dinner Sat; Ⓜ Alonso Martínez
Set in a delightful old mansion and famous for its opera arias throughout the night sung by professional opera singers, La Favorita has an ambience all of its own. The outdoor garden courtyard is delightful on a summer's evening, while the music and food (which is dominated by the cuisine of the northeastern Spanish region of Navarra) are top drawer. Although there's no opera at lunchtime, there is a €15 buffet. Our only complaint is that the tables are too close together.

EL PEDRUSCO Map pp116-17 Spanish €€
☎ 91 446 88 33; www.elpedruscodealdealcorvo .com, in Spanish; Calle de Juan de Austria 27; meals €35-40; ☽ lunch Mon-Thu, lunch & dinner Fri & Sat; Ⓜ Iglesia
If you haven't time to visit one of the *asadores* (restaurants specialising in roasted meats) of Segovia (see p240), head to this fine restaurant where the *cochinillo asado* (roast suckling pig; €65 for two or three people) and ¼ *lechazo* (quarter roast lamb; €40 for two) are succulent and as good as any in Madrid. It's the sort of place where a salad is a must and you'll be delighted to see a vegetable.

LAS TORTILLAS DE GABINO
Map pp116-17 Spanish €€
☎ 91 319 75 05; www.lastortillasdegabino.com, in Spanish; Calle de Rafael Calvo 20; meals €35-40; ☽ lunch & dinner Mon-Fri, dinner Sat; Ⓜ Iglesia
It's a brave Spanish chef that fiddles with the iconic *tortilla de patatas*, but the results here are delicious – *tortilla* with cockles, with octopus, and with all manner of surprising combinations. This place also gets rave reviews for its *croquetas*. The service is excellent and the bright yet classy dining area adds to the sense of a most agreeable eating experience. Reservations are highly recommended.

CASA JACINTO
Map pp116-17 Traditional Spanish €€
☎ 91 447 81 30; Calle de Nicasio Gallego 14; meals €30-40; ☽ lunch & dinner Sep-Jul; Ⓜ Alonso Martínez or Bilbao

All too often, bastions of traditional cooking in Madrid are stuffed full of grumpy old men. This place is different. Some of the friendliest service we've encountered in Madrid is the ideal introduction to an extensive menu of rice dishes, roast lamb, roast suckling pig and exquisite steaks. In the case of the *chuletón de buey* (large beef steak), you cook it yourself at your table. There are a range of set menus (from €26) and advance reservations are essential.

NAGOYA Map pp116-17 Japanese €€
☎ 91 448 69 07; www.nagoya.es, in Spanish; Calle de Trafalgar 7; meals €30-35; ☽ lunch & dinner daily; Ⓜ Bilbao
One of the longer-standing Japanese restaurants in Madrid, Nagoya has fast service and excellent food, from the tempura and sushi to the *kami yaki soba* (duck with noodles and teriyaki sauce). Ask for your *California maki* with *sesamo blanco por fuera* (white sesame on the outside) and you'll be in heaven.

RESTAURANTE COLLAGE
Map pp116-17 Swedish €€
☎ 91 448 45 62; www.restaurantecollage.com, in Spanish; Calle de Olid 6; meals €30-35; ☽ lunch Mon, lunch & dinner Tue-Fri, dinner Sat; Ⓜ Quevedo or Bilbao
One of our favourite restaurants in the barrio, Restaurante Collage serves wonderful food; the *rollitos de alce* (elk spring rolls) are a spectacular entrée and the *solomillo de reno* (reindeer sirloin) is tender and utterly delicious. The *menú de noche* (evening set menu; €21.95) is excellent and Swedish in orientation, while the daytime *menú del día* (€8.95) is supercheap by barrio standards, more basic and caters to hungry local workers in search of home cooking rather than exotic Scandinavian tastes. The whole atmosphere is quietly sleek in a Swedish kind of way.

COSTA BLANCA ARROCERÍA
Map pp116-17 Rice & Paella €€
☎ 91 448 58 32; Calle de Bravo Murillo 3; meals €20-30; ☽ lunch & dinner daily; Ⓜ Quevedo
Even if you don't have plans to be in Chamberí, it's worth a trip across town to this casual bar-restaurant that offers outstanding rice dishes, including paella. The quality is high and prices (around €11 per person) are among the cheapest in

town. Start with *almejas a la marinera* (baby clams) and follow it up with *paella de marisco* (seafood paella) for the full experience. As always in such places, you'll need two to make up an order.

IL CASONE Map pp116-17   Italian €€

☎ 91 591 62 66; Calle de Trafalgar 25; meals €20-25; ☽ lunch & dinner daily; Ⓜ Quevedo, Iglesia or Bilbao

With its outdoor tables on the lovely Plaza de Olavide in summer, reasonable prices and fresh and inventive Italian cooking, Il Casone is outstanding. We always order the *tagliatelle scampi*, but there are flashes of creativity, such as *fagottini* with black truffles and cream of foie gras and mushroom. The carpaccios and grilled provolone are great starters.

SAGARETXE Map pp116-17   Basque Tapas €€

☎ 91 446 25 88; www.sagaretxe.com, in Spanish; Calle de Eloy Gonzalo 26; meals €20-25; ☽ noon-5pm & 7pm-1am; Ⓜ Iglesia

One of the best Basque *pintxos* bars in Madrid, Sagaretxe takes the stress out of eating tapas, with around 20 varieties lined up along the bar (and up to 150 that can be prepared in the kitchen upon request). Simply point and any of the wonderful selection will be plated up for you. Better still, order the *surtido de 8/12 pintxos* (your own selection of eight/12 tapas) for €14/20. There's a more expensive but equally good restaurant downstairs.

BODEGA DE LA ARDOSA

Map pp116-17   Tapas €

☎ 91 446 58 94; Calle de Santa Engracia 70; meals €10-15; ☽ 9am-3pm & 6-11.30pm Thu-Tue; Ⓜ Iglesia

Tucked away in a fairly modern corner of Chamberí, this fine old relic has an extravagantly tiled facade complete with shrapnel holes dating back to the Spanish Civil War. For decades locals have been coming here for their morning tipple and for some of the best traditional Spanish *patatas bravas* (fried potatoes with a spicy tomato sauce) in town. It also has vermouth on tap.

NORTHERN MADRID

The business and well-to-do clientele who eat in the restaurants of northern Madrid know their food and they're happy to pay for it. Often it's a fair metro or taxi ride north of the centre, but well worth it for a touch of class.

SANTCELONI Map p121   Catalan €€€

☎ 91 210 88 40; www.restaurantesantceloni.com; Paseo de la Castellana 57; set menus €132-165, meals from €125; ☽ lunch & dinner Mon-Fri, dinner Sat; Ⓜ Gregorio Marañón

The Michelin-starred Santceloni is one of Madrid's best restaurants, with luxury decor that's the work of star interior designer Pascual Ortega, and nouvelle cuisine from the kitchen of master Catalan chef Santi Santamaría. Primary responsibility for the kitchen has passed to one of his acolytes, Óscar Velasco, but the quality hasn't dipped at all and Santamaría still makes regular appearances. Each dish is an exquisite work of art and the menu changes with the seasons, but we'd recommend one of the *menús gastronómicos* to really sample the breadth of surprising tastes on offer.

ZALACAÍN Map p121   Basque & Navarran €€€

☎ 91 561 48 40; www.restaurantezalacain .com; Calle de Álvarez de Baena 4; meals €90-100; ☽ lunch & dinner Mon-Fri, dinner Sat Sep-Jul; Ⓜ Gregorio Marañón

CULINARY TOURS OF MADRID

If you'd like an insider's take on Madrid's (often lesser-known) tapas restaurants, Adventurous Appetites (☎ 639 331 073; www.adventurousappetites.com; 4hr tour incl 1st drink €50, food extra; ☽ 8pm-midnight Mon-Sat) runs English-language tours through central Madrid from the bear statue in Puerta del Sol.

Also highly recommended is the 'Foodies Walking Tour' of central Madrid run by Alambique (Map pp62-3; ☎ 91 547 42 20; www.alambique.com; 3½hr tours from €50; Plaza de la Encarnación 2; Ⓜ Ópera or Santo Domingo), whose tours visit traditional bakeries and the Mercado de San Miguel; these can be extended to include lunch and a cooking class.

Other good choices are the 'Gourmet Tapas Tours' offered by Insider's Madrid (☎ 91 447 38 66; www .insidersmadrid.com) and Letango Tours (Map pp76-7; ☎ 91 369 47 52; www.letango.com; 1st fl, Plaza de Tirso de Molina 12; 3hr tour incl light tapas Mon-Fri from €95, Sat & Sun €135).

top picks

FINE DINING

- Santceloni (opposite)
- Sergi Arola Gastro (p168)
- Jockey (p168)
- Zalacaín (opposite)
- La Terraza del Casino (p149)
- Sula Madrid (p159)

Where most other fine-dining experiences centre on innovation, Zalacaín is a bastion of tradition, with a refined air and a loyal following among Spain's great and good. Everyone who's anyone in Madrid, from the king down, has eaten here since the doors opened in 1973; it was the first restaurant in Spain to receive three Michelin stars. The pig's trotters filled with mushrooms and lamb is a house speciality, as is the lobster salad. The wine list is purported to be one of the best in the city (it stocks an estimated 35,000 bottles with 800 different varieties). You should certainly dress to impress (men will need a tie and a jacket).

PUERTA 57 Map p121   Spanish €€€
☎ 91 457 33 61; www.grupolamaquina.es, in Spanish; Gate 57, Estadio Santiago Bernabéu, Calle de Padre Damián; meals €60-70; ☽ lunch & dinner Mon-Sat, lunch Sun; Ⓜ Santiago Bernabéu
There are many reasons to recommend this place, but the greatest novelty lies in its location – inside the home stadium of Real Madrid; its Salón Madrid (one of a number of dining rooms) looks out over the playing field. Needless to say, you'll need to book a long time in advance for a meal during a game. The cuisine is traditional Spanish with an emphasis on seafood and it gets rave reviews from its predominantly business clientele.

ECOCENTRO Map p121   Vegetarian €€
☎ 91 553 55 02; www.ecocentro.es, in Spanish; Calle de Esquilache 2-6; meals €25-30; ☽ lunch & dinner daily; Ⓜ Canal or Ríos Rosas
Ecocentro is a vegetarian's paradise. Depending on which door you enter, there's an extensive organic food shop, a cheap cafeteria-style eatery or a basement restaurant that serves wonderful vegie food. The *menú del día* (€10.50) changes daily and has plenty of choices.

BEYOND THE CENTRE
EL RINCÓN DE JEREZ
Map pp124-5   Andalucian €€
☎ 91 355 47 45; Calle de Rufino Blanco 5; meals €20-25; ☽ lunch & dinner Tue-Sat, lunch Sun Sep-Jul; Ⓜ Manuel Bacerra
Fried fish and seafood Andalucian-style, bull's tail and fine *jamón* from the south can be found in bars and restaurants all over Madrid, and certainly ones that are more central than El Rincón de Jerez. But this place is utterly unlike anywhere else in the capital for one reason: at 11pm from Tuesday to Saturday, they turn off the lights, light the candles and sing as one *La Salve Rociera,* a near-mythical song with deep roots in the flamenco and Catholic traditions of the south.

CASA MINGO Map pp124-5   Asturian €
☎ 91 547 79 18; www.casamingo.es, in Spanish; Paseo de la Florida 34; meals €15-20; ☽ lunch & dinner daily; Ⓜ Príncipe Pío
Built in 1916 to feed workers building the Príncipe Pío train station, Casa Mingo is a well-known and vaguely cavernous Asturian cider house. It's kept simple here, focusing primarily on the signature dish of *pollo asado* (roast chicken) accompanied by a bottle of cider. Combine with a visit to the neighbouring Ermita de San Antonio de la Florida (p122).

DRINKING & NIGHTLIFE

top picks

Nights in the Spanish capital are the stuff of legend and what Hemingway wrote of the city in the 1930s remains true to this day: 'Nobody goes to bed in Madrid until they have killed the night.'

Madrid has more bars than any other city in the world, six, in fact, for every 100 inhabitants, and, wherever you are in town, there'll be a bar close by. But bars are only half the story. On any night in Madrid, excellent flamenco venues, funky jazz clubs and an otherwise outstanding live music scene keep you going beyond midnight, then segue easily into cocktail bars and the nightclubs that have brought such renown to Madrid as the unrivalled scene of all-night fiestas.

Although you could spend your night criss-crossing the city in search of the perfect vibe, most madrileños take a fairly localised approach to a night out – once they've begun to drink and otherwise settle into the night, they tend to move from one place to the next within the same barrio. We've followed suit and to help you plan your journey through the Madrid night, we've divided each barrio throughout this chapter into five sections: Cafes, First Drinks, Live Music, Until 3am and After 3am. And in each barrio we've included a boxed text 'A Night Out in…' taking you through our favourite night-time journey through the neighbourhood.

These are intended to serve as a guide only – you could, for example, easily pass an entire night in a live music venue where pre-performance cocktails are served and DJs take up when the live performers head home, or combine first and last drinks in the same place.

Every barrio in the city (with the exception of Paseo del Prado and El Retiro) makes its contribution to the pulsating after-dark *marcha* (action), but some barrios definitely offer more than others. Los Austrias, Sol and Centro have a small selection of venues across a range of genres, while Huertas attracts a local and international crowd most nights of the week. Chueca is exuberantly and extravagantly gay (see also p216), although everyone's welcome. Neighbouring Malasaña, the spiritual home of *la movida madrileña* (see p32), has never really grown up and is the barrio of choice for grunge rockers, sideburns and an eclectic crowd; it's the antithesis of Salamanca, where it's all about hair gel and designer clothing. La Latina and, to a lesser extent, Lavapiés are gritty, groovy and cool all at once, and definitely among night-time Madrid's best-kept secrets, while Chamberí and Argüelles don't have many venues, but they're worth checking out. And northern Madrid has a handful of outstanding bars and live venues.

A final piece of advice: If you plan to stay out the whole night, sleeping the siesta the afternoon before will be the key to your staying power.

CAFES

Madrid's thriving cafe culture dates back to the early and mid-20th century, when old-style coffee houses formed the centrepiece of the country's intellectual life. Although many such cafes were torn down in the rush to modernisation, many that recall those times remain, with period architecture and an agreeable formal atmosphere; their clientele long ago broadened to encompass the entire cross-section of modern Madrid society. Added into the mix are some terrific and usually more casual modern cafes, although here, too, the principle remains the same: they're at once social and cultural meeting places, and places to escape from the often frenetic pace of city life.

Most of the cafes covered in this chapter are primarily places to take a coffee at any hour of the day or early evening, and we recommend them as such. But this being Spain, the majority stays open well beyond midnight and they

top picks

GRAND OLD CAFES

- Café Comercial (p190)
- Café-Restaurante El Espejo (p190)
- Gran Café de Gijón (p191)
- Café del Círculo de Bellas Artes (p184)
- Café Manuela (p190)
- Café de Ruiz (p190)
- Café Ajenjo (p190)
- Café de Oriente (p177)
- Nuevo Café de Barbieri (p181)

top picks

LIVE MUSIC VENUES

- Sala El Sol (p179)
- Moby Dick (p198)
- Café La Palma (p194)
- Clamores (p198)
- Galileo Galilei (p198)
- Costello Café & Niteclub (p179)
- Honky Tonk (p198)
- BarCo (p193)
- La Escalera de Jacob (p183)
- ContraClub (p184)

all serve alcohol if you're in need of something a little stronger.

FIRST DRINKS

If you're unaccustomed to Madrid's late eating hours, the upside is that it allows plenty of time for a pre-dinner drink, an activity that locals have turned into an institution. Of course, they often combine the two – eating and drinking – by starting early with a drink and some tapas, so, in addition to the bars we cover in this chapter, it's always worth considering those places that are better known for their food (see p145) when planning your first step into the night.

Madrid's bars are as diverse as the city itself and range from simple local watering holes that serve as centres of community life to sophisticated temples to good taste. The former usually open throughout the day, while the latter rarely do so before 8pm.

Most of the places which we have categorised under the heading of First Drinks stay open fairly late. We've designated them as First Drinks, however, because we see them first and foremost as fine places to start your night. But don't be surprised if you find yourself wanting to stay longer, even right through until closing time. That's the thing about Madrid's nightlife: there are no rules.

LIVE MUSIC

Madrid made its name as a live music city back in the 1980s, when drugs and rock music fuelled the decade-long fiesta known as *la movida madrileña* (see p32), although it was all pretty one-dimensional. And so it stayed until the late 1990s, when big international names began once again including the Spanish capital on their European tours and, perhaps more importantly, live music venues catering to all tastes began populating just about every barrio of the city. While rock remains a Madrid mainstay and the doors of a handful of classic venues remain open, the live music scene is in rude health, covering every genre – flamenco and jazz are the star attractions – just about every night of the week. Many concert venues double as clubs where DJs follow the live acts, making it possible to start off the night with a great concert and stay on to party until late.

In addition to checking the websites of individual clubs, a good website to find out what's happening is La Noche En Vivo (www.lanocheenvivo.com, in Spanish); click on 'Agenda de Conciertos' for upcoming concerts and on 'Salas Asociadas' for a list of venues.

Flamenco

Madrid may not be the spiritual home of flamenco, and its big names may feel more at home in the atmospheric flamenco taverns of Andalucía, but Madrid remains one of Spain's premier flamenco stages.

Seeing flamenco in Madrid is, with some worthy exceptions, expensive – at the *tablaos* (restaurants where flamenco is performed) expect to pay €25 to €35 just to see the show. The admission price usually includes your first drink, but you pay extra for meals (up to €50 per person) that, put simply, are rarely worth the money. For that reason, we suggest you eat elsewhere and simply pay for the show (after having bought tickets in advance), on the understanding that you won't have a front-row seat. The other important thing to remember is that most of these shows are geared towards tourists. That's not to say that

top picks

FLAMENCO VENUES

- Corral de la Morería (p182)
- Cardamomo (p186)
- Las Tablas (p179)
- Las Carboneras (p179)
- Casa Patas (p182)
- Café de Chinitas (p179)
- La Soléa (p182)

top picks

JAZZ VENUES

- Café Central (p186)
- El Berlín Jazz Café (p179)
- Populart (p187)
- El Junco Jazz Club (p196)
- El Despertar (p183)
- Segundo Jazz (p198)

the quality isn't top notch. On the contrary, it's often magnificent, spine-tingling stuff. It's just that it sometimes lacks the genuine, raw emotion of real flamenco.

There are alternatives, some of which are listed here, although the dark, smoky bars of flamenco's origins are now pretty thin on the ground. One bar that's always brimful of flamenco atmosphere is El Callejón (p187), while for those of you keen to dance your own version of the *sevillana* (flamenco dance style), Almonte (p189) is a good choice. And to capture the spirit of flamenco and all its associations with the south, El Rincón de Jerez (p171) is one of the briefest but most unforgettable experiences of the Madrid night.

If you don't fancy paying the steep prices of the *tablaos*, other live music venues also have live flamenco, usually one night a week. Such places include BarCo (p193), Clamores (p198), ContraClub (p184), El Juglar (p183) and Galileo Galilei (p198).

Festivals are another place to find flamenco; February's Festival Flamenco Caja Madrid (p17) and Suma Flamenca (p19) in May-June are the city's biggest flamenco events and attract the biggest names in the genre.

For more information about flamenco as an art form, turn to p45.

Jazz Clubs

Madrid was one of Europe's jazz capitals in the 1920s. It's taken a while, but it's once again among Europe's elite for live jazz. There's only a small number of places devoted exclusively to jazz, but it's all about quality rather than quantity. Put them all together and it's hard to imagine a city with a better range of venues to choose from. The range of styles on offer begins with the kind of classic jazz designed to keep the purist happy as well as Latin, nu jazz and countless other variations on the theme.

Beyond the signature jazz venues, numerous multigenre live music stages broaden out the experience, with at least one night a week at the following places dedicated to jazz (often including a jazz jam session): BarCo (p193); Clamores (p198); Marula Café (p183); ContraClub (p184); La Escalera de Jacob (p183); Casa Pueblo (p187); La Boca del Lobo (p187); Galileo Galilei (p198); and Zanzibar (p194).

For a jazz atmosphere without the live acts, try Jazz Bar (p185), where the name says it all.

Madrid also has two major jazz festivals: Jazz es Primavera (p18) in March-April, and Festival Jazz Madrid (p20) in November. The former is run by the Club de Música y Jazz San Juan Evangelista (www.sanjuanevangelista.org), a nationwide jazz club whose website sometimes has Madrid-centric jazz news and lists upcoming events.

UNTIL 3AM

If Madrid has an official closing time for the vast majority of bars and smaller nightclubs (the dividing line between the two is often decidedly blurry), then it's 3am. Some places may close half an hour earlier or later (especially on Friday and Saturday nights), but 3am operates as a threshold – it's either time to head home or give up on tomorrow and stagger onwards into the night to dance until dawn.

The hours between midnight and 3am are filled with choices, although our favourite way to pass these hours and truly embrace all that's good about Madrid's nightlife is to take up residence in one of the oh-so-cool cocktail bars.

AFTER 3AM

There's no turning back now and, unless you have to work tomorrow (although that doesn't stop some in Madrid), why would

top picks

COCKTAIL BARS

- Museo Chicote (p196)
- Del Diego (p195)
- Le Cabrera (p195)
- Bar Cock (p195)
- Mercado de la Reina Gin Club (p193)
- Areia (p195)
- Stromboli (p196)
- The Penthouse (p185)
- Real Café Bernabéu (p198)

top picks

you? People here live fully for the moment. Today's encounter can be tomorrow's distant memory, perhaps in part because Madrid's nightclubs (also known as *discotecas*) rival any in the world. The best places are usually the megaclubs, with designer decor, designer people and, sometimes, with enough space for numerous dance floors each with their own musical style to suit your mood. Themed nights are all the rage, so it's always worth checking in advance to see what flavour of the night takes your fancy.

Although you'll find a nightclub going strong until sunrise in almost every barrio, the biggest selection of clubs is to be found downtown: in Los Austrias, Sol and Centro, Huertas, and Malasaña and Chueca.

Most nightclubs don't open their doors until around midnight and don't really get going until after 1am; some won't even bat an eyelid until 3am, when the bars elsewhere have closed. Admission prices vary widely, depending on the time of night you enter, the way you're dressed and the number of people inside. The standard entry fee is €10, which usually includes the first drink, although megaclubs and swankier places charge a few euros more (listed above). Even those that let you in for free will play catch up with hefty prices for drinks, so don't plan your night around looking for the cheapest ticket.

If you're looking to find out more, a couple of websites can help you to fine tune your search. European Vibe (www.europeanvibe.com) is all about connecting you with themed expat (and predominantly student) nights, while Discotecas Gratis (www.discotecasgratis.com, in Spanish) offers on-line registration to get you into some of the bigger clubs for free.

For advice on how to get back to your hotel when the metro's not working, see the boxed text, p188.

LOS AUSTRIAS, SOL & CENTRO

A small handful of lovely cafes and bars in downtown Madrid don't provide much choice when it comes to starting your night; if these don't appeal, there are many more options close at hand in neighbouring La Latina (see p180) and Huertas (see p184). But even if you've left the barrio to begin with, make sure you return later because the live music (particularly flamenco) venues here are outstanding and there are excellent nightclubs in abundance. For cocktail bars, our choice beyond the barrio would be those along Calle de la Reina in Chueca (see p194), a very small block north of Gran Vía. Ending the night as a local is easy here, thanks to the presence of the most famous purveyor of *chocolate con churros* in perhaps all of Spain.

CAFES

CAFÉ DE ORIENTE Map pp62-3   Cafe
☎ 91 541 39 74; Plaza de Oriente 2; ⊙ 8.30am-1.30am Mon-Thu, 9am-2.30am Fri & Sat, 9am-1.30am Sun; Ⓜ Ópera
The outdoor tables of this distinguished old cafe are among the most sought-after in central Madrid, providing as they do a front-row seat for the beautiful Plaza de Oriente, with the Palacio Real as a backdrop. The building itself was once part of a long-gone, 17th-century convent and the interior feels a little like a set out of

---

A NIGHT OUT IN LOS AUSTRIAS, SOL & CENTRO

After a fortifying coffee in Café de Oriente (above), we'd start the serious business of drinking at El 44 Bar (p178) or Café del Real (p178). For live music we simply love Costello Café & Niteclub (p179) or the classic jazz at El Berlín Jazz Café (p179), before moving on to Sala El Sol (p179) for a slice of Madrid history. Then it's dancing until dawn at Charada (p180) or Cool (p180) if it's the weekend or thereabouts; if not, it has to be Oba Oba (p180). On the way home stop for *chocolate con churros* at Chocolatería de San Ginés (p179).

Mitteleuropa. It's the perfect spot for a coffee (surprisingly, only €2.50) when the weather's fine.

EL CAFÉ DE LA ÓPERA Map pp62-3   Cafe
☎ 91 542 63 82; www.elcafedelaopera.com, in Spanish; Calle de Arrieta 6; ☽ 8am-midnight; Ⓜ Ópera

Opposite the Teatro Real, this classic before-performance cafe has one unusual requirement for would-be waiters – they have to be able to sing opera. They break into song from around 9.30pm, when you'll fork out €55 for a meal – not bad value if you don't have tickets for the show across the road.

CHOCOLATERÍA VALOR
Map pp62-3   Chocolate Cafe
☎ 91 522 92 88; Postigo de San Martín 7; ☽ 8am-10.30pm Mon-Thu, 8am-1am Fri, 9am-1am Sat, 9am-10.30pm Sun; Ⓜ Callao

It may be Madrid tradition to indulge in *chocolate con churros* around sunrise on your way home from a nightclub, but for everyone else who prefers a more reasonable hour, this is possibly the best *chocolatería* in town. They serve traditional *churros,* but they're only the side event to the astonishing array of chocolates in which to dip them. Our favourite has to be *cuatro sentidos de chocolate* (four senses of chocolate; €7.95), but we'd happily try everything on the menu to make sure.

FIRST DRINKS

EL 44 BAR Map pp62-3   Bar
Cuesta de Santo Domingo 8; ☽ 8pm-2.30am Tue-Sat; Ⓜ Santo Domingo or Ópera

An intimate bar experience tucked away on a quiet street that leads down towards the opera house, El 44 Bar ranks among our favourite little bars in the centre. The cocktails are well priced (€5 to €7) and original (including *caipipretas,* a Lisbon staple that riffs on the caipirinha with black rum). The music includes '70s, '80s and detours into lounge (Gotan Project seems a particular favourite), Brazilian jazz and deep house, picking up speed as the night wears on.

ANTICAFÉ Map pp62-3   Cafe
☎ 91 559 41 63; Calle de la Unión 2; ☽ 5pm-2.30am; Ⓜ Ópera

Bohemian kitsch is the prevailing theme here and it runs right through the decor, regular cultural events (poetry readings and concerts) and, of course, the clientele. As such, it won't be to everyone's taste, but we rather think that it adds some much-needed variety to the downtown drinking scene. Coffees are as popular as the alcohol, although that rather strange predilection wears off as the night progresses.

CAFÉ DEL REAL Map pp62-3   Cafe
☎ 91 547 21 24; Plaza de Isabel II 2; ☽ 9am-1am Mon-Thu, 9am-3am Fri & Sat, 10am-midnight Sun; Ⓜ Ópera

A cafe and cocktail bar in equal parts, this intimate little place serves up creative coffees and a few cocktails to the soundtrack of chill-out music. The best seats are upstairs, where the low ceilings, wooden beams and leather chairs are a great place to pass an afternoon with friends.

HOT DRINKS – A PRIMER

Café con hielo A glass of ice and a hot cup of black coffee, to be poured over the ice; it's as close as Spaniards come to iced coffee.

Café con leche About half coffee and half hot (*templada,* literally 'tepid') milk. Ask for *grande* or *doble* if you want a large cup, *en vaso* if you want a smaller shot in a glass, or *sombra* if you want lots of milk.

Café cortado A short black with a little milk (called *macchiato* in Italy).

Café solo (un solo) A short black.

Chocolate caliente Hot chocolate – it's dark and sweet and so thick you could stand your spoon up in it. If you want something less thick, ask for a Cola Cao or Nesquik.

Infusions Herbal teas.

Té Tea; locals tend to drink tea black, so if you want milk *(leche),* ask for it to come separately *(a parte).*

LIVE MUSIC

CAFÉ DE CHINITAS Map pp62-3   Flamenco
☎ 91 547 15 02; www.chinitas.com; Calle de Torija 7; admission incl drink €25; ☺ 8pm-midnight Mon-Sat, shows 8.30pm & 10.30pm Mon-Sat; ☎ Santo Domingo

One of the most distinguished *tablaos* in Madrid, drawing in everyone from the Spanish royal family to Bill Clinton, Café de Chinitas has an elegant setting and top-notch flamenco performers. You can order a meal off the menu (around €25 per person) or simply have a drink, making this a good deal. It may attract loads of tourists, but flamenco aficionados also give it top marks. Reservations are highly recommended.

LAS CARBONERAS Map pp62-3   Flamenco
☎ 91 542 86 77; www.tablaolascarboneras.com, in Spanish; Plaza del Conde de Miranda 1; admission €30-35; ☺ shows 10.30pm Mon-Thu, 8.30pm & 11pm Fri & Sat; Ⓜ Ópera, Sol or La Latina

Like most of the *tablaos* around town, this place sees far more tourists than locals, but the quality is nonetheless unimpeachable. It's not the place for gritty, soul-moving spontaneity, but it's still an excellent introduction and one of the few places that flamenco aficionados seem to have no complaints about.

LAS TABLAS Map pp62-3   Flamenco
☎ 91 542 05 20; www.lastablasmadrid.com; Plaza de España 9; admission €24; ☺ shows 10.30pm Sun-Thu, 8pm & 10pm Fri & Sat; Ⓜ Plaza de España

One of the relatively recent newcomers to Madrid's flamenco scene, Las Tablas has quickly earned a reputation for quality flamenco and it could just be the best choice in town. Most nights you'll see a classic flamenco show, with plenty of throaty singing and soul-baring dancing. Antonia Moya and Marisol Navarro, leading lights in the flamenco world, are regular performers here.

EL BERLÍN JAZZ CAFÉ Map pp62-3   Jazz
☎ 91 521 57 52; www.cafeberlin.es, in Spanish; Calle de Jacometrezo 4; admission €6-10; ☺ 7pm-2.30am Tue-Sun Sep-Jul; Ⓜ Callao or Santo Domingo

El Berlín has been something of a Madrid jazz stalwart since the 1950s and it's the kind of place that serious jazz fans rave about as the most authentic in town – it's all about classic jazz here with none of the fusion performances tha[t]... elsewhere. The art-deco interio[r]... charm and the headline acts are... who of world jazz; in the past Al Fo... (Miles Davis' drummer), Santiago de... and the Calento Jazz Orchestra have al... taken to the stage. The headline acts take to the stage at 11.30pm on Fridays and Saturdays, with other performances sprinkled throughout the week.

COSTELLO CAFÉ & NITECLUB
Map pp62-3   Live Music

www.costelloclub.com; Calle del Caballero de Gracia 10; admission €5-10; ☺ 6pm-1am Sun-Wed, 6pm-2.30am Thu-Sat; Ⓜ Gran Vía

Very cool. Costello Café & Niteclub is smooth-as-silk ambience wedded with an innovative mix of pop, rock and fusion in Warholesque surrounds. There's live music at 9.30pm every night of the week except Sundays, with resident and visiting DJs keeping you on your feet until closing time from Thursday to Saturday. Even when there's nothing happening, it's a funky place that draws a sophisticated crowd that usually includes the odd local celebrity. Our only complaint is that they close earlier than we'd like.

SALA EL SOL Map pp62-3   Live Music
☎ 91 532 64 90; www.elsolmad.com, in Spanish; Calle de los Jardines 3; admission €8-25; ☺ 11pm-5.30am Tue-Sat Jul-Sep; Ⓜ Gran Vía

Madrid institutions don't come any more beloved than Sala El Sol. It opened in 1979, just in time for *la movida,* and quickly established itself as a leading stage for all the icons of the era, such as Nacha Pop and Alaska y los Pegamoides. *La movida* may have faded into history, but it lives on at El Sol, where the music rocks and rolls and usually resurrects the '70s and '80s, while soul and funk also get a run. It's a terrific venue and although most concerts start at 11pm and despite the official opening hours, some acts take to the stage as early as 10pm. Check the website (which also allows you to book online) for upcoming acts.

AFTER 3AM

CHOCOLATERÍA DE SAN GINÉS
Map pp62-3   Chocolate Con Churros Cafe
☎ 91 365 65 46; Pasadizo de San Ginés 5; ☺ 9.30am-7am Mon-Fri, 9am-7am Sat & Sun; Ⓜ Sol

...r the grand icons of the Madrid night, this *chocolate con churros* (Spanish donuts with chocolate) cafe sees a sprinkling of tourists throughout the day, but locals usually pack it out in their search for sustenance on their way home from a nightclub sometime close to dawn. They close for only two hours a day, and only then to give it a quick scrub. Only in Madrid…

CHARADA Map pp62-3 Nightclub

www.charadaclubdebaile.com, in Spanish; Calle de la Bola 13; admission €10-15; ⏰ midnight-6am Thu-Sat; Ⓜ Santo Domingo

Charada took the Madrid nightlife scene by storm in 2009 and hasn't looked back. Its decor is New York chic (with no hint of its former existence as a brothel), the cocktails are highly original, the clientele is well heeled and often famous, and it's the home turntable for some of the best house DJs in town. Thursday's 'Future Disco Jams' (disco-funk) is our pick of the nights.

COOL Map pp62-3 Nightclub

☎ 91 733 35 05; www.fsmgroup.es; Calle de Isabel la Católica 6; admission from €10; ⏰ midnight-6am Thu-Sat; Ⓜ Santo Domingo

Cool by name, cool by nature. One of the hottest clubs in the city, the Phillipe Starck–designed curvy white lines, discreet lounge chairs in dark corners and pulsating dance floor are accompanied by gorgeous people, gorgeous clothes and a strict entry policy. Thursday is given over to 'Sunflower Dance Sessions' (house music and a fashionista crowd), Friday is 'Stardust' (electronica and techno), while Saturdays are called 'Royal', with new house music and a predominantly gay clientele. Whatever the night, the sexy, well-heeled crowd includes a lot of sleek-looking gay men and model-like women. Things don't really get going until 3am.

OBA OBA Map pp62-3 Nightclub

Calle de Jacometrezo 4; ⏰ 7pm-5.30am Sun-Thu, 7pm-6am Fri & Sat; Ⓜ Callao

This nightclub is Brazilian down to its G-strings, with live music some nights and dancing till dawn every night of the week. You'll find plenty of Brazilians in residence, which is the best recommendation we can give for the music and the authenticity of its caipirinhas.

PALACIO GAVIRIA Map pp62-3 Nightclub

☎ 91 531 26 01; www.palaciogaviria.com; Calle del Arenal 9; admission €10-15; ⏰ midnight-6am; Ⓜ Sol

An elegant palace converted into one of the most popular dance clubs in Madrid, this is the kind of place where you're guaranteed to meet the locals, and probably even a few compatriots as it's beloved of a newly arrived international crowd. The scene can be pretty young and boisterous, the queues are long, and Thursday is international student and house-music night – international relations have never been such fun. It was closed for restoration at the time of writing, but should have reopened by the time you arrive.

TEATRO JOY ESLAVA Map pp62-3 Nightclub

Joy Madrid; ☎ 91 366 37 33; www.joy-eslava.com; Calle del Arenal 11; admission €12-15; ⏰ 11.30pm-6am; Ⓜ Sol

The only things guaranteed at this grand old Madrid dance club (housed in a 19th-century theatre) are a crowd and the fact that it'll be open (it claims to have operated every single day for the past 29 years). The music and the crowd are a mixed bag, but queues are long and invariably include locals and tourists, and even the occasional *famoso*. Every night's a little different. 'Cinema Elite Club' on Sundays is all about Ibiza-style house, Thursday is student night, Friday's 'Fabulush' is all about glamour and there's even the no-alcohol, no-smoking 'Joy Light' on Saturday evenings (5.30pm to 10pm) for those aged between 14 and 17. Throw in occasional live acts and cabaret-style performances on stage and it's a point of reference for Madrid's professional party crowd.

LA LATINA & LAVAPIÉS

For those whose idea of a night out reaches its limit at the sensible hour of 3am, La Latina and Lavapiés are ideal. Both have memorable cafes, bars and live venues that you could spend more than a single night exploring.

Most nights (and Sunday afternoons), crowds of happy madrileños hop from bar to bar across La Latina. This is a barrio beloved by a discerning crowd of 20- and 30-something urban sophisticates, who ensure that there's little room to move in the good places and that the bad ones don't survive long; the

A NIGHT OUT IN LA LATINA & LAVAPIÉS

In La Latina, start the night with an early evening coffee at Café del Nuncio (below) and choose from the countless tapas bars (see p152) around the barrio, before moving on for a *mojito* at Delic (p182) or a wine at Taberna Tempranillo (p182). For live music, the flamenco at Corral de la Morería (p182) is a once-in-a-lifetime experience; for different reasons, the same could be said of La Soléa (p182) when it's on song. And if you haven't already come to ContraClub (p184) or Marula Café (p183) earlier in the night for some live music, and even if you have, these are the two places to spend the rest of the night dancing.

Down the (steep) hill in Lavapiés, snaffle a table at Gaudeamus Café (below) and hold onto it until you're ready to move on to La Inquilina (p182). We'd stop just across the road for some sustenance at Bar Melo's (p155), a wee-small-hours Lavapiés institution, en route to a *mojito* at El Eucalipto (p184) before making for El Juglar (p183). If you're able to keep going, you'll be able to climb the hill to one of the nightclubs in the centre (see p179) or Huertas (see p188).

scene is a little more diverse on Sundays as crowds fan out from El Rastro. Most of the action takes place along Calle de la Cava Baja, the western end of Calle del Almendro and Plaza de la Paja. Many of these places are better known for their tapas (see p152), but they're equally great for a drink.

Lavapiés is a completely different kettle of fish altogether – working class and multicultural, with an alternative, often Bohemian crowd and quirky bars brimful of personality. Not everyone loves Lavapiés, but we do.

CAFES

CAFÉ DEL NUNCIO Map pp76-7 Bar

☎ 91 366 08 53; Calle de Segovia 9; ⌚ noon-2am Sun-Thu, noon-3am Fri & Sat; Ⓜ La Latina

Café del Nuncio straggles down a passage to Calle de Segovia. You can drink on one of several cosy levels inside or, better still in summer, enjoy the outdoor seating that one local reviewer likened to a slice of Rome. By day it's an old-world cafe, but by night it's one of the best bars in the barrio.

GAUDEAMUS CAFÉ Map pp76-7 Cafe

☎ 91 528 25 94; www.gaudeamuscafe.com, in Spanish; 4th fl, Calle de Tribulete 14; ⌚ 3pm-midnight Mon-Fri, 6pm-midnight Sat; Ⓜ Lavapiés

What a place! Decoration that's light and airy, with pop-art posters of Audrey Hepburn and James Bond. A large terrace with views over the Lavapiés rooftops. A stunning backdrop of a ruined church atop which the cafe sits. With so much else going for it, it almost seems incidental that it also serves great teas, coffees and snacks. The only criticism we can think of is that it doesn't stay open later. The terrace is filled to bursting on summer evenings.

NUEVO CAFÉ DE BARBIERI Map pp76-7 Cafe

☎ 91 527 36 58; Calle del Ave María 45; ⌚ 3pm-2am Sun-Thu, 3pm-3am Fri & Sat; Ⓜ Lavapiés

This barrio classic is Lavapiés' grandest old cafe, the sort of place for quiet conversation amid the columns and marble-topped tables right on the Plaza de Lavapiés. It does everything from coffees and cakes to cocktails and it's always been an intellectual hub of barrio life. If it all sounds a bit staid, it gets busy with a younger crowd on weekend nights.

FIRST DRINKS

EL VIAJERO Map pp76-7 Bar

☎ 91 366 90 64; Plaza de la Cebada 11; ⌚ 2pm-2am Tue-Thu & Sun, 2pm-3am Fri & Sat; Ⓜ La Latina

The undoubted highlight of this landmark of La Latina nights is the open-air, rooftop *terraza*, which boasts fine views down onto the thronging streets. When the weather's warm, it's nigh on impossible to get a table. Our secret? It often closes the *terraza* around 8pm to spruce it up a little; you should be ready to pounce when it reopens and thereafter guard your table with your life.

top picks

MOJITOS

- Café Belén (p192)
- El Eucalipto (p184)
- Dos Gardenias (p184)
- Delic (p182)
- Museo Chicote (p196)
- Centro Cubano de España (p189)

LA INQUILINA Map pp76-7   Bar

☎ 627 511 804; Calle del Ave María 39; ☾ 7pm-1.30am Tue-Thu, 7pm-2.30am Fri & Sat, 1pm-1am Sun; Ⓜ Lavapiés

This could just be our favourite bar in Lavapiés. It's partly about the cool-and-casual vibe and partly its community spirit, with deep roots in the Lavapiés soil. Contemporary artworks by budding local artists adorn the walls and you can either gather around the bar or take a table out the back. It's a small slice of sophistication in a barrio not known for such characteristics.

DELIC Map pp76-7   Bar-Cafe

☎ 91 364 54 50; www.deliccafe.com; Costanilla de San Andrés 14; ☾ 11am-2am Tue-Thu, 7pm-2am Mon, 11am-2.30am Fri & Sat; Ⓜ La Latina

We could go on for hours about this long-standing cafe-bar, but we'll reduce it to its most basic elements: nursing an exceptionally good *mojito* (€8) or three on a warm summer's evening at Delic's outdoor tables on one of Madrid's prettiest plazas is one of life's great pleasures. Bliss. Due to local licensing restrictions, the outdoor tables close two hours before closing time, whereafter the intimate interior is almost as good.

TABERNA TEMPRANILLO
Map pp76-7   Wine Bar

☎ 91 364 15 32; Calle de la Cava Baja 38; ☾ 8pm-midnight Mon, 1-3.30pm & 8pm-midnight Tue-Sun; Ⓜ La Latina

You could come here for the tapas, but we recommend Taberna Tempranillo primarily for its wines, of which it has a selection that puts most Spanish bars to shame, and many

---

LA HORA DEL VERMUT

Sunday. One o'clock in the afternoon. A dark bar off Calle de la Cava Baja. In any civilised city the bar would be shut tight, but in Madrid the place is packed because it's *la hora del vermut* (vermouth hour), a long-standing tradition whereby friends and families head out for a quick aperitif before Sunday lunch. Sometimes referred to as *ir de Rastro* (going to the Rastro) because so many of the traditional vermouth bars are in and around El Rastro market, this Sunday tradition is deeply engrained in madrileño culture. Some of the best bars for vermouth are along Calle de la Cava Baja (Map pp76-7), while Casa Alberto (p156) is another legendary part of this fine tradition.

---

are sold by the glass. It's not a late-night place, but it's always packed in the early evening and on Sundays after El Rastro.

BONANNO Map pp76-7   Wine & Cocktail Bar

☎ 91 366 68 86; Calle del Humilladero 4; ☾ noon-2am Sun-Thu, noon-2.30am Fri & Sat; Ⓜ La Latina

If much of Madrid's nightlife starts too late for your liking, Bonanno could be for you. It made its name as a cocktail bar, but many people come here for the great wines and it's usually full of young professional madrileños from early evening onwards. Be prepared to snuggle up close to those around you if you want a spot at the bar.

LIVE MUSIC

CASA PATAS Map pp76-7   Flamenco

☎ 91 369 04 96; www.casapatas.com, in Spanish; Calle de Cañizares 10; admission €30-35; ☾ shows 10.30pm Mon-Thu, 9pm & midnight Fri & Sat; Ⓜ Antón Martín or Tirso de Molina

One of the top flamenco stages in Madrid, this *tablao* always offers flawless quality that serves as a good introduction to the art. It's not the friendliest place in town, especially if you're only here for the show, and you're likely to be crammed in a little, but no one complains about the standard of the performances.

CORRAL DE LA MORERÍA
Map pp76-7   Flamenco

☎ 91 365 84 46; www.corraldelamoreria.com; Calle de la Morería 17; admission incl drink €27-37; ☾ 8.30pm-2.30am, shows 10pm & midnight Sun-Fri, 7pm, 10pm & midnight Sat; Ⓜ Ópera

This is one of the most prestigious flamenco stages in Madrid, with 50 years' experience as a leading flamenco venue and top performers most nights. The stage area has a rustic feel, and tables are pushed up close. We'd steer clear of the restaurant, which is overpriced (€43), but the performances have a far better price-quality ratio. This is where international celebrities (eg Marlene Dietrich, Marlon Brando, Muhammad Ali and Omar Sharif) have always gone for their flamenco fix when in town.

LA SOLÉA Map pp76-7   Flamenco

☎ 91 366 05 34; Calle de la Cava Baja 34; admission free; ☾ 8pm-2am Mon-Sat; Ⓜ La Latina

This long-standing bar has live flamenco of a much more improvised kind and which bears little resemblance to the *tablao* floor shows. Usually from around midnight, a knowledgeable crowd of flamenco insiders provides the closest flamenco comes to a jam session. Like any such session, sometimes it works and sometimes it doesn't, but when it does it has a soulful authenticity that more formal *tablaos* can't quite match.

EL DESPERTAR Map pp76-7   Jazz
☎ 91 530 80 95; www.cafeeldespertar.com, in Spanish; Calle de la Torrecilla del Leal 18; admission €2-6; ✆ 7.30pm-late Thu-Sun; Ⓜ Antón Martín
El Despertar is all about jazz down to its roots. Everything about this place harks back to the 1920s, with a commitment to old-style jazz and decor to match from its days as a meeting point for the barrio's intelligentsia. There are live performances every Friday and Saturday, as well as most Thursdays and Sundays. Concerts start between 9.30pm and 11pm; check the website for details.

EL JUGLAR Map pp76-7   Live Music
☎ 91 528 43 81; www.salajuglar.com; Calle de Lavapiés 37; admission €5-10; ✆ 9pm-3am Sun-Wed, 9pm-3.30am Thu-Sat; Ⓜ Lavapiés
One of the hottest spots in Lavapiés, this great venue hosts a largely Bohemian crowd who come from all over the city for a rock-dominated program leavened with flamenco at 10pm on Sunday and occasional reggae, folk and fusion beats. After the live acts leave the stage around midnight, it's DJ-spun Latin tunes or music from the American South.

EL RINCÓN DEL ARTE NUEVO
Map pp76-7   Live Music
☎ 91 365 50 45; www.rincondelartenuevo.com, in Spanish; Calle de Segovia 17; admission €7-10; ✆ 8pm-4am; Ⓜ La Latina
With 29 years in the business, this small venue knows what its punters like and it serves up a nightly feast of singer-songwriters for an appreciative crowd. The acts are as diverse as the genre itself, with Melendi, Fran Postigo and Diego El Negro among those to have taken the stage here. Concerts start between 9.30pm and 12.30am and sometimes stray into flamenco or pop.

MARULA CAFÉ Map pp76-7   Live Music
☎ 91 366 15 96; www.marulacafe.com, in Spanish; Calle de Caños Viejos 3; admission free-€10;

✆ 11pm-5.30am Sun-Thu, 11pm-6am Fri & Sat; Ⓜ La Latina
An Afro hairstyle would be the perfect look here, where the music (concerts at 11.30pm, DJs until sunrise) is all about funk, soul, jazz, music from the American South, Afrobeat and even a little hip hop. It's a club with attitude and always has a great rhythm. The jazz-soul jam sessions at midnight on Monday are a fine way to start the week. It's a little hard to find – it's almost under the viaduct just down the hill from Calle de la Morería.

LA ESCALERA DE JACOB
Map pp76-7   Live Music & Cocktail Bar
☎ 649 423 254; www.laescaleradejacob.es, in Spanish; Calle de Lavapiés 11; admission €6-12; ✆ 6pm-2am; Ⓜ Antón Martín or Tirso de Molina
As much a theatre-bar as a live music venue, 'Jacob's Ladder' is one of Madrid's most original stages. Magicians, storytellers, children's theatre (on Saturdays and Sundays at noon), live jazz and other genres are all part of the mix. Behind this intimate venue is a philosophy of crossing boundaries (very Lavapiés) and refusing to be contained within specific genres. This alternative slant on life makes for some terrific live performances and a crowd of like-minded patrons. And regardless of what's on, it's worth stopping by here for their creative cocktails that you won't find anywhere else – the *fray aguacate* (Frangelico, vodka,

top picks

MADRID TERRAZAS (OPEN-AIR BARS)

The perimeters of Madrid's squares and major thoroughfares are very often colonised by the outdoor tables of numerous bars. Unless you've a specific bar in mind, the choice is simple: wherever you can find a free table. The following squares and boulevards are our favourites:

- Plaza de Santa Ana (Map pp84-5)
- Paseo de la Castellana (Map p102)
- Paseo de los Recoletos (Map p102)
- Plaza de Olavide (Map pp116-17)
- Plaza de Oriente (Map pp62-3)
- Plaza de Chueca (Map p110)
- Plaza de la Paja (Map pp76-7)
- Plaza Mayor (Map pp62-3)

honey, avocado and vanilla) should give you an idea of how far they go.

CONTRACLUB Map pp76-7   Live Music & Nightclub
☎ 91 365 55 45; www.contraclub.es, in Spanish; Calle de Bailén 16; admission €6-12; ⏰ 10pm-5.30am Wed & Thu, 10pm-6am Fri & Sat; Ⓜ La Latina
ContraClub is a crossover live music venue and nightclub, with live flamenco on Wednesday and an eclectic mix of other live music (jazz, blues, world music and rock) from Thursday to Saturday; after the live acts (which start at 10.30pm), the resident DJs serve up equally eclectic beats (indie, pop, funk and soul) to make sure you don't move elsewhere.

UNTIL 3AM

EL EUCALIPTO Map pp76-7   Cocktail Bar
Calle de Argumosa 4; ⏰ 5pm-2am Sun-Thu, 5pm-3am Fri & Sat; Ⓜ Lavapiés
You'd be mad not to at least pass by this fine little bar with its love of all things Cuban. From the music to the clientele and the Caribbean cocktails (including nonalcoholic), it's a sexy, laid-back place. Not surprisingly, the *mojitos* are a cut above average, but the juices and daiquiris also have a loyal following.

AFTER 3AM

The absence of all-night *discotecas* in La Latina and Lavapiés doesn't necessarily mean that you need to head elsewhere after 3am. Both Marula Café (p183) and ContraClub (above) let DJ's do their stuff until *very* late.

HUERTAS & ATOCHA

Huertas comes into its own after dark and stays that way until close to sunrise – this is one of the iconic neighbourhoods of the Madrid night. As if keeping the rest of the barrio at arm's length, two architecturally splendid cafes sit at the northern end of Huertas, the alter ego of the barrio's loud and relentless energy. Bars are everywhere, from Sol down to the Paseo del Prado hinterland, but it's in Plaza de Santa Ana and along Calle de las Huertas that most of the action is concentrated. Huertas is good at any time of the night, but it's in the live jazz (and other music) venues and nightclubs (including two of Madrid's biggest and best) that it really comes into its own.

A NIGHT OUT IN HUERTAS

Our night out in Huertas invariably begins at the sedate Café del Círculo de Bellas Artes (below), then it's on to two of our favourite bars: La Venencia (p186) and its chic antithesis The Penthouse (opposite). After that, it just has to be jazz at Café Central (p186) or flamenco at Cardamomo (p186), followed by a lingering pina colada at El Imperfecto (p187). And dancing like there's no tomorrow has never been so much fun as at Adraba (p188).

Your standard Huertas bar has touts outside throughout the night offering a cheap first drink; we haven't bothered to list these as they'll find you before you find them. For the most part, we've concentrated instead on places with what Spaniards call *encanto* (charm) that will appeal to the more discerning among you. Down the hill, Atocha, like many Madrid barrios, has standard Spanish bars on most streets.

CAFES

CAFÉ DEL CÍRCULO DE BELLAS ARTES Map pp84-5   Cafe
☎ 91 521 69 42; Calle de Alcalá 42; ⏰ 9am-1am Sun-Thu, 9am-3am Fri & Sat; Ⓜ Sevilla
This wonderful belle-époque cafe was designed by Antonio Palacios in 1919 and boasts chandeliers and the charm of a bygone era. Unless you're here between 1.30pm and 4.30pm or after 9pm (when dinners are served), you have to buy a token temporary club membership (€1) to drink here. It does, however, include access to the centre's exhibitions and it's worth every cent, even if the waiters are not averse to looking aggrieved if you put them out. The entrance is on Calle de Marqués de Casa Riera.

FIRST DRINKS

DOS GARDENIAS Map pp84-5   Bar
Calle de Santa María 13; ⏰ 8pm-2.30am Mon-Sat, 5pm-2.30am Sun; Ⓜ Antón Martín
When Huertas starts to overwhelm, this tranquil little bar is the perfect antidote. The flamenco and chill-out music ensure a relaxed vibe, while sofas, softly lit colours and some of the best *mojitos* (and exotic teas) in the barrio make this the perfect spot to ease yourself into or out of the night.

TABERNA DE DOLORES Map pp84-5   Bar

☎ 91 429 22 43; Plaza de Jesús 4; ⏰ 11am-1am Sun-Thu, 11am-2am Fri & Sat; Ⓜ Antón Martín

Old bottles and beer mugs line the shelves behind the bar at this Madrid institution, known for its blue-and-white tiled exterior and for a 30-something crowd that often includes the odd *famoso* (celebrity) or two. It claims to be 'the most famous bar in Madrid' – that's pushing it, but it's invariably full most nights of the week, so who are we to argue? You get good house wine, great anchovies and what Spaniards like to call 'well-poured beer'.

CAFÉ DEL SOUL Map pp84-5   Chill-Out Bar

☎ 91 523 16 06; www.cafedelsoul.es, in Spanish; Calle de Espoz y Mina 14; ⏰ 4pm-2am Mon-Fri, noon-3am Sat, noon-2am Sun; Ⓜ Sol

Cocktails (with or without alcohol) for €6.50 (€4.50 without alcohol) are a big selling point these days in Madrid. If you add chill-out music (that turns to chill-house later in the night) and curious decor that incorporates Moroccan lamps, Café del Soul is more mellow than many in the area.

THE PENTHOUSE Map pp84-5   Cocktail Bar

☎ 91 701 60 20; Plaza de Santa Ana 14; ⏰ 9pm-1.30am Mon-Wed, 9pm-2am Thu, 9pm-2.30am Fri & Sat, 5pm-1.30am Sun; Ⓜ Antón Martín or Sol

High above the Plaza de Santa Ana, this sybaritic open-air (7th floor) cocktail bar has terrific views over Madrid's rooftops. It's a place for sophisticates, with chill-out areas strewn with cushions, funky DJs and a dress policy designed to sort out the classy from the wannabes, although they're less strict when things are quiet. If you suffer from vertigo, consider the equally classy Midnight Rose on the ground floor.

TABERNA ALHAMBRA

Map pp84-5   Flamenco Bar

☎ 91 521 07 08; www.tabernaalhambra.es, in Spanish; Calle de la Victoria 9; ⏰ 11am-1.30am Sun-Wed, 11am-2am Thu, 11am-2.30am Fri & Sat; Ⓜ Sol

There can be a certain sameness about the bars between Sol and Huertas, which is why this fine old *taberna* (tavern) stands out. The striking facade and exquisite tile work of the interior are quite beautiful; however, this place is anything but stuffy and the vibe is cool, casual and busy. They serve tapas and, later at night, there are some fine flamenco tunes.

JAZZ BAR Map pp84-5   Jazz Bar

☎ 91 429 70 31; www.jazzbar.es, in Spanish; Calle de Moratín 35; ⏰ 3pm-2.30am; Ⓜ Antón Martín

Jazz aficionados will love this place for its endless jazz soundtrack and discreet leather booths (at last, a bar that has gone for privacy instead of trying to cram too many people in) and there's plenty of greenery to keep you cheerful. If you want live jazz, head elsewhere, but this place is like a mellow after-party for aficionados in the know.

LAS CUEVAS DE SÉSAMO

Map pp84-5   Sangria Bar

☎ 91 429 65 24; Calle del Príncipe 7; ⏰ 7pm-2am; Ⓜ Antón Martín

Contrary to popular myth, madrileños don't drink much sangria unless they're by the beach in summer, but they love to do so here, where the quality is legendary. With besuited waiters and a formal air, this place has a vaguely anachronistic feel in casual Huertas, although it does have considerable charm. We list it here under First Drinks because, unless you get here early, you simply won't get a table.

WINE APPRECIATION COURSES & TOURS

Lavinia (p137) Wine courses (in Spanish) and tours to nearby bodegas (wineries).

Planeta Vino (☎ 91 310 28 55; www.planetavino.net) Tastings in an English-language wine school from €25.

Poncelet (p149) Monthly primers on cheese and wine appreciation for around €50.

Wellington Society (☎ 609 143 203; www.wellsoc.org; tours €85) Quirky and informative tours of the wines of La Rioja and Ribera del Duero in Madrid wine bars.

La Rebelión de los Mandiles (Map pp76-7; ☎ 91 365 62 70; www.larebeliondelosmandiles.com; Calle de San Isidro Labrador 10; Ⓜ La Latina) Two-hour wine courses for beginners for €25.

LA VENENCIA Map pp84-5   Sherry Bar
☎ 91 429 73 13; Calle de Echegaray 7;
🕑 1-3.30pm & 7.30pm-1.30am; Ⓜ Sol
This is how sherry bars should be – old
world, drinks poured straight from the
dusty wooden barrels and none of the
frenetic activity for which Huertas is
famous. La Venencia is a barrio classic, with
fine sherry from Sanlúcar and manzanilla
from Jeréz, accompanied by a small
selection of tapas with an Andalucian bent.
Otherwise, there's no music, no flashy
decorations; it's all about you, your *fino*
(sherry) and your friends.

MALASPINA Map pp84-5   Tapas Bar
☎ 91 523 40 24; Calle de Cádiz 9; 🕑 11am-2am
Sun-Thu, 11am-2.30am Fri & Sat; Ⓜ Sol
Although it serves inviting tapas, we like
this cosy bar, with its wooden tables and
semirustic decor, as a mellow place for a
quiet drink before you head home for an
early night. Many of the bars in this area
lack character or have sold their soul to the
god of tourism. This place is different.

CERVECERÍA ALEMANA Map pp84-5 Beer Bar
☎ 91 429 70 33; Plaza de Santa Ana 6; 🕑 11am-
12.30am Sun-Thu, 11am-2am Fri & Sat; Ⓜ Antón
Martín or Sol
If you've only got time to stop at one bar
on Plaza Santa Ana, let it be this classic
cervecería (beer bar), renowned for its cold,
frothy beers and a wider selection of Spanish beers than is the norm. It's fine inside,
but snaffle a table outside in the plaza
on a summer's evening and you won't be

giving it up without a fight. This was one
of Hemingway's haunts, and neither the
wood-lined bar nor the bow-tied waiters
have changed much since his day.

ØLSEN Map pp84-5   Vodka Bar
☎ 91 429 36 59; www.olsenmadrid.com; Calle
del Prado 15; 🕑 1-4pm & 8pm-2am Tue-Sun;
Ⓜ Antón Martín
This classy and clean-lined bar is a temple
to Nordic minimalism and comes into its
own after the Scandinavian restaurant out
the back closes. We think the more than
80 varieties of vodka are enough to satisfy
most tastes. You'll hate vodka the next day,
but Madrid is all about living for the night.

LIVE MUSIC
CARDAMOMO Map pp84-5   Flamenco
☎ 91 369 07 57; www.cardamomo.es; Calle de
Echegaray 15; admission incl drink €32; 🕑 9pm-
3.30am daily, live shows 9pm Tue-Sun; Ⓜ Sevilla
Until recently, this place was one of the last
bastions of flamenco served up in a dark,
smoky bar with a knowledgeable crowd. A
change of owner has brought a shift towards
a more formal flamenco show that draws
more tourists than aficionados. Despite
having lost something in atmosphere,
however, the flamenco is top-notch.

CAFÉ CENTRAL Map pp84-5   Jazz
☎ 91 369 41 43; www.cafecentralmadrid.com,
in Spanish; Plaza del Ángel 10; admission €10-15;
🕑 1.30pm-2.30am Sun-Thu, 1.30pm-3.30am Fri &
Sat; Ⓜ Antón Martín or Sol

SPANISH WINES – A PRIMER
Although beer drinking now outstrips wine, Spaniards love their wine, not least because they produce some of the
best wines in Europe. Like France but unlike many other wine-producing countries, Spanish wine is labelled primarily
according to region and quality, rather than the type of grape. Spanish wine is subject to a complicated system of wine
classification, ranging from the straightforward *vino de mesa* (table wine) to *vino de la tierra*, which is a wine from an
officially recognised winemaking area. If they meet certain strict standards for a given period, they receive *Denominación
de Origen* (DO) status. An outstanding wine region gets the *Denominación de Origen Calificada* (DOC), while *reserva* and
gran reserva are other indications of quality. The only DOC wines come from the La Rioja region in northern Spain, which
was demarcated in 1926, and the small Priorat area in Catalonia.

Most of the best Spanish wine, whether *blanco* (white), *tinto* (red) or *rosado* (rosé), is produced in northern Spain.
The most famous wine region is La Rioja, whose wines (mostly reds) are generally of the highest order. Not far behind
are the regions of Ribera del Duero (along the Duero River in Castilla y León) and Navarra, while Valdepeñas in Castilla-La
Mancha has less variety but is generally well priced. For whites, the Ribeiro wines of Galicia are well regarded and have
traditionally been popular, while the Penedès area in Catalonia produces whites and sparkling wine, such as *cava*, the
Champagne-like toasting drink of choice for Spaniards at Christmas. Jeréz sherry is the most famous alcoholic drink to
emerge from Andalucía. All are widely available in Madrid.

This art-deco bar has consistently been voted one of the best jazz venues in the world by leading jazz magazines and, with almost 9000 gigs under its belt, it rarely misses a beat. Big international names like Chano Domínguez, Tal Farlow and Wynton Marsalis have all played here, and there's everything from Latin jazz and fusion to tango and classical jazz. Performers usually play here for a week and then move on, so getting tickets shouldn't be a problem, except on weekends; shows start at 10pm and tickets go on sale an hour before the set starts.

POPULART Map pp84-5 — Jazz

☎ 91 429 84 07; www.populart.es, in Spanish; Calle de las Huertas 22; admission free; ☿ 6pm-2.30am Sun-Thu, 6pm-3.30am Fri & Sat; Ⓜ Antón Martín or Sol

One of Madrid's classic jazz clubs, this place offers a low-key atmosphere and top-quality music, which is mostly jazz with occasional blues, swing and even flamenco thrown into the mix. Compay Segundo, Sonny Fortune and the Canal Street Jazz Band have all played here. Shows start at 10.15pm but, if you want a seat, get here early.

CASA PUEBLO Map pp84-5 — Live Music

☎ 91 420 20 38; Calle de León 3; ☿ 5pm-2am Mon-Thu, 3pm-3am Fri-Sun; Ⓜ Antón Martín

The friendly owners of Casa Pueblo looked at the Madrid week and came to the conclusion that lovers of live music were left with insufficient options beyond the weekend. In compensation they send free live acts (jazz, tango and other genres) onto the stage from Sunday to Wednesday at around 8pm. The rest of the time, it's an agreeable bar serving up a winning combination of cakes and cocktails that draw a discerning 30-something crowd.

LA BOCA DEL LOBO Map pp84-5 — Live Music

☎ 91 429 70 13; www.labocadellobo.com, in Spanish; Calle de Echegaray 11; admission free-€10; ☿ 9pm-3.30am; Ⓜ Sol or Sevilla

Known for offering mostly rock and alternative concerts, La Boca del Lobo (The Wolf's Mouth) is as dark as its name suggests and has broadened its horizons to include just about anything – roots, reggae, jazz, soul, ska, flamenco, funk and fusion. Amid all the variety are some mainstays –

Wednesdays at 11pm are set aside for a roots and groove jam session, while Sunday nights are dedicated to soul music. Concerts start between 9.30pm and 11pm (check the website) most nights and DJs take over until closing time.

UNTIL 3AM

EL IMPERFECTO Map pp84-5 — Bar

Plaza de Matute 2; ☿ 3pm-2am Sun-Thu, 3pm-3am Fri & Sat; Ⓜ Antón Martín

Its name notwithstanding, the 'Imperfect One' is our ideal Huertas bar, with live jazz most Tuesdays at 9pm and a drinks menu as long as a saxophone, ranging from cocktails (€6.50) and spirits to milkshakes, teas and creative coffees. Its pina colada is one of the best we've tasted and the atmosphere is agreeably buzzy yet chilled.

VIVA MADRID Map pp84-5 — Bar

☎ 91 429 36 40; www.barvivamadrid.com; Calle de Manuel Fernández y González 7; ☿ 1pm-2am; Ⓜ Antón Martín or Sol

The tiled facade of Viva Madrid is one of Madrid's most recognisable and it's an essential landmark on the Huertas nightlife scene. It's packed to the rafters on weekends and you come here in part for fine *mojitos* and also for the casual, friendly atmosphere.

LA TERRAZA DEL URBAN

Map pp84-5 — Cocktail Bar

☎ 91 787 77 70; Carrera de San Jerónimo 34; ☿ 10pm-4am; Ⓜ Sevilla

A close thing with The Penthouse (p185) in the prize for the best rooftop bar in Madrid, this indulgent terrace sits atop the five-star Urban Hotel (p224) and has five-star views with five-star prices. Worth every euro. In case you get vertigo, head downstairs to the similarly high-class Glass Bar (☿ 11pm-3am).

EL CALLEJÓN Map pp84-5 — Flamenco Bar

☎ 91 429 83 97; Calle de Manuel Fernández y González 5; ☿ 7.30pm-2.30am Sun-Thu, 7.30pm-3.30am Fri & Sat; Ⓜ Sevilla or Antón Martín

Tiny El Callejón lives and breathes flamenco, from the music coming from the sound system to the stars of *cante jondo* (deep flamenco song) who adorn the walls. The clientele includes flamenco stars who recognise authentic flamenco when they hear it. It's a way to sample a more

GETTING HOME

Madrid's extensive metro system can get you most places, but it grinds to a halt between 2am and 6.05am. If you're trying to get back to your hotel at these hours, there are two main options (apart from walking). The first is a taxi (see p255) – although these hours attract a higher flag fall (€3.10) and per-kilometre rate (€1.18) than during daylight hours, it should rarely cost you more than €10 to get home. The other option is the night buses known as *búhos* (owls), with 26 routes fanning out across the city from Plaza de la Cibeles – see p253 for further information.

traditional flamenco-in-a-smoky-bar atmosphere than most of the flamenco stages in Madrid, albeit without the live acts.

AFTER 3AM

LA NEGRA TOMASA Map pp84-5   Cuban
☎ 91 523 58 30; Calle de Cádiz 9; admission free; ⏰ 1.30pm-5.30am; Ⓜ Sol

Bar, live music venue, restaurant and magnet for all things Cuban, La Negra Tomasa is a boisterous meeting place for the Havana set, with waitresses dressed in traditional Cuban outfits (definitely pre-Castro) and Cuban musicians playing deep into the night. Groups start at 11.30pm every night of the week, with additional performances at 2.30am on Fridays and Saturdays and 3pm on Sundays. There's even a Tarot card reader tucked away in the corner.

ADRABA Map pp84-5   Nightclub
www.fsmgroup.es, in Spanish; Calle de Alcalá 20; admission €15-18; ⏰ midnight-6am Wed-Sun; Ⓜ Sevilla

This nightclub has history. It was one of the most famous nightclubs of *la movida madrileña* until it burned down (killing 81 revellers in the process) in 1983. It finally reopened to much fanfare in 2010 and has rapidly re-established itself as one of the city's best. The designer decor is stunning, the safety provisions are second to none and there's five nights of dancing with a sophisticated crowd. Thursday night is 'Vanité' (which comes with the attached subtitle of 'The Most Fashion Night') and is devoted to glamour and lounge-bar sounds), while Friday and Saturday take you through the last three decades of dance tunes. Bookends to the rather

long Adraba weekend are provided by Wednesday ('Fever', with music from the 1970s through to the 1990s) and Sunday ('Queen's Club', an elitist party with a door policy to match). Whatever the night, the resident DJs are among the best in Madrid.

KAPITAL Map pp84-5   Nightclub
☎ 91 420 29 06; www.grupo-kapital.com, in Spanish; Calle de Atocha 125; admission €20; ⏰ midnight-6am Thu-Sat; Ⓜ Atocha

One of the most famous megaclubs in Madrid, this massive seven-storey nightclub has something for everyone: from cocktail bars and dance music to karaoke, salsa, hip hop and more chilled spaces for R&B and soul, as well as a section devoted to 'Made in Spain' music. It's such a big place that a cross-section of Madrid society (VIPs and the Real Madrid set love this place) hangs out here without ever getting in each other's way. We reckon €2 to use the cloak room cheapens an otherwise great package.

STELLA Map pp84-5   Nightclub
☎ 91 531 63 78; www.theroomclub.com, www.web-mondo.com, both in Spanish; Calle de Arlabán 7; admission €13-15; ⏰ 12.30-6am Thu-Sat; Ⓜ Sevilla

If you arrive here after 3am, there simply won't be room and those inside have no intention of leaving until dawn. The DJs here are some of Madrid's best and the great visuals will leave you cross-eyed if you weren't already from the music in this heady place. Thursday and Saturday nights ('Mondo', for electronica) rely on resident and invited DJs, while Friday nights ('The Room') are usually the preserve of Ángel García, one of the celebrated stalwart DJs of the Madrid night.

VILLA ROSA Map pp84-5   Nightclub
☎ 91 521 36 89; Plaza de Santa Ana 15; ⏰ 11pm-6am Mon-Sat; Ⓜ Sol

The extraordinary tiled facade (the 1928 work of Alfonso Romero, who was responsible for the tile work in Madrid's Plaza de Toros) of this longstanding nightclub is a tourist attraction in itself; the club even appeared in the Pedro Almodóvar film *Tacones Lejanos* (High Heels; 1991). It's been going strong since 1914 and has seen many manifestations – it made its name as a flamenco venue and it occasionally returns to its roots, which is when it's at its best. But most of the time the music is what's known as 'comercial', which basically means the latest dance hits with nothing too challenging.

SALAMANCA

Salamanca is the land of the beautiful people and it's all about gloss and glamour: heels for her and hair gel for him. As you glide through the *pijos* (beautiful people or yuppies), keep your eyes peeled for Real Madrid players, celebrities and designer clothes. If nothing else, you'll see how the other half lives. Although places do exist in Salamanca's otherwise quiet streets that enable you to spend the whole night here, we're of the view that there are far better barrios to get a feel for Madrid's famous nightlife. And many of Salamanca's celebrities would appear to agree – the clubs and cocktail bars of Malasaña, Chueca and elsewhere are where they're more likely to show up. The places we've listed here are only those we think are worth crossing town for.

FIRST DRINKS

THE GEOGRAPHIC CLUB Map p102   Bar
☎ 91 578 08 62; Calle de Alcalá 141; ⏱ 1pm-1.30am Sun-Wed, 1pm-2am Thu, 1pm-3am Fri & Sat; Ⓜ Goya
With its elaborate stained-glass windows, ethno-chic from all over the world and laid-back atmosphere, the Geographic Club is an excellent choice in Salamanca for an early evening drink. We like the table built around an old hot-air-balloon basket almost as much as the cavernlike pub downstairs.

CENTRO CUBANO DE ESPAÑA
Map p102   Cuban Bar
☎ 91 575 82 79; www.elcentrocubano.com; 1st fl, Calle de Claudio Coello 41; ⏱ 8.45pm-midnight Sun-Tue, 8.45pm-1am Wed, 8.45pm-2am Thu, 8.45pm-2.30am Fri & Sat; Ⓜ Serrano
Always dreamed of Havana, Cuba? Come here and you'll be a whole lot closer. This is where Cubans from all over Madrid come to be reminded of their homeland via the flavours (in the restaurant) and fine rum-based drinks such as *mojitos* (in the bar).

AFTER 3AM

ALMONTE Map p102   Nightclub
☎ 91 563 25 04; www.almontesalarociera.com, in Spanish; Calle de Juan Bravo 35; ⏱ 10pm-5am; Ⓜ Núñez de Balboa or Diego de León
If flamenco has captured your soul, but you're keen to do more than watch, head to Almonte, where the whitewashed facade tells you that this is all about Andalucía, the home of flamenco. The young and the beautiful who come here have *sevillanas* (a flamenco dance style) in their soul and in their feet, so head downstairs to see the best dancing. Dance if you dare.

SERRANO 41 Map p102   Nightclub
☎ 91 578 18 65; www.serrano41.com, in Spanish; Calle de Serrano 41; admission €10; ⏱ 11pm-5.30am Wed-Sun; Ⓜ Serrano
If bullfighters, Real Madrid stars and other A-listers can't drag themselves away from Salamanca, chances are that you'll find them here. Danceable pop and house dominate the most popular Friday and Saturday nights, funk gets a turn on Sunday and it's indie night on Thursday. As you'd imagine, the door policy is stricter than most.

MALASAÑA & CHUECA

Although it's a close-run thing, if you had to choose just one area in Madrid (Huertas and, to a lesser extent, La Latina are the other prime candidates) for the complete night out, we'd make it Malasaña and Chueca.

Spending a night exploring these two barrios is like taking a journey through Madrid's multifaceted past. As close as Madrid came to the intellectual cafes of Paris' Left Bank, the cafes of the Glorieta de Bilbao were in the 1950s and 1960s a centre of coffee-house intellectualism with *tertulias* (literary discussions) and intrigues – a few gems remain. Throughout Malasaña, *rockeros* nostalgic for the hedonistic Madrid of the 1970s and 1980s will find ample bars in which to indulge their memories. At the same time all across the barrios, especially in gay Chueca and away to the west in Conde Duque, modern Madrid is very much on show, with chill-out spaces and swanky, sophisticated bars. Small and intimate live venues are here in numbers, Madrid's best cocktail bars are to be found in Chueca on Calle de la Reina and Gran Vía, and nightclubs that reflect

A NIGHT OUT IN MALASAÑA

We could spend an entire night meandering among Malasaña's signature cafes, but if we had to pick just three to get things going it would be Café Comercial (below), Café Manuela (right) and Lolina Vintage Café (opposite). If we're feeling in need of a little romance and sophistication, we'd make for El Jardín Secreto (p192). But Malasaña is an indie rock barrio and that's what it's all about at Picnic (p192). For live acts, BarCo (p193) or Café La Palma (p194) fit the bill, followed by Brazilian Kabokla (p195), indie Tupperware (p195) and 1980s La Vía Láctea (p194). To end the night, we'd get all sweaty in either Morocco (p196) or Siroco (p197).

the barrios' split personalities keep things moving until dawn. For more options that cater to a predominantly gay crowd, turn to p216. In short, going out at night in Malasaña and Chueca is the stuff of Madrid legend, whatever your era, whatever your drink, whatever your sexual preference, whatever your look.

CAFES

CAFÉ AJENJO Map pp108-9 Cafe

☎ 91 447 70 76; Calle de Galería de Robles 4; ☽ 3.30pm-2.30am Tue-Sun; Ⓜ Bilbao

Malasaña's old cafes don't come any better than this one, with beguiling old-world decor, a vaguely intellectual air and some of the best cakes in the barrio. It's the sort of place to retreat if Malasaña gets too much, although it does get lively here without getting out of hand.

CAFÉ COMERCIAL Map pp108-9 Cafe

☎ 91 521 56 55; Glorieta de Bilbao 7; ☽ 7.30am-midnight Mon, 7.30am-1am Tue-Thu, 7.30am-2am Fri, 8.30am-2am Sat, 9am-midnight Sun; Ⓜ Bilbao

This glorious old Madrid cafe proudly fights a rearguard action against progress with heavy leather seats, abundant marble and old-style waiters. Café Comercial, which dates back to 1887, is the largest of the barrio's old cafes and has changed little since those days, although the clientele has broadened to include just about anyone, from writers on their laptops to old men playing chess.

CAFÉ DE MAHÓN Map pp108-9 Cafe

☎ 91 532 47 56; Plaza del Dos de Mayo 4; ☽ noon-1.30am Mon-Thu, noon-3am Fri-Sun; Ⓜ Bilbao

If we had to choose our favourite slice of Malasaña life, it would be this engaging little cafe, whose outdoor tables watch out over Plaza del Dos de Mayo. It's beloved by *famosos* as much as by the locals catching up for a quiet drink with friends. Their official opening times notwithstanding, they have a habit of opening and closing whenever the whim takes them.

CAFÉ DE RUIZ Map pp108-9 Cafe

☎ 91 446 12 32; Calle de Ruiz 11; ☽ 2.30pm-1.30am Sun-Thu, 2.30pm-2.30am Fri & Sat; Ⓜ Bilbao

Another of the old Malasaña cafes that so distinguish the northern end of the barrio, Café de Ruiz has all-wooden furniture and columns, draws a mature crowd and offers everything from creative teas and coffees to milkshakes and cocktails.

CAFÉ ISADORA Map pp108-9 Cafe

☎ 91 445 71 54; Calle del Divino Pastor 14; ☽ 4pm-2am; Ⓜ Bilbao or San Bernardo

Echoing the distinguished cafes that once dominated northern Malasaña and tucked away in one of Malasaña's quieter corners, Café Isadora has the old-world signposts of another age, with the memorabilia of high culture adorning its walls and mid-20th-century decor. This being Malasaña, it's as good for a mellow evening coffee as a middle-of-the-night cocktail.

CAFÉ MANUELA Map pp108-9 Cafe

☎ 91 531 70 37; Calle de San Vicente Ferrer 29; ☽ 4pm-2am Mon-Fri, noon-3am Sat & noon-2am Sun; Ⓜ Tribunal

Stumbling into this graciously restored throwback to the 1950s along one of Malasaña's grittier streets is akin to discovering hidden treasure. There's a luminous quality to it when you come in out of the night and, like so many Madrid cafes, it's a surprisingly multifaceted space, serving cocktails, delicious milkshakes and offering board games atop the marble tables in the unlikely event that you get bored.

CAFÉ-RESTAURANTE EL ESPEJO

Map p110 Cafe

☎ 91 308 23 47; Paseo de los Recoletos 31; ☽ 11am-2am Sun-Thu, 11am-3am Fri & Sat; Ⓜ Colón

Once a haunt of writers and intellectuals, this architectural gem blends modernista and art-deco styles and its interior could well overwhelm you with all the mirrors, chandeliers and bow-tied service of another era. The atmosphere is suitably quiet and refined, although our favourite corner is the elegant glass pavilion out on the Paseo de los Recoletos, where the outdoor tables are hugely popular in summer.

DIURNO Map p110 — Cafe
☎ 91 522 00 09; www.diurno.com, in Spanish; Calle de San Marcos 37; ☽ 10am-midnight Mon-Thu, 10am-1am Fri, 11am-1am Sat, 11am-midnight Sun; Ⓜ Chueca

One of the most important hubs of barrio life in Chueca, this cafe (with DVD store attached) has become to modern Chueca what the grand literary cafes were to another age. It's always full with a fun Chueca crowd relaxing amid the greenery. We recommend that you join them in what has become one of the most laid-back centres of barrio life. They also serve well-priced meals and snacks if you can't bear to give up your seat.

EL PARNASILLO Map pp108-9 — Cafe
☎ 91 447 00 79; Calle de San Andrés 33; ☽ 2.30pm-3am Sun-Thu, 2.30pm-3.30am Fri & Sat; Ⓜ Bilbao

Another of the grand old literary cafes to have survived close to the Glorieta de Bilbao, El Parnasillo has seigneurial decor with muted art-nouveau frescoes and stained glass adorning the walls, but it's a favourite drinking hole for the diverse crowd drawn to the Malasaña night for reasons other than the heavy rock scene.

GRAN CAFÉ DE GIJÓN Map p110 — Cafe
☎ 91 521 54 25; www.cafegijon.com; Paseo de los Recoletos 21; ☽ 7am-1.30am; Ⓜ Chueca or Banco de España

This graceful old cafe has been serving coffee and meals since 1888 and has long been a favourite with Madrid's literati for a drink or a meal – all of Spain's great literary figures of the 20th century came here for coffee and *tertulias* (literary discussions). You'll find yourself among intellectuals, conservative Franco diehards and young madrileños looking for a quiet drink.

LOLINA VINTAGE CAFÉ Map pp108-9 — Cafe
☎ 91 523 58 59; Calle del Espíritu Santo 9; ☽ 10am-1am Sun-Tue, 10am-2am Wed, 10am-2.30am Thu-Sat; Ⓜ Tribunal

Close to being our favourite recent discovery in Malasaña, Lolina Vintage Café seems to have captured the essence of the barrio in one small space. With a studied retro look (comfy old-style chairs and sofas, gilded mirrors and 1970s-era wallpaper), it confirms that the new Malasaña is not unlike the old but is a whole lot more sophisticated. It's low-key, full from the first breakfast to closing time and they cater to every taste with salads and cocktails (€6).

CAFÉ PEPE BOTELLA Map pp108-9 — Cafe-Bar
☎ 91 522 43 09; Calle de San Andrés 12; ☽ noon-2am; Ⓜ Bilbao or Tribunal

Pepe Botella has hit on a fine formula for success. As good in the hours around midnight as it is in the afternoon when its wi-fi access draws the laptop-toting crowd, it's a classy bar with green-velvet benches, marble-topped tables, and old photos and mirrors covering the walls. The faded elegance gives the place the charm that has made it one of the most enduringly popular drinking holes in the barrio.

THE SECRET LANGUAGE OF BEER

In the majority of bars you won't have much choice when it comes to beer, but thankfully Madrid's flagship beer, Mahou, goes down well. Mahou was first produced in Madrid by a French entrepreneur in 1890 and comes as both draught and bottled. Cruzcampo is a lighter beer. Otherwise, two Catalan companies, Damm and San Miguel, each produce about 15% of all Spain's beer. Foreign beers are becoming more widely available, but you'll have to ask for them and don't expect too much choice in most bars. The Mexican Coronita is also widely on sale.

The most common order is a *caña*, a small glass of *cerveza de barril* (draught beer). A larger beer (about 300ml), more common in the hipper bars and clubs, usually comes in a *tubo* (a long, straight glass). The equivalent of a pint is a *pinta*, while a *jarra* refers to a jug of beer. A *clara* is a shandy, a beer cut with *gaseosa* (lemonade or soda water) or *limón* (lemon).

A small bottle of beer is called a *botellín* or *quinto* because it contains a fifth of a litre. A larger one (330ml) is often referred to as a *tercio* (ie a third of a litre).

FIRST DRINKS

EL NARANJA Map pp108-9   Bar

Calle de San Vicente Ferrer 52; www.elnaranja.info, in Spanish; ☽ 10am-1am Tue-Thu, 10am-2.30am Fri, 6pm-2.30am Sat, 6pm-midnight Sun; Ⓜ Noviciado

Packed to its orange rafters from Thursday to Saturday, this fine little corner bar (they prefer the epithet of 'cultural space') represents the starting point for Conde Duque if you've come down the hill from the rest of Malasaña. And what a beguiling introduction it is. DJ sessions, concerts and even film nights are regular events, but even without such adornments it's always cool, casual, intelligent fun.

LA BARDEMCILLA Map p110   Bar

☎ 91 521 42 56; www.labardemcilla.com; Calle de Augusto Figueroa 47; ☽ noon-2am Mon-Fri, 6pm-2am Sat; Ⓜ Chueca

Run by the family of film heart-throb Javier Bardem, this bar has an agreeable buzz most nights of the week. A comfortable space to relax, a slightly Bohemian air and a loyal following add up to a great package. The clientele includes a regular cast of celebrities, but the atmosphere is resolutely informal, with cinema decor and allusions to the cinematic world through the menu, such as the *croquetas jamón jamón* (named after the film in which Javier Bardem made his name).

LA PALMERA Map pp108-9   Bar

Calle de la Palma 67; ☽ 7.30pm-2am Mon-Sat; Ⓜ Noviciado

Tucked away in the quiet-by-day laneways of Conde Duque, this tiny, unprepossessing place is covered in blue and yellow tiles and has an antique bar that looks like an animal eating out of a trough. La Palmera draws an artsy crowd who come to sit at the small wooden tables and nurse a drink or two. The atmosphere is very low-key. In summer the outdoor tables are the place to be.

STOP MADRID Map pp108-9   Bar

☎ 91 521 88 87; Calle de Hortaleza 11; ☽ 12.30-4pm & 6.30pm-2am; Ⓜ Gran Vía

The name may not be Madrid's most evocative but this terrific old *taberna* is friendly and invariably packed with people and wins the vote of at least one Lonely Planet author for the best sangria in Madrid. The tapas are also outstanding and there's always a buzz here in the evenings.

PICNIC Map pp108-9   Bar-Nightclub

Calle de las Minas 1; ☽ 5pm-1.30am Sun-Thu, 5pm-2am Fri & Sat; Ⓜ Noviciado

The little brother to the more-famous Tupperware (p195), Picnic is another diehard bar that gives Malasaña its indie soul. The look is retro, as you'd expect in this Malasaña subculture, and there are concerts most Sundays.

BRISTOL BAR Map p110   Cafe-Bar

☎ 91 522 45 68; www.bristolbar.es; Calle del Almirante 20; ☽ 9am-12.30am Mon-Wed, 9am-2.30am Thu & Fri, 11am-2.30am Sat; Ⓜ Chueca

You could come here for the English breakfast (€13) or the brunch (€16 to €21), but we like this place for its 75 different types of gin. By day, the atmosphere is that of a quiet cafe; after work, a busy gathering place; and, as the evening wears on, a sophisticated gin parlour.

CAFÉ BELÉN Map p110   Chill-Out Bar

☎ 91 308 24 47; Calle de Belén 5; ☽ 3.30pm-3am; Ⓜ Chueca

Café Belén is cool in all the right places – lounge and chill-out music, dim lighting, a great range of drinks (the *mojitos* are especially good) and a low-key crowd that's the height of casual sophistication. In short, it's one of our favourite Chueca watering holes.

EL JARDÍN SECRETO

Map pp108-9   Chill-Out Bar

☎ 91 541 80 23; Calle del Conde Duque 2; ☽ 5.30pm-12.30am Sun-Thu, 6.30pm-2.30am Fri & Sat; Ⓜ Plaza de España

---

A NIGHT OUT IN CHUECA

Gran Café de Gijón (p191) and Café-Restaurante El Espejo (p190) belong to another time, and they're terrific places to start. For a more gay aesthetic and ambience, it would be Mamá Inés (p217) or Café Acuarela (p216). Depending on our mood, we'd continue on to Café Belén (above), Splash Óscar (opposite) or Antigua Casa Ángel Sierra (opposite), then choose between Zanzíbar (p194) and El Búho Real (p194) for live acts. We're spoiled for choice when it comes to cocktails but, if we had to choose just three, they'd be Museo Chicote (p196), Del Diego (p195) and Le Cabrera (p195). To round out the night, we'd take in El Junco Jazz Club (p196), Pachá (p197) or Why Not? (p197).

'The Secret Garden' is intimate and romantic in a barrio that's one of Madrid's best-kept secrets. Lit by Spanish designer candles, draped in organza from India and serving up chocolates from the Caribbean, El Jardín Secreto is our favourite drinking corner in Conde Duque. They serve milkshakes, cocktails and everything in between. It's at its best on a summer's evening, but the atmosphere never misses a beat, with a loyal and young professional crowd.

OJALÁ AWARENESS CLUB
Map pp108-9   Chill-Out Bar
☎ 91 523 27 47; Calle de San Andrés 1; ⏱ 8.30am-1am Sun-Wed, 8.30am-2am Thu-Sat; Ⓜ Tribunal
From the people who brought you La Musa (p162), Ojalá is every bit as funky and has a lot more space to enjoy. Yes, you eat well here, but we love it first and foremost for a drink (especially a daiquiri) at any time of the day. Its lime-green colour scheme, zany lighting and a hip, cafe-style ambience all make it an extremely cool place to hang out, but the sandy floor and cushions downstairs take chilled to a whole new level.

SANDSET CHILL-OUT LOUNGE
Map pp108-9   Chill-Out Bar
☎ 655 585 469; www.sandset.es, in Spanish; Calle del Conde Duque 30; ⏱ 6pm-1am Sun & Tue-Thu, 6pm-2.30am Fri & Sat; Ⓜ San Bernardo or Ventura Rodríguez
Whether for your morning coffee or a weekend copa (drink) after midnight, Sandset is right at home in laid-back Conde Duque. Upstairs is a lazy cafe with a sense of light and space (it serves great cakes to accompany your coffee), but it's downstairs that wins prizes for imagination, with tinkling water, sand on the floor, cushions, wicker beach furniture and water pipes to smoke. It's an eclectic mix, but it works.

SPLASH ÓSCAR Map p110   Chill-Out Bar
☎ 91 701 11 73; Plaza de Vázquez de Mella 12; ⏱ 4.30pm-12.30am; Ⓜ Gran Vía
Another of the stunning rooftop terraces (although this one has a small swimming pool), atop Hotel Óscar (p228), this chilled space with gorgeous skyline views has become a cause célèbre among A-list celebrities.

MERCADO DE LA REINA GIN CLUB
Map p110   Cocktail Bar
☎ 91 521 31 98; www.mercadodelareina.es; Calle de la Reina 16; ⏱ 4pm-2am; Ⓜ Gran Vía
In this area of Madrid known for its classy cocktails, this gin club fits right in. But unlike other choices nearby – eg Bar Cock (p195), Del Diego (p195) and Museo Chicote (p196) – this place has no pretensions to former grandeur; the decor is supermodern and, like the clientele, all dressed in black. With 30 types of gin (€8 to €12) and DJs at night from Thursday to Saturday, it's a happening place.

CONSENTIDO Map pp108-9   Lounge Bar
☎ 91 521 16 44; www.consentido.org, in Spanish; Calle del Barco 32; ⏱ 7pm-1am Tue-Thu & Sun, 7pm-2.30am Fri & Sat; Ⓜ Tribunal
Now here's something different. Calling itself a 'Social Space for Eroticism', ConSentido combines an erotic boutique, small erotic art gallery and a basement lounge bar where they serve aphrodisiac cocktails (including, of course, Sex on the Beach) and small snacks. It's low-key, funky and never crosses the line into bad taste.

ANTIGUA CASA ÁNGEL SIERRA
Map p110   Tavern
☎ 91 531 01 26; Calle de Gravina 11; ⏱ noon-1am; Ⓜ Chueca
This historic old taberna is the antithesis of modern Chueca chic – it has hardly changed since it opened in 1917. As Spaniards like to say, the beer on tap is very 'well poured' here and it also has vermouth on tap. Fronting onto the vibrant Plaza de Chueca, it can get pretty lively of a weekend evening when it spills over onto the plaza. Just don't expect service with a smile.

LIVE MUSIC
BARCO Map pp108-9   Live Music
☎ 91 521 24 47; www.barcobar.com, in Spanish; Calle del Barco 34; admission free-€6; ⏱ 8pm-5.30am Sun-Thu, 8pm-6am Fri & Sat; Ⓜ Tribunal
Just before Malasaña spills over into the seedy backside of Gran Vía, BarCo is an outstanding live venue with jazz, flamenco (usually Thursday), Latin music, funk, rock or blues; it's also the headquarters for Madrid's School of Creative Music. There's room to dance if the mood takes you

and the crowd is almost exclusively local. There's a fantastic jazz jam session from 10pm every Sunday, and flamenco star Enrique Morente is also known to turn up here on occasion.

CAFÉ LA PALMA Map pp108-9 Live Music
☎ 91 522 50 31; www.cafelapalma.com, in Spanish; Calle de la Palma 62; admission free-€12; 🕙 4.30pm-3am Sun-Thu, 4.30pm-3.30am Fri & Sat; Ⓜ Noviciado

It's amazing how much variety Café La Palma has packed into its labyrinth of rooms. Live shows featuring hot local bands are held at the back, while DJs mix it up at the front. Some rooms have a cafe style, while others evoke an Arab tea room, pillows on the floor and all. You might find live music other nights as well, but there are always two shows at 10pm and midnight from Thursday to Saturday. Every night is a little different and the various rooms ensure that you spend the whole night here, simply moving from room to room depending on your mood.

EL BÚHO REAL Map p110 Live Music
☎ 91 319 10 88; www.buhoreal.com, in Spanish; Calle de Regueros 5; admission €5-10; 🕙 8pm-3am Sun-Thu, 8pm-3.30am Fri & Sat; Ⓜ Alonso Martínez or Chueca

It looks like your average Madrid *bar de copas* (bar serving spirits and mixed drinks), but El Buho Real (The Royal Owl) is all about acoustic music. It interprets the term pretty widely to include flamenco, rock and singer-songwriter solo acts, and it's been around long enough to have drawn a loyal following. Concerts start at 9.30pm.

LIBERTAD 8 Map p110 Live Music
☎ 91 532 11 50; www.libertad8cafe.com, in Spanish; Calle de la Libertad 8; admission free-€6; 🕙 4pm-2.30am; Ⓜ Chueca

ONE FOR THE ROAD

Spaniards can be a superstitious lot, so there's one drinking etiquette rule to be mindful of: never suggest having just one last drink. Madrileños almost always order the *penúltima* (second-last), even if it's really the last of the evening. To mention the *última* (last) is bad luck; it sounds like one's last drink on earth. Of course, the problem with ordering a *penúltima* is that it frequently leads to ordering another.

One of the most enduring live venues in Chueca, this small-stage bar attracts storytellers, poets and local and international singer-songwriters and a whole range of other acts; they also often have exhibitions. We like the mix, and it is intimate venues like these that add depth to the Madrid night.

TABOÓ Map pp108-9 Live Music
☎ 91 524 11 89; www.taboo-madrid.com, in Spanish; Calle de San Vicente Ferrer 23; admission €4-10; 🕙 10.30pm-6am Thu-Sat; Ⓜ Tribunal

With everything from pop to hard-core punk and a whole lot of house music in between, Taboó likes to keep its options open. Check out the website to see which way it's leaning, and spend as little time as possible talking to the bouncers while you wait in the queue.

ZANZIBAR Map p110 Live Music
☎ 91 319 90 64; www.zanzibarmadrid.com, in Spanish; Calle de Regueros 9; admission €4; 🕙 8pm-3am Sun-Thu, 8pm-3.30am Fri & Sat; Ⓜ Alonso Martínez or Chueca

What a fantastic little venue this is. Styled with African decor, it does indeed have world music (and sometimes a jam session) most Tuesdays, but its repertoire extends to jazz, singer-songwriter, soul-rap and even storytelling. Concerts start at 9.30pm or 11.30pm, and there's a lovely cafe-style intimacy about the place.

UNTIL 3AM

LA VÍA LÁCTEA Map pp108-9 Bar-Nightclub
☎ 91 446 75 81; Calle de Velarde 18; 🕙 9pm-3am; Ⓜ Tribunal

Another living, breathing and somewhat grungy relic of *la movida*, La Vía Láctea remains a Malasaña favourite for a mixed, informal crowd who seems to live for the 1980s. The music ranges across rock, pop, garage, rockabilly and indie. There are plenty of drinks to choose from and by late Saturday night anything goes. Expect long queues to get in on weekends.

MOLOKO Map pp108-9 Bar-Nightclub
Calle de Quiñones 12; 🕙 10pm-3.30am Tue-Sat; Ⓜ San Bernardo

Its walls plastered with old concert flyers and the odd art-house movie poster (*A Clockwork Orange*, for example), Moloko remains an excellent middle-of-the-night option in the Conde Duque area of western Malasaña. The music – indie, rock, garage and '60s – is consistently good, which is why people return here again and again.

POLYESTER Map p110 — Bar-Nightclub
Travesía de San Mateo 10; 🕐 **10pm-3am Sun-Thu, 10pm-3.30am Fri & Sat;** Ⓜ **Tribunal**
They've chosen the perfect name for this place, another essential element of the local indie circuit. Just in case you thought you'd crossed some hidden frontier to Malasaña, it attracts a mixed gay-straight crowd and the soundtrack revolves around the likes of Franz Ferdinand and The Smiths.

TUPPERWARE Map pp108-9 — Bar-Nightclub
☎ **91 446 42 04; Calle de la Corredera Alta de San Pablo 26;** 🕐 **9pm-3am;** Ⓜ **Tribunal**
A Malasaña stalwart and prime candidate for the bar that best catches the enduring *rockero* spirit of Malasaña, Tupperware draws a 30-something crowd, spins indie rock with a bit of soul and classics from the '60s and '70s, and generally revels in its kitsch (eyeballs stuck to the ceiling, and plastic TVs with action-figure dioramas lined up behind the bar). It can get pretty packed on a weekend after 1am. By the way, locals pronounce it 'Tupper-warry'.

KABOKLA Map pp108-9 — Brazilian Bar
☎ **91 532 59 66; www.kabokla.es, in Spanish; Calle de San Vicente Ferrer 55; admission free;** 🕐 **10pm-1am Tue-Thu, 6pm-3am Fri, 2.30-6.30pm & 10.30pm-3.30am Sat, 2.30-10pm Sun;** Ⓜ **Noviciado**
Run by Brazilians and dedicated to all things Brazilian, Kabokla is terrific. Live Brazilian groups play some nights from around 10pm (from percussion to samba and cover bands playing Chico Buarque). When there's no live music, the DJ gets the crowd dancing. It also serves Madrid's smoothest caipirinhas and runs samba and capoeira classes outside opening hours (see p258).

AREIA Map p110 — Chill-Out Bar & Nightclub
☎ **91 310 03 07; www.areiachillout.com; Calle de Hortaleza 92;** 🕐 **1pm-3am;** Ⓜ **Chueca or Alonso Martínez**
The ultimate lounge bar by day (cushions, chill-out music and dark secluded corners, where you can hear yourself talk or even snog quietly), this place is equally enjoyable

by night. That's when groovy DJs take over (from 11pm Sunday to Wednesday, and from 9pm the rest of the week) with deep and chill house, nu jazz, bossa and electronica. It's cool, funky and low-key all at once.

LOLA BAR Map p110 — Chill-Out Bar & Nightclub
☎ **91 522 34 83; Calle de la Reina 25;** 🕐 **6pm-3am Tue-Sun Sep-Jul;** Ⓜ **Gran Vía**
If you like your music chilled, Lola Bar is the sort of place where you'll want to find a comfy corner and remain until closing time. On weekends, the DJ ups the tempo a little, but it's more lounge than house and the volume's never excessive.

BAR COCK Map p110 — Cocktail Bar
☎ **91 532 28 26; Calle de la Reina 16;** 🕐 **8pm-3am;** Ⓜ **Gran Vía**
With a name like this, Bar Cock could go either way, but it's definitely cock as in 'rooster', so the atmosphere is elegant and classic rather than risqué. The decor resembles an old gentlemen's club, but it is beloved by A-list celebrities, those who'd like to be and a refined 30-something crowd who come here for the lively atmosphere and great cocktails. On weekends all the tables seem to be reserved, so be prepared to hover on the fringes of fame.

DEL DIEGO Map p110 — Cocktail Bar
☎ **91 523 31 06; Calle de la Reina 12;** 🕐 **7pm-3am Mon-Thu, 7pm-3.30am Fri & Sat;** Ⓜ **Gran Vía**
Calle de la Reina is much loved by *famosos*, especially models, actors and designers, as a place for terrific cocktails in stately surrounds. Del Diego fits this bill perfectly and over its 20 years of existence has become one of the city's most celebrated cocktail bars. The decor blends old-world cafe with New York style and it's the sort of place where the music rarely drowns out the conversation. Even with around 75 cocktails to choose from, we'd still order the signature 'El Diego' (vodka, advocaat, apricot brandy and lime).

LE CABRERA Map p110 — Cocktail Bar
☎ **91 319 94 57; www.lecabrera.com, in Spanish; Calle de Bárbara de Braganza 2;** 🕐 **4pm-2.30am Mon-Sat;** Ⓜ **Colón or Alonso Martínez**
In the basement below the exciting new tapas bar of the same name (see p165), this

oh-so-chic cocktail bar is every bit as appealing. The more than 60 different cocktail varieties are the work of Diego Cabrera, the long-standing barman of renowned master chef Sergi Arola and, along with the designer decor, the combination has transformed this into one of the 'in' places in not just the barrio but the entire city.

MUSEO CHICOTE Map p110 — Cocktail Bar
☎ 91 532 67 37; www.museo-chicote.com; Gran Vía 12; ☷ 6pm-3am Mon-Thu, 6pm-3.30am Fri & Sat; Ⓜ Gran Vía

The founder of this Madrid landmark is said to have invented more than a hundred cocktails, which the likes of Hemingway, Ava Gardner, Grace Kelly, Sophia Loren and Frank Sinatra all enjoyed at one time or another. It's still frequented by film stars and top socialites, and it's at its best after midnight, when a lounge atmosphere takes over, couples cuddle on the curved benches and some of the city's best DJs do their stuff (CDs are available). The 1930s-era interior only adds to the cachet of this place. We don't say this often, but if you haven't been here, you haven't really been to Madrid – it's that much of an icon.

STROMBOLI Map p110 — Cocktail Bar
☎ 91 319 46 28; Calle de Hortaleza 96; admission free; ☷ 6pm-3am Mon-Sat; Ⓜ Chueca or Tribunal

After a number of years as a fairly standard small club, Stromboli has found its niche as a minimalist cocktail bar. In addition to the cocktails – our favourite is 'Bubaloo' (vodka, syrup of bubble gum and sugar, mint and lemon) – there's also a carefully chosen menu of Champagnes and *cavas* (sparkling wines).

LAYDOWN REST CLUB
Map pp108-9 — Lounge & Cocktail Bar
☎ 91 548 79 37; www.laydown.es, in Spanish; Plaza de Mostenses 9; ☷ 9pm-3am Tue-Sun; Ⓜ Plaza de España or Noviciado

The name says it all. DJs, cabaret-style shows and cocktails are a fairly familiar Madrid mix, but this is one of few places where you get to enjoy them while reclining on a comfy bed. It's a pretty sophisticated 30-something crowd that's up for a dance when they're not flat-out drinking. It can be difficult to find – from Plaza de Mostenses, head east along Calle del General Mitre then take the first lane on the right.

SUPERSONIC Map p110 — Nightclub
Calle de Campoamor 3; www.supersonicclub.com; ☷ 10pm-3am Wed-Sat; Ⓜ Alonso Martínez

Madrid has nightclubs in the most unlikely places… On a quiet residential Chueca street, this great little *discoteca* is one of the best venues for indie music, with a mix of '70s diehard to everything that we loved to hate about Britpop (The Smiths, Oasis etc). It's slightly more downtempo on Wednesday and Thursday, but the commitment to British music never abates.

AFTER 3AM

EL JUNCO JAZZ CLUB Map p110 — Jazz
☎ 91 319 20 81; www.eljunco.com, in Spanish; Plaza de Santa Bárbara 10; admission free; ☷ 11pm-6am; Ⓜ Alonso Martínez

El Junco has established itself on the Madrid nightlife scene by appealing as much to jazz aficionados as to clubbers. Its secret is high-quality live jazz gigs from Spain and around the world at 11.30pm every night, followed by DJs spinning funk, soul, nu jazz, blues and innovative groove beats. There are also jam sessions at 11.30pm in jazz (Tuesday) and blues (Sunday). The emphasis is on music from the American South and the crowd is classy and casual.

MOROCCO Map pp108-9 — Nightclub
☎ 91 531 51 67; www.morocco-madrid.com, in Spanish; Calle del Marqués de Leganés 7; admission €10; ☷ midnight-6am Fri & Sat; Ⓜ Santo Domingo or Noviciado

Owned by the zany Alaska, the standout musical personality of *la movida,* Morocco has decor that's so kitsch it's cool, and a mix of musical styles that never strays too far from 1980s Spanish and international tunes, with electronica another recurring theme. The bouncers have been known to show a bit of attitude, but then that kind of comes with the profession.

NASTI CLUB Map pp108-9 — Nightclub
☎ 91 521 76 05; www.nasti.es, in Spanish; Calle de San Vicente Ferrer 33; admission free-€10; ☷ 11pm-5.30am Thu-Sat; Ⓜ Tribunal

It's hard to think of a more off-putting entrance than Nasti Club's graffiti and abandoned-building look. You also won't find the name outside – if you want to come here, you're supposed to know where to find it. Its staple, appropriately, is a faithfully grungy approach to the 1970s (pop, rock and punk), both in terms of music and decor. But it's not as nasty as it sounds and the crowd can span the full range of 1970s throwbacks from a who's who of Madrid's underground to some surprisingly respectable types. Above all it's a place with attitude and, as their own publicity says, they're *not* from Barcelona, they *don't* play electronica, people who come here *are* cool and no one's ever heard of the live acts who appear here until they become famous two years later. Says it all really. Very Malasaña.

PACHÁ Map p110   Nightclub
☎ 91 447 01 28; www.pacha-madrid.com; Calle de Barceló 11; admission €10; ⏲ 12.30-5am Thu-Sat; Ⓜ Tribunal
This megaclub, a branch of the international chain of clubs that earned its fame in Ibiza, became a major Madrid club during *la movida*. The name still has a certain cachet on the Madrid nightlife scene, so the odd celebrity turns up here and gets all sweaty dancing to house, R&B and other related genres across the three dance floors.

SALA FLAMINGO Map pp108-9   Nightclub
Calle de Mesonero Romanos 13; admission €10; ⏲ midnight-5.30am Thu, midnight-6am Fri & Sat; Ⓜ Callao or Gran Vía
One of the most 'in' places in Madrid for many years, Sala Flamingo is famous above all for its Friday night 'OchoyMedia' session, which seamlessly blends indie rock with electronica to create its own genre, 'rockotrónica' – this is the night when local celebrities flood through the doors. For a complete change of pace and clientele, 'Darkhole' on Saturday is all black and Gothic, while Thursday kicks it all off with 'Playback', where dressing down seems to be the only requirement.

SIROCO Map pp108-9   Nightclub
☎ 91 593 30 70; www.siroco.es, in Spanish; Calle de San Dimas 3; admission €10; ⏲ 9.30pm-5.30am Thu, 9.30pm-6am Fri & Sat; Ⓜ Noviciado
One of the most popular and eclectic nightclubs in Madrid, Siroco does everything from reggae to drum 'n' bass, funk, soul and danceable disco tunes. It gets a diverse crowd and queues can be long. The one unifying theme is the commitment to Spanish music

(there are often upcoming local rock bands at 10pm before the action really kicks off) and it's a good place to hear local music before it becomes too mainstream.

WHY NOT? Map p110   Nightclub
Calle de San Bartolomé 7; ⏲ 10.30pm-6am; admission €10; Ⓜ Chueca
Underground, narrow and packed with bodies, gay-friendly Why Not? is the sort of place where nothing's left to the imagination (the gay and straight crowd who come here are pretty amorous) and it's full nearly every night of the week. Pop and top-40 music are the standard here, and the dancing crowd is mixed and as serious about having a good time as they are about heavy petting. We're not huge fans of the bouncers here but, once you get past them, it's all about having fun.

CHAMBERÍ & ARGÜELLES

Like any barrios in the capital, Chamberí and Argüelles have bars on practically every street corner, and a couple in particular stand out. And while largely residential Chamberí may seem like an unlikely place for live music, there are three options here that are famous throughout the city.

FIRST DRINKS

DJÉNNÉ Map pp116-17   Bar
Calle de Galileo 74; ⏲ 8pm-2.30am Mon-Sat; Ⓜ Islas Filipinas
Styling itself as a bar with a passion for travel, this bar *could* be a real find. The wall-sized mural of Mali's Djenné market and photos from around the world give it something special, but the music is of a

top picks

ROOFTOP TERRAZAS (OPEN-AIR BARS)

- The Penthouse (p185)
- La Terraza del Urban (p187)
- Splash Óscar (p193)
- Gaudeamus Café (p181)
- Hotel de las Letras (p221)

fairly standard, late-night-bar variety – if only they'd play a few world music tunes, the fantastic cocktails would go down even better. We wouldn't cross town to get here, but if you're on your way to or from Galileo Galilei (below), it's worth a stop.

KRYPTON Map pp116–17   Cocktail Bar
☎ 91 591 54 32; Calle de Gonzalo de Córdoba 20;
☺ 9pm-2.30am Thu-Sat, 6-10pm Sun; Ⓜ Bilbao or Quevedo

In the heart of Chamberí, Krypton is a dimly lit, smoky bar with quirky decoration dedicated to the edgy art of Japanese manga comics, music that could be jazz, electronica or hip hop, and good cocktails (including *mojitos*). We love it, but it won't be to everyone's taste.

LIVE MUSIC

CLAMORES Map pp116–17   Live Music
☎ 91 445 79 38; www.clamores.es, in Spanish; Calle de Alburquerque 14; admission €5-15;
☺ 6pm-3am; Ⓜ Bilbao

Clamores is a one-time classic jazz cafe that has morphed into one of the most diverse live music stages in Madrid. Jazz is still a staple, but world music, flamenco, soul fusion, singer-songwriter, pop and rock all make regular appearances. Live shows can begin as early as 7pm on weekends but sometimes really only get going after 1am! On the rare nights when there's nothing live, a DJ takes over, spinning pop, indie and funk.

GALILEO GALILEI Map pp116–17   Live Music
☎ 91 534 75 57; www.salagalileogalilei.com, in Spanish; Calle de Galileo 100; admission free-€15;
☺ 6pm-4.30am; Ⓜ Islas Filipinas

There's no telling what will be staged here next, but it's sure to be good, as the list of past performers attests: Jackson Browne, El Cigala, Kiko Veneno, Niña Pastori and Brazilian songstress Cibelle among others. The program changes nightly, with singer-songwriters, jazz, flamenco, folk, fusion, indie, world music and even comedians. Most performances start at 10.30pm. Along with its sister venue Clamores, there's always something worth listening to.

HONKY TONK Map pp116–17   Live Music
☎ 91 445 61 91; www.clubhonky.com, in Spanish; Calle de Covarrubias 24; admission free; ☺ 9pm-5am; Ⓜ Alonso Martínez

Despite the name, this is a great place to see blues or local rock 'n' roll, though many acts have a little country, jazz or R&B thrown into the mix, too. It's a fun vibe in a smallish club that's been around since the heady 1980s and opens 365 days a year. It's a reliable late-night option in a barrio of few, and the range of malt whiskies is impressive. Arrive early as it fills up fast.

NORTHERN MADRID

You probably wouldn't spend a whole night in northern Madrid, although you could do so. But the four places here repay in bucketloads the taxi fare required to reach them.

LIVE MUSIC

SEGUNDO JAZZ Map p121   Jazz
☎ 91 554 94 37; www.segundojazz.es, in Spanish; Calle del Comandante Zorita 8; admission free-€10;
☺ 7pm-4am; Ⓜ Nuevos Ministerios or Cuatro Caminos

This well-regarded jazz venue focuses on up-and-coming local talents, as well as a few international acts. It's an agreeable, unpretentious place that's worth the fair hike to get here: the quality is always high and the atmosphere nice and laid-back. Monday and Tuesday are given over to jam sessions from 11pm, while other concerts start anywhere from 9pm to midnight.

MOBY DICK Map p121   Live Music
☎ 91 555 76 71; www.mobydickclub.com, in Spanish; Avenida del Brasil 5; admission free-€18;
☺ 10pm-5am Mon-Sat; Ⓜ Santiago Bernabéu

In a corner of Madrid that works hard by day and parties even harder on weekends, Moby Dick is an institution on the live music circuit. It's mostly well-known rock bands who can't quite fill the 25,000-seater venues, and there are plenty of dance bars alongside if the music's not to your liking. The house band plays at 11.30pm on Monday, with the program chosen by the punters.

UNTIL 3AM

REAL CAFÉ BERNABÉU Map p121   Bar
☎ 91 458 36 67; www.realcafebernabeu.es; Gate 30, Estadio Santiago Bernabéu, Avenida de Concha Espina; ☺ 10pm-2am; Ⓜ Santiago Bernabéu

Overlooking one of the most famous football fields on earth, this trendy cocktail

CONCERT VENUES

Madrid is a major stop on the European tour circuit. Summer is undoubtedly the best time to see the big names, but headline acts arrive in town throughout the year and, in addition to the smaller live music venues listed throughout this chapter, play at the following venues:

Auditorio Parque Juan Carlos I (off Map pp124-5; ☎ 91 721 00 79; www.parquejuancarlos.net/parquejuancarlosi/auditorio.htm; Avenida de Logroño; Ⓜ Campo de las Naciones)

Palacio de Deportes (Map pp124-5; ☎ 91 444 99 49; www.palaciodedeportes.com; Calle de Jorge Juan 99; Ⓜ Goya or O'Donnell)

Plaza de Toros Monumental de Las Ventas (off Map p102; ☎ 91 356 22 00; www.las-ventas.com, in Spanish; Calle de Alcalá 237; Ⓜ Ventas)

La Riviera (Map pp124-5; ☎ 91 365 24 15; www.salariviera.com, in Spanish; Paseo Bajo de la Virgen del Puerto; ☿ midnight-6am Tue-Sun; Ⓜ Puerta de Ángel) One of Madrid's most popular venues that morphs into a nightclub after the live acts go home.

Sala Caracol (Map pp124-5; ☎ 91 527 35 94; www.salacaracol.com, in Spanish; Calle de Bernardino Obregón 18; Ⓜ Embajadores)

Sala Heineken (Map pp116-17; ☎ 91 547 57 11; www.salaheineken.com, in Spanish; Calle de la Princesa 1; Ⓜ Plaza de España)

bar will appeal to those who live and breathe football or those who simply enjoy mixing with the beautiful people. Views are exceptional, although it closes two hours before a game and doesn't open until an hour after. There's also a good restaurant.

AFTER 3AM

MACUMBA Map p121   Nightclub
www.fsmgroup.es, in Spanish; Plaza Estación de Chamartín; ☿ midnight-6am Fri & Sat, 4pm-midnight Sun; Ⓜ Chamartín

Macumba, on the second floor of the Chamartín train station, may be a fair trip north of the centre (although still well within city limits), but it's one of the most prestigious nightclubs in Madrid. Friday nights ('Danzoo') is when a peerless cast of local and international DJs spin house and techno over the incredible sound system. It's house music again and all manner of special effects on gay-friendly Saturday ('Sunflowers'). And for something different, Sunday ('Space of Sound') is for those who can't bear their weekend to end.

THE ARTS

top picks

- Teatro Real (p203)
- Teatro de la Zarzuela (p204)
- Cine Doré (p204)
- Yelmo Cineplex Ideal (p204)

THE ARTS

Madrid is an excellent place to take in a theatre, classical music, opera or dance performance. Such performances are attended more often by locals than tourists, which may be an attraction in itself, but these genres take you deeper into the local arts scene that receives little coverage beyond the Spanish-speaking world. Indeed this is the best place in the world to see Spanish drama (both classical and modern) and *zarzuela* (a Madrid cross between opera and dance). Then again, you could always just join the throngs of Madrid's cinema-goers, either in English or in Spanish.

Although Spaniards consider those quintessentially Spanish pursuits of flamenco and bullfighting to be artistic endeavours, an overall look at flamenco appears on p45, flamenco venues are covered in the Nightlife chapter which begins on p173, and bullfighting can be found on p211.

WHAT'S ON

All of the following publications and websites provide comprehensive listings of shows at Madrid's theatres, cinemas and concert halls:

EsMadrid Magazine (www.esmadrid.com) Monthly tourist-office listings for concerts and other performances; available at tourist offices, some hotels and online.

Guía del Ocio (www.guiadelocio.com, in Spanish) A Spanish-only weekly magazine available for €1 at news kiosks.

In Madrid (www.in-madrid.com) This monthly English-language expat publication is given out free (check the website for locations) and has lots of information about what to see and do in town.

La Netro (http://madrid.lanetro.com, in Spanish) Comprehensive online guide to Madrid events.

Metropoli (www.elmundo.es/metropolis, in Spanish) *El Mundo*'s Friday supplement magazine has information on the week's offerings.

On Madrid (www.elpais.com, in Spanish) *El País* also has a Friday supplement with weekly listings.

What's on When (www.whatsonwhen.com) The Madrid page covers the highlights of sport and cultural activities, with some information on getting tickets.

CLASSICAL MUSIC & OPERA

Madrid loves to party, but scratch beneath the surface and you'll find a thriving city of high culture, with venues dedicated to year-round opera and classical music. Orchestras from all over Europe perform regularly here, but Madrid's own Orquesta Sinfónica (www.osm.es, in Spanish) also performs (or accompanies) in the Teatro Real or Auditorio Nacional de Música. The Banda Sinfónica Municipal de Madrid (www.muni madrid.es/bandasinfonica, in Spanish) plays at the Teatro Monumental.

BOOKING CONCERT & THEATRE TICKETS

Outlets selling tickets online for concerts, theatre and other live performances include the following:

Caixa Catalunya's Tel-Entrada (☎ 902 101 212; www.telentrada.com)

El Corte Inglés (☎ 902 400 222; www.elcorteingles.es, in Spanish) Click on 'Entradas' on its website.

Entradas.com (www.entradas.com, in Spanish)

Fnac (www.fnac.es) Click on 'Entradas'; it's mostly modern, big-name music groups.

Localidades Galicia (Map pp62-3; ☎ 91 531 91 31; www.bullfightticketsmadrid.com; Plaza del Carmen 1; 🕓 9.30am-1pm & 4.30-7pm Mon-Sat, 9.30am-1pm Sun; Ⓜ Sol)

Servicaixa (www.servicaixa.com) You can also get tickets in Servicaixa ATMs.

Taquilla Ultimo Minuto (Map pp62-3; www.taquillaultimominuto.com; Plaza del Carmen 1; 🕓 5-8pm Wed, Thu & Sun, 5-10pm Fri & Sat) Last-minute theatre tickets at up to 50% discount.

Tick Tack Ticket (www.ticktackticket.com)

AUDITORIO NACIONAL DE MÚSICA
Map p121

☎ 91 337 01 40; www.auditorionacional.mcu.es;
Calle del Príncipe de Vergara 146; Ⓜ Cruz del Rayo
When it's not playing the Teatro Real,
Madrid's venerable Orquesta Sinfonía plays
at this modern venue, which also attracts
famous conductors from all across the
world to its two concert halls. It's usually
fairly easy to get your hands on tickets at
the box office.

FUNDACIÓN JUAN MARCH Map p102

☎ 91 435 42 40; www.march.es; Calle de Castelló
77; Ⓜ Núñez de Balboa
A foundation dedicated to promoting
music and culture (as well as exhibitions;
see p104), the Juan March Foundation
stages free concerts throughout the year.
Performances range from solo recitals to
themed concerts dedicated to a single style
or composer.

TEATRO MONUMENTAL Map pp84-5

☎ 91 429 10 55; Calle de Atocha 65; Ⓧ ticket
office 11am-2pm & 5-7pm Mon-Fri; Ⓜ Antón
Martín
The main concert season runs from
October to March each year, when
performances include those of the Banda
Sinfónica Municipal Madrid, the Orquesta
Sinfónica de RTVE, and occasional operas,
ballets or zarzuelas. It's a modern theatre
with fabulous acoustics. Tickets are an
absolute bargain at €3 to €10.

TEATRO REAL Map pp62-3

☎ 902 244 848, 91 516 06 60; www.teatro-real
.com; Plaza de Oriente; Ⓜ Ópera
After spending €100 million-plus on a
long rebuilding project, the Teatro Real is
as technologically advanced as any venue
in Europe, and is the city's grandest stage
for elaborate operas, ballets and classical
music. You'll pay as little as €6 for a spot so
far away you'll need a telescope, although
the sound quality is consistent throughout.
For the best seats, don't expect change
from €127.

DANCE

Spain's lively Compañía Nacional de Danza (☎ 91 354
50 53; http://cndanza.mcu.es/), under director Nacho
Duato, performs worldwide and has won ac-
colades for its marvellous technicality and

original choreography. The company, made
up mostly of international dancers, performs
contemporary pieces and is considered a
main player on the international contemporary dance scene. When in town, which is not
often, it performs at various venues, including
the Teatro de la Zarzuela (p204) or Teatro de
Madrid (below).

Madrid is also home to the Ballet Nacional de
España (☎ 91 517 99 99; http://balletnacional.mcu.es/), a
classical company known for its unique mix
of ballet and traditional Spanish styles, such
as flamenco and zarzuela. When in Madrid,
it's usually on stage at the Teatro Real (left),
the Teatro de la Zarzuela (p204) or the Teatro
de Madrid.

One performer that you absolutely must
see if your visit coincides with her arrival in
town is Sara Baras (www.sarabaras.com), a
Cádiz-born performer whose flamenco ballet
is unique and soul-stirring.

TEATRO DE MADRID off Map pp58-9

☎ 91 740 52 74; www.teatromadrid.com; Avenida
de la Ilustración s/n; Ⓜ Barrio del Pilar or Herrera
Oria
A modern theatre in La Vaguada in northern
Madrid, the Teatro de Madrid is devoted
solely to dance performances, from avant-
garde contemporary dance to the Ballet
Nacional de España.

FILM

Madrileños have to be among Europe's most
devoted movie-goers and on weekend evenings just about every sala (venue) in town
is packed, with queues stretching down the
street. Most people buy tickets at the door,
but turning up a couple of hours early, booking online or phoning the cinema to make a
booking can be a good idea. Regular tickets
in most cinemas cost around €7 to €8, but can
vary depending on the cinema; prices sometimes rise by a euro or more on weekends and
there's a discount on the día de espectador
(spectator's day) which is usually a Monday
or a Wednesday, but can vary from cinema to
cinema. There are further discounts one day
a week (also usually Wednesday) for senior
citizens.

ORIGINAL-VERSION CINEMAS

Plenty of cinemas offer versión original (VO;
original version) films, which are shown in
the original language with Spanish subtitles;

otherwise foreign-language films are dubbed in mainstream cinemas. The epicentre of original-version cinemas is around Plaza de Emilio Jiménez Millas (known locally as Plaza de los Cubos), just north of Plaza de España. The major Spanish newspapers have full film listings, while most local entertainment guides (see p202) have listings of VO cinemas. The following are the best original-version cinemas:

Cines Princesa (Map pp116-17; ☎ 91 541 41 00, 902 229 122; www.cinesrenoir.com, in Spanish; Calle de Princesa 3; Ⓜ Plaza de España)

Renoir Princesa (Map pp116-17; ☎ 91 541 41 00, 902 229 122; www.cinesrenoir.com, in Spanish; Calle de Princesa 5; Ⓜ Plaza de España)

Verdi (Map pp116-17; ☎ 91 447 39 30; www.cines-verdi. com; Calle de Bravo Murillo 28; Ⓜ Canal or Quevedo) Neighbourhood cinema that cherry-picks the best, big-budget art-house movies.

Yelmo Cineplex Ideal (Map pp76-7; ☎ 902 220 922; www.yelmocines.es, in Spanish; Calle del Doctor Cortezo 6; Ⓜ Sol or Tirso de Molina)

SPANISH-LANGUAGE CINEMAS

The highest concentrations of Spanish-language cinemas are on Gran Vía and Calle Fuencarral, between the Glorieta de Bilbao and Glorieta de Quevedo. Watch in particular for the massive painted billboards outside, although this traditional form of advertising is a dying art. Those looking for cult movies in Spanish also have a couple of options:

Cine Doré (Map pp76-7; ☎ 91 369 11 25; www.mcu.es/ cine/MC/FE/CineDore/Programacion, in Spanish; Calle de Santa Isabel 3; ☉ Tue-Sun; Ⓜ Antón Martín) A wonderful old cinema that's home to the Filmoteca Nacional (National Film Library) and an excellent Spanish-language cinema bookshop. Best of all, it shows classics past and present for just €2.50 (a 10-session ticket costs €15). Four movies are shown nightly, the first at 5.30pm and the last around 10pm.

Cinesa Capitol (Map pp62-3; ☎ 902 333 231; www .cinesa.es, in Spanish; Gran Vía 41; tickets €7.60; Ⓜ Callao)

Cinesa Proyecciones (Map pp116-17; ☎ 902 333 231; www.cinesa.es, in Spanish; Calle de Fuencarral 136; tickets €7.60; Ⓜ Bilbao or Quevedo) Wonderful Art Deco exterior, modern cinema within.

La Enana Marrón (Map p110; ☎ 91 308 14 97; www .laenanamarron.org; Travesía de San Mateo 8; tickets €4; Ⓜ Alonso Martínez) Artsy, alternative and independent (mostly Spanish) films that don't get a run elsewhere. A great little cinema.

THEATRE

Madrid's theatre scene is a year-round affair, but really gets going in autumn. Most shows are in Spanish, but those who don't speak the language may still enjoy musicals or *zarzuela*, Spain's own singing-and-dancing version of musical theatre. Tickets start at around €10 and run up to €50. Mostly you can buy tickets at the box office on the day of the performance, but for new or weekend shows you should book ahead. On other days they're generally open from about 10am until 1pm and again from 5pm until the start of the evening's show. What follows is by no means an exhaustive list. For further options not listed here, visit www.teatrosdemadrid .com (in Spanish) and www.gruposmedia .com (in Spanish).

TEATRO ALFIL Map pp108-9
☎ 91 521 45 41, 91 521 58 27; www.teatroalfil .com, in Spanish; Calle del Pez 10; Ⓜ Noviciado
Staging a broad range of alternative and experimental Spanish-language theatre, Teatro Alfil is a good place to catch up-and-coming Spanish actors and comedians, and mingle with an eclectic crowd.

TEATRO CIRCO PRICE Map pp76-7
☎ 91 528 98 65 or 91 528 81 22; www.teatrocirco price.es, in Spanish; Ronda de Atocha 35; Ⓜ Lavapiés, Embajadores or Atocha
Just south of Lavapiés, this modern theatre does a little bit of everything from concerts and circuses to dance performances. It also hosts the Festival Flamenco Caja Madrid (p17) in February.

TEATRO COLISEUM Map p108-9
☎ 91 547 66 12; Gran Vía 78; Ⓜ Plaza de España
One of the largest theatres in the city, here you can expect to see major musicals, often Broadway or West End hits, but usually with an all-Spanish cast and in Spanish.

TEATRO DE LA ZARZUELA Map pp84-5
☎ 91 524 54 00; http://teatrodelazarzuela.mcu .es/; Calle de Jovellanos 4; Ⓜ Banco de España
This theatre, built in 1856, is the premier place to see *zarzuela* (see the boxed text, opposite); tickets start at €16 and climb to €40. It also hosts a smattering of classical music and opera, as well as the cutting edge Compañía Nacional de Danza.

LA ZARZUELA

What began in the late 17th century as a way to amuse King Felipe IV and his court has become Spain's own unique theatre style. With a light-hearted combination of music and dance, and a focus on everyday people's problems, *zarzuelas* quickly became popular in Madrid, which remains the genre's undoubted capital. Although you're likely to have trouble following the storyline (*zarzuelas* are notoriously full of local references and jokes), seeing a *zarzuela* gives an entertaining look into local culture. The best place to catch a show is the Teatro de la Zarzuela (opposite), while for a history of *zarzuela* in English, translations of *zarzuela* songs and storylines, CD and DVD reviews, and a critical look at current *zarzuela* shows, check out the terrific website zarzuela.net (www.zarzuela.net).

TEATROS DEL CANAL Map pp116-17

☎ 91 308 99 99; www.teatrosdelcanal.org, in Spanish; Calle de Cea Bermúdez 1; Ⓜ Canal
A state-of-the-art theatre complex opened in 2009, Teatros del Canal does major theatre performances, as well as musical and dance concerts. It also hosts the Suma Flamenca festival (p19) in June.

TEATRO ESPAÑOL Map pp84-5

☎ 91 360 14 84; www.esmadrid.com/teatro espanol; Calle del Príncipe 25; Ⓜ Sevilla, Sol or Antón Martín
This theatre, which fronts onto the Plaza de Santa Ana, has been here in one form or another since the 16th century and is still one of the best places to catch mainstream Spanish drama, from the works of Lope de Vega to more recent playwrights.

TEATRO FERNÁN GÓMEZ Map p102

☎ 91 480 03 00; http://teatrofernangomez. esmadrid.com/; Plaza de Colón; Ⓜ Colón or Serrano
Located under the waterfall at Plaza de Colón, this busy theatre has exhibition and performance spaces where it stages everything from classical to world music concerts, with comic and children's theatre, opera and flamenco.

TEATRO HAAGEN DAZS Map pp76-7

☎ 902 006 617; www.teatrohaagen-dazs.es, in Spanish; Calle de Atocha 18; Ⓜ Tirso de Molina
Big budget musicals are among those that take the stage in this grand old theatre (formerly Teatro Calderón) and stay for months.

TEATRO PAVÓN Map pp76-7

☎ 91 528 28 19; teatroclasico.mcu.es, in Spanish; Calle de los Embajadores 9; Ⓜ La Latina or Tirso de Molina
The home of the National Classical Theatre Company, this theatre has a regular calendar of classical shows by Spanish and European playwrights.

TEATRO VALLE-INCLÁN Map pp76-7

☎ 91 505 88 01; cdn.mcu.es; tickets €15-18; Plaza de Lavapiés; Ⓜ Lavapiés
The stunning refurbishment of this theatre has brought new life (and quality plays) to this once run-down corner of Lavapiés. Located on the southern end of the Plaza de Lavapiés, it is now the headquarters for the Centro Dramático Nacional (National Drama Centre) and puts on landmark plays by (mostly) Spanish playwrights such as Valle-Inclán and Fernando Arrabal.

SPORTS & ACTIVITIES

top picks

- Hammam Medina Mayrit (p208)
- Hammam Ayala (p208)
- City Yoga (p209)
- Estadio Santiago Bernabéu (p211)
- Plaza de Toros Monumental de Las Ventas (p212)

SPORTS & ACTIVITIES

The peculiarly Spanish phenomena that are Real Madrid and the controversial 'sport' of bullfighting may be the headline acts when it comes to Madrid's sporting scene and these are undoubtedly unforgettable experiences. If, however, you prefer to make your own sport, tennis, a gymnasium workout, skiing, yoga, Pilates and swimming are all options. For a complete change of pace, Madrid's terrific range of day spas offer the opportunity for some serious pampering.

HEALTH & FITNESS
HEALTH & DAY SPAS

CHI SPA Map p102

☎ 91 578 13 40; www.thechispa.com; Calle del Conde de Aranda 6; ⏰ 10am-9pm Mon-Fri, 10am-6pm Sat; Ⓜ Retiro

Wrap up in a robe and slippers and prepare to be pampered in one of Spain's best day spas. There are separate areas for men and women, and services include a wide range of massages (30/60 minutes from €35/65), facials (€45 to €125), manicures (€25) and pedicures (€35). It also offers a range of package deals from 90-minute facial, scrub and relaxation massage (€99) to a four-hour beauty session for €199. Now, what was it you were stressed about?

HAMMAM MEDINA MAYRIT Map pp62-3

☎ 902 333 334; www.medinamayrit.com; Calle de Atocha 14; ⏰ 10am-midnight; Ⓜ Sol

Medina Mayrit is both an architectural jewel and a sensory indulgence that takes your senses back in time. Housed in the excavated cellars of old Madrid, this imitation traditional Arab bath offers massages and aromatherapy beneath graceful arches and accompanied by the sound of trickling water. Prices are cheapest from 10am to 4pm Monday to Friday (from €24 for the basic bath experience); otherwise, you'll pay from €26 up to €51.50 for the full bath and massages experience; there are discounts for students and for those over 65. Reservations are required. There's also a Moroccan-style tea room and restaurant upstairs.

HAMMAM AYALA off Map p102

☎ 91 187 52 20; www.hammamayala.com, in Spanish; Calle de Ayala 126; ⏰ 10am-8pm Tue & Thu, 1-10pm Wed, Fri & Sat, 1-8pm Sun; Ⓜ Manuel Becerra

Another excellent traditional Arab bath experience, Hammam Ayala offers massages

and a range of bath treatments within a faithful re-creation of the Middle East's hammams. All-natural products and the sensory pleasures of exotic oils make this a lovely escape from modern life. Massages start at €25, while the traditional bath ritual costs €65.

SPA RELAJARSE Map p110

☎ 91 308 61 48; www.sparelajarse.es, in Spanish; Calle de Barquillo 43; ⏰ 11am-11pm Mon-Sat, 1-9pm Sun; Ⓜ Chueca

Step inside this intimate little spa and you can't help but feel relaxed. With a range of options (the Especial Spa includes a hydromassage pool with strawberries and Möet Chandon for €170, while the Especial Spa with a 'romantic dinner' costs €260), this may be one for a special occasion. Discretion and privacy are its trademarks, with most sessions popular with couples.

LAB ROOM SPA Map p110

☎ 91 781 14 11; www.thelabroom.com; Calle de Campoamor 6; ⏰ 7am-9pm Mon-Fri, 11am-7pm Sat; Ⓜ Alonso Martínez

An exclusive spa and beauty parlour whose past clients include Penélope Cruz, Jennifer Lopez, Gwyneth Paltrow and Gael García Bernal, the Lab Room is close to the ultimate in pampering for both men and women. It offers a range of make-up sessions, massages and facial and body treatments, although prices can be surprising reasonable – the 'Lab Room manicure' costs €35, massages start from €30 and it has a range of well-priced, all-inclusive package deals. There's even 'fashion and wardrobe consultancy' which starts at €180 and gets your wardrobe sorted for the season.

ZENSEI Map pp116-17

☎ 91 549 60 49; www.zensei.net, in Spanish; Calle de Blasco de Garay 64; ⏰ 10am-10pm Mon-Sat; Ⓜ Moncloa or Quevedo

Hidden away on a suburban Argüelles street, this Japanese relaxation centre is an oasis of civility and promises the ultimate in Zen massage, acupuncture, reiki, shiatsu and yoga, not to mention origami or Japanese tea-ceremony classes. The two-hour relaxation or beauty programs are also highly recommended. You'll come out floating on air.

YOGA & PILATES

In addition to the places listed here, many private gyms also offer yoga and Pilates.

CITY PILATES Map pp116-17

☎ 91 445 13 03; www.city-pilates.com, in Spanish; Calle de Ruiz 27; classes from €18; ☾ 8am-10pm Mon-Fri; Ⓜ San Bernardo or Bilbao
This state-of-the-art Pilates centre has classes across all styles of the genre and, like its sister centre City Yoga, it offers programs for soon-to-be and recovering mums.

CITY YOGA Map p121

☎ 91 553 47 51; www.city-yoga.com, in Spanish; Calle de los Artistas 43; classes from €18; ☾ 10am-10pm Mon-Fri, 10am-2pm Sat; Ⓜ Cuatro Caminos or Nuevos Ministerios
Don't be put off by the somewhat gritty surrounding streets because this yoga and Pilates centre is one of the most popular in the city, with classes suiting all styles and ability levels. It also offers massages, Pilates and pre- and post-natal activities. There's a one-off joining fee of €30.

GYMS

Public gyms and indoor pools (normally for lap swimming only) are scattered throughout Madrid. They generally charge a modest €3.50 to €7 for one-day admission and can get pretty crowded at weekends and after work hours. More expensive (€10 to €15 per one-day admission), privately owned health centres usually have less crowded workout rooms.

GIMNASIO CHAMBERÍ Map pp116-17

☎ 91 448 04 60; www.gimnasiochamberi.com, in Spanish; Calle de Raimundo Lulio 18; admission around €8; ☾ 7.45am-11pm Mon-Fri, 9am-3pm Sat & Sun; Ⓜ Iglesia
This privately run suburban gym doesn't have a pool, but it does offer yoga, Pilates, aerobics of most descriptions and a well-equipped workout room.

ÓPERA GYM Map pp62-3

☎ 91 547 26 68; Calle del Fomento 3; day admission €8; ☾ 8am-11pm Mon-Fri, 11am-4pm Sat, 11am-3pm Sun; Ⓜ Santo Domingo
Another privately run gym although this time in central Madrid, Ópera Gym offers Pilates, aerobics and kick-boxing, as well as modern gym equipment.

CENTRO DEPORTIVO LA CHOPERA
Map p91

☎ 91 420 11 54; Parque del Buen Retiro; one/10 sessions €4.35/37; ☾ 9am-9pm Mon-Sat, 9am-3pm Sun, closed August; Ⓜ Atocha
With a fine workout centre, several football fields and a few tennis courts, this centro deportivo (sports centre and gym) in the southwestern corner of the Parque del Buen Retiro is one of Madrid's most attractive and central. It also has tennis courts where court hire costs €5.60 per adult, but you'll need your own racquet.

ACTIVITIES

SWIMMING

If you'd rather splash around than labour over laps, the following public pools are worth trying, although they can be completely overwhelmed in summer.

CANAL DE ISABEL II Map p121

☎ 91 533 17 91; Avenida de Filipinas 54; admission €4; ☾ 11am-8pm Jun–early Sep; Ⓜ Ríos Rosas or Canal
Open only in summer, this large outdoor pool is easily accessible by metro from the city centre. It also has a football field, a basketball court and a weights room, and across the road there's a running track and a golf driving range.

CASA DEL CAMPO off Map pp124-5

☎ 91 463 00 50; Avenida Ángel; pool €4.50; ☾ 11.30am-9pm summer, 9am-noon & 3-7pm & 9-10pm winter; Ⓜ Lago
The outdoor pools at this sprawling park are overrun in summer. The rest of the year (October to April), swimming is indoors.

PISCINA MUNICIPAL PEÑUELAS
Map pp124-5

☎ 91 474 28 08; Calle de Arganda; admission €4; ☾ 11am-9pm Jun-Aug; Ⓜ Acacias, Pirámides or Embajadores

With two gloriously cool pools and another smaller one for infants, this outdoor complex south of the city centre is a popular place for a summer dip, but like any place where there's water in Madrid, it gets crowded on summer weekends.

SKIING

For more on skiing in the mountains north of Madrid, see p248.

MADRID XANADÚ off Map pp124-5
☎ 902 361 309; www.madridsnowzone.com; Carretera A-5, Salida 22 & 25, Arroyomolinos; 1hr adult/child €19/16, day pass €33/30, equipment rental per hr/day €36/50; ⏰ 10am-midnight
Far out to the east of Madrid, in the massive Madrid Xanadú shopping centre, you'll find the largest covered ski centre in Europe, covering 18,000 sq metres. Open 365 days a year, it's kept at a decidedly cool -2°C, so rug up before hitting the surprisingly good slopes. To get here, take bus 528 or 534 from the Intercambiador de Príncipe Pío.

SPECTATOR SPORT

Watching Real Madrid play at its world-famous Estadio de Santiago Bernabéu or taking in a bullfight at the Plaza de Toros Monumental de Las Ventas are high on the list of must-sees for a number of visitors to Madrid. There's also high-quality basketball if that's your thing.

Sports-only dailies such as *Marca* (www.marca.com, in Spanish) and *AS* (www.as.com, in Spanish) are wildly popular and will give you the inside scoop on upcoming matches and events, provided you read basic Spanish. They're available from any newspaper kiosk.

FOOTBALL

Depending on your perspective, Real Madrid (www.realmadrid.com) is either the best football club in the world (in 1998, FIFA declared it the greatest club of the 20th century) or the symbol of a game gone mad with money.

When it comes to history, no-one can match Real Madrid's record at home or abroad: 31 Spanish *liga* (league) titles, the last in 2008; 17 Copas del Rey; nine European Cups (now known as the Champions League, the last in 2002); two Uefa Cups; and the Supercopa de España eight times.

Even against such a backdrop, however, the recent headlines surrounding the club have been extraordinary. After construction magnate Florentino Perez became club president in 2000, the club spent hundreds of millions of euros buying the best players in the world, in the process building a team known as *los galacticos*. In the three seasons following its Spanish league title in 2003, however, Real Madrid won nothing (the longest drought in the club's history). In March 2006, Florentino Perez resigned, blaming the prima donnas whom he himself had brought to the club. Real Madrid won the 2007 La Liga title, and followed it up with another in 2008. Success has, however, continued to elude them on the European stage.

The sight of Barcelona winning La Liga, Copa del Rey and the European Champions League in 2009 proved too much for Florentino Perez, who returned to the Real Madrid helm. Undaunted by the failures of his first period in office, Perez launched the *galactico* era Mark II. He quickly broke the world record transfer fee (a record Real Madrid held for the 2001 purchase of Frenchman Zinedine Zidane for UK£46 million) by purchasing the Brazilian superstar Kaká for UK£56.8 million, only to break it again soon after by paying UK£80 million for Portuguese champ Cristiano Ronaldo. But in its first year together, the expensively assembled team was eliminated in the first knockout stage of the Champions League and lost twice to Barcelona en route to second place in La Liga.

Even amid all the tarnished glamour, El Estadio Santiago Bernabéu is one of the world's great football arenas; watching a game here is akin to a pilgrimage for sports fans and doing so alongside 80,000 passionate Madridistas (Real Madrid supporters) in attendance will send chills down your spine. If you're lucky enough to be in town when Real Madrid wins a major trophy, head to Plaza de la Cibeles and wait for the all-night party to begin.

It surprises many visitors that a significant proportion of the population can't stand Real Madrid and actually support the capital's other team, Atlético de Madrid (www.clubatleticodemadrid.com, in Spanish). Though existing in the shadow of its more illustrious city rivals, Atlético has won nine *liga* titles (a feat bettered only by Real Madrid and FC Barcelona), the latest in 1996, and nine Copas del Rey. In 2010 it won the UEFA Europa League. Atlético, which has a cult following, attracts passionate support and fans of the *rojiblancos* (red-and-whites) declare theirs to be the *real* Madrid team, unlike the reviled and aristocratic 'Madridistas' up the road.

ESTADIO SANTIAGO BERNABÉU
Map p121

☎ 91 398 43 00, 902 301 709; www.realmadrid .com; Calle Concha Espina 1; ☺ 10am-7.30pm Mon-Sat, 10.30am-6.30pm Sun, except match days; Ⓜ Santiago Bernabéu

Holding 80,000 delirious fans, the Santiago Bernabéu (named after the long-time club president) is a mecca for Real Madrid football fans worldwide. Those who can't come to a game can at least stop by for a tour (p120), a peek at the trophies or to buy Real Madrid memorabilia in the club shop (p144).

ESTADIO VICENTE CALDERÓN
Map pp124-5

☎ 91 366 47 07; www.clubatleticodemadrid.com, in Spanish; Calle de la Virgen del Puerto; Ⓜ Pirámides

The home of Atlético de Madrid isn't as large as Real Madrid's (the Vicente Calderón seats fewer than 60,000), but what it lacks in size it makes up for in raw energy. A game at the Estadio Vicente Calderón has a passionate, more carnivalesque feel to it than most Real Madrid games. There's also the on-site Museo Atlético de Madrid (☎ 91 365 09 31; admission €6; ☺ 11am-7pm Tue-Sun) and it offers guided tours (incl museum entry €8) of the stadium.

Prices & Reservations

The Spanish football season runs from September (or the last weekend in August) until May, with a two-week break just before Christmas until early in the New Year.

Tickets for football matches in Madrid start at around €40 and run up to the rafters for major matches; you pay in inverse proportion to your distance from the pitch. Even in a relatively unimportant game, the best seats can cost €120. For bigger games, such as Real Madrid against Barcelona or Atlético de Madrid, or a Champions League game, *entradas* (tickets) are difficult to find unless you're willing to take the risk with scalpers. For less-important matches, you shouldn't have too many problems.

Unless you book your Real Madrid ticket through a ticket agency, turn up at the Estadio Santiago Bernabéu ticket office at Gate 42

on Calle de Concha Espina early in the week before a scheduled game (eg a Monday morning for a Sunday game). The all-important telephone number for booking tickets (which you later pick up at Gate 42) is ☎ 902 324 324, which works only if you're calling from within Spain. To see an Atlético de Madrid game, try calling ☎ 91 366 47 07 or ☎ 902 530 500, but you're most likely to manage a ticket if you turn up at the ground a few days before the match. Tickets for both Real Madrid and Atlético de Madrid matches can also be bought on their respective websites – click on 'Entradas'.

If you're booking from abroad and don't have any luck online, try Localidades Galicia (Map pp62-3; ☎ 91 531 91 31; www.bullfightticketsmadrid.com; Plaza del Carmen 1; ☺ 9.30am-1pm & 4.30-7pm Mon-Sat, 9.30am-1pm Sun; Ⓜ Sol). Numerous websites also sell tickets to Real Madrid games, including www.madrid-tickets.net, www.madrid-tickets .com and www.ticket-finders.com.

BULLFIGHTING

An epic drama of blood and sand or a cruel blood 'sport' that has no place in modern Europe? This most enduring and controversial of Spanish traditions is all this and more, at once compelling theatre and an ancient ritual that sees 40,000 bulls killed in around 17,000 bullfights every year in Spain. Perhaps it was best summed up by Ernest Hemingway – a bullfighting aficionado – who described it as 'a wonderful nightmare'.

Love it or loathe it, bullfighting is a national institution. An afternoon of *la corrida* (bullfight) is still part of Madrid life and the Plaza de Toros Monumental de Las Ventas is the country's most prestigious venue. The undoubted star of modern bullfighting is the Madrid-born, José Tomás, who returned to the ring in 2007 after five years in retirement. Other respected *toreros* (bullfighters) include Jesulín de Ulbrique, Julián 'El Juli' López and Enrique Ponce.

On an afternoon ticket there are generally six bulls and three star *toreros* dressed in the dazzling *traje de luces* (suit of lights). It's a one-sided event – the death of the bull is close to inevitable – but it's still a dangerous business. Despite the spectre of death that pervades *la corrida,* a day out at the bullring is a festive occasion for aficionados.

At the same time, many animal lovers feel bullfighting is immoral, and bullfights are vehemently opposed by numerous animal-welfare organisations. Although some regions of Spain, notably Catalonia, have taken steps towards banning bullfighting, there are no signs that Madrid will follow suit. In 2010, King Juan Carlos, an enthusiastic bullfighting aficionado, publicly reiterated his support for *la corrida*. Even so, bullfighting's popularity has waned in the last few decades, especially among younger Spaniards. A recent poll found that just 17% of Spaniards under 25 had any interest in bull-fighting, compared with 41% of those aged over 64. Similar polls show that three-quarters of Spaniards have no interest in the sport.

Alternatively, organisations opposed to bullfighting worth checking out include the World Society for the Protection of Animals (www.wspa.org .uk), the League Against Cruel Sports (www.leagueagainst cruelsports.org) and the Madrid-based Equanimal (www.equanimal.org, in Spanish). For information about creative protests against bullfighting, visit www.runningofthenudes.com.

PLAZA DE TOROS MONUMENTAL DE LAS VENTAS off Map p102
☎ 91 356 22 00; www.las-ventas.com, in Spanish; Calle de Alcalá 237; Ⓜ Ventas
One of the largest rings in the bullfighting world, Las Ventas has a grand *mudéjar* (a Moorish architectural style) exterior and a suitably Coliseum-like arena surrounding the broad sandy ring. For more information, see p100.

Prices & Reservations

Spain's top *toreros* do their thing at Las Ventas bullring from early to mid-May to coincide with the Fiestas de San Isidro Labrador (see p18), continuing daily for a month, with further weekend fights until October. There are also bullfights in autumn.

Tickets for *corridas* are divided into *sol* (sun) and *sombra* (shade) seating, with the former cheaper than the latter. Ticket sales begin a few days before the fight, at Plaza de Toros Monumental de Las Ventas ticket office (off Map p102; ☎ 91 356 22 00; www.las-ventas.com, in Spanish; Calle de Alcalá 237; Ⓥ 10am-2pm & 5-8pm; Ⓜ Ventas). A few agencies sell before then, adding an extra 20% for their trouble; one of the best is Localidades Galicia (Map pp62-3; ☎ 91 531 91 31; www.bullfighttickets madrid.com; Plaza del Carmen 1; Ⓥ 9.30am-1pm & 4.30-7pm Mon-Sat, 9.30am-1pm Sun; Ⓜ Sol). You can also get tickets at La Central Bullfight Ticket Office (☎ 91 531 33 66; Map pp84-5; Calle de la Victoria) or online at www .taquillatoros.com (in Spanish). Mostly, you'll have no problem getting a ticket at the gate,

but during the Fiestas de San Isidro, or when a popular *torero* comes to town, book ahead.

The cheapest tickets (around €5) are for standing-room *sol*, though on a hot summer day you might want to pay the extra €4 for *sombra* tickets. The premium seats – on the front row in the shade – are the preserve of celebrities and cost more than €100.

For information on who'll be in the ring, check out the colourful posters tacked around town or the daily newspapers (in which bull-fighting appears in the 'Cultura', not sports pages).

BASKETBALL

Although they don't get the same publicity, the basketball players of Real Madrid de Baloncesto (www.realmadrid.com), are as much champions as their footballing counterparts and their rivalry with Barcelona is equally fierce. The team has won 30 Spanish league titles, 22 Copas del Rey and eight European championships (the last in 1995).

Also popular, although far less successful, is Asefa Estudiantes (☎ 902 400 002; www.clubestudiantes .com, in Spanish), the Atlético de Madrid of the city's basketball scene and Madrid's most popular team.

Prices & Reservations

The basketball season shadows the football season, from September through to the second half of May.

Real Madrid plays at the Palacio Vistalegre (www.palaciovistalegre.com; Calle de Utebo 1; Ⓜ Vista Alegre) in the southern Carabanchel district. To buy tickets, there are three main options: call ☎ 902 244 824; book online at www.real madrid.com; or in person at the stadium box office two hours before the game. Tickets generally start at €25 and go as high as €130.

Asefa Estudiantes plays in the excellent Telefónica Madrid Arena (off Map pp124-5; www.telefonica arenamadrid.com; Calle de las Aves, Casa de Campo; Ⓜ Lago or Alto de Extremadura), west of the centre, and usually in front of a packed house. In town, you can buy tickets at the Polideportivo Antonio Magariños (Map p121; ☎ 91 562 40 22; Calle de Serrano 127; Ⓥ 9am-8pm Mon-Fri) or online at www.clubestudiantes .com; click on 'Entradas'.

MARATHONS

In late April, the Maratón de Madrid (www.maraton madrid.org) cuts a swathe through the city and attracts athletes from all over the world.

Less-serious athletes may find the wonderfully festive San Silvestre Vallecana (www.sansilvestre vallecana.com) more to their liking. Staged on 31 December at 6pm, the 10km course leads from Plaza de Castilla all the way down Paseo de la Castellana to Vallecas, to the southeast. Although the professional section of the race attracts leading runners, the amateur section is one of the more unusual races in Europe. Many athletes wear fancy dress; musicians line the route and runners, who must pass through streets warming up for New Year's Eve, are pelted with eggs and tomatoes.

GAY & LESBIAN MADRID

top picks

- Black & White (p217)
- Café Acuarela (p216)
- Hostal La Zona (p218)
- Librería Berkana (p216)
- Mamá Inés (p217)
- Sala Bash/Ohm (p217)

What's your recommendation? www.lonelyplanet.com/madrid

GAY & LESBIAN MADRID

Madrid has always been one of Europe's most gay-friendly cities. The city's gay community is credited with reinvigorating the once down-at-heel inner-city barrio of Chueca, where Madrid didn't just come out of the closet, it ripped the doors off in the process. Today the barrio is one of Madrid's most vibrant and it's very much the heart and soul of gay Madrid. Cafes, bars and nightclubs clearly oriented to a gay clientele abound, and new book, video and adult-toy shops aimed at gay people continue to spring up in and around Chueca, as well as gay-friendly hostels. But there's nothing ghetto-like about Chueca. Its extravagantly gay-and-lesbian personality is anything but exclusive and the crowd is almost always mixed gay-straight. As gay and lesbian residents like to say, Chueca isn't gay-friendly, it's hetero-friendly.

It's a great time to be gay in Madrid. Under laws passed by the Spanish Congress in June 2005, same-sex marriages now enjoy the same legal protection as those between heterosexual partners. At the time there was a conservative backlash, but opinion polls showed that the reforms were supported by more than two-thirds of Spaniards. The best time of all to be in town if you're gay or lesbian is around the last Saturday in June for Madrid's gay and lesbian pride march (p19).

On the pages that follow, we have covered the best shopping, nightlife and sleeping options. For eating choices, just about every restaurant in Chueca is a gay meeting place of sorts – see p165 for full listings.

SHOPPING

LIBRERÍA BERKANA Map p110   Bookshop
☎ 91 522 55 99; www.libreriaberkana.com, in Spanish; Calle de Hortaleza 64; ⏱ 10.30am-9pm Mon-Fri, 11.30am-9pm Sat, noon-2pm & 5-9pm Sun; Ⓜ Chueca
One of the most important gay and lesbian bookshops in Madrid, Librería Berkana stocks gay books, movies, magazines, music, clothing, and a host of free magazines for nightlife and other gay-focused activities in Madrid and around Spain; this is the place to pick up your copy of *Shanguide*, *Shangay Express* and *MENsual* (see p218).

A DIFFERENT LIFE Map p110   Sex Shop
☎ 91 532 96 52; www.adifferentlife.es, in Spanish; Calle de Pelayo 30; ⏱ 11am-10pm Mon-Fri, 11am-midnight Sat, 11am-3pm & 5-10pm Sun; Ⓜ Chueca
Yes, A Different Life has the usual sex-shop products – DVDs, magazines and erotic gifts – but it also does a line in gay novels and DVDs focusing on gay themes or with predominantly gay characters. As such, it's somewhat less in-your-face than other shops.

NIGHTLIFE

Chueca lives for the night and the possibilities are endless. The action fans out from the Plaza de Chueca (Map p110), and this is where

you should get your bearings and linger at the outdoor tables as you plan your night. Apart from the Chueca landmarks that follow, other good watering holes with a partly gay or lesbian vibe include Antigua Casa Ángel Sierra (p193) and Diurno (p191).

CAFES & FIRST DRINKS

Any bar in Chueca (and arguably most bars in Madrid whatever the barrio) can be considered reliably gay-friendly. One with a particularly strong following among the gay community is the sleek Splash Óscar (p193), with views out over the rooftops.

B AIRES CAFÉ Map p110   Cafe-Bar
☎ 91 532 98 79; Calle de Gravina 4; ⏱ 3pm-1am Sun-Wed, to 2am Thu & Fri, to 2.30am Sat; Ⓜ Chueca
This oasis of sophistication in anything-goes Chueca is perfect for a quiet conversation, and most gays and lesbians passing through Chueca spend some time here, either resting from nights of partying, taking some down time in preparation for the night ahead or simply as an end in itself.

CAFÉ ACUARELA Map p110   Cafe-Bar
☎ 91 522 21 43; Calle de Gravina 10; ⏱ 11pm-2am Sun-Thu, 11pm-3am Fri & Sat; Ⓜ Chueca
A few steps up the hill from Plaza de Chueca and long a centrepiece of gay

Madrid – a huge statue of a nude male angel guards the doorway – this is an agreeable, dimly lit salon decorated with, among other things, religious icons! It's ideal for quiet conversation and catching the weekend buzz as people plan their forays into the more clamorous clubs in the vicinity.

CAFÉ LA TROJE Map p110 Cafe-Bar
☎ 91 531 05 35; Calle de Pelayo 26; 🕑 2pm-2am; Ⓜ Chueca
A gay reference point for a quiet drink in Chueca, this lovely cafe with ochre shades and candles on the tables is a more sedate alternative to the nonstop action elsewhere in Chueca. Apart from coffee and alcohol, it serves more than 50 different types of tea.

MAMÁ INÉS Map p110 Cafe-Bar
☎ 91 523 23 33; Calle de Hortaleza 22; 🕑 10am-2am Sun-Thu, to 3am Fri & Sat; Ⓜ Gran Vía or Chueca
A gay meeting place with its low lights and low music, this cafe-bar is never sleazy and has a laid-back ambience by day and a romantic air by night. You can get breakfast, yummy pastries and all the gossip on where that night's hot spot will be. There's a steady stream of people coming and going throughout the day and they turn the lights down low and crank up the music as evening turns into night.

UNTIL 3AM
In addition to the places listed here, Polyester (p195) is another good choice.

CLUB 54 STUDIO Map p110 Nightclub
www.studio54madrid.com, in Spanish; Calle de Barbieri 7; 🕑 11.30pm-3.30am Thu-Sat; Ⓜ Chueca
Modelled on the famous New York club Studio 54, this nightclub draws a predominantly gay crowd, but its target market (and door policy) is more upmarket than many in the barrio. Unlike other Madrid nightclubs where paid dancers up on stage try to get things moving, here they let the punters set the pace.

LIQUID MADRID Map p110 Nightclub
www.liquid.es; Calle de Barbieri 7; 🕑 9am-3am Mon-Thu, 9am-3.30am Fri & Sat; Ⓜ Chueca
An essential stop on any gay itinerary through Chueca, Liquid is a little overwhelming with its multiple video screens and endless movement of people (mostly men, mostly

gay, but it's friendly and inclusive whatever your gender or orientation).

AFTER 3AM
A number of Madrid's biggest and best nightclubs have nights aimed squarely at the gay community. For example, Saturday ('Royal') night at Cool (p180) is one of the biggest events on Madrid's weekly gay calendar, as is Saturday ('Sunflowers') night at Macumba (p199). The same could also be said of every night at Why Not? (p197).

SALA BASH/OHM Map pp108-9 Nightclub
Sala Bash; ☎ 91 531 01 32; Plaza del Callao 4; 🕑 midnight-6am Fri & Sat; Ⓜ Callao
The DJs who get you waving your hands in the air like you just don't care have made this club, and its sessions that go by the name of 'Ohm', arguably the No 1 nightspot for Madrid's gay community. The music never strays far from techno-house. Saturdays are slightly more mixed, but it remains a gay icon.

BLACK & WHITE Map p110 Nightclub
☎ 91 531 11 41; www.discoblack-white.net; Calle de la Libertad 34; 🕑 10pm-5.30am Sun-Thu, 10pm-6am Fri & Sat; Ⓜ Chueca
People still talk about the opening party of Black & White way back in 1982 and ever since, it has been a pioneer of Chueca's gay nights. This place is extravagantly gay with drag acts, male strippers (every night except Saturday) and a refreshingly no-holds-barred approach to life. From Wednesday to Saturday, resident DJs Kike Medina and Daniel Colombo prize younger punters out of their embraces and onto the lower dance floor for the Rainbow Party Zone.

SLEEPING
Most Madrid hotels won't bat an eyelid if you're a same-sex couple asking for a double bed. In addition to the budget options listed below, two places that go out of their way to make gay couples welcome are Me by Meliá (p224) and Hotel Óscar (p228). For a guide to price symbols, see p221.

ATRIUM Map pp108-9 Hostel €
☎ 91 523 47 78; www.atriummadrid.es; 3rd fl, Calle de Valverde 3; s/d/tr from €40/60/90; Ⓜ Gran Vía

Playfully bright colours dominate the rooms at this lovely little *hostal* (hostel) which receives an almost exclusively gay clientele. Some of the single rooms are a little small, but it's a five-minute walk from most of the Chueca action and rooms have air-con, a safe and free internet.

CASA CHUECA Map p110 Hostel €

☎ 91 523 81 27; www.casachueca.com; 2nd fl, Calle de San Bartolomé 4; s/d/tr from €40/55/75; Ⓜ Gran Vía

If you don't mind lugging your suitcase up to the 2nd floor, Casa Chueca is outstanding. The rooms are modern, colourful and a cut above your average *hostal*; in keeping with the barrio that it calls home, Casa Chueca places a premium on style. Add casual, friendly service and you'd be hard pressed to find a better price-to-quality ratio anywhere in central Madrid.

CHUECA PENSIÓN Map p110 Hostel €

☎ 91 523 14 73; www.chuecapension.com; 2nd fl, Calle de Gravina 4; s/d/tr €40/60/85; Ⓜ Gran Vía

There are few better Chueca bases than this lovely *pensión*. Features include hardwood floors, free wi-fi and large rooms, while the bright bedspreads add a splash of colour lacking in many *hostales* in this price range. Best of all, Beni Uria, the owner, is a welcoming host. There's no lift (elevator).

HOSTAL LA ZONA Map pp108-9 Hostel €

☎ 91 521 99 04; www.hostallazona.com; 1st fl, Calle de Valverde 7; s/d/tr from €50/60/85; Ⓜ Gran Vía

Catering primarily to a gay clientele, the stylish Hostal La Zona has exposed brickwork, subtle colour shades and wooden pillars. We like a place where a sleep-in is encouraged – breakfast is served from 9am to noon, which is exactly the understanding Madrid's nightlife merits. There's free internet and wi-fi, Arnaldo and Vincent are friendly hosts, and every room has air-con and heating.

FURTHER RESOURCES
MAGAZINES

A few informative free magazines are in circulation in gay bookshops (especially Librería

Berkana (p216), and gay-friendly bars. One is the biweekly *Shanguide*, which is jammed with listings (including saunas and hardcore clubs) and contact ads. Its companion publication *Shangay Express* is better for articles, with a handful of listings and ads. The *Mapa Gaya de Madrid* lists gay bars, clubs and saunas. Also useful is the *Punto Guía de España para Gays y Lesbianas*, a guide for gay and gay-friendly bars, restaurants, hotels and shops around the country. The monthly *MENsual* costs €2.20 at newsstands; there's a web version at www.mensual.com.

WEBSITES

You can also check out the following sites:

Chueca.com (www.chueca.com, in Spanish) Forums, news and reviews.

Gay Madrid 4 U (www.gaymadrid4u.com) A good overview of gay bars and nightclubs.

Night Tours.com (www.nighttours.com/madrid/) A reasonably good guide to gay nightlife and other attractions in Madrid.

Orgullo Gay (www.orgullogay.org, in Spanish, www.gaypridemadrid.com) Website for the gay and lesbian pride march and links to gay organisations across the country.

Shangay (www.shangay.com, in Spanish) Good for upcoming events, music and other reviews.

ORGANISATIONS

The Colectivo de Gais y Lesbianas de Madrid (Cogam; Map pp108-9; ☎ 91 522 45 17; www.cogam.es; Calle de la Puebla 9; Ⓜ Callao or Gran Vía) offers activities, has an info office and social centre, and runs an information line (☎ 91 523 00 70; ☉ 5-9pm Mon-Fri).

The Comunidad de Madrid's Programa de Información y Atención a Homosexuales y Transexuales (Map pp84-5; ☎ 91 701 07 88; 5th fl, Calle de Alcalá 22; ☉ 9am-9pm mid-Sep–mid-Jun, 8am-3pm Mon-Fri mid-Jun–mid-Sep; Ⓜ Sol or Sevilla) also has a toll-free information line (☎ 900 720 569).

The Federación Estatal de Lesbianas, Gays, Transexuales & Bisexuales (Felgt; Map p110; ☎ 91 360 46 05; www.felgt.org; 1st fl, Calle de las Infantas 40; Ⓜ Chueca) is a national advocacy group that played a leading role in lobbying for the legalisation of gay marriages.

Fundación Triángulo (Map pp116-17; ☎ 91 593 05 40; www.fundaciontriangulo.es; 1st fl, Calle de Melendez Valdés 52; Ⓜ Iglesia) is another source of information on gay issues; it has a separate information line, Información LesGai (☎ 91 44 66 394).

lonely planet Hotels & Hostels

Want more sleeping recommendations than we could ever pack into this little ol' book? Craving more detail – including extended reviews and photographs? Want to read reviews by other travellers and be able to post your own? Just make your way over to **lonelyplanet.com/hotels** and check out our thorough list of independent reviews, then reserve your room simply and securely.

SLEEPING

top picks

- **Albergue Juvenil** (p229)
- **Antigua Posada del Pez** (p229)
- **Cat's Hostel** (p223)
- **Hotel Abalú** (p228)
- **Hotel Meninas** (p221)
- **Hotel Óscar** (p228)
- **Hotel Puerta América** (p230)
- **Hotel Urban** (p224)
- **Quo** (p225)

SLEEPING

Madrid's hotel scene is the equal of anywhere in Europe with high-quality accommodation across all price ranges and catering to every taste.

Each barrio has its own distinctive identity and where you decide to stay will play an important role in your experience of Madrid, although all are just a few metro stops from each other. Los Austrias, Sol and Centro put you in the heart of the busy downtown area, while La Latina (the best barrio for tapas) and Lavapiés, and Huertas (nightlife), are good for those who love Madrid nights but don't want to stagger too far to get back to their hotel in the wee small hours. Staying along the Paseo del Prado is ideal for those here to spend most of their time in galleries, while Salamanca is quiet, upmarket and perfect for serial shoppers. You don't have to be gay to stay in Chueca, but you'll love it if you are, while Malasaña is another inner-city barrio with great restaurants and bars. Chamberí removes you from the tourist scrum and lets you experience Madrid as the locals do.

Accommodation that caters primarily (but by no means exclusively) to a gay clientele is found on p217.

ACCOMMODATION STYLES

At the budget end of the market, there are plenty of buzzing backpacker places and cheap hostels for those who value a private room. You'll rarely pay more than €60 for a double room with private bathroom, TV and towels.

Midrange is where there's the widest variety of choice, with charming traditional architecture converted into chic designer hotels offering rooms for prices not seen in other European capitals in decades. These *hoteles con encanto* (hotels with charm) share the market with stylish, modern monuments to 21st-century fashions. Devoid of stuffiness, hotels and *hostales* (hostels) in this category enable you to feel pampered without the price tag.

At the top end of the market, the sky's the limit when it comes to luxury and price, with refined hotels valuing old-world elegance as well as innovative temples to modern design.

Three final things: in Spain a *habitación doble* (double room) usually indicates a room with two single beds; cuddly couples should request a *cama de matrimonio* (literally, a marriage bed). All but the most basic *hostales* have free internet access. And check-out in almost all places is noon.

ROOM RATES

Some top-end places have separate price structures for *temporada alta* (high season), *temporada media* (midseason) or *temporada baja* (low season), all usually displayed on a notice in reception. But there's little agreement among hoteliers about when the seasons actually begin and end, and prices can vary on a daily basis according to occupancy, trade fairs and other major events in Madrid. Many of the top, business-oriented hotels cut good deals for weekend stays. Given this occasionally fluid price structure, accommodation prices in this book are a guide only and you should always check room charges before putting down your bags; and remember that prices can and do change with time. Booking ahead is always a good idea.

APARTMENTS

If you'll be in Madrid for more than a few days and you'd like the comfort and space of your own apartment, consider Apartasol (☎ 91 521 32 42; www.apartasol.com; apt per night €50-115). This traveller-friendly agency has well-equipped modern apartments scattered around the vicinity of the Puerta del Sol and Gran Vía. Prices are first-rate and there are discounts available for longer stays.

Another option are the excellent apartments of Hostal Madrid (p222).

Alternatively, check out the excellent Reserva Madrid (☎ 91 000 69 19; www.reservamadrid.com).

Other places offering apartments or suite-only accommodation include: Hotel Amador de los Ríos (p230); Hostal Madrid (p222); and Suite Prado Hotel (p225).

Virtually all accommodation prices are subject to 7% IVA (the Spanish version of value-added tax). This is often included in the quoted price at cheaper places, but less often at more expensive ones. To check, ask: *'¿Está incluido el IVA?'* ('Is IVA included?'). In some cases you will be charged the IVA only if you ask for a receipt.

LOS AUSTRIAS, SOL & CENTRO

With a wealth of historical sites, accommodation across a range of budgets, transport links fanning out across the city and traditional taverns, restaurants and shops within a stone's throw, this area is a good place to be based. It's also where old Madrid meets the new and can be at once exhilarating and slightly seedy (especially along Calle de la Montera). For more information on the barrio, see p61.

CASA DE MADRID Map pp62-3   Hotel €€€
☎ 91 559 57 91; www.casademadrid.com; 2nd fl, Calle de Arrieta 2; s €195, d €230-285, ste €390; Ⓜ Gran Vía
Refined, extravagantly decorated rooms make Casa de Madrid a luxurious choice overlooking the Teatro Real. The rooms, in an 18th-century building, are awash in antique furnishings and marble busts, with each built around a theme (eg the Spanish Room, the Indian Room, the Damascus Suite) and it's difficult not to feel like royalty here. It's a little like staying at the Ritz but without the price tag.

HOTEL SENATOR Map pp62-3   Hotel €€€
☎ 91 531 41 51; www.playasenator.com; Gran Vía 21; s/d from €145/163; Ⓜ Gran Vía
One of central Madrid's prettiest facades conceals some of the most attractive accommodation in the city centre. Unusually, only one room on each floor doesn't face

onto the street and the views down Gran Vía from the corner rooms are brilliant. Rooms are sophisticated and come with armchairs and, wait for it, reclinable beds.

HOTEL MENINAS Map pp62-3 Boutique Hotel €€
☎ 91 541 28 05; www.hotelmeninas.com; Calle de Campomanes 7; s/d from €109/129; Ⓜ Ópera
This is a classy, cool choice. Opened in 2005, it's the sort of place where an interior designer licked their lips and created a master work of understated, minimalist luxury. The colour scheme is blacks, whites and greys, with dark-wood floors and splashes of fuchsia and lime-green. Flat-screen TVs in every room, modern bathroom fittings, internet access points, and even a laptop in some rooms, round out the clean lines and latest innovations. We love the location as well. We've yet to hear a bad word about this place, and past guests include Viggo Mortensen and Natalie Portman.

HOTEL DE LAS LETRAS
Map pp62-3 Boutique Hotel €€
☎ 91 523 79 80; www.hoteldelasletras.com; Gran Vía 11; d from €100; Ⓜ Gran Vía
If you want to cause a stir in Madrid with a new hotel, make sure it has a rooftop bar overlooking the city. They're all the rage, but Hotel de las Letras started the craze. The bar's wonderful, but the entire hotel is excellent, with individually styled rooms, each with literary quotes from famous writers written on the walls. We don't always get the colour scheme, but it may just come down to personal taste. The building dates from 1917 and the public areas retain original features, including mosaic tiles.

HOTEL VINCCI CAPITOL Map pp62-3 Hotel €€
☎ 91 521 83 91; www.vinccihoteles.com; Gran Vía 41; d €90-206; Ⓜ Callao
Opened in 2007 in the landmark Carrión building, this modern hotel has large rooms with muted tones, and some even have the novelty of circular beds. But what makes it stand out are the views – straight down Gran Vía with its life and grandeur. Not all rooms have views, but there's a 9th-floor viewing area for guests. One local newspaper gave the hotel a '9' for architecture, a '4' for decoration and a '6'

for the comfort of the rooms; they're being a little harsh, but we know what they mean.

HOTEL PRECIADOS Map pp62-3 Hotel €€
☎ 91 454 44 00; www.preciadoshotel.com; Calle de Preciados 37; d €125-200; M Santo Domingo or Callao

With a classier feel than many of the other business options around town, the Preciados gets rave reviews for its service. Soft lighting, light shades and plentiful glass personalise the rooms and provide an intimate feel.

PETIT PALACE POSADA DEL PEINE
Map pp62-3 Boutique Hotel €€
☎ 91 523 81 51; www.hthoteles.com; Calle de Postas 17; d from €130; M Sol

This hotel combines a splendid historic building (dating to 1610), brilliant location (just 50m from the Plaza Mayor) and modern hi-tech rooms. The bathrooms sparkle with stunning fittings and hydromassage showers, and the rooms are beautifully appointed; many historical architectural features remain *in situ* in the public areas. It's just a pity some of the rooms aren't larger.

MARIO ROOM MATE
Map pp62-3 Boutique Hotel €€
☎ 91 548 85 48; www.room-matehoteles.com; Calle de Campomanes 4; s €90-120, d €100-140; M Ópera

Entering this swanky boutique hotel is like crossing the threshold of Madrid's latest nightclub – staff dressed all in black, black walls and swirls of red lighting in the lobby. Rooms can be small but with high ceilings and simple furniture, light tones contrasting smoothly with muted colours and dark surfaces; some rooms are pristine white, others have splashes of colour with zany murals. The first of the Room Mate chain of hotels to open, Mario prides itself on being 'intimate, elegant and serene', and we have to agree with it.

BOOK YOUR STAY ONLINE

For more accommodation reviews and recommendations by Lonely Planet authors, check out the online booking service at lonelyplanet.com. You'll find the true, insider lowdown on the best places to stay. Reviews are thorough and independent. Best of all, you can book online.

HOTEL EUROPA Map pp62-3 Hotel €€
☎ 91 521 29 00; www.hoteleuropa.es; Calle del Carmen 4; s/d from €79/99; M Sol

Around since 1917 but with tastefully renovated rooms, Hotel Europa combines excellent service with modern midrange comforts just a few steps from Puerta del Sol. Here you'll find all the benefits of the central location (including unrivalled convenience and a sense of Madrid's nonstop energy swirling around you) with few of its drawbacks – windows are double-glazed. You pay more for the rooms that overlook the square.

HOTEL LAURA Map pp62-3 Boutique Hotel €€
☎ 91 701 16 70; www.room-matehoteles.com; Travesía de Trujillos 3; d €90-200, ste €150-280; M Sol or Ópera

Another fine offering from the Room Mate chain, Hotel Laura combines location with interiors that are the work of the famous interior designer Tomas Alia. It's all very slick, contemporary and colourful behind the somewhat staid facade. It gets rave reviews from travellers.

HOTEL PLAZA MAYOR Map pp62-3 Hotel €€
☎ 91 360 06 06; www.h-plazamayor.com; Calle de Atocha 2; s €50-70, d €60-130; M Sol or Tirso de Molina

We love this place. Sitting just across from the Plaza Mayor, here you'll find stylish decor, charming original elements of this 150-year-old building and helpful staff. The rooms are attractive, some with a light colour scheme and wrought-iron furniture. The attic rooms (doubles from €130) boast dark wood and designer lamps, and have lovely little terraces with wonderful rooftop views of central Madrid.

HOSTAL MADRID Map pp62-3 Apartments €€
☎ 91 522 00 60; www.hostal-madrid.info; 2nd fl, Calle de Esparteros 6; s €40-60, d €50-78, apt per night €60-150, per month €1200-2100; M Sol

The 19 excellent apartments here range in size from 33 sq metres to 200 sq metres and each has a fully-equipped kitchen, its own sitting area, bathroom and, in the case of the larger ones (room 51 on the 5th floor is one of the best), an expansive terrace with good views over central Madrid. It's a favoured haunt of writers (Gunter Grass wrote one of his novels in room 53), and tastefully modern wrought-iron furniture and attractive colour schemes combine with period pieces throughout. The double rooms are comfortable and well-sized and the service is extremely friendly. It has plans to move the reception down to the ground floor and add more rooms.

HOSTAL ACAPULCO Map pp62-3   Hostel €
☎ 91 531 19 45; www.hostalacapulco.com; 4th fl, Calle de la Salud 13; s/d/tr €52/62/79; Ⓜ Gran Vía
A cut above many other hostels in Madrid, this immaculate little *hostal* has marble floors, recently renovated bathrooms (with bathtubs), double-glazed windows and comfortable beds. Street-facing rooms have balconies overlooking a sunny plaza and are flooded with natural light. The staff are also friendly and always more than happy to help you plan your day in Madrid. There's also free wi-fi and a coffee machine.

HOSTAL LUIS XV Map pp62-3   Hostel €
☎ 91 522 10 21; www.hrluisxv.net, in Spanish; 8th fl, Calle de la Montera 47; s €45-50, d €59-70, tr €80; Ⓜ Gran Vía
Everything here – especially the spacious rooms and the attention to detail – makes this family-run place feel pricier than it is. You'll find it hard to tear yourself away from the balconies outside every exterior room, from where the views are superb (especially from the triple in room 820) and you're so high up that noise is rarely a problem. When you come out the door, head left onto Gran Vía, rather than seedy Calle de la Montera. If the *hostal*'s full, try downstairs at its sister hostel, Hostal Jerez (☎ 91 532 90 73; www.hrjerez.net; 6th fl, Calle de la Montera 47), which has the same prices and similar views.

HOSTAL RIESCO Map pp62-3   Hostel €
☎ 91 522 26 92; www.hostalriesco.es, in Spanish; Calle del Correo 2; s/d €42/55; Ⓜ Sol
Billing itself as Madrid's most central accommodation, Hostal Riesco is a simple, friendly and well-maintained *hostal* with a number of balconies overlooking the Puerta del Sol itself – at least one LP author fell in love with Madrid from one of these balconies.

HOSTEL METROPOL Map pp62-3   Hostel €
☎ 91 521 29 35; www.metropolhostel.com; 1st fl, Calle de la Montera 47; dm €16-21, s/d €45/60; Ⓜ Gran Vía

top picks
FOR BACKPACKERS

- Albergue Juvenil (p229)
- Cat's Hostel (p223)
- International Youth Hostel – La Posada de Huertas (p226)
- Los Amigos Sol Backpackers Hostel (below)
- Mad Hostel (p224)

It's not that the rooms here are great; in fact, they're simple and don't have a whole lot of character. But young travellers congregate here for the easy-going attitude and youthful vibe. You'll also find occasional art exhibitions, plenty of tourist information, staff that merge seamlessly with the travellers, a few comfy chairs, picnic lunches, a laundry and alternative, street-wise advice.

LOS AMIGOS SOL BACKPACKERS HOSTEL Map pp62-3   Hostel €
☎ 91 559 24 72; www.losamigoshostel.com; 4th fl, Calle de Arenal 26; dm €17-20, d €50; Ⓜ Ópera or Sol
If you arrive in Madrid keen for company, this could be the place for you – lots of students stay here, the staff are savvy (and speak English) and there are bright dorm-style rooms (with free lockers) that sleep from two to four people. Prices include breakfast and there's a kitchen for guests. A steady stream of repeat visitors is the best recommendation we can give.

LA LATINA & LAVAPIÉS
Places to stay are pretty thin on the ground in these two barrios, but the entirely budget choices here are removed from the clamorous streets of downtown and yet still close enough to get around the centre on foot. For more information on the barrio, see p74.

Although yet to open at the time of writing, Posada del Dragón (Map pp76-7; Calle de la Cava Baja 14), a new boutique hotel set in a historic building in one of La Latina's best locations promises to be one of the best places to stay.

CAT'S HOSTEL Map pp76-7   Hostel €
☎ 91 369 28 07; www.catshostel.com; Calle de Cañizares 6; dm/d from €15/42; Ⓜ Antón Martín

Forming part of a 17th-century palace, the internal courtyard here is Madrid's finest – lavish Andalucian tilework, a fountain, a spectacular glass ceiling and stunning Islamic decoration, surrounded on four sides by an open balcony. There's a super-cool basement bar with free internet and fiestas, often with live music. One small complaint: Cat's standards of maintenance haven't quite kept pace with its popularity.

MAD HOSTEL Map pp76-7 Hostel €
☎ 915 06 48 40; www.madhostel.com; Calle de Cabeza 24; dm from €15; Ⓜ Antón Martín
From the people who brought you Cat's Hostel, Mad Hostel is similarly filled with life. The 1st-floor courtyard – with retractable roof – re-creates an old Madrid *corrala* (a traditional Madrid tenement block with long communal balconies built around a central courtyard) and is a wonderful place to chill, while the four- to eight-bed rooms are smallish but clean. There's a small, rooftop gym equipped with state-of-the-art equipment. Great choice.

HOSTAL HORIZONTE Map pp76-7 Hostel €
☎ 91 369 09 96; www.hostalhorizonte.com; 2nd fl, Calle de Atocha 28; s with shared/private bathroom €29/40, d €44/55; Ⓜ Antón Martín
Billing itself as a hostel run by travellers for travellers, Hostal Horizonte is a well-run place. The rooms have far more character than your average hostel, with high ceilings, deliberately old-world furnishings and modern bathrooms. The King Alfonso XII room (€72) is especially well presented. All in all, it's a good package.

HOSTAL BARRERA off Map pp76-7 Hostel €
☎ 91 527 53 81; www.hostalbarrera.com; 2nd fl, Calle de Atocha 96; s/d €50/65; Ⓜ Antón Martín
This place gets consistently good reports from travellers, as much for its clean rooms and friendly service as for the terrific location just up the hill from Madrid's big three art galleries. All rooms face onto the street and have double-glazed windows.

HUERTAS & ATOCHA

If you're opening a swish new designer hotel in Madrid, Huertas seems to be the place to do it. Some of the most exciting new upmarket hotels are here in a barrio that seems hell-bent on reinventing itself as the Spanish capital's home of accommodation chic. Huertas nights will, however, quickly bring you back down to earth: going to sleep in Huertas can seem like something of a lost cause on weekends, although, thankfully, most newer places have double-glazed windows. For more information on the sights of the barrio, see p82.

Although not yet open at the time of writing, the respected NH chain of hotels (www.nh-hotels.com) was due to inaugurate a new landmark property, the NH Palacio de Teda (Map pp84-5; Calle de San Sebastián 2). The combination of location, a mere stone's throw from the Plaza de Santa Ana, and the heritage properties of this 18th-century building suggest that this will be one to watch.

HOTEL URBAN Map pp84-5 Hotel €€€
☎ 91 787 77 70; www.derbyhotels.com; Carrera de San Jerónimo 34; d/ste from €190/250; Ⓜ Sevilla
This towering glass edifice is the epitome of art-inspired designer cool. With its clean lines and original artworks from Africa and Asia (there's a small museum dedicated to Egyptian art in the basement), it's a wonderful antidote to the more classic charm of Madrid's five-star hotels of longer standing. Dark-wood floors and dark walls are offset by plenty of light, while the dazzling bathrooms have wonderful designer fittings – the washbasins are sublime. The rooftop swimming pool is one of Madrid's best and the gorgeous terrace is heaven on a candle-lit summer's evening. If money were no object, we would need a good reason to stay anywhere else.

ME BY MELIÁ Map pp84-5 Hotel €€€
☎ 91 701 60 00; www.me-by-melia.com; Plaza de Santa Ana 14; d without/with plaza view from €182/230; Ⓜ Sol or Antón Martín
Once the landmark Gran Victoria Hotel, the Madrid home of many a famous bullfighter, this audacious new hotel is fast becoming a landmark of a different kind. Overlooking the western end of Plaza de Santa Ana, this luxury hotel is decked out in minimalist white with curves and comfort in all the right places; this is one place where it's definitely worth paying extra for the view, quite apart from the additional space that you'll have in the plaza-facing Supreme rooms. Its two bars – the Penthouse and Midnight Rose (see p185) – are as lavish as the hotel.

CATALONIA LAS CORTES
Map pp84-5   Hotel €€
☎ 91 389 60 51; www.hoteles-catalonia.es; Calle del Prado 6; d €99-169; Ⓜ Antón Martín
Occupying an 18th-century palace and renovated in a style faithful to the era, this elegant hotel is a terrific choice right in the heart of Huertas. It's something of an oasis surrounded by the nonstop energy of the barrio's streets and the service is discreet and attentive. It gets plenty of return visitors which is just about the best recommendation we can give.

QUO
Map pp84-5   Boutique Hotel €€
☎ 91 532 90 49; www.hotelesquo.com; Calle de Sevilla 4; d €90-217; Ⓜ Sevilla
Quo is one of Madrid's boutique hotels of longer standing and it's still deservedly popular. The rooms have minimalist designer furniture, tall ceilings and huge windows that let light flood in. The colour scheme is black and red, with light surfaces providing perfect contrast and a resolutely contemporary look. We're also big fans of the bathrooms, with glass doors, glass benches and stainless-steel basins. All rooms have flat-screen TVs, black-and-white photos of Madrid, dark-wood floors and comfy armchairs; rooms on the 7th floor have Jacuzzis and private terraces with terrific views over the rooftops.

HOTEL ALICIA
Map pp84-5   Boutique Hotel €€
☎ 91 389 60 95; www.room-matehoteles.com; Calle del Prado 2; d €105-165, ste from €200; Ⓜ Sol, Sevilla or Antón Martín
One of the landmark properties of the designer Room Mate chain of hotels, Hotel Alicia overlooks Plaza de Santa Ana with beautiful, spacious rooms. The style (the work of designer Pascua Ortega) is a touch more muted than in other Room Mate hotels, but the supermodern look remains intact, the downstairs bar is oh-so-cool, and the service is young and switched on. Two of the duplex suites have their own terrace with a small private pool.

SUITE PRADO HOTEL
Map pp84-5   Suites €€
☎ 91 420 23 18; www.suiteprado.com; Calle de Manuel Fernández y González 10; s €99-126, d €115-160; Ⓜ Sevilla
The spacious modern suites at this centrally located hotel have plenty of space and are semi-luxurious, although they don't have a

whole lot of character; some are cavernous, as if the decorators didn't quite know what to do with so much space. All have sitting rooms, good bathrooms and kitchenettes, and the location is good.

HOTEL EL PASAJE
Map pp84-5   Hotel €€
☎ 91 521 29 95; www.elpasajehs.com; Calle del Pozo 4; d Sun-Thu €91, Fri & Sat €113; Ⓜ Sol
If you were to choose your ideal location in Huertas, Hotel El Pasaje would be hard to beat. Set on a quiet lane largely devoid of bars, yet just around the corner from the Plaza de la Puerta del Sol, it combines a central location with a quiet night's sleep, at least by the standards of Huertas. The feel is intimate and modern (except for the tired-coloured bedspreads – what were they thinking?), with good bathrooms, minibars and enough space to leave your suitcase without tripping over it. The twins have balconies; the doubles are on the inside of the building.

HOTEL MIAU
Map pp84-5   Hotel €€
☎ 91 369 71 20; www.hotelmiau.com; Calle del Príncipe 26; s/d from €85/95; Ⓜ Sol or Antón Martín
If you want to be close to the nightlife of Huertas or can't tear yourself away from the beautiful Plaza de Santa Ana, then Hotel Miau is your place. Light tones, splashes of colour and modern art adorn the walls of the rooms, which are large and well equipped. It can be noisy, but you chose Huertas…

HOTEL EL PRADO
Map pp84-5   Hotel €€
☎ 91 369 02 34; www.pradohotel.com; Calle del Prado 11; s €70-140, d €75-195, ste €100-250; Ⓜ Antón Martín or Sevilla
This is one of Madrid's most welcoming three-star hotels, offering style and service beyond its modest rating. There's a wine theme running throughout the spacious rooms, which have parquet floors, light tones, and places to sit and write. The double-glazed windows are also important, especially if you're here on a weekend, when prices are at their cheapest.

CHIC & BASIC COLORS
Map pp84-5   Hostel €€
☎ 91 429 69 35; www.chicandbasic.com; 2nd fl, Calle de las Huertas 14; s/d from €62/78, apt from €96; Ⓜ Antón Martín
It's all about colours here at this fine little hostel. The rooms are white in a minimalist

style with free internet, flat-screen TVs, dark hardwood floors with a bright colour scheme superimposed on top, with every room a different shade. It's all very comfortable, contemporary and casual. Only three of the rooms look out onto the street, but those on the inside of the building don't feel quite as claustrophobic as in some places. Prices increase by €10 per room on Friday and Saturday. It also has some apartments in the same building and the slightly more upmarket hotel Chic & Basic Atocha (Map pp84-5; ☎ 91 369 2895; Calle de Atocha 113; s/d from €80/100; Ⓜ Antón Martín).

HOTEL VICTORIA 4 Map pp84-5 Hotel €€
☎ 91 523 84 30; www.hotelvictoria4.com; Calle de Victoria 4; d incl breakfast €75-150; Ⓜ Sol
We like a place where you can feel like you're in an oasis of calm even as carousing crowds pass by your front door. A great location, handy for some of Madrid's best nightlife, and attractive, well-equipped rooms add up to a package that represents outstanding value for the centre of a major European capital. It also has plans for a rooftop bar.

HOSTAL SARDINERO Map pp84-5 Hostel €
☎ 91 429 57 56; www.hostalsardinero.com; 3rd fl, Calle del Prado 16; s €42-52, d €50-65, tr €68-75; Ⓜ Sol or Antón Martín
A change of owners here has brought more than just a fresh lick of paint, new mattresses and new TVs. The cheerful rooms, which have high ceilings, air-conditioning, a safe, hairdryers and renovated bathrooms, are complemented nicely by the equally cheerful Nieves and Jimmy who are attentive without being in your face. We especially like the light-filled room 5 (a triple), but all the rooms are well turned out.

HOSTAL ADRIANO Map pp84-5 Hostel €
☎ 91 521 13 39; www.hostaladriano.com; 4th fl, Calle de la Cruz 26; s/d/tr €53/65/85; Ⓜ Sol
They don't come any better than this bright and friendly hostel wedged in the streets that mark the boundary between Sol and Huertas. Most rooms are well sized and each has its own colour scheme. Indeed, more thought has gone into the decoration than in your average hostel, from the bed covers to the pictures on the walls. On the same floor, the owners run the Hostal Adria Santa Ana (Map pp84-5; www.hostaladriasantaana.com;

top picks

LAP OF LUXURY

- Hotel Ritz (below)
- Westin Palace (opposite)
- Hotel Puerta América (p230)
- Hotel Urban (p224)
- Hotel AC Santo Mauro (p229)

s/d/tr €60/70/90), which is a step up in price, style and comfort. Both hostels drop their prices even further in the height of summer.

INTERNATIONAL YOUTH HOSTEL – LA POSADA DE HUERTAS
Map pp84-5 Hostel €
☎ 91 429 55 26; www.posadadehuertas.com; Calle de las Huertas 21; dm €18-21; Ⓜ Antón Martín
There's no better place to base yourself if you've come to Madrid to party and prefer to spend your money on your drinks rather than your bed. Rooms are simple, modern bog-standard four- to 10-bed dorms (separated by gender), and include free internet, breakfast, locker, and your own key that lets you come and go as you please. Staff are young and live Madrid's nightlife when they're not working; they're happy to advise on the latest in places.

PASEO DEL PRADO & EL RETIRO

If your main reason for being in Madrid is to visit the three major art galleries – the Museo del Prado, Museo Thyssen-Bornemisza and Centro de Art Reina – the elegant surrounds of the Paseo del Prado should be your location of choice. The lovely Parque del Buen Retiro is another of the joys of staying here. For more information on the barrio, see p90.

HOTEL RITZ Map p91 Hotel €€€
☎ 91 701 67 67; www.ritzmadrid.com; Plaza de la Lealtad 5; d from €280, ste €1100-5000; Ⓜ Banco de España
The grand old lady of Madrid, the Hotel Ritz is the height of exclusivity. One of the most lavish buildings in the city, it has classic style and impeccable service that is second to none. Unsurprisingly it's the favoured

hotel of presidents, kings and celebrities. The public areas are palatial and awash with antiques, while the rooms are extravagantly large, opulent and supremely comfortable. In the Royal Suite, the walls are covered with raw silk and there's a personal butler to wait upon you. We challenge you to find a more indulgent hotel experience anywhere in Spain.

WESTIN PALACE Map p91 Hotel €€€

☎ 91 360 80 00; www.westinpalacemadrid.com; Plaza de las Cortes 7; d from €215, ste from €650; Ⓜ Banco de España or Antón Martín

An old Madrid classic, this former palace of the Duque de Lerma opened as a hotel in 1911 and was Spain's second luxury hotel. Ever since, it has looked out across Plaza de Neptuno at its rival, the Ritz, like a lover unjustly scorned. Its name may not have the world-famous cachet of the Ritz, but it's not called the Palace for nothing and is extravagant in all the right places. After the snooty Ritz banned actors and other public performers in the early 20th century, the Palace became the hotel of choice for celebrities – Mata Hari lived here during WWI and her ghost reportedly occupies the corridors, while Hemingway, Dalí and Lorca were all regulars in the cocktail bar. The 1999 renovations cost €144,000 per room.

NH PASEO DEL PRADO Map p91 Hotel €€

☎ 91 330 24 00; www.nh-hotels.com; Plaza de Cánovas del Castillo 4; d €96-200, ste from €165; Ⓜ Atocha or Banco de España

A stone's throw from both the Museo del Prado and Museo Thyssen-Bornemisza, this fine hotel, which belongs to the excellent NH chain of hotels, is probably the pick of the midrange choices arrayed along the *paseo's* shores. The standard or superior rooms have a contemporary look with muted colour tones, while the suites favour a more classic look with antique furnishings. The onsite tapas bar, Estado Puro (p91), is a terrific place to eat.

HOTEL MORA Map p91 Hotel €

☎ 91 420 15 69; www.hotelmora.com; Paseo del Prado 32; s €46-65, d €58-83; Ⓜ Atocha

Alongside the landmark Caixa Forum, close to the main museums and a short (uphill) walk from the city centre, this simple, friendly hotel is a well-located and extremely well-priced option. Rooms are a little sparse

top picks

DESIGNER HOTELS

- Hotel Puerta América (p230)
- Hotel Urban (p224)
- Hotel Meninas (p221)
- Hotel Óscar (p228)
- Quo (p225)
- Me by Meliá (p224)
- Adler Hotel (below)
- Amador de los Ríos Espahotel (p230)
- Hotel Abalú (p228)

and the furnishings a little tired, but they're spacious and clean, and some look out across the Paseo del Prado.

SALAMANCA

Salamanca is Madrid's most exclusive address, home to suitably grand sights and the best shopping that the city has to offer. It's generally a quieter choice than anywhere else in the capital and good restaurants abound. For more information on the barrio, see p100.

ADLER HOTEL Map p102 Boutique Hotel €€€

☎ 91 426 32 20; www.adlermadrid.com; Calle de Velázquez 33; d from €250; Ⓜ Velázquez

A five-star boutique hotel at the intersection of two of Salamanca's iconic streets, the Adler combines classy and supremely comfortable rooms with near-faultless service. Room decor subscribes to a vaguely old-world elegance, but is light-filled and never stuffy.

PETIT PALACE ART GALLERY

Map p102 Hotel €€

☎ 91 435 54 11; www.hthoteles.com; Calle de Jorge Juan 17; d €120-220; Ⓜ Serrano

Occupying a stately 19th-century Salamanca building, this relatively new addition to the Petit Palace chain, this lovely designer hotel combines hi-tech facilities with an artistic aesthetic with loads of original works dotted around the public spaces and even in some of the rooms. Hydro-massage showers, laptop computers and exercise bikes in many rooms are just some of the extras, and the address is ideal for the best of Salamanca.

HESPERÍA HERMOSILLA Map p102 Hotel €€
☎ 91 246 88 00; www.hesperia.com; Calle de la
Hermosilla; d from €84; Ⓜ Serrano
If you're here on a mission to shop or you
otherwise value quiet, exclusive streets away
from the noise, this modern and subtly
stylish hotel is a terrific choice. The furnishings
are vaguely minimalist, especially in the
public areas, and LCD flat-screen TVs and
other creature comforts are rare luxuries in
this price range.

MALASAÑA & CHUECA
Staying in Malasaña or Chueca keeps you
within walking distance of (or a short metro
ride from) most of Madrid's major sights but
immerses you in the sometimes gritty, usually cool personalities of these two inner-city
barrios. There's not a lot to see here – a few
museums is about it – but both barrios are
wonderful places to eat out or drink the night
away. It's a generally young vibe, and Chueca
can be extravagantly gay, but it's almost
always inclusive regardless of your age or
sexual orientation.

For a list of particularly gay-friendly places
to stay, see p217.

SIETE ISLAS HOTEL Map pp108-9 Hotel €€
☎ 91 523 46 88; www.hotelsieteislas.com;
Calle de Valverde 14-16; s/d from €103/114;
Ⓜ Gran Vía
Rooms here are attractive and although
probably not quite worth the four stars it
claims, very comfortable. They come with
generous, marble-lined bathrooms and
cool beige-and-navy-blue tones throughout.
The owners hail from the Canary Islands
and each room is themed to a different
village from the islands.

PETIT PALACE HOTEL DUCAL
Map pp108-9 Hotel €€
☎ 91 521 10 43; www.hthoteles.com; Calle de
Hortaleza 3; d from €80; Ⓜ Gran Vía
Fusing elegant old buildings with state-of-
the-art rooms and hi-tech facilities is the
hallmark here. The rooms boast strong,
contrasting colours, polished floorboards,
clean lines, comfy beds and armchairs, and
plenty of light and mirrors. Each room also
has its own computer with free internet.
The hi-tech theme continues in the bathrooms, where hydromassage showers
are standard.

top picks

HOTEL CHAINS
- AC (www.ac-hoteles.com)
- Hi Tech (www.hthoteles.com)
- NH (www.nh-hotels.com)
- Room Mate (www.room-matehoteles.com)
- Vincci (www.vinccihoteles.com)

HOTEL ABALÚ Map pp108-9 Boutique Hotel €€
☎ 91 531 47 44; www.hotelabalu.com; Calle del Pez
19; s/d from €74/90, ste from €140; Ⓜ Noviciado
You may love the mean streets of Malasaña,
but that doesn't mean you want to sleep
rough. At last, Malasaña has its own
boutique hotel, an oasis of style amid the
barrio's timeworn feel. Suitably located on
the uncharacteristically cool Calle del Pez,
each room here has its own design drawn
from the imagination of Luis Delgado, from
retro chintz to Zen, Baroque and pure white
and most aesthetics in between. Some of
the suites have Jacuzzis and large-screen
home cinemas. You're close to Gran Vía,
but away from the tourist scrum.

HOTEL ÓSCAR Map p110 Boutique Hotel €€
☎ 91 701 11 73; www.room-matehoteles.com;
Plaza Vázquez de Mella 12; d €90-200, ste €150-
280; Ⓜ Gran Vía
Outstanding. Hotel Óscar belongs to the
highly original Room Mate chain of hotels
and the designer rooms ooze style and
sophistication. Some have floor-to-ceiling
murals, the lighting is always funky, and
the colour scheme is asplash with pinks,
lime greens, oranges or a more minimalist
black and white. Like all Room Mate hotels,
this one's themed around an individual
personality, in this case Óscar, who describes
himself as 'nocturnal, cosmopolitan and
ready for anything'. The facade – with
thousands of hanging Coca-Cola bottles –
is a striking local landmark, there's a fine
street-level tapas bar and a rooftop
terrace (p193).

FLAT 5 MADRID Map pp108-9 Hostel €
☎ 91 127 24 00; www.flat5madrid.com; 5th fl, Calle
de San Bernardo 55; d with shared bathroom €40-60,
with private bathroom €60-100; Ⓜ Noviciado
Unlike so many other hostels in Madrid
where the charm depends on a timeworn

air, Flat 5 Madrid has a fresh, clean-lined look with bright colours, flat-screen TVs, free wi-fi, air-con and heating and flower boxes on the window sills. Even the rooms that face onto a patio have partial views over the rooftops. If the rooms and bathrooms were a little bigger, we'd consider moving in.

ANTIGUA POSADA DEL PEZ
Map pp108-9   Hostel €

☎ 91 531 42 96; www.antiguaposadadelpez.com; Calle de Pizarro 16; s €40-120, d €50-150; Ⓜ Noviciado

If only all places to stay were this good. This place inhabits the shell of an historic Malasaña building, but the rooms are slick and contemporary with designer bathrooms. You're also just a few steps up the hill from Calle del Pez, one of Malasaña's most happening streets. It's an exceptionally good deal, even when prices head upwards.

HOSTAL SAN LORENZO Map p110   Hostel €
☎ 91 521 30 57; www.hotel-sanlorenzo.com; Calle de Clavel 8; s/d/tr from €40/50/70; Ⓜ Gran Vía

Hostal San Lorenzo is generally an excellent deal: original stone walls and some dark-wood beams from the 19th century in the public areas, and modern, comfortable and bright rooms (some with splashes of old-world charm) that you'll be more than happy to return to at the end of the day. Some of the rooms could be larger and, depending on who you encounter, the service can be a little off-hand.

HOSTAL DON JUAN Map p110   Hostel €
☎ /fax 91 522 31 01; 2nd fl, Plaza de Vázquez de Mella 1; s/d/tr €38/53/71; Ⓜ Gran Vía

Paying cheap rates for your room doesn't mean you can't be treated like a king. This elegant two-storey *hostal* is filled with original artworks and antique furniture that could grace a royal palace, although mostly it's restricted to the public areas. Rooms are large and simple but luminous; most have a street-facing balcony. The location is good, close to where Chueca meets Gran Vía.

HOSTAL AMÉRICA Map p110   Hostel €
☎ 91 522 64 48; www.hostalamerica.net; 5th fl, Calle de Hortaleza 19; s/d €38/48; Ⓜ Gran Vía

Run by a lovely mother-son-dog team, the América has super-clean, spacious and IKEA-dominated rooms. As most rooms face onto the usual interior 'patio' of the build-

ing, you should get a good night's sleep despite the busy area. For the rest of the time, there's an expansive terrace – quite a luxury for a hostel in downtown Madrid – with tables, chairs and a coffee machine. There's free wi-fi, but if you're too far down the hall, the connection can be tenuous.

ALBERGUE JUVENIL Map p110   Hostel €
☎ 91 593 96 88; www.ajmadrid.es; Calle de Mejía Lequerica 21; dm €19-25; Ⓜ Bilbao or Alonso Martínez

If you're looking for dormitory-style accommodation, you'd need a good reason to stay anywhere other than here while you're in Madrid. Opened in 2007, the Albergue has spotless rooms, no dorm houses more than six beds (each has its own bathroom), and facilities include a pool table, a gymnasium, wheelchair access, free internet, laundry and a TV/DVD room with a choice of movies. All the facilities are super-modern, and breakfast is included in the price. Yes, there are places with more character or a more central location, but we'd still rate this as one of Madrid's best hostels for backpackers.

CHAMBERÍ & ARGÜELLES

The least-touristed of Madrid's major barrios, Chamberí offers the chance to closely experience Madrid life as locals live it. Although there are few major sights to speak of, you'll share the barrio's streets with local children in playgrounds or on their way to and from school, and people popping down to their local bar for a drink – it has bars, shops, cinemas, restaurants and open squares in just the right measure. There aren't many places to stay (and none in Argüelles), but those that are here are excellent, and you're only a short metro ride from the main sites of interest. For more information on the barrio, see p114.

HOTEL AC SANTO MAURO
Map pp116-17   Hotel €€€

☎ 91 319 69 00; www.ac-hotels.com; Calle de Zurbano 36; d €200-375, ste €425-1150; Ⓜ Alonso Martínez

Everything about this recently renovated place oozes exclusivity and class, from the address – one of the elite patches of Madrid real estate – to the 19th-century mansion that's the finest in a barrio of many.

It's a place of discreet elegance and warm service, and rooms are suitably lavish, with a predominantly modern aesthetic in some rooms and a more old-world look (with Persian carpets on the floor) in others; the Arabian-styled indoor pool isn't bad either. David Beckham may well be derided for many things, but the fact that he chose to make this his home for six months certainly suggests he has a higher degree of taste than people usually give him credit for. Madonna and Richard Gere have been other notable guests.

HOTEL AMADOR DE LOS RÍOS
Map pp116-17   Boutique Hotel €€
☎ 91 310 75 00; www.amadordelosrios.com; Calle de Amador de los Ríos 3; s/d from €80/92; Ⓜ Colón
Tucked away in an exclusive corner of Chamberí and just set back in behind the Paseo de la Castellana, Amador de los Ríos is a terrific hotel where all the rooms are apartments or suites. The interior design by Pascual Ortega blends the classic with the contemporary and the rooftop swimming pool is pure luxury. The rooms themselves are bathed in warm colours with soft lighting.

HOTEL TRAFALGAR Map pp116-17   Hotel €€
☎ 91 445 62 00; www.hotel-trafalgar.com; Calle de Trafalgar 35; s/d from €70/100; Ⓜ Quevedo
If you asked madrileños where they would most like to live, the chances are it would be within a 1km radius of this hotel. The hotel itself is modern and comfortable, with good-sized rooms and all the mod-cons (in-room movies, internet and good bathrooms). There's not a lot of character, but you'll love strolling down to the Plaza de Olavide for breakfast.

NORTHERN MADRID
It may not be the most romantic barrio in which to stay, but Northern Madrid is home to what is arguably the city's most original hotel.

HOTEL PUERTA AMÉRICA
Map p121   Hotel €€€
☎ 917 44 54 00; www.hotelpuertamerica.com; Avenida de América 41; d/ste from €117/235; Ⓜ Cartagena
When the owners of this hotel saw their location – halfway between the city and the airport – they knew they had to do something special, to build a self-contained world so innovative and luxurious that you'll never want to leave. Their idea? Give 22 of world architecture's most creative names (eg Zaha Hadid, Sir Norman Foster, Ron Arad, David Chipperfield, Jean Nouvel) a floor each to design. The result? An extravagant pastiche of styles, from zany montages of 1980s chic to bright-red bathrooms that feel like a movie star's dressing room. Even the bar ('a temple to the liturgy of pleasure'), restaurant, facade, gardens, public lighting and car park had their own architects. It's an extraordinary, astonishing place.

DAY TRIPS

DAY TRIPS

Located as it is in the geographical heart of Spain, Madrid is an ideal base for exploring the country. Well-developed road and rail networks fan out across the peninsula, with a host of beautiful historical towns and other sights within easy reach of the capital.

If you're a city person, Toledo, Segovia and Ávila are an hour away from Madrid by train. A visit to these cities takes you on a journey through the country's polyglot history, from the soaring Roman remains of Segovia, to the medieval defensive battlements of Ávila and the grand monuments to religious enlightenment in Toledo.

If you're needing a break from city life, villages like Chinchón and those of the Sierra de Guadarrama or Sierra Pobre provide an antidote. In the sierras, you can also leave behind the last outposts of civilisation and hike out into the wilderness and still be back in Madrid for a late dinner. Alcalá de Henares straddles the two experiences, with all the life and energy of an elegant university town and the intimacy of a large village.

The royals who have always made Madrid their capital also understood that a country retreat was sometimes necessary from all the noise of the city. From a ledge in the mountains to the west of the city, San Lorenzo de El Escorial is one of the most extraordinary palace-monasteries in Spain. South of Madrid, Aranjuez is equally eye-catching, with a stately palace surrounded by monumental gardens. And on any of the day trips covered in this chapter, you'll find restaurants where you can eat like a king.

Although you could easily stray further and make it back to Madrid by nightfall, you'd be rushing to do so. For this reason, we have restricted our coverage in this chapter to places that require no more than a two-hour round trip. We understand, however, that if you have more time, you may wish to stay overnight in cities such as Toledo, Segovia and Ávila with their many attractions – for this reason we've included a handful of sleeping options.

BEAUTIFUL CITIES

Toledo (p234) is a grandly austere city that once rivalled Madrid for the role of capital. Coming here is like stepping back into the Middle Ages, into a history when Christians, Muslims and Jews turned this into one of Spain's most enlightened cities. Ávila (p241), too, resonates with history, most notably in its imposing cathedral and encircling medieval walls. The Unesco World Heritage-listed old city of Segovia (p238) has an entirely different, light-filled charm as it surveys the surrounding mountains from its hill-top perch. The exceptional *alcázar* (Muslim-era fortress) and Roman-era aqueduct are its signature sights, but it's also a place where eating is an art form.

ROYAL PLAYGROUNDS

The imposing 16th-century monastery and palace complex of San Lorenzo de El Escorial (p244) guards the gateway to Madrid from the northwest and is a terrific excursion. Nearby the Valle de los Caídos (p245) is a curious monument to General Francisco Franco's delusions of grandeur – not royalty, but he would have liked to have been. Graceful Aranjuez (p246) is home to a magnificent palace and expansive

---

FIESTAS & FESTIVALS

It's worth planning a trip to coincide with some of the extravagant fiestas going on in the towns around Madrid:

- Semana Santa (Easter week) Elaborate, sombre processions by pointy-hatted penitents fill Toledo, Ávila and Chinchón for one of the year's holiest festivals.
- Corpus Christi, Toledo (on the Thursday after Trinity Sunday, eight weeks after Easter Sunday) Several days of festivities culminate in a solemn procession.
- Fiesta Mayor, Chinchón (2nd to 3rd week of August) The town's splendid plaza is turned into a bullring each morning.
- Santa Teresa, Ávila (around 15 October) Held in honour of Saint Teresa, this festival sees the town indulge in days of celebrations and processions.

Olmedo
To Valladolid (112km)
Coca
Arévalo
N-601
N-VI
CASTILLA Y LEÓN
N-403
To Salamanca (138km)
Villacastín
A6
N-VI
Zarzuela del Monte
Cuéllar
Navalmanzano
Carbonero el Mayor
Turégano
N-110
Segovia (p238)
La Granja de San Ildefonso
Sierra de Guadarrama (p248)
N-603
Puerto de Navacerrada
Navacerrada

Parque Natural del Hoz Duratón
Sepúlveda
Riaza
Ayllón
Atienza
Puerto de Somosierra
Sierra Pobre (p248)
N-1
Buitrago
Embalse de El Villar
Canencia
Embalse de El Atazar
M-604
To Zaragoza (248km); Barcelona (549km)
Río Henares
Brihuega
Torija
N-II

Manzanares el Real
Soto del Real
Guadalix de la Sierra
El Molar
N-320
Guadalajara
Moralzarzal
M-614
M-607
N1
Río Jarama
Azuqueca de Henares
CASTILLA-LA MANCHA

Ávila (p241)
Valle de Los Caídos (p245)
San Lorenzo de El Escorial (p244)
Guadarrama
El Escorial
Collado-Villalba
COMUNIDAD DE MADRID
Colmenar Viejo
San Sebastián de los Reyes
Alcobendas
M-100
Barajas Airport
Alcalá de Henares (p247)
Pastrana
M-505
N-403
CASTILLA Y LEÓN
El Barraco
El Tiemblo
Sierra de Gredos
San Martín de Valdeiglesias
M-600
A6
Majadahonda
MADRID
Alcorcón
Móstoles
Leganés
Getafe
San Fernando de Henares
Nuevo Baztán
Arganda del Rey
M-404
M-311
San Martín de la Vega
Escalona
N-V
Río Alberche
N-IV
N-III
Tarancón
N-400

Val de Santo Domingo
N-V
Río Guadarrama
N-401
Chinchón (p247)
Río Tajo
Aranjuez (p246)
Ocaña
N-400
N-III
N-403
CASTILLA-LA MANCHA
Olías del Rey
N-400
La Puebla de Montalbán
Río Tajo
Toledo (p234)
Nambroca
N-301
Los Navalmorales
Mascaraque
N-IV
Los Navalucillos
Navahermosa
Orgaz
Quintanar de la Orden
Montes de Toledo
C-400
Mota del Cuervo
Consuegra
Madridejos
Camuñas
Campo de Criptana
N-420
N-403
Alcázar de San Juan
Puerto Lapice
Río Guadiana
0   50 km
0   30 miles
Malagón
Parque Nacional De Las Tablas De Daimiel
To Córdoba (310km); Sevilla (360km); Málaga (380km)

gardens, and now serves as a fine retreat from the noise and bustle of Madrid just as it did for Spanish royalty down through the ages.

VILLAGES & MOUNTAINS

Chinchón (p247), southeast of Madrid, has a stunning, ramshackle charm; its uneven, porticoed Plaza Mayor ranks among Spain's most enchanting plazas. Chinchón is also a fine place for eating. Alcalá de Henares (p247), east of the capital, has almost outgrown its village origins, but is worth as much time as you can give it. It was the birthplace of Miguel de Cervantes and is still home to one of Spain's oldest universities and distinguished architecture. Protecting Madrid from the north, the Sierra de Guadarrama (p248) and Sierra Pobre (p248) shelter charming old villages, including Manzanares El Real (p248) and Buitrago (p248).

TOLEDO

Toledo is an imperial and imperious city, a one-time crossroads of religions, its architecture looking for all the world like the Middle East grafted onto Spanish soil with mosques, synagogues and a labyrinth of narrow streets, plazas and inner patios. Rising above it all is the Gothic grandeur of the cathedral and forbidding *alcázar*, which survey the surrounding country from a rocky ridge high above the Río Tajo.

'Toletum', as the Romans called it, was always a strategically important city. In the 6th century it was the capital of the Visigoth empire and after AD 711 it became an important Muslim centre of power. Under the Muslims Toledo was a flourishing centre of art, culture and religion, a multifaith city, which was home to peacefully coexisting Jews, Christians and Muslims. Alfonso VI wrestled the city back into Christian hands in 1085, and shortly after it was declared 'the seat of the Church' in Spain. This marked the beginning of a golden age where Toledo's power knew few limits, a state of affairs that lasted through the Inquisition and into the 16th century.

But too powerful for its own good, Toledo was bypassed as capital in 1561 as a nervous Felipe II favoured the more compliant and then-less-grand Madrid as its seat of power. Ever since, Toledo has glowered out across the plains.

The old city and the most important sights are stacked stone upon stone in a crook of the Río Tajo. The hills here make for a steep climb up to the centre; for a more relaxing view of the old city, hop on the Zoco Tren (☎ 925 23 22 10; www.zocotren.com; adult/child €4.25/1.85), a small train that does a 45-minute loop up the hill and through Toledo. The train leaves hourly into the early evening and tickets are available from the tourist office.

Toledo lacks a true centre – its rich concentration of monuments is scattered throughout the old city – but the Plaza de Zocodover, at the northeastern end of the old city, is a good place to start. This oddly shaped plaza was once an Arab livestock market and later became the main city market, but is now lined with terrace cafes and filled with day-trippers. On the eastern side of the square, pass through the Arco de la Sangre (Gate of Blood), which once marked the city's walls, and down to the rewarding Museo de Santa Cruz (☎ 925 22 10 36; Calle de Cervantes 3; admission free; ☒ 10am-6.30pm Mon-Sat, 10am-2pm Sun), a splendid early 16th-century pastiche

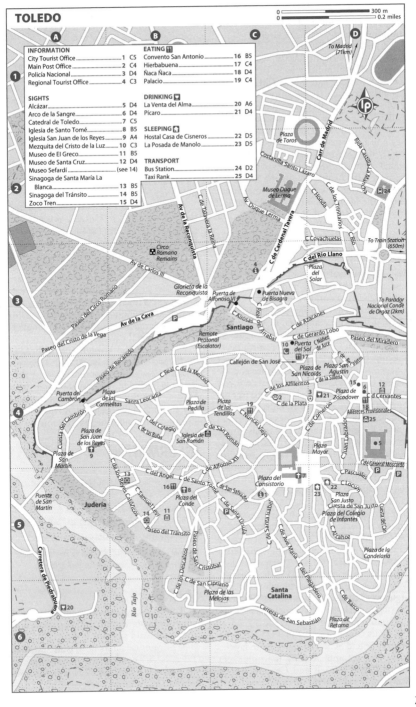

TOLEDO

| 0 | 300 m |
| 0 | 0.2 miles |

INFORMATION
City Tourist Office........................1 C5
Main Post Office...........................2 C4
Policía Nacional............................3 D4
Regional Tourist Office................4 C3

SIGHTS
Alcázar...5 D4
Arco de la Sangre........................6 D4
Catedral de Toledo......................7 C5
Iglesia de Santo Tomé................8 B5
Iglesia San Juan de los Reyes.....9 A4
Mezquita del Cristo de la Luz....10 C3
Museo de El Greco.....................11 B5
Museo de Santa Cruz................12 D4
Museo Sefardí.................(see 14)
Sinagoga de Santa María La
  Blanca.....................................13 B5
Sinagoga del Tránsito................14 B5
Zoco Tren..................................15 D4

EATING
Convento San Antonio...............16 B5
Hierbabuena.............................17 C4
Ñaca Ñaca.................................18 D4
Palacio......................................19 C4

DRINKING
La Venta del Alma.....................20 A6
Pícaro.......................................21 D4

SLEEPING
Hostal Casa de Cisneros............22 D5
La Posada de Manolo.................23 D5

TRANSPORT
Bus Station...............................24 D2
Taxi Rank..................................25 D4

235

of Gothic and Spanish Renaissance styles, fine cloisters and a number of El Greco paintings, including *La Asunción de la Virgen*.

Up the hill to the south is Toledo's signature fortress, the four-spired Alcázar, which began life as a Roman military base, later became an Arab fortress and then a Christian one rebuilt by Alfonso VI in the 11th century. Later, Carlos V converted the harsh square block of a building into a royal visitors palace until it was damaged by fire in 1710. The palace burned again in 1810 (thanks to Napoleon) and was nearly destroyed yet again during the civil war. It remains closed while restoration works prepare it for its new role as the Museo del Ejército (Army Museum). In the meantime, this is the highest point in Toledo and just beyond the Alcázar to the east are some fine views out over the Río Tajo.

Follow the spires west down the hill to Catedral de Toledo (☎ 925 22 22 41; Plaza de Ayuntamiento; adult/child €7/free; ☸ 10am-6.30pm Mon-Sat, 2-6.30pm Sun), the spiritual home of Catholic Spain and one of the largest and most opulent cathedrals in the world. An essentially Gothic creation with a few *mudéjar* (a Moorish architectural style) afterthoughts, it was built in the 13th century atop an earlier mosque. All the chapels and side rooms are worth peeking into, especially the Capilla de la Torre (Tower Chapel) in the northwestern corner and the Sacristía (Sacristy). The latter boasts a lovely vaulted ceiling and works by El Greco (see the boxed text, opposite), Rubens, Zubarán, Titian and Velázquez, while the Tower Chapel has one of the most extraordinary monstrances in existence, the 16th-century Custodia de Arfe. With 18kg of gold and 183kg of silver, this shimmering mass of metal has an astonishing 260 statuettes. Behind the main altar, the Transparente is a mesmerising piece of churrigueresque baroque. A lavish 18th-century embellishment, it also serves to remedy the lack of light in the cathedral.

Down the hill is a cluster of must-sees for El Greco fans, among them the wonderful Iglesia de Santo Tomé (☎ 925 25 60 98; www.santotome .org; Plaza del Conde; admission €2.30; ☸ 10am-6pm mid-Oct–Feb, 10am-6.45pm Mar–mid-Oct), which houses arguably El Greco's greatest work, *El Entierro del Conde de Orgaz* (The Burial of the Count of Orgaz). The painting tells the legend of the pious count's funeral in 1323, when St Augustine and St Steven appeared to lay the body in the tomb. Among the onlookers are El Greco himself and Cervantes. The Museo de El Greco (☎ 925 22 44 05; Calle Samuel Leví) is

nearby, with around two dozen of the master's minor works, although it, too, was closed for restoration at the time of research.

You're now in the heart of the judería (Toledo's old Jewish Quarter). Here, the Sinagoga del Tránsito (☎ 925 22 36 65; Calle Samuel Leví; adult/child €3/1.50; ☸ 9.30am-7pm Tue-Sat, 10am-2pm Sun Mar-Sep, 9.30am-6pm Tue-Sat, 10am-2pm Sun Oct-Feb) should on no account be missed. Built in 1355 by special permission of Pedro I (construction of synagogues was by then prohibited in Christian Spain), the rich *mudéjar* decoration in the main prayer hall has been expertly restored. It's now the Museo Sefardí, which provides an insight into the history of Jewish culture in Spain.

A short way northwest, the Sinagoga de Santa María La Blanca (☎ 925 22 72 57; Calle de los Reyes Católicos 4; admission €2.30; ☸ 10am-7pm Apr-Oct, 10am-6pm Nov-Mar) is less grand but definitely worthwhile for its 29 horseshoe arches. Further along Calle de los Reyes Católicos is the imposing Iglesia San Juan de los Reyes (☎ 925 22 38 02; Plaza de San Juan de los Reyes 2; admission €2.30; ☸ 10am-6.45pm Apr-Sep, 10am-6pm Oct-Mar), a fine Franciscan monastery and church with tranquil cloisters and the chains of Christian prisoners liberated in Granada dangling from the walls.

For a glimpse of Muslim Toledo, head to the Mezquita del Cristo de la Luz (☎ 925 25 41 91; Cuesta de los Carmelitas Descalzas 10; admission €2.30; ☸ 10am-2pm & 3.30-7pm Mon-Fri, 10am-7pm Sat & Sun). During Muslim rule, there were 10 mosques in the city; this one, quite beautiful, is typical of its style and is the only one that remains.

INFORMATION

City Tourist Office (☎ 925 25 40 30; www.t-descubre. com, www.toledo-turismo.com; Plaza del Consistorio 1; ☸ 10.30am-6pm) Across from the cathedral.

Main Post Office (☎ 925 28 44 37; Calle de la Plata 1; ☸ 8.30am-8.30pm Mon-Fri, 9.30am-1pm Sat)

Policía Nacional (☎ 091; Plaza de la Ropería)

Regional Tourist Office (☎ 925 22 08 43; Puerta de Bisagra; ☸ 9am-6pm Mon-Fri, 9am-7pm Sat, 9am-3pm Sun)

EATING

Of Toledo's specialties, *cuchifritos* (a potpourri of lamb, tomato and egg cooked in white wine with saffron) is especially good, while *carcamusa* (a pork dish) is also popular. Otherwise, it's good, hearty Castilian fare.

Hierbabuena (☎ 925 22 39 24; www.restaurante hierbabuena.com, in Spanish; Callejón de San José 17; meals

EL GRECO IN TOLEDO

Few artists are as closely associated with a city as El Greco is with Toledo – many travellers come here for his paintings alone.

Born in Crete in 1541, Domenikos Theotokopoulos (El Greco; the Greek) moved to Venice in 1567 to be schooled as a Renaissance artist. Under the tutelage of masters, such as Tintoretto, he learned to express dramatic scenes with few colours, concentrating the observer's interest in the faces of his portraits and leaving the rest in relative obscurity, a characteristic that remained one of his hallmarks.

El Greco came to Spain in 1577 hoping to get a job decorating El Escorial, although Felipe II rejected him as a court artist. In Toledo, the painter managed to cultivate a healthy clientele and command good prices. His rather high opinion of himself and his work, however, did not endear him to all. He had to do without the patronage of the cathedral administrators, who were the first of many clients to haul him to court for his obscenely high fees. El Greco liked the high life and took rooms in a mansion on the Paseo del Tránsito, where he often hired musicians to accompany his meals.

As Toledo's fortunes declined, so did El Greco's personal finances, and although the works of his final years are among his best, he often found himself unable to pay the rent. He died in 1614, leaving his works scattered about the city.

€35-40; ☺ lunch & dinner Mon-Sat, lunch only Sun) Classy Hierbabuena is a dress-for-dinner restaurant serving food that's a cut above the usual traditional cooking with plenty of steaks, pâté and artichokes stuffed with Catalan sausages and creamed leeks.

Palacio (☎ 925 21 59 72; Calle de Alfonso X el Sabio 3; meals €15-20) An unpretentious place where stained glass, beams and old-fashioned service combine with traditional no-nonsense cuisine.

Ñaca Ñaca (Plaza de Zocodover; bocadillos €2.50-4.50; ☺ 9am-11pm Mon-Thu, 9am-4am Fri, 9am-6am Sat, 11am-11pm Sun) This place is good for chunky *bocadillos* (filled rolls) deep into the night.

Convento San Antonio (☎ 925 22 40 47; Plaza San Antonio 1; ☺ 11.15am-1.30pm & 4-6pm) The Franciscan nuns here sell their sweet speciality, *corazones de San Antonio* (San Antonio hearts) for around €8 a box.

DRINKING

La Venta del Alma (☎ 925 25 42 45; Carretera de Piedrabuena 35; ☺ 3.30pm-2am Sun & Tue-Thu, 3.30pm-6am Fri & Sat) Mild-mannered during the day, La Venta del Alma is a lively spot on Friday and Saturday. It's just outside the city; cross Puente de San Martín, turn left up the hill and it's 200m up on your left.

Pícaro (☎ 925 22 13 01; Calle de las Cadenas 6; ☺ 4pm-2.30am Sun-Wed, 4pm-6am Thu-Sat) Pícaro is a popular café-*teatro* (theatre) serving an eclectic range of *copas* (drinks) and there's live music most Friday nights. It really gets going after 2.30am on weekends.

SLEEPING

Toledo's charms can be diminished somewhat when it's overwhelmed by tour groups, so staying after dusk rewards those eager to experience the city when it returns to the locals and the streets take on a brooding, other-worldly air.

La Posada de Manolo (☎ 925 28 22 50; www.laposadademanolo.com; Calle de Sixto Ramón Parro 8; s/d from €42/66) This boutique hotel has themed floors with furnishings and decor reflecting one of the 'three cultures' of Toledo. The views of the old city and cathedral from the rooftop terrace are stunning.

Hostal Casa de Cisneros (☎ 925 22 88 28; www.hostal-casa-de-cisneros.com; Calle del Cardinal Cisneros; d/tr €80/105) Just across from the cathedral, this upmarket *hostal* is built on the site of an 11th-century Muslim palace, which is visible through the lobby floor. The rooms are decked out in stone and pretty wood beams and have renovated bathrooms.

Parador Nacional Conde de Orgaz (☎ 925 22 18 50; d from €171, d with views from €185) High above the southern bank of the Río Tajo, Toledo's

TRANSPORT: TOLEDO

Distance from Madrid 71km

Direction Southwest

Car From Madrid, head south on the A-42 highway, which leads to Toledo. In town, follow the signs to the *centro urbano* (town centre). Driving time is around one hour.

Bus Buses (€4.40) make the 50-minute trip from Madrid's Estación Sur (ticket windows 12 and 13) to Toledo every half-hour.

Train Renfe's new high-speed AVANT rail link (☎ 902 240 202; www.renfe.es; one way/return €9.90/€17.50) is the best way to get to Toledo, with around 11 trains daily. The trip takes 30 minutes.

parador boasts a classy interior and breath-taking views of the city although you pay extra for a view.

SEGOVIA

Strewn with monuments and filled with life, this beautiful town was inscribed on Unesco's World Heritage List for its extraordinary Roman monuments, fine medieval monuments, fairytale *alcázar* and lovely setting amid the rolling hills of Castile.

Segovia has always had a whiff of legend about it. Perhaps it's because some city historians have claimed that Segovia was founded by Hercules or by the son of Noah. It may also have something to do with the fact that nowhere else in Spain has such a stunning monument to Roman grandeur survived in the heart of a vibrant modern city. Or maybe it's because art really has imitated life Segovia style – Walt Disney is said to have modelled Sleeping Beauty's Castle in California's Disneyland on Segovia's *alcázar*. Whatever it is, the effect is stunning with a city of warm terracotta and sandstone hues set against the backdrop of the often-snowcapped Sierra de Guadarrama.

The medieval walled city is in the far western corner of modern Segovia. The 11th-century walls stretch from the Roman aqueduct to the *alcázar* on the edge of town, enclosing just about everything worth seeing in a short visit. Two major plazas, the Plaza del Azoguejo near the aqueduct and the Plaza Mayor by the cathedral, are the nerve centres of the city. The lively commercial streets of Calle de Cervantes and Calle de Juan Bravo (together referred to as 'Calle Real') serve as the main artery connecting the two plazas.

Start your visit at the Roman aqueduct (El Acueducto), an 894m-long engineering wonder that looks like an enormous comb plunged into Segovia. It's 28m high, has 163 arches and was built without a drop of mortar, just good old Roman know-how using more than 20,000 uneven granite blocks. It was most probably built around AD 50 to bring water to the Roman settlement from 18km away. The aqueduct's pristine condition is attributable to a major restoration project in the 1990s.

From the Plaza del Azoguejo, climb Calle Real into the ancient heart of Segovia, passing the sunny Plaza de San Martín, crowned with the lovely 13th-century Romanesque Iglesia de San Martín ($\circledS$ for Mass), with a *mudéjar* tower and arched gallery. The interior boasts a Flemish Gothic chapel. Well worth a brief detour is the Museo de Arte Contemporáneo Esteban Vicente ($\textcircled{a}$ 921 46 20 10; www.museoestebanvicente.es; Plazuela de las Bellas Artes; admission €3, free Thu; $\circledS$ 11am-2pm & 4-7pm Tue & Wed, 11am-2pm & 4-8pm Thu & Fri, 11am-8pm Sat & Sun), which showcases modern artworks in a 15th-century palace of Enrique IV, complete with Renaissance chapel and *mudéjar* ceiling.

Calle de Isabel la Católica leads to the shady, elongated Plaza Mayor, which is adorned by a fine pavilion. At the western end of the plaza the Catedral ($\textcircled{a}$ 921 46 22 05; Plaza Mayor; admission €3; $\circledS$ 9.30am-5.30pm Oct-Mar, 9.30am-6.30pm Apr-Sep) towers over the plaza. Completed in 1577, 50 years after its Romanesque predecessor had been destroyed in the revolt of the Comuneros, the cathedral is one of the most homogenous Gothic churches in Spain. The austere, three-naved interior is delicate and refined, with a handful of side chapels, a fine choir stall and stained-glass windows dating from the 1600s. You can visit the cloister and museum, with its fantastic collection of sacred art and 17th-century Belgian tapestries. The smaller Iglesia de San Miguel recedes humbly into the shadows by comparison to the cathedral, despite its historical significance – Isabel was crowned Queen of Castile in this small church.

From the Plaza Mayor head down Calle Marqués del Arco to reach the fortified Alcázar ($\textcircled{a}$ 921 46 07 59; www.alcazardesegovia.com; Plaza de la Reina Victoria Eugenia; admission €4, tower €2, EU citizen 3rd Tue month free; $\circledS$ 10am-6pm Oct-Mar, 10am-7pm Apr-Sep), a fairytale castle perched dramatically on the western edge of Segovia. Fortified since Roman times, the site takes its name from the Arabic *al-qasr* (castle), but what you see today is a reconstruction of a 13th-century structure that burned to the ground in 1862. Inside is an interesting collection of armour and military

THE DEVIL'S WORK

Although no-one really doubts that the Romans built the aqueduct, a local legend asserts that two millennia ago a young girl, tired of carrying water from the well, voiced a willingness to sell her soul to the devil if an easier solution could be found. No sooner said than done. The devil worked throughout the night, while the girl recanted and prayed to God for forgiveness. Hearing her prayers, God sent the sun into the sky earlier than usual, catching the devil unawares with only a single stone lacking to complete the structure. The girl's soul was saved, but it seems like she got her wish anyway. Perhaps God didn't have the heart to tear down the aqueduct.

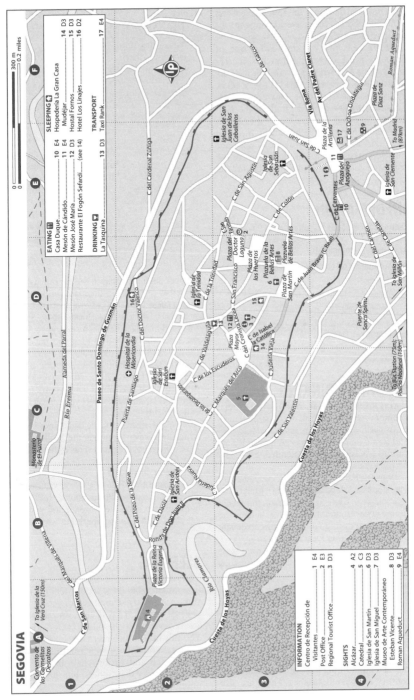

SEGOVIA

EATING 🍴
Casa Duque	10 E4
Mesón de Candido	11 E4
Mesón José María	12 D3
Restaurante El Fogón Sefardí	(see 14)

DRINKING 🍷
La Tasquina	13 D3

SLEEPING 🛏️
Hospedería La Gran Casa Mudéjar	14 D3
Hostal Fornos	15 D3
Hotel Los Linajes	16 D2

TRANSPORT 🚕
Taxi Rank	17 E4

INFORMATION
Centro de Recepción de Visitantes	1 E4
Post Office	2 E3
Regional Tourist Office	3 D3

SIGHTS
Alcázar	4 A2
Catedral	5 C3
Iglesia de San Martín	6 D3
Iglesia de San Miguel	7 D3
Museo de Arte Contemporáneo Esteban Vicente	8 D3
Roman Aqueduct	9 E4

Convento de los Carmelitas Descalzos
To Iglesia de la Vera Cruz (150m)

C de San Marcos

Río Eresma

Monasterio de El Parral

Paseo de Santo Domingo de Guzmán

Alameda del Parral

Río Clamores

Cuesta de los Hoyas

Cuesta de los Hoyos

Río Clamores

Plaza de la Reina Victoria Eugenia

C del Pozo de la Nieve

C de Daoíz

Ronda de Don Juan II

Iglesia de San Andrés

Puerta Nueva

Hospital de la Misericordia

Puerta de Santiago

Iglesia de San Esteban

C de los Desamparados

C del Doctor Velasco

C de Valdeláguila

Iglesia de la Trinidad

C de la Trinidad

C San Francisco

Plaza del Doctor Laguna

C San Esteban

Plaza de los Huertos

Plazuela de Bellas Artes

Plazuela de Bellas Artes

C de Juan Bravo

Plaza de San Martín

Plaza Mayor

C del Cronista Lecea

C de Isabel la Católica

Ciudela Vieja

C Marqués del Arco

C de San Valentín

Puente de Sancti Spíritu

C de los Escuderos

C del Cardenal Zúñiga

Iglesia de San Juan de los Caballeros

C del Carmen

C de San Agustín

Iglesia de San Sebastián

C de Colón

Iglesia de San Millán

To Iglesia de San Millán

C de Cervantes

Plaza de Azoguejo

Plaza de la Artillería

Vía Roma

Av del Padre Claret

C de Gascos

Roman Aqueduct

C de Ochoa Ondátegui

Plaza de Díaz Sanz

To Madrid (87km)

C de Carretas

Iglesia de San Clemente

To Bus Station (75m); Policía Nacional (150m)

300 m
0.2 miles

239

gear, but even better are the 360-degree views from the *alcázar's* tower overlooking the hills and pastures of Castile.

From here you can make out one of Segovia's most interesting churches, the 12-sided Iglesia de la Vera Cruz (Church of the True Cross; ☎ 921 43 14 75; Carretera de Zamarramala; admission €1.75; ⏲ 10.30am-1.30pm & 3.30-7pm Tue-Sun Mar-Aug, 10.30am-1.30pm & 4-6pm Tue-Sun Sep-Feb), built in the 13th century following the floor plan of the Church of the Holy Sepulchre in Jerusalem. A relic of what was said to be the 'true cross' was once housed in the church. For great views of the town and countryside, hike uphill behind the church.

INFORMATION

Centro de Recepción de Visitantes (Tourist Office; ☎ 921 466 720; www.turismodesegovia.com; Plaza del Azoguejo 1; ⏲ 10am-8pm)

Policía Nacional (☎ 091; Paseo de Ezequiel González 22; ⏲ 24hr)

Post Office (☎ 921 461 616; Plaza Doctor Laguna 5; ⏲ 8.30am-8.30pm Mon-Fri, 9.30am-2pm Sat)

Regional Tourist Office (☎ 921 460 334; www.turismo castillayleon.com; Plaza Mayor 10; ⏲ 9.30am-2pm & 4-7pm Mon-Sat, 9.30am-5pm Sun mid-Sep–Jun, 9am-8pm Jul–mid-Sep)

EATING & DRINKING

If you love your meat, you'll love Segovia. People come here from all over Spain for delicious *cochinillo asado* (roasted suckling pig) and *asado de cordero* (roasted lamb). Reservations are highly recommended, especially on weekends.

Mesón José María (☎ 921 46 11 11; www.rtejosemaria .com, in Spanish; Calle del Cronista Lecea 11; meals €35-40; ⏲ lunch & dinner) Close to Plaza Mayor, this *mesón* (home-style restaurant) offers great tapas in the bar and five dining rooms serving exquisite *cochinillo* and other local specialties.

Mesón de Cándido (☎ 921 42 59 11; www.mesonde candido.es; Plaza del Azoguejo 5; meals €35-45; ⏲ lunch & dinner) Set in a delightful 18th-century building in the shadow of the aqueduct, Mesón del Cándido is famous throughout Spain for its suckling pig and roast lamb.

Restaurante El Fogón Sefardí (☎ 921 46 62 50; www .lacasamudejar.com; Calle de Isabel La Católica 8; meals €35-40; ⏲ lunch & dinner) This place serves Sephardi cuisine in a restaurant with an intimate patio or a splendid dining hall with original, 15th-century *mudéjar* flourishes. There are also

cheaper Sephardi tapas in the bar downstairs, as well as *cochinillo* in the main restaurant.

Casa Duque (☎ 921 46 24 86; www.restauranteduque .es, in Spanish; Calle de Cervantes 12; meals €35-45; ⏲ lunch & dinner) This place has been serving suckling pig since the 1890s and long ago mastered the art. For the uninitiated, try its *menú segoviano* (€33), which includes *cochinillo*, or the *menú gastronómico* (€42), which gives a taste of many local specialties. Downstairs is the informal *cueva* (cave), where you can get tapas and *cazuelas* (stews).

By night, head for Calle de Infanta Isabel, which is known locally as the 'Calle de los Bares' (Street of the Bars). This is the destination for serious drinking, cheap eating and merriment all around.

La Tasquina (☎ 921 461 954; Calle de Valdeláguila 3; ⏲ 9pm-late) Just off Plaza Mayor, this wine bar spills out onto the footpath and you can get good wines, *cavas* (sparkling wines) and cheeses.

SLEEPING

You can get a taste of Segovia as a day trip from Madrid, but there are outstanding hotel choices if you'd like to linger longer.

Hostal Fornos (☎ 921 46 01 98; www.hostalfornos .com, in Spanish; Calle de Infanta Isabel 13; s €34-41, d €48-55) This tidy little hostel has a cheerful air thanks to its tasteful rooms, which have that fresh white-linen-and-wicker-chair look. Some are a bit larger than others, but the value is unimpeachable.

Hotel Los Linajes (☎ 921 46 04 75; www.hotelloslinajes .com; Calle del Doctor Valesco 9; s €73-87, d €99-118) For some of the best views in Segovia, Hotel Los Linajes is exceptionally good. The rooms are large and all look out onto the hills; many also have cathedral and/or *alcázar* views.

Hospedería La Gran Casa Mudéjar (☎ 921 46 62 50; www.lacasamudejar.com; Calle de Infanta Isabel 8; d €60-175) Spread over two buildings, this place has been magnificently renovated, blending genuine, 15th-century *mudéjar* ceilings with modern amenities. In the newer wing, where the building dates from the 19th century, the rooms on the top floors have fine mountain views out over the rooftops of Segovia's old Jewish quarter.

ÁVILA

The walled city of Ávila provides Spain with one of its most spectacular skylines. Medieval kingdoms battled over Ávila for centuries and each ruler in his turn reinforced the city until it reached its current, stunning manifestation of eight monumental gates, 88 watchtowers and more than 2500 turrets (to protect archers); the walls are illuminated to magical effect at night. If you're here in winter when an icy wind whistles in off the plains, it can seem as if the walls were built to protect the city from the harsh Castilian climate – Ávila is one of the highest and windiest cities in Spain and winters can be bitterly cold – with the old city huddling behind the high stone walls. Within the walls, Ávila can appear as if caught in a time warp. Its many churches, convents and high-walled palaces, all built of sombre stone, date back to the city's golden age, the 15th century, when the city's defining figure, Santa Teresa (see the boxed text below), was born. Shortly after her death in 1582, the city's fortunes began a downward spiral that ended in its economic ruin; Ávila has only recently shaken off its slumber.

The Catedral (☎ 920 21 16 41; Plaza de la Catedral; admission €4; ✆ 10am-7.30pm Mon-Fri, 10am-8pm Sat, noon-6.30pm Sun Jun-Sep, shorter hr rest of year) is embedded in the eastern wall of the old city. Although the main facade hints at the cathedral's 12th-century Romanesque origins, the church was finished 400 years later in a predominantly Gothic style, making it the first Gothic church in Spain. The grey, sombre facade betrays some unhappy 18th-century meddling in the main portal, but within are rich walnut choir stalls, a dazzling altar painting begun by Pedro de Berruguete showing the life of Jesus in 24 scenes and a long, narrow central nave that makes the soaring ceilings seem all the more majestic. The cloisters, sacristy and small museum are superb; the latter includes a painting by El Greco.

Among Ávila's highlights are splendid 12th-century walls (murallas; ☎ 920 25 50 88; adult/child €3.50/2; ✆ 10am-8pm Apr–mid-Oct, 11am-6pm

IN THE FOOTSTEPS OF SANTA TERESA

Probably the most important woman in the history of the Catholic church in Spain, Santa Teresa spent most of her life in Ávila. From the convent, plaza and gate that bear her name to the sweet *yemas de Santa Teresa* (yummy biscuits made with egg yolk and supposedly invented by the saint) her trail seems to cover every inch of the city.

Teresa de Cepeda y Ahumada – a Catholic mystic and reformer – was born in Ávila on 28 March 1515, one of 10 children of a merchant family. Raised by Augustinian nuns after her mother's death, she joined the Carmelite order at age 20. After her early, undistinguished years as a nun, she was shaken by a vision of Hell in 1560, which crystallised her true vocation: she would reform her order.

With the help of many supporters Teresa founded convents of the Carmelitas Descalzas (Shoeless Carmelites) all over Spain. She also co-opted San Juan de la Cruz (St John of the Cross) to begin a similar reform in the masculine order, a task that earned her several stints of incarceration by the mainstream Carmelites. Santa Teresa's writings were first published in 1588 and proved enormously popular, perhaps partly for their earthy style. She died in 1582 in Alba de Tormes, where she is buried. She was canonised by Pope Gregory XV in 1622.

After a visit to the Convento de Santa Teresa (☎ 920 21 10 30; Plaza de la Santa; museum/relic room/church €2/free/free; ✆ 9am-1.30pm & 3.30-7.30pm Tue-Sun), you can pop into the nearby Iglesia de San Juan Bautista (☎ 920 21 11 27; Plaza de la Victoria; admission free; ✆ before & after Mass), where she was baptised. The first convent she founded, Convento de San José (☎ 920 22 21 27; Calle del Duque de Alba; admission €1; ✆ 10am-1.30pm & 3-6pm Nov-Mar; ✆ 10am-1.30pm & 4-7pm Apr-Oct), is here, too, and you can visit its small museum packed with Teresa artefacts and memorabilia. To see a replica of her monastic cell, head to the Monasterio de la Encarnación (☎ 920 21 12 12; Paseo de la Encarnación; admission €1.50; ✆ 9.30am-1.30pm & 4-6pm Mon-Fri, 10am-1pm & 4-6pm Sat & Sun) outside the city walls where she lived and worked for 27 years.

ÁVILA

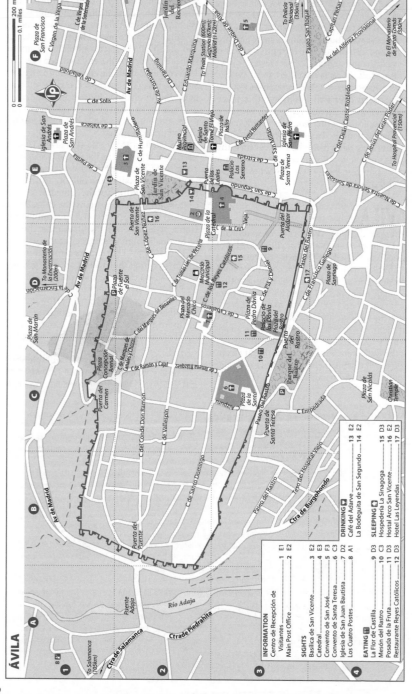

INFORMATION
Centro de Recepción de	
Visitantes............................ 1	E1
Main Post Office......................... 2	E2

SIGHTS
Basílica de San Vicente............ 3	E2
Catedral..................................... 4	E3
Convento de San José.............. 5	F3
Convento de Santa Teresa....... 6	C3
Iglesia de San Juan Bautista.... 7	D2
Los Cuatro Postes.................... 8	A1

EATING
La Flor de Castilla..................... 9	D3
Mesón del Rastro.................... 10	C3
Posada de la Fruta................... 11	D3
Restaurante Reyes Católicos... 12	D3

DRINKING
Café del Adarve....................... 13	E2
La Bodeguita de San Segundo... 14	E2

SLEEPING
Hospedería La Sinagoga......... 15	D3
Hostal Arco San Vicente......... 16	E2
Hotel Las Leyendas................. 17	D3

mid-Oct–Mar), which rank among the world's best-preserved medieval defensive perimeters. At the time of writing, the two access points are at the Puerta del Alcázar and the Puerta de los Leales, which allow walks of 300m and 800m respectively; the same ticket allows you to climb both sections of the wall. There are also plans to open a third section of the wall from Puerta del Carmen to Puerta del Puente. The most impressive gates are the Puerta de San Vicente and Puerta del Alcázar, which are flanked by towers more than 20m high and stand on either side of the cathedral's apse. The last tickets are sold 45 minutes before closing time.

From close to the Plaza de la Catedral, the pedestrianised Calle de los Reyes Católicos, which is lined with shops and bars, runs down into the pretty Plaza del Mercado Chico. Southwest of the plaza, the Convento de Santa Teresa is even more beloved by locals and pilgrims than the cathedral because it was built on the site where Santa Teresa was born. This church was built in 1636 and today you can see its simple interior and the gold-smothered chapel that sits atop Teresa's former bedroom, though more interesting are the relics (including a piece of the saint's ring finger!) and the small museum about her life.

So much of Ávila's religious architecture is brooding and sombre, but the graceful Basílica de San Vicente (☎ 920 25 52 30; admission €1.40; ☼ 10am-1.30pm & 4-6.30pm) is a masterpiece of the subdued elegance of the Romanesque style. Work started in the 11th century, supposedly on the site where three martyrs – San Vicente and his sisters – were slaughtered by the Romans in the early 4th century. Their canopied sepulchre is an outstanding piece of Romanesque with nods to the Gothic.

Just northwest of the city on the road to Salamanca, Los Cuatro Postes affords the finest views of Ávila's walls; it marks the place where Santa Teresa and her brother were caught by their uncle as they tried to run away from home. They were hoping to achieve martyrdom at the hands of the Muslims.

INFORMATION

Centro de Recepción de Visitantes (Tourist Office; ☎ 920 22 59 69; www.avilaturismo.com; Avenida de Madrid 39; ☼ 10am-6pm Nov-Mar, 9am-8pm Apr-Oct)

Hospital Provincial (☎ 920 35 72 00; Calle de Jesús del Gran Poder 42; ☼ 24hr)

Main Post Office (☎ 920 35 31 06; Plaza de la Catedral 2; ☼ 8.30am-8.30pm Mon-Fri, 9.30am-2pm Sat)

Policía Nacional (☎ 091; Paseo San Roque 34; ☼ 24hr)

EATING

Ávila is famous for its *chuleton de avileño* (T-bone-steak) and *judias del barco de Ávila* (white beans, usually with chorizo, in a thick sauce).

La Flor de Castilla (☎ 920 25 28 66; Calle de San Gerónimo; ☼ 10am-2pm & 5-8pm Mon-Sat) This is a fine place to buy the *yema de Santa Teresa*, a sticky ultra-sweet biscuit made of egg yolk and sugar, which is said to have been invented by the saint.

Posada de la Fruta (☎ 920 22 09 84; www.posadadela fruta.com, in Spanish; Plaza de Pedro Dávila 8; meals €10-20; ☼ lunch & dinner) Simple, informal meals can be had at the cafe-bar in a light-filled, covered courtyard, while the traditional *comedor* (dining room) serves *menús* (fixed-price meals) and a la carte dishes.

Mesón del Rastro (☎ 920 21 12 19; Plaza del Rastro 1; meals €25-35; ☼ lunch & dinner Thu-Sat, lunch only Sun-Wed) The dining room at Mesón del Rastro, with its dark-wood beams, announces immediately that this is a bastion of Castilian cooking. Expect hearty, delicious mainstays, such as *chuleton de avileño, judias del barco de Ávila* and *cordero asado* (roast lamb).

Restaurante Reyes Católicos (☎ 920 25 56 27; www .restaurante-reyescatolicos.com, in Spanish; Calle de los Reyes Católicos 6; set menus €16-26, meals €25-35; ☼ lunch & dinner) Most *asadors* (restaurants serving roasted meats) in Ávila are old-school with dark, wood-panelled dining areas, whereas this slick, modern restaurant is a refreshing change. The cuisine offers a mix of traditional and fusion dishes.

DRINKING

La Bodeguita de San Segundo (☎ 920 25 73 09; www .vinoavila.com, in Spanish; Calle de San Segundo 19; ☼ 11am-midnight Thu-Tue) This gem of a wine and tapas

---

TRANSPORT: ÁVILA

Distance from Madrid 101km

Direction West

Car From Madrid, take the A-6 motorway northwest, then take the N-110 west. Driving time is around one hour.

Bus Up to nine buses (fewer on weekends) connect Madrid's Estación Sur and Ávila (1¼ hours, €8.54). Contact the bus station (☎ 920 25 65 05; Avenida de Madrid 2) for more information.

Train The company Renfe (☎ 902 240 202; www .renfe.es) has up to 30 trains to Ávila daily. The trip takes up to two hours (one way from €7.20), although the occasional train runs express, takes 1¼ hours and costs €9.70.

bar is standing-room only most nights and more tranquil in the quieter afternoon hours. The setting in the 16th-century Casa de la Misericordia is superb and the wines here are excellent.

Café del Adarve (Calle de San Segundo 40; ☼ 5pm-late) About as lively as Ávila gets, Café del Adarve has quirky decor, weekend DJs and occasional live music during winter.

SLEEPING

Given that Ávila nights can be pretty quiet, the only real reason to linger after dark (or overnight) is to catch a glimpse of the city's walls lit up like in a fairytale.

Hostal Arco San Vicente (☎ 920 22 24 98; www.arcosanvicente.com; Calle de López Núñez 6; s/d from €50/70) A terrific option is this engaging *hostal*, which has lovely, brightly painted rooms and friendly owners. The location, just inside the city walls, is also a winner.

Hospedería La Sinagoga (☎ 920 35 23 21; lasinagoga@vodafone.es; Calle de los Reyes Católicos 22; s/d/ste from €52/72/88) This delightful little hotel incorporates details from Ávila's main 15th-century synagogue with bright, spacious rooms. Rates for doubles can drop to as low as €42 on weekdays in winter.

Hotel Las Leyendas (☎ 920 35 20 42; www.lasleyendas.es; Calle de Francisco Gallego 3; s €55-61, d €67-79) Occupying the house of 16th-century Ávila nobility, this intimate hotel is wonderful, with period touches (original wooden beams, exposed brickwork) wedded to modern amenities.

SAN LORENZO DE EL ESCORIAL

Home to the majestic monastery and palace complex of San Lorenzo de El Escorial (☎ 91 890 59 03; www.patrimonionacional.es; adult/student €8/3.50, guided visits €10, EU citizen Wed free, combined ticket with Valle de los Caídos €8.50/5; ☼ 10am-6pm Tue-Sun Apr-Sep, 10am-5pm Tue-Sun Oct-Mar), this one-time royal getaway rises up from the foothills of the mountains that shelter Madrid from the north and west. Although it attracts its fair share of foreign tourists, this prim little town is overflowing with quaint shops, restaurants and hotels (many of which close when things are quiet) that cater primarily to madrileños who are intent on escaping the city on weekends: the fresh, cool air, among other things, has been drawing city dwellers here since the complex was first built on the orders of King Felipe II

in the 16th century. Admission to the basilica is free.

Several villages were razed to make way for the massive project, which included a monastic centre, a decadent royal palace and a mausoleum for Felipe's parents, Carlos I and Isabel. Architect Juan de Herrera (see p47) oversaw the project.

The monastery's main entrance is to the west. Above the gateway a statue of St Lawrence stands watch, holding a symbolic gridiron, the instrument of his martyrdom (he was roasted alive on one). From here you'll first enter the Patio de los Reyes (Patio of the Kings), which houses the statues of the six kings of Judah.

Directly ahead lies the sombre basilica. As you enter, look up at the unusual flat vaulting by the choir stalls. Once inside the church proper, turn left to view Benvenuto Cellini's white Carrara marble statue of Christ crucified (1576).

The remainder of the ground floor contains various treasures, including some tapestries and an El Greco painting – impressive as it is, it's a far cry from El Greco's dream of decorating the whole complex – and then downstairs to the northeastern corner of the complex. You pass through the Museo de Arquitectura and the Museo de Pinturaf. The former tells (in Spanish) the story of how the complex was built, the latter contains a range of 16th- and 17th-century Italian, Spanish and Flemish art.

Head upstairs into a gallery around the eastern part of the complex known as the Palacio de Felipe II or Palacio de los Austrias. You'll then descend to the 17th-century Panteón de los Reyes (Crypt of the Kings), where almost all

TRANSPORT: SAN LORENZO DE EL ESCORIAL

Distance from Madrid 59km

Direction Northwest

Car Take the A-6 motorway to the M-600 highway, then follow the signs to El Escorial. Driving time 40 minutes.

Bus Every 15 minutes (every half-hour on weekends), Herranz bus company (Map pp116-17; ☎ 91 890 41 00) runs a service (buses 661 and 664) to El Escorial from platform 3 of Madrid's Moncloa Intercambiador de Autobuses station. The one-hour trip costs €3.35.

Train A few dozen Renfe (☎ 902 240 202; www.renfe.es) C8 *cercanía* (local train network) trains make the one-hour trip (€1.25) daily from Madrid's Atocha or Chamartín stations to El Escorial.

Spain's monarchs since Carlos I are interred. Backtracking a little, you'll find yourself in the Panteón de los Infantes (Crypt of the Princesses).

Stairs lead up from the Patio de los Evangelistas (Patio of the Gospels) to the Salas Capitulares (chapterhouses) in the southeastern corner of the monastery. These bright, airy rooms, whose ceilings are richly frescoed, contain a minor treasure chest of works by El Greco, Titian, Tintoretto, José de Ribera and Hieronymus Bosch (known as El Bosco to Spaniards).

Just south of the monastery is the Huerta de los Frailes (Friars Garden; ☎ 10am-7pm Apr-Sep, 10am-6pm Oct-Mar), which merits a stroll, while the Jardín del Príncipe (☎ 10am-7pm Apr-Sep, 10am-6pm Oct-Mar), which leads down to the town of El Escorial (and the train station), contains the Casita del Príncipe (guided visits adult/student €3.60/2; ☎ 10am-1pm & 4-6.30pm Tue-Sun) a little neo-Classical gem built in 1772 by Juan de Villanueva (see p48) under Carlos III for his heir, Carlos IV.

INFORMATION

Pullmantur (p262) Half-day bus tours to San Lorenzo El Escorial and Valle de los Caídos for €50.

Tourist Office (☎ 91 890 53 13; www.sanlorenzoturismo .org; Calle de Grimaldi 2; ☒ 10am-2pm & 3-6pm Tue-Sat, 10am-2pm Sun, longer hr summer)

EATING

The tourist office's website has a list of restaurants and bars in town. These are two of our favourites.

Charolés (☎ 91 890 59 75; Plaza de San Lorenzo 2; meals €35; ☒ lunch & dinner) Famous throughout the Madrid region for its *cocido* (meat and chickpea stew) which is served on Wednesday lunchtime (when reservations are essential), Charolés also serves seasonal dishes, red meats and there's a lengthy wine list.

La Cueva (☎ 91 890 15 16; www.mesonlacueva.com; Calle de Floridablanca 24; meals €50-60; ☒ lunch & dinner) Just a block back from the monastery complex, La Cueva has been around since 1768 and it shows in the heavy wooden beams and hearty, traditional Castilian cooking – roasted meats and steaks are the mainstays, with a few fish dishes.

VALLE DE LOS CAÍDOS

This extraordinary basilica and stone monument, the Valle de los Caídos (Valley of the Fallen; ☎ 91 890 56 11; www.patrimonionacional.es; Carretera 600; adult/ student €5/2.50, combined ticket with El Escorial €8.50/5; ☒ 10am-6pm Tue-Sat Apr-Sep, 10am-5pm Tue-Sat Oct-Mar), is built into the side of a mountain 15km north of San Lorenzo de El Escorial. Conceived in the grandiose imagination of the dictator Francisco Franco, it served as a memorial of those who died during the Spanish Civil War (1936–39), though in reality it has always glorified Franco's side and was constructed by Franco's prisoners of war, many of whom died in the process. It has long been a pilgrimage site for the small reactionary rump of Franco supporters, who come here especially on 20 November – the anniversary of Franco's death – to reminisce about Franco's rule, complete with stiff-armed fascist salutes. Spain's Socialist government has plans to transform the site into a broader memorial, and at the time of writing, large sections of the complex (including the basilica) were closed as part of this process. Check with the Comunidad de Madrid tourist office (p265) before setting out.

The mammoth stone cross sits atop a bunker-like basilica dug into the mountainside in the middle of a pristine pine forest. Walking into the basilica, you enter into the heart of the mountain. Franco's body is interred by the altar, although given the unclear changes proposed for the site by the national government, no-one knows how long his body will remain there. Near the basilica are walking trails and a picnic area.

You can take a funicular (one way/return €1.50/2.50; ☒ 11am-4.30pm Tue-Sat Oct-Mar, 11am-5.30pm Tue-Sat Apr-Sep) up the mountain to the base of the cross, where, if the wind doesn't blow you away, you can enjoy great views of the surrounding sierra.

The site is almost impossible to reach via public transport. Unless you have your own wheels, the best option is the half-day bus tour (€50) from Madrid to San Lorenzo El Escorial and Valle de los Caídos run by Pullmantur (p262).

TRANSPORT: VALLE DE LOS CAÍDOS

Distance from Madrid 45km
Direction Northwest
Car Take the A-6 motorway to the M-600 highway, then follow the signs. Driving time 35 minutes.

ARANJUEZ

Aranjuez was founded as a royal pleasure retreat, away from the riff-raff of Madrid, and it remains a place to escape the rigours of city life. The palace is opulent and its grandeur is amplified by its setting amid the greenery of lovely, expansive gardens.

The Palacio Real (☎ 91 891 07 40; www.patrimonio nacional.es; child, EU senior & student/adult €2.50/5, EU citizens free Wed, gardens free; ☉ palace 10am-5.15pm Tue-Sun Oct-Mar, 10am-6.15pm Tue-Sun Apr-Sep, gardens 8am-8.30pm mid-Jun–mid-Aug, shorter hr rest of year) started as one of Felipe II's modest summer palaces but took on a life of its own as a succession of royals, inspired by the palace at Versailles in France, lavished money upon it. By the 18th century, its 300-plus rooms had turned the palace into a sprawling, gracefully symmetrical complex filled with a cornucopia of ornamentation. Of all the rulers who spent time here, Carlos III and Isabel II left the greatest mark.

The obligatory guided tour (in Spanish) provides insight into the palace's art and history. And a stroll in the lush gardens takes you through a mix of local and exotic species, the product of seeds brought back by Spanish botanists and explorers from Spanish colonies all over the world. Within their shady perimeter, which stretches a few kilometres from the palace, you'll find the Casa de Marinos, which contains the Museo de Faluás (admission €3; ☉ 10am-4pm Oct-Mar, 10am-6.15pm Apr-Sep), a museum of royal pleasure boats from days gone by. The 18th-century neo-classical Casa del Labrador (☎ 91 891 03 05; adult/child, senior or student €5/2.50; ☉ 10am-6pm Tue-Sun Apr-Sep, 10am-5pm Tue-Sun Oct-Mar) is also worth a visit. Further away, towards Chinchón, is the Jardín del Príncipe, an extension of the massive gardens. The Chiquitren (☎ 902 088 089; www

.arantour.com; adult/child €5/3; ☉ 11am-5.30pm Tue-Sun Oct-Feb, 10am-8pm Tue-Sun Mar-Sep), a small tourist train, loops through town and stops at all the major sites.

INFORMATION

Tourist Office (☎ 91 891 04 27; www.aranjuez.es, in Spanish; Antigua Carretera de Andalucía s/n; ☉ 10am-6.30pm Nov-Apr, 10am-8.30pm May-Oct)

EATING

Pabelete (☎ 91 891 03 81; Calle de Stuart 108; meals €25-30; ☉ lunch & dinner Wed-Mon) Going strong since 1946, this casual tapas bar has a loyal following far beyond Aranjuez. Its *croquetas* (croquettes) are a major drawcard, as is the stuffed squid and it's all about traditional cooking at its best without too many elaborations.

Casa José (☎ 91 891 14 88; www.casajose.es; Calle de Abastos 32; meals €50-60; ☉ lunch & dinner Tue-Sat, lunch only Sun) The quietly elegant Casa José is the

---

THE STRAWBERRY TRAIN

You could take a normal train from Madrid to Aranjuez, but for romance it's hard to beat the Tren de la Fresa (Strawberry Train; ☎ 902 240 202, 902 228 822; www.museodelferrocarril.org, in Spanish; return adult/child €26/18; ☉ May-Oct). Begun in 1985 to commemorate the Madrid-Aranjuez route – Madrid's first and Spain's third rail line, which was inaugurated in the 1850s – the *Strawberry Train* is a throwback to the time when Spanish royalty would escape the summer heat and head for the royal palace at Aranjuez.

The journey begins at 10am on Saturday and Sunday between early May and late October when an antique Mikado 141F-2413 steam engine pulls out from Madrid's Museo del Ferrocarril, pulling behind it four passenger carriages that date from the early 20th century and have old-style front and back balconies. During the 50-minute journey, rail staff in period dress provide samples of local strawberries – one of the original train's purposes was to allow royalty to sample the summer strawberry crop from the Aranjuez orchards. Upon arrival in Aranjuez, your ticket fare includes a guided tour of the Palacio Real, Museo de Faluás and other Aranjuez sights, not to mention more strawberry samplings. The train leaves Aranjuez for Madrid at 6.25pm for the return journey.

Tickets can be purchased at any Renfe office or any travel agency that sells train tickets.

proud owner of a Michelin star and is packed on weekends with madrileños drawn by the beautifully prepared meats and local dishes with some surprising innovations. It's pricey but worth every euro.

CHINCHÓN

Chinchón is just 45km from Madrid yet worlds away. Although it has grown beyond its village confines, visiting here is like stepping back into a charming, ramshackle past. The heart of town is its unique, almost circular Plaza Mayor, which is lined with sagging, tiered balconies – it gets our vote as one of the most evocative *plazas mayores* in Spain. In summer the plaza is converted into a bullring (see the boxed text, p232). It's also the stage for a popular passion play shown at Easter. Chinchón's other main attraction is made up of the traditional mesón-style restaurants scattered in and around the plaza, some with wonderful balcony tables.

There are a few other sights worth seeking out, particularly the 16th-century Iglesia de la Asunción that rises above the Plaza Mayor and the late-16th-century Renaissance Castillo de los Condes, which is about 1km south of Chinchón and which was abandoned in the 1700s; the tourist office has details of their irregular opening hours (usually weekends). But Chinchón's real charm lies in the Plaza Mayor and eating fine *cordero asado* (roast lamb).

INFORMATION

Tourist Office (☎ 91 893 53 23; www.ciudad-chinchon .com; Plaza Mayor 6; ☼ 10am-7pm) Small office but helpful staff.

EATING

Café de la Iberia (☎ 91 894 08 47; www.cafedelaiberia.com; Plaza Mayor 17; meals €35-40; ☼ lunch & dinner) This is definitely our favourite of the *mesones* (home-style restaurants) on the Plaza Mayor perimeter. It offers wonderful food, including succulent roast lamb, served by attentive staff in an atmospheric dining area set around a light-filled internal courtyard (where Goya is said to have visited) or, if you can get a table, out on the balcony.

Mesón Cuevas del Vino (☎ 91 894 02 06; www .cuevasdelvino.com; Calle Benito Hortelano 13; meals €35-40; ☼ lunch & dinner Wed-Sat & Mon, lunch Sun) From the huge goatskins filled with wine and the barrels covered in famous signatures, to the atmos-

TRANSPORT: CHINCHÓN

Distance from Madrid 45km
Direction Southeast
Car Head out of Madrid on the N-IV motorway and exit onto the M-404, which winds its way to Chinchón.
Bus The La Veloz (Map pp124-5; ☎ 91 409 76 02) bus 337 leaves half-hourly to Chinchón. The buses leave from Avenida del Mediterráneo, 100m west of Plaza del Conde de Casal. The 50-minute ride costs €3.35.

pheric caves underground, this is sure to be a memorable eating experience with delicious home-style cooking.

ALCALÁ DE HENARES

So close to Madrid and just off an unappealing motorway, Alcalá de Henares is full of surprises with historical sandstone buildings seemingly at every turn. Throw in some sunny plazas and a legendary university, and Alcalá de Henares is a terrific place to go to escape the city.

The university (☎ 91 883 43 84; 6 free guided tours per day Mon-Fri, 11 per day Sat & Sun; ☼ 9am-9pm), founded in 1486 by Cardinal Cisneros, is one of the country's principal seats of learning. A guided tour gives a peek into the *mudéjar* chapel and the magnificent Paraninfo auditorium, where the King and Queen of Spain give out the prestigious Premio Cervantes literary award every year. The town is also dear to Spaniards because it is the birthplace of the country's literary figurehead, Miguel de Cervantes Saavedra (see p36). The site believed by many to be Cervantes' birthplace is re-created in the illuminating Museo Casa Natal de Miguel de Cervantes (☎ 91 889 96 54; www.museo-casa-natal-cervantes.org; Calle Mayor 48; admission free; ☼ 10am-6pm Tue-Sun), which lies along the beautiful, colonnaded Calle de Mayor.

TRANSPORT: ALCALÁ DE HENARES

Distance from Madrid 35km
Direction East
Car Head towards Zaragoza on the N-II highway. Driving time is 40 minutes.
Bus There are regular departures (every five to 15 minutes) from the Intercambiador de Avenida de América. The trip takes about one hour (€2.99).
Train C2 and C7 Renfe (☎ 902 240 202; www.renfe .es) *cercanía* trains make the 50-minute trip to Alcalá de Henares daily. The trip costs €1.25.

INFORMATION

Tourist Office (☎ 91 881 06 34; www.turismoalcala.com, in Spanish; Plaza de los Santos Niños; ⏰ 10am-2pm & 5-7.30pm Jun-Sep, 10am-2pm & 4-6.30pm Oct-May) Free guided tours of 'Alcalá Monumental' at noon and 4.30pm Saturday and Sunday.

EATING

Barataria (☎ 91 888 59 25; Calle de los Cerrajeros 18; meals €25-35; ⏰ lunch & dinner Mon-Sat, lunch Sun) A wine bar, tapas bar and restaurant all rolled into one, Barataria is a fine place to eat whatever your mood. Grilled meats are the star of the show, with the ribs with honey in particular a local favourite.

Hostería del Estudiante (☎ 91 888 03 30; www.parador .es; Calle de los Colegios 3; meals €40-50) Based in the parador, this charming restaurant has wonderful Castilian cooking and a classy ambience in a dining room decorated with artefacts from the city's illustrious history.

SIERRA DE GUADARRAMA

North of Madrid lies the Sierra de Guadarrama, a popular skiing destination and home of several charming towns. In Manzanares El Real you can explore the small 15th-century Castillo de los Mendoza (☎ 91 853 00 08; Manzanares El Real; admission incl guided tour €2.50; ⏰ 10am-2pm & 3-6pm Tue-Sun Apr-Sep, 10am-5pm Tue-Sun Oct-Mar), a storybook castle with round towers at its corners and a Gothic interior patio.

Cercedilla is a popular base for hikers and mountain bikers. There are several marked

trails through the sierra, the main one known as the Cuerda Larga or Cuerda Castellana. This is a forest track that takes in 55 peaks between the Puerto de Somosierra in the north and Puerto de la Cruz Verde in the southwest. Get more information at the Centro de Información Valle de la Fuenfría. Small ski resorts, such as Valdesqui (☎ 902 886 446; www.valdesqui.es, in Spanish; Puerto de Cotos; day/afternoon lift tickets €36/21; ⏰ 9am-4pm) or Navacerrada (☎ 902 882 328; www.puertonavacerrada.com, in Spanish; lift tickets €25-30; ⏰ 9.30am-5pm) welcome weekend skiers from the city.

INFORMATION

Ayuntamiento de Manzanares El Real (www.manzanares elreal.org, in Spanish) Great website.

Centro de Información Valle de la Fuenfría (☎ 91 852 22 13; Carretera de las Dehesas; ⏰ 10am-6pm) Information centre located 2km outside Cercedilla on the M-614.

Navacerrada Tourist Office (☎ 91 856 03 08; www .navacerrada.es, in Spanish)

SIERRA POBRE

The 'Poor Sierra' is a toned-down version of its more refined western neighbour, the Sierra de Guadarrama. Popular with hikers and others looking for nature without quite so many creature comforts or crowds, the sleepy Sierra Pobre has yet to develop the tourism industry of its neighbours. And that's just why we like it.

Head first to Buitrago, the largest town in the area, where you can stroll along part of the old city walls. You can also take a peek into the 15th-century *mudéjar* and Romanesque Iglesia de Santa María del Castillo and into the small and unlikely Picasso Museum (☎ 91 868 00 56; Plaza Picasso 1; admission free; ⏰ 11am-1.45pm & 4-6pm Tue, Thu & Fri, 11am-1.45 Wed, 10am-2pm & 4-7pm Sat, 10am-2pm Sun), which contains a few works that the artist gave to his barber, Eugenio Arias.

Hamlets are scattered throughout the rest of the sierra; some, like Puebla de la Sierra and El Atazar, are pretty walks and are the starting point for winding hill trails.

INFORMATION

Buitrago Tourist Office (☎ 91 868 16 15; ⏲ 9am-3pm Jul-Sep)

EATING

El Arco (☎ 918 68 09 11; Calle Arco 6; meals €35-45; ⏲ lunch only Fri-Sun mid-Sep–mid-Jun, lunch & dinner Tue-Sat & lunch Sun mid-Jun–mid-Sep) The best restaurant in the region, El Arco is located in Villavieja del Lozoya, close to Buitrago, and known for its fresh, creative cuisine based on local, seasonal ingredients and traditional northern Spanish dishes such as the classic Basque *Bacalao al Pil-Pil*. The desserts and wine list also stand out.

TRANSPORT

Madrid is served by almost 100 airlines, excellent bus networks and trains that radiate into and out from the Spanish capital. The ongoing expansion of Spain's high-speed rail network has dramatically cut travel times and, with the link between Madrid and Barcelona, has brought Madrid that much closer to the rest of Europe.

Madrid's extensive, modern metro system is all you're likely to need for getting around the city. There's also an extensive bus network, as well as reasonably priced taxis.

Flights, tours and rail tickets can be booked online at www.lonelyplanet.com /travel_services.

AIR

Madrid's Barajas airport is Europe's fourth-busiest hub, trailing only London Heathrow, Paris Charles de Gaulle and Frankfurt.

For intercontinental flights, the best connections are through South America, but there are also direct flights from Asia, North America and the Middle East.

Within Europe, the cheapest way to fly to Madrid is with low-cost airlines such as easyJet, Air Berlin, German Wings, Ryanair and Vueling. The earlier you book a flight, the less you pay.

Iberia, Air Europa and Spanair once had a stranglehold over the domestic market, but now compete with international low-cost airlines on a number of domestic routes out of Madrid. Carriers and routes include easyJet (Ibiza), Ryanair (Alicante, Almería, Canary Islands, Fuerteventura, Girona, Granada, Jerez, Palma de Mallorca, Santander and Santiago de Compostela), Air Berlin (Barcelona, Seville, Valencia, Palma de Mallorca, Bilbao, Alicante, Jerez and Málaga) and Vueling (Barcelona, Canary Islands, Menorca, Ibiza and Seville). Andalus also flies from Madrid to Almería, San Sebastián and Gibraltar.

Airlines

A full list of airlines flying to Madrid is available on the Madrid-Barajas section of www .aena.es; click on 'Airlines'.

Aer Lingus (☎ 902 502 737; www.aerlingus.com) To Madrid from Dublin and Washington.

THINGS CHANGE...

The information in this chapter is particularly vulnerable to change. Check directly with the airline or a travel agent to make sure you understand how a fare (and ticket you may buy) works and be aware of the security requirements for international travel. Shop carefully. The details given in this chapter should be regarded as pointers and are not a substitute for your own careful, up-to-date research.

Air Berlin (☎ 902 320 737; www.airberlin.com) German budget airline with flights to Madrid from around 15 cities across western Europe and domestic flights within Spain.

Air Europa (☎ 902 401 501; www.aireuropa.com) Connects Madrid with London, Paris, Milan, Venice, Rome and Lisbon, as well as destinations in Africa, the Caribbean, South America and dozens of Spanish airports.

Air France (☎ 902 207 090; www.airfrance.com)

Alitalia (☎ 902 100 323; www.alitalia.it)

American Airlines (☎ 902 887 300; www.aa.com) Madrid from New York, Miami and Dallas/Fort Worth.

Andalus (☎ 902 887 300; www.andalus.es) Flights to Almería, San Sebastián and Gibraltar.

Austrian Airlines (☎ 902 551 257; www.aua.com) Madrid direct from Frankfurt and from Vienna via Munich and Barcelona.

British Airways (☎ 902 111 333; www.britishairways .com) London Heathrow to Madrid.

Continental Airlines (☎ 900 961 266; www.continental .com) Daily flights to New York with connections to other US cities.

easyJet (☎ 807 260 026; www.easyjet.com) Madrid from 18 European and Moroccan cities, with some domestic Spanish routes.

Emirates (www.emirates.com) Due to begin Madrid–Dubai services some time in 2010, with connections throughout Asia, the Middle East and Australia.

German Wings (☎ 807 070 025; www.germanwings .com) Flies to Madrid from more than 20 European cities.

Iberia (☎ 902 400 500; www.iberia.es) Spain's national airline with flights throughout Spain, Europe, Asia and the Americas.

KLM (☎ 902 222 747; www.klm.com) Madrid to Amsterdam.

INTERNET AIR FARES

Most airlines, especially budget ones, encourage you to book on their websites. Other useful general sites to search for competitive fares include the following:
www.atrapalo.com, in Spanish
www.cheaptickets.com
www.ebookers.com
www.expedia.com
www.lowestfare.com
www.opodo.com
www.orbitz.com
www.planesimple.co.uk
www.rumbo.es, in Spanish
www.sta.com
www.travel.com.au
www.travelocity.com

Lufthansa (☎ 902 883 882; www.lufthansa.com) Madrid from Hamburg, Frankfurt, Toulouse and Milan.

Malev Hungarian Airlines (☎ 902 104 786; www.malev .hu) Madrid to Budapest.

Qatar Airways (☎ 902 627 070; www.qatarairways.com) Madrid to Doha and connections across the Middle East and Australia.

Royal Air Maroc (☎ 902 210 010; www.royalairmaroc .com) Madrid to Moroccan cities with connections across Africa and the Middle East.

Ryanair (☎ 807 220 032; www.ryanair.com) Madrid from 15 European airports as well as domestic Spanish routes from Madrid.

Scandinavian SAS (☎ 802 112 117; www.flysas.es) Madrid to Copenhagen.

Spanair (☎ 902 131 415; www.spanair.com) Flights from dozens of destinations throughout Spain and Europe, as well as the US, Africa and Bangkok.

Swiss International Airlines (☎ 901 116 712; www .swiss.com) Madrid to Zurich.

TAP Air Portugal (☎ 901 116 718; www.flytap.com) Madrid from Lisbon and Porto.

Thai Airways (☎ 91 782 05 21; www.thaiairways.com) Madrid to Bangkok with connections in Asia, Australia and New Zealand.

Turkish Airlines (☎ 902 124 440; www.turkishairlines .com) Madrid to Istanbul.

Vueling (☎ 807 200 200; www.vueling.com) Spanish low-cost company with flights between Madrid and European destinations, as well as domestic Spanish flights.

Airport

Madrid's Barajas airport (☎ 902 404 704; www.aena.es) lies 12km northeast of the city, and every year almost 50 million passengers pass through here.

Terminal 4 (T4) is the airport's architectural showpiece and deals mainly with flights of Iberia and its partners (eg British Airways, American Airlines and Vueling), while the remainder leave from the conjoined T1, T2 and (rarely) T3. Iberia's Puente Aereo (air shuttle) between Madrid and Barcelona, which operates like a bus service with no advance booking necessary, operates from T4 with 30 flights per day. To match your airline with a terminal, visit the Madrid-Barajas section of www.aena.es and click on 'Airlines'.

TRANSPORT AIR

CLIMATE CHANGE & TRAVEL

Climate change is a serious threat to the ecosystems that humans rely upon, and air travel is the fastest-growing contributor to the problem. Lonely Planet regards travel, overall, as a global benefit, but believes we all have a responsibility to limit our personal impact on global warming.

Flying & Climate Change

Pretty much every form of motor transport generates carbon dioxide (the main cause of human-induced climate change) but planes are far and away the worst offenders, not just because of the sheer distances they allow us to travel but because they release greenhouse gases high into the atmosphere. The statistics are frightening: two people taking a return flight between Europe and the US will contribute as much to climate change as an average household's gas and electricity consumption over a whole year.

Carbon Offset Schemes

Climatecare.org and other websites use 'carbon calculators' that allow travellers to offset the greenhouse gases they are responsible for with contributions to energy-saving projects and other climate-friendly initiatives in the developing world – including projects in India, Honduras, Kazakhstan and Uganda.

Lonely Planet, together with Rough Guides and other concerned partners in the travel industry, supports the carbon offset scheme run by climatecare.org. Lonely Planet offsets all of its staff and author travel.

For more information check out our website: www.lonelyplanet.com.

Although all airlines conduct check-in (*facturación*) at the airport's departure areas, some also allow check-in at the Nuevos Ministerios Metro stop and transport interchange in Madrid itself – ask your airline.

Parking is available outside T1, T2 and T4. Rates are €1.65 per hour, up to €18 for 24 hours. Further away from the terminals and linked by a free shuttle bus is the Parking de Largas Estancias (Long-term Carpark; ☎ 91 393 69 37; www.largaestancias.com; 1/2/5/10 days €10.60/21.20/50/78). If you plan to leave a vehicle in one of the car parks for several days, bookings must be made in advance.

Other important airport services include:

ATMs & exchange booths All terminals.

Ayuntamiento tourist information office (☎ 91 588 16 36; ☺ 9am-8pm) In the T4 arrivals hall.

Car-rental companies In the arrivals area of T1, T2 and T4.

Comunidad de Madrid tourist office (☎ T1 91 305 86 56; T4 902 100 007; ☺ 9am-8pm) In the arrivals areas of T1 and T4.

Left-luggage offices (consignas; ☎ 902 404 704; ☺ 24hr; 1 day €3.85, 2 to 15 days per day per small/large bag €3.83/4.93; more than 15 days per day €1.97 plus 1-off transfer fee to storage €39.34) Located in T1, T2 and T4.

Post office (☎ T1 8.30am-8.30pm Mon-Fri, 9.30am-1pm Sat, T4 8.30am-2.30pm Mon-Fri, 9.30am-1pm Sat) In the arrivals lounges of T1 and T4.

Pharmacy (☺ T4 24hr; T1 & T2 7am-11pm)

BICYCLE

Lots of people zip around town on *motos* (mopeds), but little has been done to encourage cyclists in Madrid and bike lanes are almost as rare as drivers who keep an eye out for cyclists.

You can transport your bicycle on the metro from 10am to 12.30pm and after 9pm Mondays to Fridays and all day on weekends and holidays. You can also take your bike aboard *cercanías* (local trains serving big cities and nearby towns) from 10am onwards Monday to Friday and all day on weekends.

For cycling tours, see p262.

Hire

Bike Spain (Map pp62-3; ☎ 91 559 06 53; www.bikespain.info; Plaza de la Villa 1, Calle del Codo; per half-/full day €10/15, Sat & Sun €30; ☺ 10am-2pm & 4-7pm Mon-Fri) Also good for practical information and finding bike-friendly accommodation.

By Bike (Map p91; ☎ 902 876 483; www.bybike.info; Avenida de Menédez Pelayo 35; per hr/day €4/20; ☺ 10am-9pm Mon-Fri, 9.30am-9.30pm Sat & Sun Jun-Sep, 10am-3pm & 5-9pm Mon-Fri, 9am-9pm Sat & Sun Oct-May; Ⓜ Ibiza) Ideally placed for the Parque del Buen Retiro and with child seats/trailers (€5/10), roller blades and electric bikes for hire. Prices vary depending on the length of hire and number of people.

Trixi.com (Map pp62-3; ☎ 91 523 15 47; www.trixi.com; Calle de los Jardines 12; per 4/8/24 hr €8/12/15, helmet

---

GETTING INTO TOWN

Metro
The easiest way into town from the airport is line 8 of the metro (www.metromadrid.es, in Spanish; entrances in T2 & T4) to the Nuevos Ministerios transport interchange, which connects with lines 10 and 6 and the local overground *cercanías* (local trains serving suburbs and nearby towns). It operates from 6.05am to 2am. A single ticket costs €1 (10-ride Metrobús ticket €9); there's a €1 supplement if you're travelling to/from the airport in addition to the prices listed above. The journey to Nuevos Ministerios takes around 15 minutes, around 25 minutes from T4.

Bus & Minibus
Alternatively from T1, T2 and T3 take bus 200 to/from the Intercambiador de Avenida de América (transport interchange on Avenida de América; Map p121). From T4 take bus 204. The same ticket prices apply as for the metro. The first departures from the airport are at 5.36am (T1, T2 and T3) or 5.50am (T4). The last scheduled service from the airport is 11.30pm; buses leave every 12 to 15 minutes. There's also a free bus service connecting all four terminals.

AeroCITY (☎ 91 747 75 70; www.aerocity.com; per person €5-19) is a private minibus service that takes you door-to-door between central Madrid and the airport (T1 in front of arrivals gate 2, T2 between gates 5 and 6, and T4 ground level). It operates 24 hours and you can book by phone or online.

Taxi
A taxi to the city centre costs around €25 in total (up to €35 from T4), depending on traffic and where you're going; rates can be between €5 and €10 higher at night; in addition to what the meter says, you pay a €5.50 supplement. There are taxi ranks outside all four terminals.

€2.50; ☺ 10am-2pm & 4-8pm Mon-Fri, 10am-8pm Sat & Sun Mar-Oct, 10am-3pm daily Nov, Dec & Feb; Ⓜ Gran Vía)

Urban Movil (Map pp62-3; ☎ 91 542 77 71; Plaza de Santiago 2; per hr/half-/full day €4.50/14/19)

BUS
Long Distance

Estación Sur de Autobuses (☎ 91 468 42 00; www.estacion deautobuses.com, in Spanish; Calle de Méndez Álvaro 83; Ⓜ Méndez Álvaro), just south of the M-30 ring road, is the city's principal bus station. It serves most destinations to the south and many in other parts of the country. Most bus companies have a ticket office here, even if their buses depart from elsewhere.

The station operates a consigna (left-luggage office; ☺ 6.30am-midnight) on the first subterranean level. There are cafes, shops, exchange booths, a bank and a police post; there's also direct access to metro line 6.

Eurolines (www.eurolines.com), in conjunction with local carriers all over Europe, is the main international carrier connecting Spain to cities across Europe and Morocco from the Estación Sur. For information and tickets contact Eurolines Peninsular (☎ 902 405 040, 91 506 33 60; www.eurolines.es). ALSA Internacional (☎ 902 422 242; www.alsa.es) is another international operator.

Most domestic services operate from the Estación Sur, although some services leave from other terminals around the city, including the Intercambiador de Autobuses de Moncloa (Map pp116-17) and the Intercambiador de Avenida de América (Map p121).

Major companies:

ALSA (☎ 902 422 242; www.alsa.es) One of the largest Spanish companies with many services throughout Spain. Most depart from Estación Sur but some buses headed north (including to Bilbao and Zaragoza, and some services to Barcelona) leave from the Intercambiador de Avenida de América with occasional services from T4 of Madrid's Barajas Airport.

Avanzabus (☎ 902 020 052; www.avanzabus.com) Services to Extremadura (eg Cáceres), Castilla y León (eg Salamanca and Zamora) and Valencia via Cuenca, as well as Lisbon, Portugal. All leave from the Estación Sur.

Autocares Herranz (Map pp116-17; ☎ 91 890 41 00; Intercambiador de Autobuses de Moncloa; Ⓜ Moncloa) Buses 661 and 664 to San Lorenzo de El Escorial from platform 3 at the Moncloa train station.

La Sepulvedana (Map pp124-5; ☎ 91 541 32 83; www .lasepulvedana.es, in Spanish; Paseo de la Florida 11; Ⓜ Príncipe Pío) Buses to Segovia leave from Platforms 6 and 7 of the Intercambiador de Príncipe Pío.

La Veloz (Map pp124-5; ☎ 91 409 76 02; Avenida del Mediterráneo 49; Ⓜ Conde de Casal) Half-hourly buses (route 337) to Chinchón from 100m west of Plaza del Conde de Casal.

Within Madrid

Buses operated by Empresa Municipal de Transportes de Madrid (EMT; ☎ 902 507 850; www.emtmadrid.es, in Spanish) travel along most city routes regularly between about 6.30am and 11.30pm. Twenty-six night-bus *búhos* (owls) routes operate from 11.45pm to 5.30am, with all routes originating in Plaza de la Cibeles. Fares for day and night trips are the same: €1 for a single trip, €9 for a 10-trip Metrobús ticket. Single-trip tickets can be purchased on board.

For details of the Madrid Visión sightseeing buses, see p262.

CAR & MOTORCYCLE

Madrid is 2622km from Berlin, 2245km from London, 1889km from Milan, 1836km from Paris, 1470km from Geneva, 690km from Barcelona and 610km from Lisbon. The A-1 heads north to Burgos and ultimately to Santander (for the UK ferry), the A-2 wends its way northeast to Barcelona and ultimately into France (as the AP-7), while the A-3 heads down to Valencia. The A-4 takes you south to Andalucía, while the A-5 and A-6 respectively take you west towards Portugal via Cáceres and northwest to Galicia. The A-42 goes south to Toledo.

The city is surrounded by two main ring roads, the outermost M-40 and the inner M-30; there are also two additional partial ring roads, the M-45 and the more-distant M-50. The R-5 and R-3 are part of a series of toll roads built to ease traffic jams.

Coming from the UK you can put your car on a ferry from Plymouth or Portsmouth to Santander with Brittany Ferries (www.brittany-ferries .com; 4 departures per wk). Sailing times vary from 24 to 35 hours. Santander is 399km by road to Madrid. Otherwise you can opt for a ferry to France or the Channel Tunnel car train, Eurotunnel (www.eurotunnel.com).

Vehicles must be roadworthy, registered and insured (third-party at least). Also ask your insurer for a European Accident Statement form, which can simplify matters in the event of an accident. A European breakdown-assistance policy is a good investment – ask your insurance company for details.

If you're here on a tourist visa, you only need your national driving licence, although it's wise to also carry an International Driving Permit (available from the automobile association in your home country and valid for one year).

Driving

The Spanish drive on the right-hand side. The morning and evening rush hours frequently involve snarling traffic jams. They're even possible in the wee hours of the morning, especially on weekends when the whole city seems to be behind the wheel or in a bar. The streets are dead between about 2pm and 4pm, when people are either eating or snoozing.

Hire

The big-name car-hire agencies have offices all over Madrid. Avis, Europcar, Hertz and National/Atesa have booths at the airport. Some also operate branches at Atocha and Chamartín train stations. If prices at the bigger agencies seem too high, try Auto Europe (www .auto-europe.com), which operates as a clearing house for the best deals by the major companies. The rental agencies' most central offices include the following:

Avis (Map pp108-9; ☎ 902 180 854; www.avis.es; Gran Vía 60; Ⓜ Santo Domingo or Plaza de España)

Blazer Motos (Map p121; ☎ 91 413 00 47; www.blafer motos.com; Calle de Clara del Rey 17; ⏰ 8.30am-6pm Mon-Fri, 10am-1.30pm Sun; Ⓜ Cartagena) Rents 50cc to 1100cc motorcycles.

Europcar (Map pp108-9; ☎ 902 105 030; www.europcar. es; Calle de San Leonardo de Dios 8; Ⓜ Plaza de España)

Hertz (Map pp108-9; ☎ 902 402 405; www.hertz.es; Edificio de España, Calle de Princesa 14; Ⓜ Plaza de España)

National/Atesa (Map pp116-17; ☎ 902 100 101; www .atesa.es; underground parking area, Plaza de España; Ⓜ Plaza de España)

Pepecar (Map pp116-17; ☎ 807 414 243; www .pepecar.com; underground parking area, Plaza de España; Ⓜ Plaza de España) Specialises in low-cost rentals. Bookings are best made over the internet.

Parking

Most of Madrid is divided into clearly marked blue or green street-parking zones. In both areas parking meters apply from 9am to 8pm Monday to Friday and from 9am to 3pm on Saturday; the Saturday hours also apply daily in August. In the green areas you can park for a maximum of one hour (or keep putting money in the meter every hour) for €2. In the

blue zones you can park for two hours for €2.80. There are also private parking stations all over central Madrid.

You'll see local cars parked in the most unlikely of places, but following their example by parking (or double-parking) in a designated no-parking area exposes you to the risk of being towed. Should your car disappear, call the Grúa Municipal (city towing service; ☎ 91 787 72 92). Getting it back costs €144.70 plus whatever fine you've been given.

METRO & CERCANÍAS

Madrid's modern metro (☎ 902 444 403; www.metro madrid.es), Europe's second-largest, is a fast, efficient and safe way to navigate Madrid, and generally easier than getting to grips with bus routes. There are 11 colour-coded lines in central Madrid, in addition to the modern southern suburban MetroSur system as well as lines heading east to the major population centres of Pozuelo and Boadilla del Monte. Colour maps showing the metro system are available from any metro station. The metro operates from 6.05am to 2am.

The short-range *cercanías* regional trains operated by Renfe (☎ 902 320 320; www.renfe.es /cercanias/madrid), the national railway, go as far afield as El Escorial, Alcalá de Henares, Aranjuez and other points in the Comunidad de Madrid. Tickets range between €1.25 and €4.25 depending on how far you're travelling. In Madrid itself they're handy for making a quick, north–south hop between Chamartín and Atocha train stations (with stops at Nuevos Ministerios and Sol).

Tickets

Unless you're only passing through en route to elsewhere, you should buy a Metrobús ticket valid for 10 rides (bus and metro) for €9; single-journey tickets cost €1. Tickets can be purchased at stations from manned booths or machines in the metro stations, as well as most *estancos* (tobacconists) and newspaper kiosks. Metrobús tickets are not valid on *cercanías* services. Children under four travel free.

Monthly or season passes *(abonos)* only make sense if you're staying long term and use local transport frequently. You'll need to get a *carnet* (ID card) from metro stations or tobacconists – take a passport-sized photo and your passport. A monthly ticket for central Madrid (Zona A) costs €46.

An Abono Transporte Turístico (Tourist Ticket; per 1/2/7 days €5.20/8.80/23.60) is also possible.

The fine for being caught without a ticket on public transport is €20 – in addition to the price of the ticket, of course.

TAXI

You can pick up a taxi at ranks throughout town or simply flag one down. Flag fall is €2.05 from 6am to 10pm daily, €2.20 from 10pm to 6am Sunday to Friday and €3.10 from 10pm Saturday to 6am Sunday. You pay between €0.98 and €1.18 per kilometre depending on the time of day. Several supplementary charges, usually posted inside the taxi, apply; these include €5.50 to/from the airport; €2.95 from taxi ranks at train and bus stations, €2.95 to/from the Parque Ferial Juan Carlos I; and €6.70 on New Year's Eve and Christmas Eve from 10pm to 6am. There's no charge for luggage.

Among the 24-hour taxi services are Tele-Taxi (☎ 91 371 21 31, 902 501 130) and Radio-Teléfono Taxi (☎ 91 547 82 00, 91 547 82 00; www.radiotelefono-taxi .com).

A green light on the roof means the taxi is libre (available). Usually a sign to this effect is also placed in the lower passenger side of the windscreen.

Tipping taxi drivers is not common practice, although most travellers round fares up to the nearest euro or two.

TRAIN

Spain's rail network is one of Europe's best, with Madrid well-connected to cities and towns across Spain. A handful of international trains also serves the city.

For information on travelling from the UK contact Rail Europe (☎ 08448 484 064; www.raileurope .co.uk).

For travel within Spain, information (including timetables) is available from your nearest train station or travel agent, or from the operator of the rail network, Renfe (☎ 902 240 202; www.renfe.es).

There are different types of service, but remember that saving a couple of hours on a faster train can mean a big hike in the fare. Most trains have preferente (1st class) and turista (2nd class) and have dining cars.

High-speed Tren de Alta Velocidad Española (AVE) services connect Madrid with Seville (via Córdoba), Valladolid (via Segovia), Toledo, Málaga and Barcelona (via Zaragoza, Huesca and Tarragona). Most high-speed services operate from Madrid's Puerta de Atocha station. The Madrid-Segovia/ Valladolid service leaves from the Chamartín station. Extensions to the AVE network are planned to Valencia, Cuenca, Cádiz, Albacete, Alicante and Girona. AVE trains can reach speeds of 350km/h.

Train Stations

Two train stations serve the city. Note that many trains call in at either one or the other (but only sometimes both), so check when buying tickets. At Puerta de Atocha train station (Map pp84-5; Ⓜ Atocha Renfe), south of the city centre, there's an information and ticket centre for long-distance services (including the high-speed AVE) in the station (the part now serving as a tropical garden). In the same area are luggage lockers available from 6.30am to 10.20pm. Another information office (☒ 7am-11pm) near platforms 9 and 10 (look for the 'Atención al Cliente' sign) deals with regional and cercanías trains, and property lost on these trains. Tickets for regional trains can be bought at a separate counter.

In Chamartín train station (Map p121; Ⓜ Chamartín) information and tickets are available at the Centro de Viajes (☒ 7am-11pm) between platforms 7 and 10. Exchange booths and ATMs are scattered about the station. Lockers are located outside the main station building (take the exit opposite platform 18) and are available between 7am and 11pm.

DIRECTORY

BUSINESS HOURS

Standard working hours are Monday to Friday from 8am or 9am to 2pm and then again from 3pm or 4pm for another three hours.

Banks open from 8.30am to 2pm or 2.15pm Monday to Friday; some branches also open 4pm to 7pm on Thursday and/or 9am to 1pm on Saturday.

The Central Post Office opens from 8.30am to 9.30pm Monday to Friday and 8.30am to 2pm Saturday; most suburban post offices open from 8.30am to 8.30pm Monday to Friday and from 9.30am to 1pm on Saturday.

Opening hours for shops are covered on p130, while restaurant times are on p148.

CHILDREN

For madrileños (and Spaniards in general), going out to eat or sipping a beer late on a summer evening at a *terraza* (open-air bar) rarely means leaving kids with minders. Locals take their kids out all the time and don't worry too much about keeping them up late, at least in summer. That, of course, doesn't apply to late-night revelling, when Madrid's army of willing grandparents are called into baby-sitting action.

Madrid has plenty of child-friendly sights and activities. Most churches and museums probably aren't among them, but the Museo de Cera (Wax Museum; p111) usually works for kids old enough to recognise the famous figures.

If your boy's a typical boy, he'll most likely love the Museo del Ferrocarril (p127) and the Museo Naval (p96), the railway and navy museums respectively. A trip to the Estadio Santiago Bernabéu (p120) to see Real Madrid and some of the greatest names in football or to stand on the hallowed turf is also a must for those who love their sport.

Riding the Teleférico (p115) can also score points. The Parque del Buen Retiro (p97) has ample space to run around or you can rent a boat; on weekends and holidays you may catch some marionette theatre or see jugglers. Check it out at www.titirilandia.com (in Spanish).

Not especially typical of Madrid, but fun nonetheless, are the amusement parks such as the Parque de Atracciones (p127) or Warner Brothers Movie World (p127), outside the city. For some animal fun, try Faunia (p128) or the Zoo Aquarium de Madrid (p126).

In the hot summer months you'll doubtless be rewarded by squeals of delight if you take the bairns to one of the city's municipal pools (p209). For something a little more exhilarating, try the Parque de Nieve (Ski Park) at Madrid Xanadú (p210) for year-round skiing. Other possibilities for something a little bit different include:

Teatro Fernán Gómez (Map p102; ☎ 91 480 03 00; http://teatrofernangomez.esmadrid.com/; Plaza de Colón; Ⓜ Colón or Serrano) Reasonably regular program of children's theatre.

Escuela Popular de Musica y Danza (Map pp116-17; ☎ 91 447 56 82; www.popularedemusica.com, in Spanish; Calle de Trafalgar 22; Ⓜ Bilbao) Classes in music (instruments and appreciation) and dance for kids, although little for the short-term visitor.

La Escalera de Jacob (p183) Children's theatre Saturdays and Sundays at 5pm.

For great ideas and general advice on travelling with children, grab Lonely Planet's *Travel with Children*.

Baby-sitting

There's no real tradition in Spain of professional baby-sitting services – most Spaniards have *abuelos* (grandparents) or other extended family at the ready. That said, some midrange and most top-end hotels in Madrid can organise baby-sitting. Or you can try to line something up through www.canguroencasa .com (in Spanish; *canguro* or 'kangaroo' also

---

CHILDREN'S ACTIVITIES – FIND OUT MORE

To get a grip on what Madrid has to offer for children during your visit, start by looking in the various weekly activities guides (see p202 for details on where to pick them up). The *Guía del Ocio* has a 'Niños' section with children's theatre and sights listing, while 'El Madrid de los niños' in *On Madrid* is similar. The Ayuntamiento's Centro de Turismo de Madrid (p265) also has a children's section in its weekly *EsMadrid Magazine*, and a brochure entitled *For Your Family* with a list of child-friendly museums and entertainment.

means baby-sitter in Spanish), although it's based around baby-sitters advertising their services rather than functioning as a central-ised booking service; baby-sitters who speak English and other languages are highlighted.

CLIMATE

For Spaniards who don't live in Madrid, the capital's weather is a source of amusement. It has, they say, a climate of extremes, as summed up by the phrase *nueve meses de invierno y tres de infierno* (nine months of winter and three of hell). To a certain extent they're right: the *meseta* (high inland plateau) where the city is located indeed ensures scorching summers and bitterly cold winters. But Madrid's climate is not without its staunch supporters, among them Hemingway (who described Madrid's climate as the best in Spain) and fashion de-signer Agatha Ruiz de la Prada (who told us that 'it's a climate that can make you feel quite euphoric'). Personally, we love the absence of humidity, the piercing blue skies for much of winter, and the hot, dry summer days.

July is the hottest month, with August running a close second. Average highs hover above 30°C, but the maximum is frequently in excess of 35°C and sometimes nudges 40°C. When a heat wave sweeps through, it can get uncomfortable, but it's rare that the heat gets too oppressive for more than a couple of weeks a year. Air-conditioning in your room is, at such times, a godsend.

The coldest months are January and Feb-ruary, when daily average highs are less than 10°C, although as high as 15°C, or as low as 0°C, is not uncommon. At night it frequently drops below freezing, yet it rarely snows in Madrid. Whatever the official temperature, you'll really notice the cold when an icy wind blows in off the snowcapped sierra.

Spring and autumn are lovely times to be in Madrid, although you can be unlucky. In Spain they say *cuando en marzo mayea, en mayo marzea*. In other words, if you get nice, warm dry days in March (weather more typical of May), you'll be wiping that grin off your face in May, when the wet spells you missed earlier catch up with you! Never short of a saying, Spaniards say of April, *mes de abril, aguas mil* – it rains a lot in this spring month.

COURSES

Madrid is a good place to base yourself for learning Spanish or flamenco. If you're inter-ested in shorter-term cooking courses, turn to p148, while wine appreciation courses are covered on p185.

Spanish Classes

Madrid is jammed with language schools of all possible categories, as eager to teach foreign-ers Spanish as locals other languages.

Non-EU citizens who want to study at a university or language school in Spain should, in theory, have a study visa. These visas can be obtained from your nearest Spanish embassy or consulate. You'll normally require confir-mation of your enrolment, payment of fees and proof of adequate funds to support your-self before a visa is issued. This type of visa is renewable within Spain but, again, only with confirmation of ongoing enrolment and proof that you're able to support yourself.

The tourist office hands out the helpful brochure *Studying Spanish in Madrid* (it's also available for download as a pdf at www .esmadrid.com), which lists language schools that are members of the Professional Asso-ciation of Spanish Schools of Madrid. These include:

Academia Inhispania (Map pp62-3; ☎ 91 521 22 31; www.inhispania.com; Calle de la Montera 10-12; Ⓜ Sol) Intensive four-week courses start at €460.

Academia Madrid Plus (Map pp62-3; ☎ 91 548 11 16; www.madridplus.es; 6th fl, Calle del Arenal 21; Ⓜ Ópera) Four-week courses start from €310, and go up to €710 for intensive courses.

Don Quijote Madrid (Map pp108-9; ☎ 91 360 41 33; www.donquijote.org; Calle del Duque de Liria 6; Ⓜ Ventura Rodríguez or Plaza de España) Intensive four-week courses from €716.

Estudio Sampere (Map p102; ☎ 91 431 43 66; www .sampere.es; Calle de Lagasca 16; Ⓜ Retiro or Serrano) Intensive classes (20 hours a week) cost €784.

Eureka (Map pp62-3; ☎ 91 548 86 40; www .eurekamadrid.com; 3rd fl, Calle de Arenal 26; Ⓜ Sol or Ópera) Intensive 20-hour per week courses cost €685.

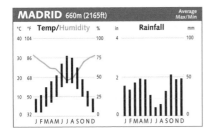

MADRID 660m (2165ft)			Average Max/Min
°C °F **Temp/Humidity** %	in	**Rainfall**	mm

International House (Map pp116-17; ☎ 91 319 72 24; www.ihmadrid.es; Calle de Zurbano 8; Ⓜ Alonso Martínez) Intensive courses cost €744 (20 hours per week) to €1109 (30 hours per week). Staff can organise accommodation with local families.

Universidad Complutense (Map pp58-9; ☎ 91 394 53 25; www.ucm.es/info/cextran/Index.htm; Secretaria de los Cursos para Extranjeros, Facultadole Filologia [Edificio A] Universidad Complutense, Cuidad Universitaria, 28040 Madrid; Ⓜ Cuidad Universitaria) A range of language and cultural courses throughout the year. An intensive semester course of 120 contact hours costs €1100, while month-long courses (48 hours) start from €442.

Flamenco

There are plenty of places where you can learn to dance *sevillanas* or strum the guitar like the greats.

Academia Amor de Dios (Map pp76-7; ☎ 91 360 04 34; www.amordedios.com, in Spanish; 1st fl, Calle de Santa Isabel 5; Ⓜ Antón Martín) The best-known course for flamenco dancing (and probably the hardest to get into), although it's more for budding professionals (as the list of past graduates attests) than casual visitors. It's on the top floor of the Mercado de Antón Martín.

El Flamenco Vive (Map pp62-3; ☎ 91 547 39 17; www.elflamencovive.com; Calle del Conde de Lemos 7; ⊙ 10.30am-2pm & 5-9pm Mon-Sat; Ⓜ Ópera) Guitar lessons for €25 per hour.

Fundación Conservatorio Casa Patas (Map pp76-7; ☎ 91 429 84 71; www.conservatorioflamenco.org, in Spanish; Calle de Cañizares 10; Ⓜ Antón Martín or Tirso de Molina) Every conceivable type of flamenco instruction (€28 to €129 per month, plus around €30 joining fee), including dance, guitar, singing and much more. It's upstairs from the Casa Patas flamenco *tablao*.

Other Courses

Cultural centres around Madrid offer courses in just about anything, while a handful of places teach music and dance.

Centro Cultural de Lavapiés (Map pp76-7; ☎ 91 506 07 12; Calle del Olivar 46; ⊙ 9am-2pm & 5-7pm Mon-Fri; Ⓜ Lavapiés) A range of (mostly Spanish-language) courses spanning ceramics, photography, t'ai chi, guitar, reflexology and more.

Escuela Popular de Musica y Danza (Map pp116-17; ☎ 91 447 56 82; www.populardemusica.com, in Spanish; Calle de Trafalgar 22; Ⓜ Bilbao) Classes in music, dance and drama.

Kabokla (p195) Samba, capoeira, salsa, merengue and bachata classes in this fine Brazilian live-music venue.

CUSTOMS REGULATIONS

People entering Spain from outside the EU are allowed to bring in duty-free one bottle of spirits, one bottle of wine, 50mL of perfume and 200 cigarettes. There are no duty-free allowances for travel between EU countries. For duty-paid items bought at normal shops in one EU country and taken into another, the allowances are 90L of wine, 10L of spirits, unlimited quantities of perfume and 800 cigarettes. For more information on obtaining VAT refunds, see the boxed text, p131.

DISCOUNT CARDS

The International Student Identity Card (ISIC; see www.isic.org) and the Euro<26 card (www.euro26.org), for people aged under 26, are available from most national student organisations and can gain you discounted access to sights.

If you're over 65, you may be eligible for a discount on admission to some attractions. In most cases, however, such discounts are restricted to those with a Seniors Card issued by an EU country or other country with which Spanish senior citizens enjoy reciprocal rights. It always pays to ask.

If you intend to do some intensive sightseeing and travelling on public transport, it might be worth looking at the Madrid Card (☎ 91 588 29 00; www.madridcard.com). It includes free entry to more than 40 museums in and around Madrid (including the Museo del Prado, Museo Thyssen-Bornemisza, Centro de Arte Reina Sofía, Estadio Santiago Bernabéu and Palacio Real) and free Descubre Madrid (p262) walking tours and the Madrid Visión tourist bus (p262), as well as discounts on public transport and in certain shops and restaurants. The ticket is available for one/two/three days (€47/60/74). There's also a cheaper version (€31/35/39), which just covers cultural sights.

The Madrid Card can be bought online, over the phone (☎ 91 360 47 72, 902 088 908), or in person at the tourist offices on Plaza Mayor or Terminal 4 in Barajas Airport (see p265), the Metro de Madrid ticket office in Terminal 2 of the airport, the Museo-Thyssen-Bornemisza (p94) and in some tobacconists and hotels; a list of major sales outlets appears on the website.

ELECTRICITY

The electric current in Madrid is 220V, 50Hz, as in the rest of continental Europe. Several countries outside Europe (such as the USA and Canada) use 110V, 60Hz, which means that it's safest to use a transformer. Plugs have two round pins, as in the rest of continental Europe.

EMBASSIES

Most countries have an embassy or consulate in Madrid.

Australia (off Map p121; ☎ 91 353 66 00; www.spain .embassy.gov.au; 24th fl, Paseo de la Castellana 259D, Torre Espacio; Ⓜ Begoña)

Canada (Map p102; ☎ 91 423 32 50; www.espana.gc.ca; Calle de Núñez de Balboa 35; Ⓜ Velázquez)

France (Map p102; ☎ 91 423 89 00; www.ambafrance-es .org/ Calle de Salustiano Olózaga 9; Ⓜ Retiro)

Germany (Map pp116-17; ☎ 91 557 90 00; www.madrid .diplo.de; Calle de Fortuny 8; Ⓜ Rubén Dario)

Ireland (Map p102; ☎ 91 436 40 93; embajada@irlanda .es; 4th fl, Paseo de la Castellana 46; Ⓜ Rubén Dario)

Japan (Map p121; ☎ 91 590 76 00; www.es-emb-japan .jp/; Calle de Serrano 109; Ⓜ Gregorio Marañon)

New Zealand (Map p121; ☎ 91 523 02 26; www.nzembassy .com/spain; 3rd fl, Calle de Pinar 7; Ⓜ Gregorio Marañón)

UK (off Map p121; ☎ 91 714 63 00; www.ukinspain.com; Paseo de la Castellana 259D, Torre Espacio; Ⓜ Colón)

USA (Map p102; ☎ 91 587 22 00; www.embusa.es; Calle de Serrano 75; Ⓜ Núñez de Balboa)

EMERGENCY

For practical information on keeping your wits about you in Madrid, see p263. To report thefts or other crime-related matters, your best bet is the **Servicio de Atención al Turista Extranjero** (Foreign Tourist Assistance Service; Map pp62-3; ☎ 91 548 85 37, 91 548 80 08; www.esmadrid.com/satemadrid; Calle de Leganitos 19; ⏰ 9am-10pm; Ⓜ Plaza de España or Santo Domingo), which is housed in the central police station or *comisaría* of the National Police. Here you'll find specially trained officers working alongside representatives from the tourism ministry. They can also assist in cancelling credit cards, as well as contacting your embassy or your family. There's also a **general number** (☎ 902 102 112; ☎ 24hr English & Spanish, 8am-midnight other languages) for reporting crimes.

Ambulance (☎ 061)

EU standard emergency number (☎ 112)

Fire brigade (Bomberos; ☎ 080)

Local police (Policía Municipal; ☎ 092)

Military police (Guardia Civil; ☎ 062)

National police (Policía Nacional; ☎ 091)

Teléfono de la víctima (Hotline for victims of racial or sexual violence; ☎ 902 180 995)

HOLIDAYS

For madrileños the main holiday periods are during summer (July and especially August), Christmas–New Year and Easter. August can be a peculiar time as locals make their annual migration to the beach and the city they leave behind falls quiet and grinds to a halt – this is a bad time to be trying to do business, although the change is less pronounced than it used to be. When a holiday falls close to a weekend, madrileños like to make a *puente* (bridge) and take the intervening day off. On the odd occasion when a couple of holidays fall close, they make an *acueducto* (aqueduct)!

For more information on the city's festivals and other events, turn to p16.

Public Holidays

Madrid's 14 public holidays are as follows:

Año Nuevo (New Year's Day) 1 January – see p16.

Reyes (Epiphany or Three Kings' Day) 6 January – see p17.

Jueves Santo (Holy Thursday) March/April – see p18.

Viernes Santo (Good Friday) March/April – see p18.

Labour Day (Fiesta del Trabajo) 1 May.

Fiesta de la Comunidad de Madrid 2 May – see p18.

Fiestas de San Isidro Labrador 15 May – see p18.

La Asunción (Feast of the Assumption) 15 August.

Día de la Hispanidad (Spanish National Day) 12 October – a fairly sober occasion with a military parade along the Paseo de la Castellana.

Todos los Santos (All Saints' Day) 1 November.

Día de la Virgen de la Almudena 9 November – see p20.

Día de la Constitución (Constitution Day) 6 December.

La Inmaculada Concepción (Feast of the Immaculate Conception) 8 December.

Navidad (Christmas) 25 December – see p20.

INTERNET ACCESS

If you're toting a laptop, most midrange and top-end hotels have either wi-fi or cable ADSL in-room connections; even some of the better hotels can run out of cables for the latter so ask for one as soon as you arrive. For everyone else, there are plenty of internet cafes around town.

WI-FI ACCESS

The expansion of free public wi-fi hotspots around Madrid has stalled somewhat under pressure from internet service providers eager to make a profit. In the meantime, Plaza de Santo Domingo (Map pp62-3) and the Biblioteca Nacional (p103) are among those places where you can get online for free. An increasing number of cafes – Diurno (p191) in Chueca is a particularly agreeable example – offer free wi-fi access. Chueca Wifi (www.chuecawifi.com) is a barrio initiative aimed at transforming Chueca into one big wi-fi hotspot and dozens of businesses have signed up; check out its website for more details. Otherwise, check out www.totalhotspots.com/directory/es for a list of businesses offering wi-fi access.

If you're going to be in town a little longer, monthly subscriptions and prepaid accounts are possible through Telefonica (www.telefonica.es, in Spanish), as well as private operators such as Yacom (www.ya.com, in Spanish), Orange (www.orange.es, in Spanish) and Jazztel (www.jazztel.com, in Spanish). Vodafone (www.vodafone.es, in Spanish) and Telefónica also offer wireless internet connections through a variety of plans that work throughout Spain via a USB modem that plugs into your laptop. It's ideal if you'll be travelling around in Spain.

Internet Cafes

In this era of wi-fi and laptop-bearing travellers, most of Madrid's better internet cafes have fallen by the wayside. You'll find plenty of small *locutorios* (small shops selling phone cards and cheap phone calls) all over the city and many have a few computers out the back, but we haven't listed these as they come and go with monotonous regularity. In the downtown area, your best option is the Ayuntamiento's Centro de Turismo de Madrid (p265) on Plaza Mayor which offers free internet for up to 15 minutes; its quieter branch beneath Plaza de Colón offers free and unlimited access. Otherwise, your best bet is Café Comercial (Map pp108-9; Glorieta de Bilbao 7; per 50 min €1; 🕒 7.30am-midnight Mon, 7.30am-1am Tue-Thu, 7.30am-2am Fri, 8.30am-2am Sat, 9am-midnight Sun; Ⓜ Bilbao), one of Madrid's grandest old cafés (p190) with internet upstairs.

MAPS

The maps in this book should be more than enough for most travellers. Long-termers seeking comprehensive map books and atlases are spoiled for choice. A good one is Almax's *Callejero de Madrid*, scaled at 1:12,000. The same publisher produces *Atlas de Madrid*, which covers Madrid and the surrounding municipalities. You could also try the superdetailed *Guía Urbana*. Michelin's *Madrid* (No 42) map is also excellent and far less cumbersome to carry around.

For something far less detailed, any of the tourist offices have maps of central Madrid.

If you're looking for a specific address, check out www.qdq.com and click on the pull-down menu under 'Callejero', then select 'Callejeros Fotográficos' where you can type in the street name and number and you'll get a photo of the building you're looking for and its map location.

MEDICAL SERVICES

All foreigners have the same right as Spaniards to emergency medical treatment in a public hospital. European Union (EU) citizens are entitled to the full range of health-care services in public hospitals free of charge, but you'll need to present your European Health Insurance Card (EHIC); inquire at your national health service before leaving home. Even if you have no insurance, you'll be treated in an emergency, with costs in the public system ranging from free to €112. Non-EU citizens have to pay for anything other than emergency treatment – one good reason among many to have a travel-insurance policy.

Your embassy should be able to refer you to doctors who speak your language. If you have a specific health complaint, obtain the necessary information and referrals for treatment before leaving home.

Some useful numbers and addresses for travellers:

Anglo-American Medical Unit (Unidad Medica; Map p102; ☎ 91 435 18 23; www.unidadmedica.com; Calle del Conde de Aranda 1; 🕒 9am-8pm Mon-Fri, emergencies 10am-1pm Sat; Ⓜ Retiro) A private clinic with a wide range of specialisations and where all doctors speak Spanish and English. Each consultation costs around €125.

Hospital General Gregorio Marañón (Map pp124-5; ☎ 91 586 80 00; www.hggm.es, in Spanish; Calle del Doctor Esquerdo 46; Ⓜ Sainz de Baranda or O'Donnell) One of the city's main hospitals.

Pharmacies

For minor health problems, you can try your local *farmacia* (pharmacy), where pharmaceuticals tend to be sold more freely without prescription than in other countries, such as the USA, Australia or the UK.

At least one pharmacy is open 24 hours per day in each district of Madrid. They mostly operate on a rota and details appear daily in *El País* and other papers. Otherwise call ☎ 010. Most pharmacies have a list in its window indicating the location of nearby after-hours pharmacies – if it says 'Dia y noche', it's open 24 hours. Pharmacies that always remain open include:

Farmacia Velázquez 70 (Map p102; ☎ 91 575 60 28; Calle de Velázquez 70; Ⓜ Velázquez)

Farmacia Mayor (Map pp62-3; ☎ 91 366 46 16; Calle Mayor 13; Ⓜ Sol)

MONEY

As in most other EU nations, Spain uses the euro. The easiest way to travel is to take a small amount of cash and withdraw money from ATMs as you go along.

Changing Money

You can change cash or travellers cheques in currencies of the developed world without problems at virtually any bank or bureau de change (usually indicated by the word *cambio*). Central Madrid also abounds with banks – most have ATMs.

Exchange offices are open for longer hours than banks but generally offer poorer rates. Also, keep a sharp eye open for commissions at bureaus de change.

Credit Cards & ATMs

Major cards, such as Visa, MasterCard, Maestro, Cirrus and, to a lesser extent, Amex, are accepted throughout Spain. They can be used in many hotels, restaurants and shops; in doing so you'll need to show some form of photo ID (eg passport) or, increasingly, you'll be asked to key in your PIN. Credit cards can also be used in ATMs displaying the appropriate sign (if there's no sign, don't risk it), or, if you have no PIN, you can obtain cash advances over the counter in many banks. Check charges with your bank.

If your card is lost, stolen or swallowed by an ATM, you can call the following numbers tollfree to have an immediate stop put on its use:

Amex (☎ 902 375 637)

Diners Club (☎ 91 211 43 00)

MasterCard (☎ 900 971 231)

Visa (☎ 900 991 216, 900 991 124)

NEWSPAPERS & MAGAZINES

There's a wide selection of national newspapers from around Europe (including most of the UK dailies) available at newsstands all over central Madrid. The *International Herald Tribune (IHT)*, *Time*, the *Economist*, *Der Spiegel* and a host of other international magazines are also available. The *IHT* includes an eight-page supplement of articles from *El País* translated into English; it's also available online at www.elpais.com/misc/herald/herald.pdf.

Madrid's bilingual, bi-annual magazine *Madriz* (www.madriz.com; €4.95) covers the latest trends and quirks of the city. The free English-language monthly *InMadrid* (www.in-madrid.com) is a handy newspaper-format publication with articles on the local scene and classifieds. It's available in some bars and pubs, English-language bookshops, language schools, consulates and some tourist offices; see the website for a full list of outlets.

Spanish Press

The main Spanish dailies are divided roughly along political lines, with the old-fashioned *ABC* (www.abc.es, in Spanish) representing the conservative right, *El País* (www.elpais.com, in Spanish) identified with the centre-left and *El Mundo* (www.elmundo.es, in Spanish) with the centre-right. Further to the right than all others is *La Razón* (www.larazon.es, in Spanish), while *El Público* (www.publico.es, in Spanish) is associated with the left. For a good spread of national and international news, *El País*, the largest-selling of the news dailies, is the pick of the bunch. But the best-selling daily of all is *Marca* (www.marca.com, in Spanish), which is devoted exclusively to sport.

Free morning dailies that you're likely to find outside metro stations and busy intersections in the morning are *AND* (www.adn.es, in Spanish), *20 Minutos* (www.20minutos.es /madrid, in Spanish) and the sensationalist *Que!* (www.que.es/madrid, in Spanish). Of the magazines devoted to Spanish politics, *Tiempo* (www.tiempodehoy.com, in Spanish) is probably the best pick.

ORGANISED TOURS

For organised culinary or tapas tours around Madrid, see the boxed text, p170. Otherwise, the following offer tours around the city and some outlying sights.

Walking Tours

Descubre Madrid (Discover Madrid; ☎ 91 588 29 06; www.esmadrid.com/descubremadrid; walking tours adult/child, student, under 25yr or senior €3.90/3.12, bus tours €6.45/5.05, bicycle tours €3.90/3.12 plus €6 bike rental) Twenty highly recommended guided tours conducted in Spanish and English. Organised by the Centro de Turismo de Madrid (Tourist Office; Map pp62-3) at Plaza Mayor 27.

Insider's Madrid (☎ 91 447 38 66; www.insidersmadrid .com) An impressive range of tailor-made tours that include walking, tapas, flamenco and bullfighting tours.

Letango Tours (Map pp76-7; ☎ 91 369 47 52; www .letango.com; 1st fl, Plaza de Tirso de Molina 12; Mon-Fri €95, Sat & Sun €135; Ⓜ Tirso de Molina) Walking tours through Madrid with additional excursions to San Lorenzo El Escorial, Segovia and Toledo.

Madrid Original (☎ 91 521 04 49; www.madridoriginal .com; per hr per group Mon-Fri/Sat/Sun from €71/95/125) Privately run tours (for up to six people) in English, Spanish or French by professional guides. Tours include the major museums, historical eras, Gran Vía, the Parque del Buen Retiro and tailor-made itineraries.

Wellington Society (☎ 609 143 203; www.wellsoc.org; tours from €60) A handful of quirky historical tours laced with anecdotes and led by the inimitable Stephen Drake-Jones. Possibilities include Bullfights, Hemingway's Madrid, Curiosities & Anecdotes of Old Madrid.

Cycling & Segway Tours

Bike Spain (Map pp62-3; ☎ 91 559 06 53 www.bikespain .info; Plaza de la Villa 1, Calle del Codo; tours €35; Ⓨ 10am-2pm & 4-7pm Mon-Fri; Ⓜ Ópera or Sol) English-language guided city tours by bicycle, by day or (Friday) night, plus longer expeditions to San Lorenzo de El Escorial (€75).

Madrid Bike Tours (☎ 680 581 782; www.madribike tours.com; 4hr tour per person €55) Londoner Mike Chandler offers a guided two-wheel tour of Madrid as well as tours further afield.

Madrid en Bicicleta (☎ 91 559 06 53; www.mtb-spain .com; day tour per person €38) Mountain-bike tours in the mountains surrounding Madrid. It also runs the two-day Guadarrama Extreme (€185). Bookings can be made through Bike Spain.

Seg City Tours (Map pp84-5; ☎ 91 127 43 93; www.seg city.es; Calle de Cervantes 22, Bajo Izq; 2-/4hr tours from €36/60; Ⓜ Antón Martín) Authorised Segway operator using the latest Segway i2 PT.

Trixi.com (Map pp62-3; ☎ 91 523 15 47; www.trixi.com; Calle de los Jardines 12; 3hr tours €22; Ⓜ Gran Vía) Cycling tours of central Madrid.

Urban Movil (Map pp62-3; ☎ 91 542 77 71, 687 535 443; www.urbanmovil.com; Plaza de Santiago 2; 1-/2hr Segway tours €40/65; Ⓨ 10am-8pm) Segway tours around Madrid. Prices include 10-minutes worth of training before you set out and it also organises bike tours.

Bus Tours

Madrid Visión (☎ 91 779 18 88, 91 765 10 16; www .madridvision.es; adult 1-/2-day ticket from €16/19, child 7-16yr & senior over 65yr 1-/2-day ticket from €7.50/10, child under 7yr free; Ⓨ 9.30am-midnight 21 Jun-20 Sep, 10am-7pm 21 Dec-20 Mar, 10am-9pm rest of year) Hop-on, hop-off open-topped buses that run every 10 to 20 minutes along two routes: Historical Madrid and Modern Madrid. Information, including maps, is available at tourist offices, most travel agencies and some hotels, or you can get tickets on the bus.

Pullmantur (Map pp62-3; ☎ 91 541 18 07; www .pullmantur.es; Plaza de Oriente 8; half-day tours from €21; Ⓜ Ópera) One of several private companies offering tours of Madrid and excursions beyond, including to San Lorenzo de El Escorial and the Valle de los Caídos, Toledo, Segovia and Ávila.

POST

Correos (☎ 902 197 197; www.correos.es), the national postal service, has its **main office** (Map p91; ☎ 91 523 06 94; Paseo del Prado 1; Ⓨ 8.30am-9.30pm Mon-Fri, 8.30am-2pm Sat; Ⓜ Banco de España) in the ornate Palacio de Comunicaciones.

Sellos (stamps) are sold at most *estancos* (tobacconists' shops with *Tabacos* in yellow letters on a maroon background), as well as post offices.

A postcard or letter weighing up to 20g costs €1.07 from Spain to other European countries, and €1.38 to the rest of the world. For a full list of prices for certified *(certificado)* and express post *(urgente)*, go to www.correos. es (in Spanish) and click on 'Calculador de Tarifas'.

All Spanish addresses have five-digit postcodes; using postcodes will help your mail arrive quicker.

Lista de correos (poste restante) mail can be addressed to you anywhere that has a post office. It will be delivered to the main post office unless another is specified in the address. Take your passport when you pick up mail. A typical *lista de correos* address looks like this:
Your name
Lista de Correos
28014 Madrid
Spain
Delivery times are erratic but ordinary mail to other Western European countries can take

up to a week; to North America up to 10 days; and to Australia or New Zealand anywhere between one and three weeks.

RADIO

The Spanish national network Radio Nacional de España (RNE) can be heard on RNE 1 (88.2 FM in Madrid) and has general interest and current affairs programs. Spaniards also divide between those who listen to the left-leaning Cadena SER (105.4 FM or 810AM) and the conservative, right-wing COPE network (100.7 FM). Among the most listened-to music stations are 40 Principales (97.7 FM), Onda Cero (98 FM) and Kiss FM (102.7 FM).

You can pick up BBC World Service (www.bbc .co.uk/radio/) and Voice of America (VOA; www.voanews .com) on a host of short-wave frequencies; check the websites for details.

RELOCATING

If you're moving to Madrid and looking for somewhere to live, try Room Madrid (Map pp108-9; ☎ 91 548 03 35; www.roommadrid.es; Calle de Conde Duque 7; ☺ 11am-2pm & 5-8pm Mon-Fri; Ⓜ Plaza de España), a booking service that arranges medium- to long-term accommodation. Within its portfolio is everything from apartments to shared flats. Though it can be a bit slow to answer (make contact well in advance of arriving in Madrid), it's generally reliable.

Several real estate and relocation companies specialise in helping foreign clients; try Solution Relocation Services (☎ 91 550 03 97; www .solucionmad.com) or Immo Madrid (☎ 91 766 06 61; www.immomadrid.com). Another good resource is www.expatica.com.

Once you're living here, pick up a copy of *The Notebook Madrid – Settling & Living in Madrid*, a locally produced publication (€20) with loads of useful tips and contacts; in English and French, it can be found at the English-language bookshops listed on its website (http://thenotebookmadrid.com).

SAFETY

Madrid is a generally safe city, although you should, as in most European cities, be wary of pickpockets on transport and around major tourist sights. Although you should be careful, don't be paranoid; remember that the overwhelming majority of travellers to Madrid rarely encounter any problems.

You're most likely to fall foul of pickpockets in the most heavily touristed parts of town, notably the Plaza Mayor and surrounding streets, the Puerta del Sol, El Rastro and around the Museo del Prado. Tricks abound. They usually involve a team of two or more (sometimes one of them an attractive woman to distract male victims). While one attracts your attention, the other empties your pockets. Be wary of jostling on crowded buses and the metro and, as a general rule, dark, empty streets are to be avoided; luckily, Madrid's most lively nocturnal areas are generally busy with crowds having a good time.

More unsettling than dangerous, the central Madrid street of Calle de la Montera has long been the haunt of prostitutes, pimps and a fair share of shady characters, although the street has recently been pedestrianised, installed with CCTV cameras and a police station. The same applies to the Casa de Campo, although it, too, has been cleaned up a little. The Madrid barrio of Lavapiés is a gritty, multicultural melting pot. We love it, but it's not without its problems, with drug-related crime an occasional but persistent problem; it's probably best avoided if you're on your own at night.

Where possible, only keep strictly necessary things on your person. Never put anything in your back pocket; small day bags are best worn across your chest. Money belts or pouches worn *under* your clothing are also a good idea. The less you have in your pockets or exposed bags the less you stand to lose if you're done. As with any travel, you should always keep a photocopy of important documents separate from the originals and travel insurance against theft and loss is also highly recommended.

For information on who to contact should you find yourself in difficulties, turn to p259. The phone numbers for reporting lost or stolen credit cards are on p261.

TELEPHONE

To call Spain, dial the international access code (00 in most countries), followed by the code for Spain (34) and the full nine-digit number. The access code for international calls from Spain is 00.

International reverse-charge (collect) calls (*una llamada a cobro revertido*) are simple:

Australia (☎ 900 99 00 61)

Canada (☎ 900 99 00 15)

France (☎ 900 99 00 33)

Germany (☎ 900 99 00 49)

Ireland (☎ 900 99 03 53)

New Zealand (☎ 900 99 00 64)

UK (☎ 900 99 00 44)

USA (☎ AT&T 900 99 00 11, Sprint & various others 900 99 00 13, MCI 900 99 00 14)

You'll get straight through to an operator in the country you're calling. There are changes afoot, so try an '800' prefix to the above numbers instead of '900' if the latter doesn't work.

If for some reason the above information doesn't work for you, in most places you can get an English-speaking Spanish international operator on ☎ 1008 (for calls within Europe or for Morocco) or ☎ 1005 (for the rest of the world).

For international directory inquiries dial ☎ 11825. Be warned, a call to this number costs €2! Dial ☎ 1009 to speak to a domestic operator, including for a domestic reverse-charge (collect) call. For national directory inquiries dial ☎ 11818.

Mobile (cell) phone numbers start with 6. Numbers starting with 900 are national toll-free numbers, while those starting 901 to 905 come with varying conditions. A common one is 902, which is a national standard rate number, but which can only be dialled from within Spain. In a similar category are numbers starting with 800, 803, 806 and 807.

Mobile Phones

You can buy SIM cards and prepaid time in Spain for your mobile phone (provided you own a GSM, dual- or tri-band cellular phone). This only works if your national phone hasn't been code-blocked; check before leaving home. Only consider a full contract unless you plan to live in Spain for a while.

All the Spanish mobile phone companies (Telefónica's MoviStar, Orange, Vodafone and Amena) offer *prepagado* (prepaid) accounts for mobiles. The SIM card costs from €50, which includes some prepaid phone time. Phone outlets are scattered across the city. You can then top up in their shops or by buying cards in outlets, such as tobacconists *(estancos)* and newsstands.

You can rent a mobile phone through the Madrid-based OnSpanishTime.com (www.onspanishtime.com/web). Delivery and pickup start from

US$16. The basic service costs US$8/49/117 per day/week/month for the phone. You pay a US$150 deposit and the whole operation is done over the internet.

Phonecards

Blue payphones are easy to use for international and domestic calls. They accept coins, *tarjetas telefónicas* (phonecards) issued by the national phone company Telefónica and, in some cases, credit cards. Phones in hotel rooms are more expensive than street payphones. The Telefónica phonecards are best for domestic calls.

For international calls you have two cut-price options. Most internet cafes recommended in this book (see p260) are Skype enabled, allowing you to call (with your Skype user id and password) for no more than the cost of your internet time. The other option is an international phonecard, which can be bought from *estancos,* some small convenience stores and newsstands in central Madrid. Most outlets display the call rates for each card. For calls to Australia, USA or Western Europe, Euro Hours has a phonecard costing €6, for more than 600 minutes of call time (plus the cost of the local call) or more than 200 minutes calling a toll-free local number.

TIME

Like most of Western Europe, Madrid is one hour ahead of Greenwich Mean Time/Coordinated Universal Time (GMT/UTC) during winter, two hours during the daylight-saving period from the last Sunday in March to the last Sunday in October. Spaniards use the 24-hour clock for official business (timetables etc), but often in daily conversation switch to the 12-hour version.

TOILETS

Public toilets are almost nonexistent in Madrid and it's not really the done thing to go into a bar or cafe solely to use the toilet; ordering a quick coffee is a small price to pay for relieving the problem. Otherwise you can usually get away with it in a larger, crowded place where they can't really keep track of who's coming and going. Another option is the department stores of El Corte Inglés (p131) that are dotted around the city.

TOURIST INFORMATION

Ayuntamiento de Madrid

The Madrid government's Centro de Turismo de Madrid (Map pp62-3; ☎ 91 588 16 36; www.esmadrid .com; Plaza Mayor 27; 🕙 9.30am-8.30pm; M Sol) is terrific. Housed in the delightful Real Casa de Panadería on the north side of the Plaza Mayor, it allows free access to its outstanding website and city database, and offers free downloads of the metro map to your mobile; staff are helpful. It also runs a useful general information line (☎ 010; Spanish only) dealing with anything from transport to shows in Madrid (call ☎ 91 540 40 10 from elsewhere in Spain, or 91 529 82 10 from outside Spain). There's a smaller tourist office (Map p102; Plaza de Colón; 🕙 9.30am-8.30pm; M Colón), which is accessible via the underground stairs on the corner of Calle de Goya and the Paseo de la Castellana, while smaller, bright orange tourist information points can be found at the following:

Barajas Airport, T4 (🕙 9am-8pm; M Aeropuerto T4)

Plaza de Cibeles (Map p91; 🕙 9.30am-8.30pm; M Banco de España)

Plaza del Callao (Map pp62-3; 🕙 9am-midnight; M Callao)

Paseo del Arte (Map pp84-5; cnr Calle de Santa Isabel & Plaza del Emperador Carlos V; 🕙 9.30am-8.30pm; M Atocha)

Comunidad de Madrid

The regional Comunidad de Madrid government runs the helpful Comunidad de Madrid Tourist Office (Map pp84-5; ☎ 902 100 007, 91 429 49 51; www.turismo madrid.es; Calle del Duque de Medinaceli 2; 🕙 8am-8pm Mon-Sat, 9am-2pm Sun; M Banco de España) covering the city and surrounding region. It also has a telephone information service (☎ 012) and branches at the following places:

Atocha train station (☎ 902 100 007; 🕙 9am-8pm Mon-Sat, 9am-2pm Sun; M Atocha Renfe)

Barajas airport (Aeropuerto de Barajas; ☎ 91 305 86 56; T1 & T4; 🕙 9am-8pm; M Aeropuerto or Aeropuerto T4)

Chamartín train station (☎ 91 315 99 76; 🕙 9am-8pm Mon-Sat, 9am-2pm Sun; M Chamartín)

TRAVELLERS WITH DISABILITIES

Although things are slowly changing, Madrid remains something of an obstacle course for travellers with a disability. Your first stop for more information on accessibility for travellers should be the Madrid tourist office website section known as Madrid Accesible (www.esmadrid.com), where you can download a list of wheelchair-accessible hotels, and a pdf called 'Lugares Accesibles', a list of wheelchair-friendly restaurants, shopping centres and museums; among the latter are the Museo del Prado (p90), Museo Thyssen-Bornemisza (p94) and the Centro de Arte Reina Sofía (p82), although few museums have guides in Braille or allow visually impaired people to touch objects.

The Ayuntamiento's program of guided tours (www.esmadrid.com/descubremadrid) includes tours for blind, deaf and wheelchair-bound travellers, as well as travellers with an intellectual disability; click on 'Rutas Accesibles'. Audio loops for the hearing impaired in cinemas are almost nonexistent, although most Spanish TV channels allow you to turn on subtitles.

When it comes to transport, metro lines built (or upgraded) since the late 1990s generally have elevators for wheelchair access, but the older lines are generally ill equipped; the updated metro maps available from any metro station (or at www.metromadrid.es, in Spanish) show stations with wheelchair access. On board the metro the name of the next station is usually announced (if the broadcast system is working…). The single-deck *piso bajo* (low floor) buses have no steps inside and in some cases have ramps that can be used by people in wheelchairs. In the long term, there are plans to make at least 50% of buses on all routes accessible to people with a disability. Radio-Teléfono Taxi (☎ 91 547 82 00; www .radiotelefono-taxi.com) runs taxis for people with a disability in addition to standard taxis. Generally, if you call any taxi company and ask for a 'eurotaxi' you should be sent one adapted for wheelchair users.

One attraction specifically for visually impaired travellers and Spaniards is the Museo Tiflológico (Museum for the Blind; Map p121; ☎ 91 589 42 19; http://museo.once.es/; Calle de la Coruña 18; admission free; 🕙 10am-2pm & 5-8pm Tue-Fri, 10am-2pm Sat; M Estrecho). Run by the National Organisation for the Blind (ONCE; see p266), its exhibits (all of which may be touched) include paintings, sculptures and tapestries, as well as more than 40 scale models of world monuments, including Madrid's Palacio Real and Cibeles fountain, as well as La Alhambra in Granada and the aqueduct in Segovia. It also provides leaflets in Braille and audio guides to the museum.

Further Information

The Spanish association for the blind, ONCE (Organización Nacional de Ciegos Españoles; Map p110; ☎ 91 577 37 56, 91 532 50 00; www.once.es; Calle de Prim 3; Ⓜ Chueca or Colón) occasionally publishes guides in Braille.

Hearing-impaired travellers can contact the Comunidad de Madrid's Federation for the Deaf, Fesorcam (Federación de Personas Sordas de la Comunidad de Madrid; Map p121; ☎ 91 725 37 57; www .fesorcam.org, in Spanish; Calle de Ferrer del Rio 33; Ⓜ Diego de León).

Travellers with an intellectual disability may wish to contact FEAPS Madrid (Map pp124-5; Federación de Organizaciones en Favor de Personas con Discapacidad Intelectual; ☎ 91 501 83 35; www .feapsmadrid.org, in Spanish; Avenida de la Ciudad de Barcelona 108; Ⓜ Menéndez Pelayo).

Outside Spain, national associations that can offer (sometimes including Madrid-specific) advice:

Access-able Travel Source (☎ 303-232 2979; www.access -able.com; PO Box 1796, Wheatridge, CO, USA)

Accessible Travel & Leisure (☎ 0145 272 9739; www .accessibletravel.co.uk; Naas Lane, Quedgeley, Gloucester, GL2 2SN, UK) Claims to be the biggest UK travel agency dealing with travel for the disabled. The company encourages the disabled to travel independently.

Holiday Care (☎ 0845 124 9971; www.holidaycare.org .uk; Shap Rd, Kendal, Cumbria LA9 6NZ, UK)

Mobility International USA (☎ 541-343 1284; www .miusa.org; 132 East Broadway, Ste 343, Eugene, Oregon 97401, USA)

Royal Association for Disability & Rehabilitation (Radar; ☎ 020-7250 3222; www.radar.org.uk; 12 City Forum, 250 City Rd, London, EC1V 8AF, UK)

Society for Accessible Travel & Hospitality (☎ 212-447 7284; www.sath.org; 347 5th Ave, Ste 610, New York, NY 10016, USA)

VISAS

Spain is one of 25 member countries of the Schengen Convention, under which EU member countries (except the UK and Ireland) plus Switzerland, Iceland and Norway have abolished checks at common borders. Legal residents of one Schengen country do not require a visa for another Schengen country. Citizens of the UK and Ireland are also exempt. Nationals of many other countries, including Australia, Canada, Israel, Japan, New Zealand and the USA, do not require visas for tourist visits of up to 90 days. All non-EU nationals entering Spain for any reason other than tourism (such as study or work) should contact a Spanish consulate, as they may need a specific visa.

If you're a citizen of a non-Schengen country not mentioned in this section, check with a Spanish consulate about whether you need a visa. The standard tourist visa issued by Spanish consulates (and usually valid for all Schengen countries unless conditions are attached) is valid for up to 90 days and is not renewable inside Spain.

WOMEN TRAVELLERS

As Spanish women will attest, women travellers need take no special precautions in Madrid: serious harassment of women travellers is rare and seldom extends beyond stares, occasional catcalls and unnecessary comments that you find in most Western European cities. Think twice about walking alone down empty city streets at night.

In the extremely rare event that you are the victim of sexual violence, contact the police (p259), while the Asociación de Asistencia a Víctimas de Agresiones Sexuales (Association for Assistance to Victims of Sexual Agression [CAVAS]; Map pp124-5; ☎ 91 574 01 10; Calle de O'Donnell 42; ☒ 10am-2pm & 4-7pm Mon-Thu, 10am-4pm Fri; Ⓜ O'Donnell) offers advice and help to rape victims; staff speak only limited English. You could also call the hotline for victims of sexual violence on ☎ 902 180 995.

WORK

Nationals of EU countries, Iceland, Norway and Switzerland are able to work in Spain without a visa, but for stays of more than three months they should apply for a *tarjeta de residencia* (residence card). That said, as EU integration evolves laws may change, so check with a Spanish embassy or consulate for the latest situation.

Virtually everyone else seeking to work in Spain is supposed to obtain, from a Spanish consulate in their country of residence, a work permit and, if they plan to stay more than 90 days, a residence visa. These procedures are well nigh impossible unless you have a job contract lined up before you begin them (or unless you're married to a Spaniard). Many people do, however, work without tangling with the bureaucracy.

Perhaps the easiest source of work for foreigners is teaching English (or another foreign language), but, even with full qualifications, non-EU citizens will find permanent positions scarce. Most of the larger, more reputable schools will hire only non-EU citizens who already have work and/or residence permits, but their attitude becomes more flexible if demand for teachers is high and you have particularly good qualifications. In the case of EU citizens, employers will generally help you through the bureaucratic minefield.

Madrid is loaded with 'cowboy outfits' that pay badly and often aren't overly concerned about quality. Reputable schools are listed in the brochure 'Study Spanish in Madrid' which is available from tourist offices.

Sources of information on possible teaching work include foreign cultural centres (the British Council, Alliance Française etc), foreign-language bookshops and university notice boards. Many language schools have notice boards where you may find work opportunities, or where you can advertise your own services. Cultural institutes you may want to try include the following.

Alliance Française (Map pp62-3; ☎ 91 435 15 32; www.alliancefrancaisemadrid.net, in Spanish; Cuesta de Santo Domingo 13; Ⓜ Santo Domingo)

British Council (Map pp116-17; ☎ 91 337 35 01; www.britishcouncil.es; Paseo del General Martínez Campos 31; Ⓜ Rubén Darío)

Goethe Institut (Map pp116-17; ☎ 91 391 39 44; www.goethe.de/madrid, in German or Spanish; Calle de Zurbarán 21; Ⓜ Colón)

Translating and interpreting could be an option if you are fluent in Spanish and speak another language that's in demand.

Another option might be au pair work, organised before you come to Spain. A useful guide is *The Au Pair and Nanny's Guide to Working Abroad,* by Susan Griffith and Sharon Legg. Griffith has also written *Work Your Way Around the World* and *Teaching English Abroad.*

Doing Business

Madrid has, in the past decade, imposed itself as the financial as well as political capital of Spain, much to the chagrin of eternal rival Barcelona, which was once considered the country's economic motor. The kind of comparison people used to draw between the two cities and Rome and Milan (respectively the political and financial capitals of Italy) increasingly seems misplaced.

People looking to expand their business into Spain should contact their own country's trade department (such as the DTI in the UK). The commercial department of the Spanish embassy in your own country should also have information – at least on negotiating the country's epic red tape. The trade office of your embassy may be able to help.

The **Cámara Oficial de Comercio e Industria de Madrid** (City Chamber of Commerce; off Map pp124-5; ☎ 91 538 35 00; www.camaramadrid.es or www.descubremadrid.com, in Spanish; Calle de Ribera del Loira 56-58; Ⓜ Campo des las Naciones) offers advisory services on most aspects of doing or setting up business in Madrid, as well as video-conferencing facilities and an accessible business database.

Exhibitions & Conferences

The **Oficina de Congresos de Madrid** (Madrid Convention Bureau; Map pp62-3; ☎ 91 480 24 05; Patronato de Turismo office, Plaza Mayor 27; Ⓜ Sol) publishes the *Guía de Congresos e Incentivos* (also in a CD-ROM version), in Spanish and English, which can be helpful for those interested in organising meetings or conventions.

Madrid's main trade-fair centre is the **Feria de Madrid** (IFEMA; ☎ 902 221 515; www.ifema.es, in Spanish; Parque Ferial Juan Carlos I; Ⓜ Campo de las Naciones) in Campo de las Naciones, one metro stop from the airport. It hosts events throughout the year. Another important trade-fair centre is the **Palacio de Congresos y Exposiciones** (Map p121; ☎ 91 337 81 00; www.pcm.tourspain.es; Paseo de la Castellana 99; Ⓜ Santiago Bernabéu). The auditorium can seat 2000 people and there are smaller meeting rooms, with technical support and secretarial services.

You can review the month's upcoming trade fairs in the free *EsMadrid.com* booklet available at tourist offices.

LANGUAGE

Spanish *(Español)*, often referred to as *castellano* (Castilian) to distinguish it from other regional languages spoken in Spain, is the language of Madrid. The conservative Real Academia Española, located near the Prado, watches over the national tongue with deadly solemnity and issues the country's version of the *Oxford English Dictionary*, the weighty *Diccionario de la Lengua Española*.

While you'll find an increasing number of madrileños who speak some English, especially younger people and hotel and restaurant employees, don't count on it. Those who learn a little Spanish will be amply rewarded as Spaniards appreciate the effort, no matter how basic your understanding of the language. Madrileños tend to talk at high volume and high velocity. Although the Spanish you learnt at school will be fine for most situations, it may take a little more effort to master some local *cheli* (slang).

If you want to learn more Spanish than we've included here, pick up a copy of Lonely Planet's comprehensive and user-friendly *Spanish* phrasebook. Lonely Planet iPhone phrasebooks are available through the Apple App store.

SOCIAL
Meeting People

Hello.	¡Hola!
Goodbye.	¡Adiós!
Please.	Por favor.
Thank you.	(Muchas) Gracias.
Yes./No.	Sí./No.
Excuse me.	Perdón.
Sorry.	¡Perdón!/¡Perdóneme!

Do you speak English?
¿Habla inglés?
Does anyone speak English?
¿Hay alguien que hable inglés?
Do you understand?
¿Me entiende?
Yes, I understand.
Sí, entiendo.
No, I don't understand.
No, no entiendo.
Pardon?; What?
¿Cómo?

Could you please ...?	¿Puede ... por favor?
speak more slowly	hablar más despacio
repeat that	repetir
write it down	escribirlo

Going Out

What's on ...?	¿Qué hay…?
locally	en la zona
this weekend	este fin de semana
today	hoy
tonight	esta noche

Where are the ...?	¿Dónde hay ...?
clubs	discotecas
gay venues	lugares gay
places to eat	lugares para comer
pubs	pubs

PRACTICAL
Question Words

Who? (sg/pl)	¿Quién?/¿Quiénes?
What?	¿Qué?
Which? (sg/pl)	¿Cuál?/¿Cuáles?
When?	¿Cuándo?
Where?	¿Dónde?
How?	¿Cómo?
How much?	¿Cuánto?
How many?	¿Cuántos?
How much is it?	¿Cuánto cuesta?
Why?	¿Por qué?

Numbers & Amounts

0	cero	17	diecisiete
1	una/uno	18	dieciocho
2	dos	19	diecinueve
3	tres	20	veinte
4	cuatro	21	veintiuno
5	cinco	22	veintidós
6	seis	30	treinta
7	siete	31	treinta y uno
8	ocho	32	treinta y dos
9	nueve	40	cuarenta
10	diez	50	cincuenta
11	once	60	sesenta
12	doce	70	setenta

13	trece	80	ochenta
14	catorce	90	noventa
15	quince	100	cien
16	dieciséis	1000	mil

Days

Monday	lunes
Tuesday	martes
Wednesday	miércoles
Thursday	jueves
Friday	viernes
Saturday	sábado
Sunday	domingo

Banking

I'd like to change some money.
Quería cambiar dinero.
I'd like to change a travellers cheque.
Quería cobrar un cheque de viaje.

ATM	el cajero automático
credit card	tarjeta de crédito
foreign exchange office	la oficina de cambio
travellers cheques	cheques de viaje

Post

Where's the post office?
¿Dónde está la oficina de correos?

envelope	sobre
fax	fax
parcel	paquete
postcard	postal
stamp/stamps	sello/sellos

Phones & Internet

I want to make a ...	Quería hacer ...
call (to ...)	una llamada a ...
reverse-charge/ collect call	una llamada a cobro revertido

I'd like a/an ...	Quería un/a ...
charger for my phone	cargador para mi teléfono
mobile/cell phone for hire	móvil para alquilar
phonecard	tarjeta telefónica
prepaid mobile/ cell phone	móvil de prepago
SIM card for your network	tarjeta SIM para su red

Where's the local internet cafe?
¿Dónde hay un cibercafé cercano?

I'd like to ...	Quería ...
get internet access	conectarme (a internet)
check my email	revisar mi correo electrónico

Transport

What time does the ... leave?
¿A qué hora sale el ...?

bus	autobús
bus (intercity)	autocar
plane	avión
train	tren

Is this taxi available?
¿Está libre este taxi?
Please put the meter on.
Por favor, ponga el taxímetro.
How much is it to ...?
¿Cuánto cuesta ir a ...?
Please take me (to this address).
Por favor, lléveme (a esta dirección).

FOOD

breakfast	desayuno
lunch	comida
dinner	cena
snack	tentempié

bar	bar
cafe	café
coffee bar	cafetería
restaurant	restaurante

A table for ..., please.
Una mesa para ..., por favor.
Is service/cover charge included in the bill?
¿Está incluido el servicio en la cuenta?
Do you have a menu in English?
¿Tienen un menu en inglés?
Do you have any vegetarian dishes?
¿Tienen algún plato vegetariano?
I'm allergic to peanuts.
Soy alérgico/a a los cacahuetes. (m/f)
What is today's special?
¿Cuál es el plato del día?
What would you recommend?
¿Qué recomienda?
The bill, please.
La cuenta, por favor.
Good health/Cheers!
¡Salud!
Thank you, that was delicious.
Muchas gracias, estaba buenísimo.

EMERGENCIES

Help!
¡Socorro!
Where are the toilets?
¿Dónde están los servicios?

Call ...!	¡Llame a ...!
the police	la policía
a doctor	un médico
an ambulance	una ambulancia

HEALTH

Where's the nearest ...?
¿Dónde está ... más cercano?

(night) chemist	la farmacia (de guardia)
doctor	el médico
hospital	el hospital

I need a doctor (who speaks English).
Necesito un doctor (que hable inglés).

GLOSSARY

abierto – open
abono – season pass
aduana – customs
albergue juvenil – youth hostel; not to be confused with *hostal*
alcalde – mayor
alcázar – Muslim-era fortress
Almoravid – Islamic Berbers who founded an empire in North Africa that spread over much of Spain in the 11th century and laid siege to Madrid in 1110
auto-da-fé – elaborate execution ceremony staged by the Inquisition
autonomía – autonomous community or region; Spain's 50 provincias are grouped into 17 of these
autopista – motorway (with tolls)
AVE – Tren de Alta Velocidad Española; high-speed train
Ayuntamiento – city or town hall; city or town council
asador – restaurant specialising in roasted meats

bailaores – flamenco dancers
baño completo – full bathroom, with a toilet, shower and/or bath, and washbasin
barrio – district, quarter (of a town or city)
biblioteca – library
billete – ticket (see also *entrada*)
bodega – literally, 'cellar' (especially a wine cellar); also means a winery or a traditional wine bar likely to serve wine from the barrel
bomberos – fire brigade
botellón – literally 'big bottle'; young adolescents partying outdoors

cajero automático – automated teller machine (ATM)
calle – street
callejón – lane
cama – bed
cambio – change; currency exchange
cantaor/cantaora – flamenco singer (male/female)
capilla – chapel
Carnaval – carnival; a period of fancy-dress parades and merrymaking, usually ending on the Tuesday 47 days before Easter Sunday

carnet – identity card or driving licence
carretera – highway
casa de comidas – the most basic restaurants specialising in simple, cheap Spanish cooking; aimed at workers on their lunch breaks, they're often only open for lunch Monday to Friday
casco – literally, 'helmet'; often used to refer to the old part of a city
castillo – castle
castizo – literally 'pure'; refers to people and things distinctly from Madrid
catedral – cathedral
centro de salud – health centre
cercanías – local trains serving big cities, suburbs and nearby towns; local train network
cerrado – closed
certificado – registered mail
cervecería – bar where the focus is on beer
churrigueresque – ornate style of Baroque architecture named after the brothers Alberto and José Churriguera
comedor – dining room
comunidad – fixed charge for maintenance of rental accommodation
Comunidad de Madrid – Madrid province
consigna – a left-luggage office or lockers
coro – choirstall
Correos – post office
corrida (de toros) – bullfight
Cortes – national parliament
cuesta – lane (usually on a hill)

día del espectador – cut-price ticket day at cinemas
discoteca – nightclub
documento nacional de identidad (DNI) – national identity card
ducha – shower
duende – an indefinable word that captures the passionate essence of flamenco

embajada – embassy
entrada – entrance; ticket for a performance
estación de autobuses – bus station
estanco – tobacconist shop

farmacia – pharmacy

feria – fair; can refer to trade fairs as well as city, town or village fairs, bullfights or festivals lasting days or weeks

ferrocarril – railway

fiesta – festival, public holiday or party

fin de semana – weekend

flamenco – traditional Spanish musical form involving any or all of guitarist, singer and dancer and sometimes accompanying musicians

fútbol – football (soccer)

gasóleo – diesel

gasolina – petrol (a *gasolinera* is a petrol station)

gatos – literally 'cats'; colloquial name for madrileños

gitanos – the Roma people (formerly known as the Gypsies)

glorieta – big roundabout

guiri – foreigner

habitaciones libres – rooms available

habitación doble – twin room

horno de asador – restaurant with a wood-burning roasting oven

hostal – hostel; not to be confused with *albergue juvenil*

iglesia – church

infanta – princess

IVA – impuesto sobre el valor añadido (value-added tax)

judería – Jewish quarter

largo recorrido – long-distance train

lavabo – washbasin; a polite term for toilet

lavandería – laundrette

librería – bookshop

llamada a cobro revertido – reverse-charges (collect) call

locutorio – telephone centre

luz – electricity

macarras – Madrid's rough but usually likable lads

madrileño – a person from Madrid

marcha – action, life, 'the scene'

marisquería – seafood eatery

media raciones – a serving of tapas, somewhere between the size of tapas and raciones

menú del día – fixed-price meal available at lunchtime, sometimes evening, too; often just called a *menú*

mercado – market

meseta – the high tableland of central Spain

mezquita – mosque

monasterio – monastery

morería – former Islamic quarter in town

moro – 'Moor' or Muslim, usually in medieval context

moto – moped or motorcycle

movida madrileña – the halcyon days of the post-Franco years when the city plunged into an excess of nightlife, drugs and cultural expression

mozarab – Christians who lived in Muslim-ruled Spain; also style of architecture

mudéjar – Muslim living under Christian rule in medieval Spain, also refers to their style of architecture

muralla – city wall

museo – museum

objetos perdidos – lost-and-found office

oficina de turismo – tourist office

Páginas Amarillas – *Yellow Pages* phone directory

parador – state-owned hotel in a historic building

pensión – guesthouse

pijo/pija – male/female yuppie (can also mean snob, beautiful people)

piscina – swimming pool

plaza mayor – main plaza; square

provincial – (call) within the same province

pueblo – village

puente – bridge

puerta – door or gate

RACE – Real Automóvil Club de España; Royal Automobile Club of Spain

ración – meal-sized serve of tapas

rastro – flea market, car-boot (trunk) sale; El Rastro is Madrid's (and Europe's) largest flea market

ronda – ring road

salida – exit or departure

Semana Santa – Holy Week; the week leading up to Easter Sunday

servicios – toilets

sierra – mountain range

sol – sun

sombra – shade

tabernas – taverns

taifa – small Muslim kingdom in medieval Spain

tapas – bar snacks traditionally served on a saucer or lid ('tapa' literally means a lid)

taquilla – ticket window/office

tarde – afternoon

tarjeta de crédito – credit card

tarjeta de residencia – residence card

tarjeta telefónica – phonecard

tasca – tapas bar

temporada alta/media/baja – high, mid- or low season

terraza – terrace; usually means outdoor tables of a café, bar or restaurant; can also mean rooftop open-air place

tienda – shop or tent

torero – bullfighter or matador

toro – bull

turismo – means both tourism and saloon car

urgencia – first-aid station

villa – town

vinoteca – wine bar

zarzuela – form of Spanish dance and music, usually satirical

zona de movida – an area of town where lively bars and discos are cluttered

BEHIND THE SCENES

THIS BOOK

The 1st and 2nd editions of Madrid were written by Damien Simonis. For the 3rd edition he was joined by Sarah Andrews. The 4th, 5th and this edition were written by Anthony Ham. This guidebook was commissioned in Lonely Planet's London office, and produced by the following:

Commissioning Editors Lucy Monie, Joe Bindloss

Coordinating Editors Justin Flynn, Thomas Lee

Coordinating Cartographer Anthony Phelan

Coordinating Layout Designer Paul Queripel

Managing Editors Imogen Bannister, Sasha Baskett

Managing Cartographers Owen Eszeki, Adrian Persoglia, Herman So

Managing Layout Designer Celia Wood

Assisting Editors Robyn Loughnane, Nigel Chin, Kathryn Glendenning, Michala Green, Hazel Meek

Assisting Cartographer Jacqueline Nguyen

Cover Research Pepi Bluck, lonelyplanetimages.com

Internal Image Research Aude Vauconsant, lonelyplanetimages.com

Indexer Amanda Jones

Language Content Laura Crawford

Thanks to Lisa Knights, Melanie Dankel, Michelle Glynn, Helen Christinis, Katie Lynch, Carol Jackson, Naomi Parker

Cover photographs Painted tiles on the wall of Los Gabrieles Cage, Oliver Strewe (top), Statue of Felipe III in Plaza Mayor, David Tomlinson (bottom)

Internal photographs
All images are copyright of the photographer unless otherwise indicated. Many of the images in this guide are available for licensing from Lonely Planet Images: www .lonelyplanetimages.com.

THANKS
ANTHONY HAM

In eight years of living in Madrid, I have been welcomed and assisted by too many people to name and whose lives and stories have become a treasured part of the fabric of my own. Special thanks to Ron, Jan, Lisa, Greg, Alex, Greta and Damien whose visits to Madrid have deepened my ties to my homes on both sides of the world. At LP, a big thank you to the wonderful production team of Lucy Monie, Justin Flynn, Robyn Loughnane and Anthony Phelan. It was my great fortune a week after arriving in Madrid to meet my wife and soulmate, Marina, who has made this city a true place of the heart. And to my daughter, Carlota: truly you are Madrid's greatest gift of all.

OUR READERS

Many thanks to the travellers who used the last edition and wrote to us with helpful hints, useful advice and interesting anecdotes:

THE LONELY PLANET STORY

Fresh from an epic journey across Europe, Asia and Australia in 1972, Tony and Maureen Wheeler sat at their kitchen table stapling together notes. The first Lonely Planet guidebook, Across Asia on the Cheap, was born.

Travellers snapped up the guides. Inspired by their success, the Wheelers began publishing books to Southeast Asia, India and beyond. Demand was prodigious, and the Wheelers expanded the business rapidly to keep up. Over the years, Lonely Planet extended its coverage to every country and into the virtual world via lonelyplanet.com and the Thorn Tree message board.

As Lonely Planet became a globally loved brand, Tony and Maureen received several offers for the company. But it wasn't until 2007 that they found a partner whom they trusted to remain true to the company's principles of travelling widely, treading lightly and giving sustainably. In October of that year, BBC Worldwide acquired a 75% share in the company, pledging to uphold Lonely Planet's commitment to independent travel, trustworthy advice and editorial independence.

Today, Lonely Planet has offices in Melbourne, London and Oakland, with over 500 staff members and 300 authors. Tony and Maureen are still actively involved with Lonely Planet. They're travelling more often than ever, and they're devoting their spare time to charitable projects. And the company is still driven by the philosophy of Across Asia on the Cheap: 'All you've got to do is decide to go and the hardest part is over. So go!'

Luis Alberto, Ingrid Albrecht, Andreas Barczyk, Candice Barnett, Sheila Bloomquist, Ansgar Bode, Mary Brooks, Christian Byhahn, R Capriotti, Malcolm Defries, Dana Fillion, Caroline Garrido, Kathy Goss, Jerneja Grasic, Susan Hart, Jane Hawkins, Muriel Hayden, Kelvin Hayes, Alison Herbert, Anna Hickl, Susan Holmes, James Igoe, Joy Jaffe, Andres Jarabo, Philip Kiernan, Evelyn Kimber, Mary Learn, Marilaura Levantino, Colin Lillicrapp, Peter Long, Beatriz Lozano, Laela Mahjoub O'Kelly, Bob Makransky, Syd Marcus, Ana Marta Arevalo, Jose Mejias, Michel Michaeljohn, Lucy Monie, Peter Moore, Eureka Morrison, Andre O'Campo-Dos Santos, Mr O'Neil, Daniel ONeill, Saskia Oskam, Jürgen Ott, Dogan Ozkan, Anna Pollard, Jacek Radwanski, Zane Rebronja, Verver Rgbrb, Jay Roberts, Sean Rooney, Stéphanie Rossenu, Mario Salgado, Irene Sanchez Moyano, Ricardo Santa Maria, Mario Schumacher, Vicki Soutar, Judith Swain, Laura Tatti, Jan Thomas, Elizabeth Thompson, John Thompson, Susan Trout, Javier Urberuaga, C Wesley, Julie Ann Zserdin

SEND US YOUR FEEDBACK

We love to hear from travellers – your comments keep us on our toes and help make our books better. Our well-travelled team reads every word on what you loved or loathed about this book. Although we cannot reply individually to postal submissions, we always guarantee that your feedback goes straight to the appropriate authors, in time for the next edition. Each person who sends us information is thanked in the next edition and the most useful submissions are rewarded with a free book.

To send us your updates – and find out about Lonely Planet events, newsletters and travel news – visit our award-winning website: lonelyplanet.com/contact.

Note: We may edit, reproduce and incorporate your comments in Lonely Planet products such as guidebooks, websites and digital products, so let us know if you don't want your comments reproduced or your name acknowledged. For a copy of our privacy policy visit lonelyplanet.com/privacy.

Notes

A

accommodation 220-30, *see also* Sleeping *subindex*
apartments 220
Chamberí & Argüelles 229-30
costs 220-1
gay travellers 217-18
Huertas & Atocha 224-6
La Latina & Lavapiés 223-4
lesbian travellers 217-18
Los Austrias, Sol & Centro 221-3
Malasaña & Chueca 228-9
Northern Madrid 230
Paseo del Prado & El Retiro 226-7
reservations 221
Salamanca 227-8
activities 208-13, *see also individual activities,* Sports & Activities *subindex*
Adrià, Ferran 149, 151
Aguirre, Esperanza 35, 52
air travel 250-2
Alcalá de Henares 247-8
Alfonso VI 23, 24
Alfonso XII 29
Alfonso XIII 29-30, 66
Almodóvar, Pedro 33, 42, 43

Álvarez del Manzano, José María 33
ambulance 259
Amenábar, Alejandro 42
Año Nuevo (New Year) 16-17
antiques, *see also* Shopping *subindex*
fairs 18
apartments, *see* Sleeping *subindex*
aquariums, *see* Sights *subindex*
Aranjuez 246-7
architecture 46-50
Argüelles, *see* Chamberí & Argüelles
Arola, Sergi 165, 168
Arroyo, Eduardo 40
art galleries, *see* Sights *subindex*
arts 36-46, 202-5, *see also individual arts,* Arts *subindex*
festivals 17
tickets 202
walking tour 98-9, **99**
ATMs 261
Atocha, *see* Huertas & Atocha
Ávila 241-4, **242**

B

babysitters 256-7
Balaguer, Oriol 138, 154
Banderas, Antonio 44
Barca, Calderón de la 45
Bardem, Javier 42, 43, 192
Barrio de las Letras 87
barrios 65
bars, *see* Drinking, Nightlife *subindexes*
opening hours 175
basketball 212
bathrooms 264
bicycle travel 252-3
Bonaparte, Joseph 27-8
Bonaparte, Napoleon 27
books 23, 36-38, *see also* Shopping *subindex*
fairs 19, 36

buildings, *see* Sights *subindex*
bullfighting 100, 101, 211-12
Buñuel, Luis 43
bus travel 252, 253
business hours 256, *see also inside front cover*
bars 175
cafes 174
nightlife 176-7
restaurants 148
shops 133

C

cafes, *see* Drinking, Eating *subindexes*
opening hours 174
car travel 253-4
Carlos I 24, 25
Carlos III 27
Carnaval 17
cathedrals, *see* Sights *subindex*
Cela, Camilo José 37
cell phones 264
cemeteries, *see* Sights *subindex*
Centro, *see* Los Austrias, Sol & Centro
Centro de Arte Reina Sofía 82-3, **7**
cercanías 254-5
Cervantes Saavedra, Miguel de 36-7, 70, 87, 234
Chamberí & Argüelles 114-19, **116-17**, **11**
accommodation 229-30
drinking & nightlife 197-8
food 168-70
shopping 142-4
transport 114
walking tour 118-19, **119**
chemists 260-1
children, travel with 256-7
sights 98
Chinchón 247
chocolate con churros **4**
Chueca *see* Malasaña & Chueca

churches, *see* Sights *subindex*
cinema 42-4
cinemas, *see* Arts *subindex*
civil war 30
classical music 202-3
climate 16, 257
climate change & travel 251
clothes, *see* Shopping *subindex*
clothing sizes 135
clubs, *see* Nightlife *subindex*
consulates 259
convents, *see* Sights *subindex*
costs 20-1, 258, *see also inside front cover*
accommodation 220-1
food 148
free sights 123
museums 93
nightlife 175, 177
value-added tax 131
courses 257-8
cooking 148
flamenco 258
language 257-8
wine appreciation 185
credit cards 261
Cruz, Penélope 43
cultural centres, *see* Sights *subindex*
customs regulations 258
cycling 252-3, 262

D

Dacosta, Quique 159
Dalí, Salvador 39-40
dance 203
day spas 208-9
day trips 232-49, **233**
Alcalá de Henares 247-8
Aranjuez 246-7
Ávila 241-4, **242**
Chinchón 247
San Lorenzo de El Escorial 244-5
Segovia 238-41, **239**
Sierra de Guadarrama 248

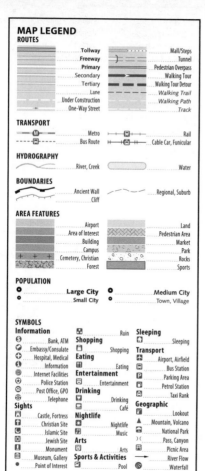

MAP LEGEND

ROUTES

Tollway
Freeway
Primary
Secondary
Tertiary
Lane
Under Construction
One-Way Street

Mall/Steps
Tunnel
Pedestrian Overpass
Walking Tour
Walking Tour Detour
Walking Trail
Walking Path
Track

TRANSPORT

Metro
Bus Route

Rail
Cable Car, Funicular

HYDROGRAPHY

River, Creek
Water

BOUNDARIES

Ancient Wall
Cliff
Regional, Suburb

AREA FEATURES

Airport
Area of Interest
Building
Campus
Cemetery, Christian
Forest

Land
Pedestrian Area
Market
Park
Rocks
Sports

POPULATION

● Large City
○ Small City
● Medium City
● Town, Village

SYMBOLS

Information
Ⓢ Bank, ATM
Ⓒ Embassy/Consulate
⊕ Hospital, Medical
ⓘ Information
@ Internet Facilities
Ⓟ Police Station
Ⓟ Post Office, GPO
☎ Telephone

Sights
Castle, Fortress
Christian Site
Islamic Site
Jewish Site
Monument
Museum, Gallery
Point of Interest

Shopping
Shopping

Eating
Eating

Entertainment
Entertainment

Drinking
Drinking
Café

Nightlife
Nightlife
Music

Arts
Arts

Sports & Activities
Pool

Ruin

Sleeping
Sleeping

Transport
Airport, Airfield
Bus Station
Parking Area
Petrol Station
Taxi Rank

Geographic
Lookout
Mountain, Volcano
National Park
Pass, Canyon
Picnic Area
River Flow
Waterfall

Published by Lonely Planet Publications Pty Ltd
ABN 36 005 607 983

Australia (Head Office)
Locked Bag 1, Footscray, Victoria 3011,
☎ 03 8379 8000, fax 03 8379 8111,
talk2us@lonelyplanet.com.au

USA 150 Linden St, Oakland, CA 94607,
☎ 510 250 6400, toll free 800 275 8555,
fax 510 893 8572, info@lonelyplanet.com

UK 2nd fl, 186 City Rd, London, EC1V 2NT,
☎ 020 7106 2100, fax 020 7106 2101,
go@lonelyplanet.co.uk

Printed by Toppan Security Printing Pte. Ltd.
Printed in Singapore

MIX
Paper from
responsible sources
FSC
www.fsc.org
FSC™ C021741